· *Festivals and the French Revolution* ·

F·E·S·T·I·V·A·L·S

and the

French Revolution

Mona Ozouf

Translated by Alan Sheridan

Harvard University Press
Cambridge, Massachusetts
London, England
1988

Copyright © 1988 by the President and Fellows
of Harvard College
All rights reserved
Printed in the United States of America
10 9 8 7 6 5 4 3 2

First published as *La fête révolutionnaire, 1789–1799,*
© Editions Gallimard, 1976

First Harvard University Press paperback edition, 1991

The publication of this volume was assisted by a grant from the
French Ministry of Culture.

Library of Congress Cataloging-in-Publication Data
Ozouf, Mona.
Festivals and the French Revolution.
Translation of: La fête révolutionnaire, 1789–1799.
Bibliography: p.
Includes index.
1. France—Social life and customs—1789–1815.
2. France—History—Revolution, 1789–1799.
3. Festivals—France—History—18th century.   I. Title.
DC159.09613   1988   944.04   87-14958
ISBN 0-674-29883-7 (alk. paper) (cloth)
ISBN 0-674-29884-5 (paper)

Designed by Gwen Frankfeldt

Contents

Foreword

by Lynn Hunt

In *Festivals and the French Revolution* Mona Ozouf has written one of those rare works of scholarly history that opens up new ways of thinking about the meaning of culture and revolution in general. At first glance, the topic might seem a clearly delimited one: the festivals of the French Revolution from 1789 to 1799. The subject conjures up visions of goddesses of Liberty, strange celebrations of Reason, and the oddly pretentious Cult of the Supreme Being. Every history of the period includes some mention of these festivals, although most historians have been content either to ridicule them as ineffectual or to bemoan them as repugnant examples of a sterile official culture. In these pages the reader will discover that the festivals were more than bizarre marginalia to the Revolutionary process. The festivals offer critical insights into the meaning of the French Revolution; they show a society in the process of creating itself anew. Under the scrutiny of a keenly perceptive historian, the festivals are revealed to be the most fascinating example of the working of Revolutionary culture.

Historians of the French Revolution have been incorporating Mona Ozouf's insights into their work for some time. Now, thanks to this excellent translation by Alan Sheridan, a much broader English-speaking public will be able to appreciate the significance of her book. In recent years there has been a resurgence of interest in the French Revolution, and studies of it have become models for understanding the revolutionary process in general. Mona Ozouf has been in the forefront of this resurgence, along with François Furet, her colleague at the Ecole des Hautes Etudes in Paris, and Maurice Agulhon of the University of Paris. Ozouf, Furet in *Interpreting the French Revolution,* and Agulhon in *Marianne into Battle: Republican Imagery and Symbolism in France, 1789–1800,* have drawn our attention away from fruitless debates about the Marxist interpretation of the French Revolution toward a new consideration of the role and significance of revolutionary political culture. Rather than focusing on the part played by different social classes or trying to trace economic trends, they have shown the importance of symbols, language, and ritual in inventing and transmitting a tradition of revolutionary action.

Mona Ozouf does not ignore the long and venerable tradition of Revolutionary historiography; she situates herself carefully vis-à-vis it by showing how an understanding of the festivals can change our thinking about the Revolution. She argues against the view long held by most historians that the festivals were simply another instrument of political struggle, more spectacular than speeches in the Convention or votes in the Jacobin Club but essentially the same in intent. In this view, the radicals, for example, used the celebrations of Reason to fortify their position, and then Robespierre created the Cult of the Supreme Being in order to defeat the radicals. While the author recognizes the differences between festivals and demonstrates their connections to unfolding events, her main interest is in their common characteristics, or what she calls their "identical conceptualization." She traces the similarities through the many stages in Revolutionary festive life: first the "wild" festivals of 1789 and 1790, which were often not very different from riots; then the grandiose and moving festivals of Federation in July 1790; the subsequent official conflicts over which events to celebrate; the alternative, locally inspired festivals of 1793 and 1794, which often included violent satires of Catholicism, the rich, and figures of political authority; and finally the official systems of festivals designed to keep unruly elements under control.

By taking the larger view of the festivals, Ozouf is able to develop the links between them and more general structures of culture. In two path-breaking pieces (Chapters VI and VII), she shows how the festivals were designed to recast space and time. The revolutionaries sought to efface the spatial reminders of the Catholic religion and of monarchical and feudal authority. Festival itineraries carefully avoided the religious processional routes of the past or showed off new symbolic representations that purposely overshadowed those reminders. Some festivals included the ceremonial burning of royalist and Catholic symbols; in these, the symbols of the new world would emerge out of the ashes of the old. Revolutionary festive space was always large and open: festival organizers preferred large, open fields or squares, where equality could be conveyed by horizontality and freedom by the lack of boundaries. Closed and vertical spaces were associated with hierarchy and lack of freedom, and they were avoided as much as possible.

The planners of the festivals were even more preoccupied with time. Catholic feast days were abolished, and new Revolutionary ones were instituted. In 1793, the entire calendar was redrawn. "Decades" of ten days replaced the weeks, and the new names given to the months and days recalled nature and reason while replacing the names associated with the Christian calendar. The Revolutionary festivals were essential to this new sense of time, because they both gave shape to the yearly cycle and established the history of the Revolution itself. Whenever the regime changed, the festival calendar had to be rearranged. New festivals were created to celebrate each major alteration, and objectional reminders from the preceding regime were eliminated. The festivals can be understood, then, as the Revolution's own history in the making.

The concern with space and time followed from the Revolutionary desire to form a new community based on new values. This is, no doubt, the book's most important and fruitful insight, for it restores to the Revolution the emphasis on creativity and inventiveness that has long been forgotten in the standard histories. As the author concludes, the festivals inaugurated a new era because they made sacred the values of a modern, secular, liberal world. In more concrete terms, this meant that the nation required new categories of social definition, the old categories having disappeared with the abolition of Old Regime corporations and titles of nobility. Processions based on rank and precedence therefore had to give way to processions grouped more neutrally by function and age. For the most part, however, the festivals emphasized consensus and oneness rather than distinctions within the community.

The emphasis on the drive toward unanimity and the recasting of the categories of social experience make the festivals seem very much like a new secular religion. Here Ozouf is following the lead given by Emile Durkheim in his influential study *The Elementary Forms of the Religious Life.* Durkheim argued that the essential function of religion was to provide social solidarity. Religion was society's way of making itself sacred; religion created the emotional bonds that made people obey social rules willingly. No society could exist without this sense of its sacredness. All societies set *themselves* up as gods, according to Durkheim; they give these gods different names, but they all serve the same social purposes. According to Durkheim, the French Revolution was an especially dramatic ex-

ample of this principle: "This aptitude of society for setting itself up as a
god or for creating gods was never more apparent than during the first
years of the French Revolution" (pp. 244–245).

Mona Ozouf is not the first historian to use Durkheim's insight into
the relationship between society and religion. A contemporary of Durkheim's and one of the renowned fathers of Revolutionary historiography,
Albert Mathiez, published a self-consciously Durkheimian study of Revolutionary symbolism in 1904, *Les origines des cultes révolutionnaires (1789–
1792)*. He argued that the new symbolic system with its oaths and festivals constituted a Revolutionary religion, by Durkheim's definition of
religion. Ozouf is more cautious about the parallel with religion and
much less sanguine than Mathiez about the results. As she shows, the
festivals did not succeed as a religious ritual even in the short run; most
French people retained their allegiance to Catholicism and never demonstrated much enthusiasm for cults of Revolutionary martyrs, the new Revolutionary calendar, or the often-printed Revolutionary catechisms. Revolutionary religion was too negative; it was dominated by the urge to
purify and subtract, to efface reminders of the past, to root out superstition.

Yet, at the same time, Mona Ozouf does valorize the religious impulse
as Durkheim defined it. In her concluding chapter she argues much like
Durkheim that "a society instituting itself must sacralize the very deed of
institution . . . Beginning a new life cannot be imagined without faith."
The chief aim of the Revolutionary festivals was "the transfer of sacrality"
from the Old Regime to the new. The model of antiquity was essential to
this transfer because it was not tainted by the feudal and monarchical
regime. Greece and Rome came before; they could serve as the "eternal
model of communal togetherness" because they had a kind of pristine,
almost prehistorical quality for the French of the eighteenth century. They
represented the utopia that was so important to the Revolutionary imagination; antiquity replaced Scripture as the sacred point of reference.

French history has often been at the forefront of historical research and
conceptualization, and this book is a good example of why this should be
so. Mona Ozouf has delineated a new method in Revolutionary studies;
with enormously rich original materials, she has fashioned a means of
understanding Revolutionary culture through its symbolic forms. She has
already reshaped our understanding of the French Revolution by showing
how the revolutionaries revealed their most profound intentions in the
festivals. Her work has just begun to influence more general thinking

about cultural theory. Sociologists, anthropologists, and political scientists, especially those interested in the revival of Durkheimianism, will find this book essential reading. Ozouf gives weight and specificity to the now general claim that social and political action can be analyzed as texts or languages; yet at the same time, she avoids the usual pitfalls of the linguistic analogy. At every moment in her analysis, we can hear the voices of the participants themselves. These are never drowned out by facile or brittle theorizing.

Chapters VIII and IX, on pedagogy and popular life, will be especially interesting to those concerned with the theory of culture. They are, moreover, typical of the brilliance of the author's analysis. In Chapter VIII, she moves from the important recognition that the festivals served an educational function to a consideration of Revolutionary theories of psychology, and from there to a fascinating discussion of visual and verbal representation generally. In Chapter IX, revolutionary officials appear as ethnographers (albeit not very good ones), and she uses their reports to do an ethnography (a very good one indeed) of popular symbolism. The analysis of the Liberty Tree in this chapter is characteristic of the book as a whole; it teases out of a rich historical record an amazingly acute and often surprising set of historiographical, sociological, and philosophical generalizations. Every paragraph will reward the reader's attention.

This is a characteristically French book in that it is more an extended essay than a monographic study. It reminds me of the great essays of the French ethnographer Marcel Mauss, or of the sociologist Roger Caillois. Like those essays, it takes an aspect of social life, investigates it, turns it around and upside down, and suggests, without being programmatic, a new understanding of the workings of society and culture. It is unusual for historians to accomplish the feat; this book should serve as inspiration to us all.

The Republican Calendar

Vendémiaire (*September 22–October 21*)

Brumaire (*October 22–November 20*)

Frimaire (*November 21–December 20*)

Nivôse (*December 21–January 19*)

Pluviôse (*January 20–February 18*)

Ventôse (*February 19–March 20*)

Germinal (*March 21–April 19*)

Floréal (*April 20–May 19*)

Prairial (*May 20–June 18*)

Messidor (*June 19–July 18*)

Thermidor (*July 19–August 17*)

Fructidor (*August 18–September 21*)

Brief Chronology of the
French Revolution

1788	August 8	Louis XVI agrees to convoke the Estates General, which has not met since 1614
	September 21	Parlement of Paris recommends that the Estates General follow the same procedures as in 1614
1789	May 5	Estates General open at Versailles
	June 17	Third Estate decides to call itself the National Assembly
	July 11	Louis XVI dismisses his popular minister Necker
	July 14	Fall of the Bastille
	July 15	First mention of a celebration of the event of July 14
	October 5–6	"October Days," during which a large crowd marches from Paris to Versailles to bring the royal family back to the capital
1790	Winter and spring	Series of federative festivals in the provinces
	July 12	Civil Constitution of the Clergy
	July 14	Festival of Federation celebrating Bastille Day
	September 20	Festival celebrated in the Champ-de-Mars in honor of the national guardsmen who died at Nancy
	October 21	Tricolor flag replaces the white flag

	November 27	Decree requiring oath of loyalty from clergy
1791	April 4	Pantheonization of Mirabeau
	June 20	Louis XVI attempts to flee Paris in disguise and is captured at Varennes
	July 11	Pantheonization of Voltaire
	October 1	Newly elected Legislative Assembly opens
1792	April 15	Festival in honor of the Swiss of Châteauvieux
	April 20	Declaration of war on Austria
	June 3	Festival in honor of Simonneau
	June 20	Invasion of the Tuileries palace by mob
	August 10	Insurrection in Paris and attack on Tuileries leads to suspension of the king
	September 2	Verdun lost to Prussian army
	September 2–6	Murder of prisoners in "September Massacres"
	September 21	Newly elected National Convention meets for the first time and abolishes the monarchy
1793	January 14–17	Voting in trial of Louis XVI
	January 21	Execution of Louis XVI
	February 1	Declaration of war on the United Kingdom and the Dutch Republic
	March 10	Revolutionary Tribunal established
	March 11	Beginning of uprising in the Vendée
	May 4	First "Maximum" on grain prices
	May 31–June 2	Insurrection leading to arrest of the "Girondins" in the Convention
	July 27	Robespierre elected to the Committee of Public Safety
	August 10	Festival of Republican Reunion
	September 5	Demonstration in the Convention leads to adoption of "terror" as the order of the day
	October 5	Adoption of Revolutionary calendar
	October 16	Execution of Marie Antoinette
	November 10	Festival of Reason at Notre-Dame

	November 21	Robespierre condemns the de-Christianization campaign
1794	January–March	Debate on the general bill to establish civic festivals
	February 4	Slavery abolished in French colonies
	March 13–24	Arrest, trial, and execution of "Hébertists"
	March 30–April 5	Arrest, trial, and execution of "Dantonists"
	May 7	Robespierre's report to the Convention on Republican principles and national festivals
	June 8	Festival of the Supreme Being
	July 27	"The Ninth of Thermidor"—arrest of Robespierre, Saint-Just, and their supporters (executed July 28–29)
	September 21	Pantheonization of Marat
	October 11	Pantheonization of Rousseau
	November 12	Closing of Paris Jacobin Club
	December 24	Abolition of the "Maximum"
1795	April 1–2	Popular uprising in Paris fails
	May 20–23	Second popular uprising also fails
	May–June	"White Terror" in south against former terrorists
	August 22	Convention approves Constitution of the Year III
	October 5	Right-wing insurrection in Paris against new Constitution defeated
	October 25	Major law on public education and the organization of festivals
	October 26	Directory government begins after elections of Year IV (October 1795)
1796	April–October 1797	Series of Italian victories by Bonaparte
	May 29	Festival of Gratitude and of Victories
1797	January 15	Inauguration of the theophilanthropic cult
	March–April	Elections of Year V register royalist gains
	May 27	Execution of Babeuf

	September 4	Coup of 18 Fructidor, Year V, in which legislature is purged of supposed royalists
	October 1	Hoche's funeral
1798	March–April	Elections of Year VI mark Jacobin resurgence
	May 11	Coup of 22 Floréal, Year VI, against the Jacobins in the councils
	May–October 1799	Bonaparte campaigns in Egypt and Middle East
	July 29	Festival of Liberty and the triumphal entry of objects of sciences and art collected in Italy
1799	September 18	Joubert's funeral
	November 9–10	Bonaparte's coup of 18–19 Brumaire

· *Festivals and the French Revolution* ·

Introduction

PEOPLE nowadays often bemoan the disappearance of festivals. It was the same in the eighteenth century. The criticisms leveled at festivals in that century, however, were so constant, so unanimous, that any attempt to draw up a typology of festivals seems almost pointless. And yet there were so many different kinds of festivals—royal and corporate celebrations, religious feast days, popular holidays, and so on—that we should hesitate before speaking, in the singular, of "the traditional festival." If it is at all possible to do so, it is only because all festivals were the object of general disapproval. The traditional festival conjured up a repellent image, the product of the incomprehension of "enlightened minds" certain, as we are today, that truly festive celebration was a thing of the past.

Yet if everyone thought that the true meaning of the festival had been lost, it is because there were too many festivals, not, as today, too few. Paris had thirty-two feast days, Nicolas de La Mare tells us, without counting the fifty-two Sundays of the year. In view of their number, attempts to eliminate some of the feast days appear timid indeed. The slogan "Cut down on the number of holidays" echoed throughout the century, finally finding a place in the *cahiers de doléances*. Behind this demand was a concern for greater economic efficiency. This above all was what condemned the endless succession of festivals: palace festivities, celebrations in the schools, academic processions, and craftsmen's and tradesmen's parades, all deriving from "our love of idleness."[1] It was this that inspired the (often quite detailed) calculation of lost national revenue that so preoccupied Montesquieu. The Protestant religion at least had the advantage of adding fifty working days to the year. Little wonder that

"Protestant commerce" competed so successfully with "Catholic commerce"![2] This observation gave rise to a host of projects for moving feast days to the nearest Sunday, or even for permitting work after Sunday morning mass and instruction.[3] Both labor and commerce would thus be given their due, and God would be honored by men, sickle in hand, albeit at the risk of annoying a saint or two. This risk was taken well before the Jacobins loosed their furies, and well before Charles Villette dared to suggest that the interests of the saints ran counter to the interests of the people.[4]

Continuous activity, furthermore, was the "mother of innocence." This aphorism of the Abbé de Saint-Pierre, repeated ad nauseam throughout the century, lent support to the project of wresting Sunday hours from the wine shop, gaming, women, and senseless sporting competitions. A hatred of wastefulness went hand in hand with a fear of the indiscipline that festivals brought with them. What was rational from an economic point of view accorded with moral and religious teaching, since the "holy days devoted to piety" had in practice become occasions for drunkenness and riotous living, for brawls, and even for murder. There was no sign in the festivals of that "serious-minded" populace that enlightened opinion so hoped for until, with the Revolution, it had supposedly been created at last. Instead the festivals were occasions of confusion, indecency, the improper mingling of the sexes, the blurring of social roles, the reign of night and of wine—in short, all that was contained in the Pandora's box labeled "abuses." The obsessive reiteration of this convenient euphemism was an admission of complicity: when the encyclopedists denounced the "abuses" of the festivals, they did not hesitate to repeat the arguments of the episcopal authorities, who had also been convinced of the advisability of reducing the number of feast days, and of the civil authorities, who had always tended to see festive crowds as unlawful assemblies all too likely to harbor elements ready, at any moment, to erupt into violence[5]— a constant threat to religion, to the state, or to morality.

Yet the festivals gave a little glory and beauty to an impoverished existence, and it might seem surprising that the dazzling sense of wonder they aroused was no longer able to justify their continued existence. The century that was to end in a blaze of spectacle at first acquired a pronounced distaste for it. For the spectacle of the festival to work its spell, one must be willing to give oneself to it; one's heart must be in it. But for those who resist the spell of illusion, the whole machinery creaks; the effects become tawdry, incongruous, ridiculous. When Venus made her way through the heavens at the Paris Opéra, what did Mably actually see? "An extremely heavy cart, a trembling Venus, and Cupids of so constrained a countenance that I could not but laugh in expectation of some tragic catastrophe."[6] Similarly, the brilliant costumes of the festive spectacle could no longer give pleasure to men insensitive to the magical, who recoiled from disguises and masks out of both socially based fears and an aesthetic reaction of repugnance. The eighteenth century saw more artifice than fire in its *feux d'artifice*. Fireworks now seemed an absurd waste of money, a fortune going up in smoke.

Thus a childlike taste for illusion had been lost. When the reports of Revolutionary celebrations refer by way of contrast to the "insignificant" ceremonies of the ancien régime, this epithet should be taken quite literally. The traditional festivals had become enigmatic to the "enlightened" sensibility. For one Diderot who still marveled at the Corpus Christi celebrations, how many were there who, like Marmontel, had to restrain his laughter at a passing religious procession in Aix; like Boulainvilliers, rendered speechless by the "giants" of Douai; or like Voltaire, pouring scorn on the Flemish Christmas![7] It seems that there were only two ways of looking at the popular festivals at this time. They were seen either as bizarre (but with no trace of curiosity: their predicted demise aroused no regrets, no nostalgia, not even a scholarly description) or as barbarous. The popular festival meant the senseless din of coal shovels and pans; crowds obstructing the streets and public squares; barbarous "sports" like shooting birds or tearing a goose limb from limb; the veiled threat of masks; the disgusting spectacle of people fighting over loaves of bread or sausages. In short, popular excitement disconcerted, or worse "offended," reason.

Finally, and most important, the traditional festival was the realm of distinctions. This was true of the royal festivities,[8] which, with exemplary rigidity, articulated the hierarchy of rank between corporate persons and bodies. It was just as true of religious celebrations, in which the ceremonial had become "arrogant and despotic, almost an opera,"[9] and had taken on an ostentation that many found scandalous. It was also true, finally, of theatrical performances, which concentrated in themselves the defects of other sorts of festivities, all of which tended toward the spectacular. Treatises on architecture had for decades denounced the theater as a place in which social hierarchy and an intoxicating display of social stratification had reached their apogee. The theater was the "dark little place" that Diderot judged incapable of "holding the attention of an entire nation."[10]

According to Mercier, it embodied a pettiness that made the audience itself the chief object of attention[11] and gave the festival, which ought to have expressed the sheer marvel of human existence as a whole, the fractional, unsharable character of a private entertainment.

The episode that epitomized for the collective imagination all the vices of the traditional festival—decreed from above, hierarchical, artificial, coercive, and, in the long run, murderous—was the catastrophe of the wedding of Louis XVI and Marie Antoinette, which turned out to be a symbol heavy with premonition. There are innumerable descriptions of the "fire breaking out in the fireworks scaffolding, lack of foresight on the part of the magistrates, the cupidity of swindlers, the lethal advance of the carriages"; or of "how the dauphin's young wife, who had arrived from Versailles by way of the Cours la Reine—happy, radiant, adorned in all her finery—to bask in the joy of an entire nation, fled in confusion, her eyes filled with tears, pursued by that frightful image and believing she still heard the cries of the dying." This scene is highly retouched.[12] Nevertheless, it is a striking example of the divorce between enlightened opinion and the festival.

Should the festivals be done away with altogether, then? No, it was not quite as simple as that. Even the advocates of the economic arguments against them—those who rubbed their hands with glee at each reduction in their number and who, like the Marquis de Mirabeau, welcomed one such reduction as a step in the right direction—even they were aware of the advantages of the festivals. Feast days structured the flow of time and gave a regular pattern to everyday life. Paradoxically, they were a guarantee of acceptable behavior, for the excesses they authorized served as a safety valve: they prevented intemperance from spreading to daily life and throughout the social body as a whole. They provided a powerful bond within the community by dramatizing reconciliation in the companionship of a shared table at which everything is of value: the roast chestnuts of Christmas, the bean in the Galette des Rois at Epiphany, Easter eggs, and the early fruit of Pentecost. Without festivals, without their capacity to embellish everything, life would have appeared what it indeed was, "a shapeless, deathly trunk." Festivals were seen as necessary, then, by anyone who considered himself to be Mirabeau's "Friend of Man"—as everyone did by that time.[13]

ONCE, long ago, there had been another sort of festival. In the remote past, the festival had been something like the contract in the *Essai sur l'origine des langues,* with no binding clauses, "a happy age when nothing marked the hours."[14] There had been a time without routine, a festival without divisions and almost without spectacle. Far back in the mists of time, a festive assembly had been held in which the participants found their satisfaction simply in the fact of being together. There had been a primitive, a primordial festival; it would be enough to return to it. But the model seemed to have been lost.

Fortunately, it had not been entirely lost. Athens and Rome had just been "unveiled"[15] through their customs, and although the practices of ancient peoples were themselves, as Court de Gébelin repeated, merely a decadent version of a more primitive—hence even truer—mythology, at least their proximity to history's origins gave them status as models. The collective imagination compensated for the mediocrity of latter-day festivals by emigrating to Greece, the national ceremonies of which the Abbé Barthélemy offered as an example to the Frenchmen of 1788, or to Rome, where, according to Bernardin de Saint-Pierre, the civic crown was the object of public homage. The desire for new festivals was projected not only into the future of the French people but also into the past. Time opened up in both directions, forward and backward. It was with images of chariots, athletes, gymnastic competitions, palms, and laurel crowns that the man of the Enlightenment climbed onto the stage of the Revolution.

Furthermore, when temporal exoticism failed, this century of voyagers could call on space to feed its dreams. There were the Abbé Mallet's Danes, who held pure religious festivities in the woods to worship a God who was already a "Supreme Being."[16] There were Mirabeau's Chinese, who had invented symbolic festivals in which the emperor himself bowed low "before the nourishing plow"[17] (and who were recalled by the organizers of the Revolutionary Festival of Agriculture, along with the Peruvians, to whom the same rite was attributed). Then there were the civilized nations of the New World, who, Mably declared, had returned to the principles of Nature herself; Raynal added that they were capable of renewing the world a second time; Grégoire later recalled that they already had their own civic festivities and their Liberty Trees as a focus for community rejoicing.[18]

Closer to hand there were "the simple inhabitants of happy Helvetia," with their winegrowers' festivals and their military celebrations, about which J.-L. Mollet gave such an enthusiastic report to Rousseau on June 10, 1761. What aroused Mollet's enthusiasm was not merely the general review of five hundred men, parading before twelve thousand spectators in a Prussian-style exercise recently introduced into Geneva. It was above all the resulting sense of communion: "The outpouring of the public's joy could be seen at every crossroads; business was suspended; people wanted to love one another and nothing more; everyone was pleasant, gracious, affable; if the word *contagion* could be taken in a positive sense, I would say that the contagion of public friendship had reached every individual in society." Rousseau gave a warm welcome to this report, expressing the hope that "these tastes, these games, these patriotic celebrations—which accord with morality and virtue, which we enjoy with rapture and recall with delight—be revived among us."[19]

But there was no need for costly voyages. The French village, that exotic but temperate region, had festivals that could serve as a model, if one knew how to look for them. It could hardly be said that pastoral literature, which did so much to shape the sensibility of the age, *contained* festivals: it *was* a festival, from beginning to end. Florian's *Galatée* contains all the elements later used by the Revolutionary festival: a busy community that prefigures the activities on the Champ-de-Mars; exercises performed by joyous young bodies, anticipating the gymnastic festivals of the Directoire; tables set up under shady trees like those of the *repas civiques*. Funeral celebrations for Hoche and Joubert would be copied from the funeral rites of Florian's shepherds, with cypress crowns and shepherds' staffs decked with an abundance of black ribbons. This pastoral, for us so unreal, so proudly detached from popular custom, the very symbol of a society in flight, seemed to many contemporary observers to be a reality taking place under their very eyes. Karamzine lends the realism of an eyewitness account to his description of the *fête de la rosière* (crowning of the "rose queen") at Suresnes.[20] The allegory of equality had at last found its incarnation: he notes that the young peasants in their Sunday best, boasting of the good wine and the good morals of their village, dared to dance with the ladies of Paris, who, "as always, were curious to see innocence so close to the capital." In 1785 Madame Jullien described at length to her ten-year-old son Marc-Antoine (later known as Jullien *fils*) a *fête champêtre* that included work in common (lending a hand during the grape harvest, an ancient feudal obligation), as well as sheer pleasure (dancing in the meadows). What a pity, she exclaims, that the child was not there to benefit from such an agreeable lesson![21] The "primal scene" that fired the imagination of La Révellière-Lépeaux was the country wedding of a cousin. It combined all that could be asked of a festival: beauty without display, abundance without waste, and everyone under the eyes of everyone else—in sum, "decency always respected in the midst of the liveliest joy and the most animated pleasures."[22] Memories of this sort made such a strong impression on people that the Revolutionary festivals were to seem no more than reminiscences of them. The Revolutionary festival would try to give new life to the cast of characters of a country celebration—the good friend, the good son, the good mother, the benevolent lord, the generous *curé*—as well as to their setting—a few barrels in a barn, flowers in a basket, and always forests of branches in all the luxuriance of an earthly paradise.

Yet all this amounted to no more than isolated, fragmented impressions of festivities, like memories of a journey. No time and no place offered the total system that men of the century sought, the network of festivals able to embrace and to sustain the whole of human life—no place but utopia, a favorite resort of the time. In those ideal lands of moderate living, moderate labor, and pleasures in moderation, what need had anyone for celebrations? In such a land there would be no need for a break: each day would be like another, and in a world free of conflict, where nobody moved about, all days would be holidays. If utopias still had holidays galore, it was first of all because their founding—the creative rupture, the lucky shipwreck—had to be remembered. This was not simply a memorable date; it was the only date in utopian history, and therefore fully deserved commemoration. Furthermore, it was linked with the memory of heroic acts and useful inventions: thus a grateful utopia dedicated new festivals to its great men. Then came the cycle of the seasons, such as the start and the end of the great communal tasks, which called for celebration, as did all the important moments in private life, such as weddings and funerals. These became, in the limpid world of the Philadelphians, celebrations for the whole of society. Thus, there were innumerable occasions to be celebrated.

It is easy to see what the pre-Revolutionary sensibility found so charming in these utopian festivals. In addition to the fiction of embarking on a voyage, the equivalent in the sphere of the imagination of a revolutionary break with the past, a number of factors found satisfaction in such festivals: the passion for classification in the order imposed by their regular occurrence, an antidote to the irregularities of the calendar; a hatred of scandal in a festival that was entirely at one with everyday life, to which it added an extra intensity, but never in any sense denied or undermined it; a fear of secrecy in a public festival in which everything was declared, even love and friendship (as Saint-Just was to remember when he tried to have bonds between individuals publicly renewed every year in the temple during the month of Ventôse); lastly, a totalizing tendency, such as is to be found in the *Constitution de la Lune*,[23] which declared that the fusion of various kinds of festivity always benefits the nation.

The utopian festival (and this is really why it was referred to so constantly) put everyone on the same level. When it assigned different roles to old people and to children, it did so on grounds of nature, not privilege. It managed (or at least it seemed to manage) to square the circle of the social problem of how to achieve variety without resorting to distinctions. Whereas actual festivals, like the rose festival at Suresnes, offered only an allegorical, ephemeral image of equality, the utopian festival ruled over a world in which the multicolored variety of humankind was, in theory, annihilated, and in which the intellectualization of activities and roles was total. All the celebrants described in the *Etudes de la nature* wear the same costume; their heads bear identical flowered crowns ("a more august spectacle than the lackeys of the great bearing their masters' crests stuck onto candles"); they make the same codified gestures, pronounce the same words, and exchange roles in perfect reciprocity.[24]

This was the model, this was the dream. The most astonishing part is the unanimity with which it was called for or experienced. Before they organized the festival that they held to be the only way to bring men together, enlightened men had already reached agreement in its imaginary working out.

THE meeting of this dream with the French Revolution is the subject of this book. The Revolution offered these dreamers an unheard-of opportunity. The austere tabula rasa that had become such a cliché for the eighteenth century had apparently been rediscovered. There would be no more royal festivities, no more religious feasts—or only the vital minimum that Rousseau was willing to grant in his projects for Corsica.[25] Even popular festivals would soon be opposed. Luxurious display would disappear, more by the force of circumstance than by the will of men. There would be no more constricting "customs." Everything became possible. The Revolution, which, as Jean Starobinski has so clearly seen, seemed to have been set up in a field open on all sides to enlightenment and to law, was felt to be an unhoped-for opportunity for realizing utopia. The Fortunate Islands had ceased to drift. They had belonged (it was their luck and fatal flaw) to no time and no country. They had at last reached port and were securely moored, here and now.

In the clean-swept world that the Revolution seemed to offer the utopian dreamers, the suppression of hierarchies and the homogenization of
the human condition left men alone. Men were individuals, in theory all
identical, all equal, but solitary. It was now the task of the legislator to
connect them, a task that all the utopias of the century took up with
meticulous relish. The men of the Revolution also took on the task of
finding an efficacious form of association for beings whom they thought
of as having returned to the isolation of nature. The festival was an indispensable complement to the legislative system, for although the legislator
makes the laws for the people, festivals make the people for the laws.
According to Michel Foucault, there were two great mythical experiences
in the eighteenth century: the person blind from birth who regains his
sight and the foreign spectator who is thrown into an unfamiliar world.
We might add to the list the individual who is rebaptized as citizen in
the festival.

This is the source of the extraordinary interest—particularly extraordinary in view of all the other things that required their energies—that
the men of the Revolution took in festivals. Through the festival the new
social bond was to be made manifest, eternal, and untouchable. Hence
nothing about festivals was unimportant: neither the objects proposed for
general contemplation and admiration, which had clearly to appear as
common property; nor the pictures portraying Revolutionary history, in
which the founding event had to be celebrated quite unambiguously; nor
the repetition of the choruses or the intoning of invocations in which a
common will found expression; nor the spectacle created by processions,
restructuring the huge crowd of isolated individuals into an organized
community; nor the publicity given to private engagements or the solemnity lent to public engagements; nor, finally, the search for transcendence.
The elaboration of the festival—where desire and knowledge met, where
the education of the masses gave way to joy—combined politics and psychology, aesthetics and morality, propaganda and religion.

Little wonder, then, that the Revolutionary festival, for so long neglected, is now attracting the attention of historians.[26] This is undoubt-
edly because their study of the work of folklorists and ethnographers has
shown them the importance of the festival. It is also because the festival
has now become a multiform reality for us, as it was for the men of the
Revolution: one has only to think how our various vocabularies—in political essays, in literary commentaries, in theater criticism—have been
invaded by the notion of the festival. If we too dream of the festival it is
often with the nostalgic intention of restoring it, for a society that expa-

tiates at length on the festivals has little left but impoverished versions of it in a neofolklore entrusted with the task of keeping up a false collective memory. Often, too, we speak of the festival in a spirit of prophetic expectation: since the events of May 1968, a moment that has been described as a reprisal for our ceremonial impoverishment, we have been awaiting the festival promised us by both political and theological thought. Theology is concerned with rehabilitating festive spontaneity in opposition to the patient, unremitting values of work,[27] while politics seems to expect the revolution to deliver happiness, not when it is due but at once, and to become one with the eternal present into which the festival is absorbed.[28] Always, however—and our own time shares this with the endless round of festivals of the French Revolution—the festival is therapeutic, a reconstruction, as in the utopias of the eighteenth century, of a social bond that has come undone.

It is difficult to believe, however, that the voyage from utopia to revolution is an easy one or that its outcome is desirable. In reality, utopia in the eighteenth century contained very little collective dynamism and very little revolutionary hope. When he had taken his stroll among the clouds of the Land of Cockaigne, the utopian returned home with a model, but not with a program. The distance that he put between himself and society sharpened his vision and his judgment, but it bought him neither hope nor even confidence. We do not move forward from utopia to revolution, then, but, on the contrary, back from revolution to utopia: it is the birth of a historical optimism that retrospectively provides utopia with an activism that it in no way possessed. Thus it is revolution that sees utopian forms as desirable and reads in them a project for a new world. It is revolution that attributes to utopia an idea that is utterly alien to it: that there are, in the course of human history, propitious and unpropitious times, and that "good" events need to ripen just like good fruit.

From the outset, then, there was a misunderstanding between revolution and utopia. The Revolution imagined itself, and willed itself, to be the daughter of utopia. What is more, it saw itself as a peaceable daughter; as the transition, without ruinous revolt, from fiction to reality, from the optative to the normative; as the embodiment, once the old order was abolished, of a new order. It was unaware of its mysterious ability to produce an irrational succession of disasters. It lived in an intellectualized overestimation of itself. It dreamed only of establishing itself once and for all. Take the description of Saint-Just left by an anonymous companion: "He yearned for the Revolution to be over so that he could give himself to his usual preoccupations, to the contemplation of nature, and to the enjoyment of a restful private life in some country haven with a young woman whom heaven seemed to have intended as his companion." But did it need a revolution to realize this pastoral dream?

The festival provides good evidence of the false view of itself that the Revolution inherited from its fascination with utopia. The entire history of the Revolutionary festivals might be presented as an illustration of this blindness: they aimed at spontaneity, yet they were really a combination of precautionary and coercive measures. Their purpose was to bring together the entire community, but they never ceased to exclude some people and to engender pariahs. They turned into parody and ended in solitude. The Revolutionary mania for festivals is the story of an immense disillusionment.

Whose fault was it? The most common response is to blame the actual historical reality of the Revolution, in which the utopian project could certainly find no place without becoming distorted. The utopian project was as luminous as the reality was somber; it remained reassuringly fixed, while the unpredictable consequences of reality were endless. Utopia was geometrical; revolutionary reality was monstrously luxuriant. Moreover—and this sums it all up—the Revolution never managed to break with the initial violence that made it possible but that also made its completion impossible. In these circumstances, the festivals were merely a false celebration of peace and unanimity of feeling; they became a camouflage, a facade plastered onto a gloomy reality that it was their mission to conceal. This was, in an ironic twist, the very definition that the century had given to the traditional festival.

These contradictions might not have been fatal, however, as long as ideology had enough resources to combat the disobliging character of events. If the Revolutionary festival found it so difficult to turn its dreams into reality, it was perhaps less because it contradicted utopia than because it made evident precisely what the very coherence of the utopian project concealed. Utopia was a less pleasant place than had been thought. All the "Land of Cockaigne" of the eighteenth century were Spartas. When utopia decreed that "everything must be displayed before the eyes of all, that the most useful customs are not those that men follow in silence, each on his own and in an isolated manner; that there is from now on only a public, national, common, and indivisible existence"[29] (even if what is spoken of here is its most idle form, the pastoral), it left no room for the free play of liberty. Utopian festivals always have that air of order and regulation that begins by discouraging fantasy and ends by punishing it, as in Rousseau's projects for Corsica or for the government of Poland. Such festivals have no place for deviants; they make a crime of isolation, excluding the atheist and his disciples, as Mercier demanded, but also excluding the rebellious child, as, Marmontel noted with satisfaction, among the Incas. Unanimity appeared to be such a clear precondition for the festival that interest soon shifted to ways of creating it. A preliminary separation of the good from the bad and a ferreting out of saboteurs and traitors seemed to be the best way of guaranteeing that the festival would take place in a world that had abolished distinctions. When this proved impossible, the festival itself took on the sorting process: anyone who failed to find pleasure in this exemplary gathering of the people would be declared, ipso facto, a public enemy.[30]

The guillotine functioned even better than the regulations on participating in the festivals as an instrument for choosing between vice and virtue. Thus Revolutionary violence appears as not that which perverted the utopian festival but that which brought it to fulfilment: Prairial, Year II, was the radiant month in which the Festival of the Supreme Being claimed to establish regenerated mankind in an innocent dawn; it was also the baleful month in which the mechanics of the Terror went into operation.

We must reverse our point of view, therefore: far from utopia's providing the French Revolution with a mirror in which it recognized itself for what it was, it was the Revolution that held up the glass in which utopia could see its true features. These were the features not of happiness but of an inflexible order that was to prepare the way for happiness; not of the imagination but of a deadly passion for detail, which Bernardin de Saint-Pierre sensed would encourage the Terror. They were the features of a violence that was the price to be paid for the abolition of differences. As Edgar Quinet put it, "Unfortunately, our utopias are almost all born in servitude, and they have preserved its spirit. That is why they are inclined to see an ally in any emergent despotism. Our system makers dedicate their dreams to absolute power. As their ideas often contradict human nature, they often entrust the task of establishing them to despotism. When the course of things does not go their way, it must be forced to do so by arbitrary authority. Hence their definite liking for the strongest. For them, however, it is never strong enough."

· I ·

The History of the
Revolutionary Festival

FOR ten years the dialogue between the utopian project and the Revolutionary festival continued through a remarkably rich proliferation of ceremonies. We tend to speak of *the* Festival of the Federation, *the* Festival of the Supreme Being, forgetting that, duplicating and echoing the celebrations in Paris, there were thousands of festivals of the Federation, thousands of festivals of the Supreme Being. Furthermore, references are always being made to these two examples and to that of the Festival of Reason; many historians look no further. Yet one has only to open the cardboard boxes containing the archives of the festivals to be struck at once by their sheer variety and abundance: festivals to celebrate Youth, Victories, Old Age, Agriculture, Spouses, the Republic, the Sovereignty of the People—there seems to be no end to the number of festivals! And they were celebrated everywhere. In the smallest municipality, several times a year and sometimes even several times a month, the flags and drums were taken out, the joiners and painters summoned, songs rehearsed, and programs drawn up. The momentum was sustained over the ten years of Revolution, leaving the researcher with bundle after bundle of reports. These dry, usually monotonous reports, whose sheer volume is impressive enough, have nevertheless been neglected in favor of the more highly colored versions to be found in memoirs and newspapers.

Is this why there is so little information about the festival in the histories of the Revolution? Take Lamartine, whom Daniel Halévy described as "endlessly talking,"[1] in 1848, in the midst of a crowd wild with joy, busy reconstituting and imitating the festivals of the first Revolution. One might have expected Lamartine to detect a certain festive exuberance in such manifestations, but in fact he leaves very little room for the Revolutionary festivals, which he tends to see as an expression of murderous fury rather than of joy.[2] Most historians reveal a similar reticence on the subject. They may find room for the obligatory accounts of the festivals of the Federation and of the Supreme Being, but these are isolated purple patches; more usually the festivals are given no more than a passing mention or a sarcastic remark. This general attitude of disapproval or neglect probably derives from the fact that the description of the Revolutionary festival is tied up with political success or failure. Once everything is related to this problem (whose relevance is not demonstrated), one is obviously inclined to stress that no festival fulfilled the remoter consequences expected of it, or even kept its immediate promises; one describes the bitter aftermath of the festival and shows how the very men whom it was intended to bring together were even more divided than ever. And this went on for the ten years of the Revolution. Beyond that, it is all too easy to observe that this great collection of rituals ended with the Revolution itself.

Interest in the festivals revived to some extent at the end of the nineteenth century, at a time when the separation in the Republic between church and state was being pushed through; for this divorce, by the unspoken fears that it aroused, brought back, in terms very close to those used by the men of the Revolution, the theme of a revival of religious enthusiasm in the civic festival. Indeed, what was taking place was another attempt at a graft or substitution: the thinking of the Republican historians went back to those Revolutionary years when men also dreamed of restoring national morale by means of festivals. Inspired by a sense of emergency, an interest in festivals lies at the heart of the dialogue, stormy as always, between Aulard and Mathiez; though less clearly expressed, it also inspired innumerable local monographs.

But the historians of the time were as certain as their predecessors of the overall failure of the Revolutionary festivals, whether they described that failure in terms of the successive policies of the men of the Revolution (and, for them, the festivals failed because those policies failed), or in terms of the content of the festivals (and the festivals failed because that content was uninteresting). Before we set out to look for the reasons for such unanimity, and therefore to draw up a list of the problems that this depressing historiography has bequeathed us, let us turn to the historian who must be excluded from this general lack of enthusiasm: Michelet, who, while he was almost exclusively concerned with the Parisian scene, never ceased to reflect on the meaning and function of the festival in the Revolution.

The Revolution as Festival

"Not to have had any festivals": that, for Michelet, was a truly impoverished childhood. "My childhood never blossomed in the open air, in the warm atmosphere of an amiable crowd, where the emotion of each individual is increased a hundredfold by the emotion felt by all."[3] And yet in Paris there was a splendid festival for each great imperial victory, when the wine flowed freely and flares lit up the sky. For the young Michelet, taken there by his father and mother, these were wonderful spectacles, but nonetheless depressing. Why? As a child Michelet did not yet know that a festival made to order inevitably has something sad about it; but the presentiment that he had of this is enough to explain the passionate attention that he was later to give to the festivals of the French Revolution. Indeed, what strikes one in his account of them—especially in comparison to the alternative accounts—is the absence of exclusion, derision, or anathema. We read of no secret festivals, no mock festivals, no condemned festivals. Even the enthusiasm aroused in him by the Festival of the Federation (in the case of almost all the other historians, this enthusiasm implies contempt for the festivals that followed) does not make Michelet indifferent to less successful festivals. One certainly senses this in the 1847 preface to his *Histoire de la Révolution française*.[4]

Michelet chooses two dates to illustrate the importance of festivals in the Revolution: July 14, 1792, and August 10, 1793. What he does is contrast them: the August 10 festival was "quite different" from its predecessor. Yet an awareness of this difference does not lead to any rigidity of judgment; it suggests not so much a definitive typology as an infinite gradation. For although Michelet had intended to show the great disjunctions that could exist between two Revolutionary festivals, other comparisons would have been more telling: between the Festival of the Federation and the Festival of Reason, for example, or between the Festival of the Federation and that of the Supreme Being. But Michelet makes little attempt to classify his material. His account includes the funeral festivals (that for the dead of August 10) and the triumphs (that of Voltaire, for instance), and he is not even averse to using the word *festival* for such unexpected occasions as the giving of tokens of gratitude to Dumouriez.

In his descriptions of these various ceremonies Michelet does not, of course, accord them equal importance or show the same liking for them; nevertheless, they are all treated as festivals.

We may begin, therefore, with this question: how does Michelet define a festival? That is, what ingredients are necessary for an occasion to be a festival in the full sense? This question is all the more pressing in that, in Michelet's mind, it is always related to another: what does a revolution have to be in order to be a revolution?

A people setting out: this is the first image of a festival, and the first sign that one has occurred. The people set out in some unpremeditated way; no one has ordered them to do so; their movement precedes any call. Their action is subject neither to laws nor to institutions nor even to concerted direction: the festivals of the Federation exemplify the spontaneous convergence of different wills rather than the education or infection of one person by another. The image is one of energy and spontaneity, which are almost enough in themselves: the people take off, that is all.

And where are they going? Nobody really knows. The movement scarcely needs any other orientation than a promise or a hope. Once the crowd is on its way, the rest follows of its own accord—just as when Rouget de Lisle had found the word *allons,* he had found everything; the rest of the *Marseillaise,* according to Michelet, wrote itself. Men set out for the sheer pleasure of doing so, to go beyond the familiar bounds—and already a festival is in existence. This was to become one of Péguy's favorite themes.[5] "The French set out—that was their glory," wrote Daniel Halévy[6] in his brilliant commentary on Péguy's idea of the Revolution. The festival is a *levée en masse*; the *levée en masse* is a festival.

This explains how a festival comes about and what is required for a festival to exist at all. It also helps us to differentiate between the festivals: the Federation, which was initially just such a taking to the road—a journey, even a pilgrimage—is obviously a festival; for Michelet it is even the archetypal festival. This is even more the case with the Federation*s*, for in the provincial *levées* it was not only those men appointed to do so who set out but a whole people, and in response to no call.[7] Similarly, the France of 1792, which rose up at the first sound of the trumpet, set out in a mood that was much more festive than warlike: "The great wind of Danton's words and the joyful sound of the cannon of August 10 carried her off to many another festival." The predilection that Michelet shows for this mass taking to the high road even makes him see the festival of Châteauvieux (which he does not find attractive and whose polemical procession he would prefer to forget) as a true festival, simply because convicts and national guardsmen walked side by side from Brest to Paris.[8]

A journey, however, is not a sufficient qualification in itself: the people may take to the road without there being any festival. This is because, in addition to a certain charge of energy, the movement of men must also possess a certain self-confidence that derives neither from overexcitement nor from resentment. This is why Michelet does not dwell on those festivals in the aftermath of Varennes, on July 14, 1791, and the triumph of his beloved Voltaire: there was a tremendous "concourse of people" in the streets, but they were overexcited, and the feverish atmosphere of the capital made the air unbreathable. Similarly, the return from Varennes, though accompanied by a living sea of people around the humiliated royal carriage, could not be regarded as a festival, because the men had come from far and wide with the intention of shedding blood. The triumphal march must also possess a certain serenity and discipline; and there is no contradiction here between this requirement and the presentation of the proclamation of national emergency as a festival: the war into which the France of 1792 plunged was a sublime war, a war of peace.

Indeed the people, who decked themselves out for both festival and war, had little reason to fear that violence would affect their progress. In fact, their appearance was enough; they hardly had to fight. This advance was not an action but an "appearance," before which any difficulties vanished. This was the language of magic, and this brings us to what, for Michelet, is a second, indispensable ingredient of the festival: it lies outside all art and all systems. Nobody can propose it, nobody knows how it is carried out; it is the gratuitous triumph of an ephemeral rationality, a miracle. Take the Federation: as men took to the road, goods too were also "miraculously" freed. During the winter of the Federations, "foodstuffs began to circulate easily, like a miraculous harvest." Take another "miracle": when Voltaire's carriage entered Paris, kings and priests fled, as if they could not bear this excess of light. It is pointless to ask for the reasons behind these miracles. *Quia est absurdum,* Michelet replies, with Pascal. The "absurd" recurs over and over again in the account of the victory over the Austrians at Jemmapes. The war was absurd; the victory too was absurd. And that is precisely why Jemmapes was commemorated in a festival.[9] The festival is a victory over rationality, over space (for Michelet the Federation was "the death of geography"), and over time. It is an effortless victory, to the accompaniment of singing.

It is also a victory over solitude. The festival brings about an emotional contagion hitherto unimaginable, and unimaginable without it; it restores harmony to the world. "To believe that the world is in harmony," Michelet writes in *Nos fils,* "to feel oneself in harmony with it, that is peace; that is the inner festival." This is a thoroughly religious definition: there is a festival when what is isolated is reunited with its own kind.[10] He is using the action of reunion in the sense in which the word is used by Lamennais, who criticizes the philosophers for failing to understand that, even before any laws had been passed to this effect, men were reunited in a "religion" that had its own specific aims: the abolition of divisions between rich and poor, nobles and commoners; the extinction of religious and personal animosities; the loss too—and in this the festival is very close to heroism—of the sense of individuality. This "religion" also had its symbols: the crowd, the dance in a ring or farandole, and of course the banquet, that key word of Michelet's sensibility, the title of a posthumous work in which, in terms very close to those used by the men of the Revolution themselves, he calls for festivals[11]—the *agape,* the love feast: that is what a true festival must be.

In the absence of the "great, universal banquet," Michelet had to be satisfied if he saw in any particular festival some "touching glimmer of religion." One senses this in his hesitation over the festival of August 10, 1793: "It was scarcely a festival." This was because it was difficult to detect any joyful spontaneity in the somewhat stiff, forced ceremony of Reunion. Above all it was because, despite the name of this festival, the theme of reunion played a secondary role (even though France was uniting symbolically to accept the Constitution, and the festival welcomed the disinherited of the earth). And yet, when Michelet's account reaches 1794, the festival of August 10, 1793, changes its meaning and character. From this terrible standpoint, Michelet now sees the place de la Bastille, when everyone drank from the cup, the "communion of holy water between the départements." From that later standpoint, August 10 had certainly been a reunion, a true festival. And the transfer of the archives from Liège had also been a festival, on account of the effusive welcome given the Liégeois. Even the tokens of gratitude and friendship given to Dumouriez could claim the name of festival: though confined within the space of a bourgeois home, inspired by the private motives of pro-Danton politicians, this occasion seemed nevertheless to transport the Revolution into "the higher region where men's hatreds die"—or at least until the sinister appearance of Marat sent everyone back to his own faction and shattered the festival.

Finally, one indispensable element in a festival is the presence of women and children. For Michelet one of the major virtues of the Revolution was that it brought women and children into public life, thus providing a heart in an otherwise heartless world. Their usual exclusion lends an extra charge of indignation to the works in which Michelet demands that the national festivals should include something for women and children, apart from the gloomy church where a "moral night" also reigns.[12] So, for Michelet, the presence of women and children in the Revolutionary festival is essential. Whether summoned or not, women lent charm to the Revolution. It was their overwhelming presence that transformed the procession of October 6, 1789, into a festival. Michelet hardly sees the barbaric procession described by Burke and so many historians after him, the heads stuck on poles, a funeral march "in the midst of horrible cries, shrieks, frantic dances, filthy words."[13] He sees instead the loaves of bread held aloft, the poplar branches, and everywhere women, representing "all that is most instinctive, most inspired" in the people. Again, the "gentle thoughts of childhood" lighten Lepelletier's gloomy, glacial funeral. It is the presence of women, with their children in their arms, that saves the Festival of the Supreme Being, the triumph of a man whom Michelet nevertheless detests. He is less indulgent toward the Festival of Reason: here there are no women, their arms encircling their children, but stiff, well-drilled "little innocents," a "chaste, boring, desiccated" festival. This judgment does not prevent him, however, from defending the Festival of Reason against the attacks leveled at it by Quinet: in spite of everything, the goddess is embodied by a woman. The festival of festivals, however, the one that accords best with Michelet's sensibility—again so close to the Revolutionary sensibility itself—is the one organized around a pure ceremonial based on age groups: girls watched over by married women, old men watched over by children, youths watched over by fathers. This living exchange of models and lessons accounts for Michelet's enthusiasm for the Festival of the Calendar at Arras, where the separation of the age groups echoed the new division of the Republican calendar.

An impetus verging on the miraculous; the communion of the people as a whole, women and children included: when these elements are present together, Michelet's prose itself takes on an especially festive character. But even if only one of those elements is present, Michelet still tries to convince himself that a true festival has taken place. August 10, 1793, which lacks spontaneous energy and miraculous improvisation, nevertheless has for Michelet the moving presence of sorrow, a reflection of communion. Voltaire's triumph, which lacks serenity, nevertheless has the living, swirling mass of the people. The identity that Michelet establishes between the Revolution and the festival is strikingly apparent here: even when the Revolutionary festivals have this tumultuous, vehement character, which he sees at work on July 14, 1791, the festival of Châteauvieux, Voltaire's triumph, and so many others, he finds in them a "substratum that redeemed everything"; this, as in the Revolution itself, is the devotion of a people to the world, to sacrifice.

There are in Michelet innumerable instances of this consubstantiality of festival and Revolution. Like the Revolution, the festival does not imitate but improvises: at first, nothing could be further from Michelet's thinking than what is for him the monstrous notion of a festival program. (This attitude was to change when he himself began to initiate festivals: we then see him criticizing Béranger for an excessive trust in the improvisational abilities of the people and resigning himself to programs.) Like the Revolution, the festival is a religion unaware of itself; like it, the festival is an imperious, almost instinctual creation. Lastly, like the Revolution, the festival, which is universal, has no conquering hero. If it does have one, as in the case of the Festival of the Supreme Being, then the sense of festival is extinguished and the Revolution dies. The people desert the streets and squares for their own homes; it becomes each man for himself. Festival and Revolution can live only when people breathe together.

To pose the problem of the "true" festival is obviously to go outside the typology suggested by the Revolutionary writings themselves; it is not necessarily to look for festivals where their presence is announced and not to give up seeing their presence where there is no mention of them. This is what Michelet does; he may describe as a festival an occasion that does not bear the name officially (for instance, the night of August 4) or reluctantly accept as such what was nevertheless a festival in due and proper form, like the events of August 10, 1793. Sometimes, of course, he indignantly refuses to use the name at all: when, just after the death of the Dantonians in 1794 (15–16 Germinal), the question of a festival is raised, he protests: "What! On the morrow of such a day! And the grave still open!" If we follow in detail Michelet's account, we might sometimes be led to believe that for him, as for Sébastien Mercier, the most perfect Revolutionary festival was the Revolutionary *journée,* for his sensibility responds very easily to the possibility of a barbarous festival: "a great festival, great carnage," he said of the Roman circus.[14] But the fact is quite different: almost invariably the presence of violence stops Michelet from acknowledging that an occasion was a festive one. One does not speak of festivals when "butchery" is taking place. Tragedy is compatible with festive rejoicing, but not threats, not oppression, not the shadow of the guillotine. This antinomy may be carried to the point of the mutual exclusion of the actual and the represented: when the sword is everywhere, one dares not show it in the festival.[15] In 1793 it was hidden all the more assiduously because it was present in everybody's mind; consequently, the festival must not only abandon any attempt to mimic the Revolutionary day but sometimes even deny it. October 6, therefore, is a festival only on condition that one shuts one's eyes. Unlike Péguy, who makes the storming of the Bastille a festival of festivals,[16] the first Federation, Michelet does not see July 14, 1789, as a festival. If even that first Revolutionary day cannot claim to be a festival, it is because it contains a degree of violence unassimilable by the festival, even if it is sometimes very difficult not to confuse violence with energy.

To the enormous problem of the close contact between violence and the festival Michelet adds that of festive unanimity and draws our attention to those excluded from the festival, for no festival, in his book, can be solely that of a faction. We see this in the case of Châteauvieux, and one senses it even in the Festival of Reason. Over and above individual differences and intentions, for him the ultimate reason for the need and the creation of festivals is to be found in the great common substratum of the Revolution. For Michelet, the festival, like the Revolution, lives only through its power to unite.

History of the Festivals, History of the Sects

Such language is exceptional. For most historians the festival suggests, on the contrary, the proliferation of factions, the splits within the Revolution—hardly, therefore, a festival at all in Michelet's terms.

The model of this essentially political interpretation of the Revolutionary festivals is found in Aulard.[17] For him, even the Festival of the Federation illustrates a particular political policy: it is "Fayettist," sometimes even royalist. He reduces August 10, 1793, to the proclamation of the constitutional act, so that for him the entire ceremony seems to stem from Hérault de Séchelles's declaration in the Champ-de-Mars. The cult of Marat is simply the cult of the nation. This "simply" is in fact the last word of Aulard's history; the Revolutionary festival as a whole is for him "simply" an "expedient of patriotism." It prospers as long as patriotism is fearful; it disappears when patriotism is reassured. Furthermore, each particular festival is "simply" the means imagined by a particular sect to defeat an opposing one. Let us check these two statements against the example of the Festival of Reason. On the one hand, it was the expression not of a religious consciousness but of the political intentions of the Hébertists; and on the other hand, it was a means of reassurance during the critical hours of national defense. If the festival was not the same at Strasbourg and Chartres, this had nothing to do with local tradition (which, indeed, played no role in the festival, contrary, says Aulard naively, to the usual expectation that the festival would be less dreary at Marseille than at Rennes!). It was because from the top of the steeple at Strasbourg, one could see the Austrian outposts. Both these ways of accounting for the Festival of Reason explain how easily it disappeared. As an expression of the Hébertist movement, the cult of Reason collapsed with it; as a means of waging war, it became obsolete as soon as the political imagination found a more adequate weapon. For, just as it is always possible to oppose one expedient to another, it is easy, for perfectly political reasons, to shift from Reason to the Supreme Being. Moreover, the new cult was susceptible to an interpretation identical on every point and, like the earlier one, double. The new expedient of patriotism began to fade as soon as the Austrians had been beaten. And it disappeared as soon as the tyrant Robespierre had disappeared. It might be objected that at least one of these two explanations is unnecessary. Aulard might reply that Fleurus killed both Robespierre and his cult. But the main point is to be found not here but in the consequence of the political interpretation that stresses, in diametrical opposition to Michelet, the fragility of the Revolutionary festivals, their lack of roots—in short, the absence of a collective need.

The success of Aulard's interpretation may be seen in the fact that such very different historians share it, as if the thesis had nothing to do with the degree of sympathy or antipathy shown by the historians to the Revolution itself. If, for Taine[18] or Duruy,[19] the Revolutionary festival expresses a political purpose, it also does for Cabet[20] or Jaurès.[21] Indeed, Jaurès, like Aulard, sees the Festival of the Supreme Being as an act of posthumous revenge on Hébertism: he sees behind it the decree of Floréal and the "decisive political mistake" that it embodied. Furthermore, in the account of the festival itself, Jaurès is much less susceptible to the ceremonial than to the physical distance that the festival seems to have placed between Robespierre and the Conventionnels: like so many others, like Quinet[22] or Albert Sorel,[23] he sees it as the symbol of a moral distance, a prophecy of Thermidor. Indeed, the political interpretation is still as vigorous as ever: opening the Clermont Conference in 1974, Albert Soboul reminded us how decisive it still is in understanding the festival; and Claude Mazauric, speaking of the Rouen example, showed how the festivals were dependent on the struggles being waged by the local leaders.[24] We must, then, try to understand the reasons for such unanimity.

The first is certainly that the texts emanating from the revolutionaries themselves overwhelmingly support this interpretation. Each of the generations that the Revolution brought to the fore wanted to establish the originality of the festivals that it had invented. This is apparent at each new upheaval. Thus the Festival of the Supreme Being took the place of the Festival of Reason. In his speech to the Convention of 25 Floréal, Payan was quite obviously anxious to distinguish the Robespierrist festivals from those that had preceded them. Payan attributed the Festival of Reason entirely to the "latest conspirators," Hébert and Chaumette, whom he also held responsible for the trappings of the festival: "the wife of a conspirator borne aloft in triumph in the midst of the people; the actress who the night before had played the role of Juno; the fanatical priest renouncing his religion." He attributed all this "mythology" to a particular political end: the destruction of liberty by atheism. Lastly, he lay particular stress on the new political purpose and suggested the urgency of "replacing" all superstitions with principles "worthy of the advocates of Liberty." This is, point by point, Aulard's interpretation. We find the same language, the same preoccupations with the Festival of Victories recurring in Vendémiaire, Year III. Parliamentary debates, speeches, and newspaper accounts repeatedly stress how important it is to distinguish this festival from the Robespierrist ceremonial and suggest ways in which this might be done. Chénier, who made a distinguished contribution to the debate, expressed his determination to have done with the "pretentious rags" of the other festivals and his hopes that a substitute would be found for them yet again.[25] In short, there is abundant evidence in the writings of the time for linking each festival with a particular historical purpose.

The advantage of placing such trust in the evidence of the men of the Revolution is that the festivals then provide a mirror in which the Revolution as a whole may be viewed. Take the Festival of the Federation: its joyful character reflects a Revolution that is still open, still filled with hope. The creaking stiffness of the Festival of the Supreme Being, by contrast, foreshadows the sclerosis of the Revolution. In the festival of 1 Vendémiaire, Year VII, with its gymnastic competitions and its exhibitions of work and skill, there is already an atmosphere of the nineteenth century. Seen in the developing context of Revolutionary events, the festivals seem to enjoy very little independence from them. But, by the same token, they allow us to follow and to understand the gradual "seizing up" of the Revolution: this is certainly what Quinet describes. From the Federation (already a somewhat lukewarm celebration compared to the dizzy expectations that it aroused), we fall into cold Reason, and then into the even chillier Supreme Being. There is no better witness to the tragedy of the Revolution than the festival, which had necessarily to exclude tragedy.

There is a second advantage, a corollary of the first. If there is such a consubstantiality between the festivals and the events of the Revolution, it should be possible to draw up a rich typology of the festivals, not as Michelet did—by describing a festival as more or less a festival according to the degree to which it approached or fell away from an ideal model—but by categorizing the festivals according to the various political intentions to which they remained subject. What variety is to be found from the Festival of the Federation to that of 1 Vendémiaire, Year VIII! The cult of Reason is sometimes seen (by Aulard) as the special creation of Hébertism, sometimes (by Auguste Comte)[26] as the sketchy but prophetic invention of the "Dantonians," the sole interpreters of a "true religion." The Festival of the Supreme Being is at one and the same time an embodiment of Robespierre's mysticism and an allegory of his fall. The festival of Thermidor, Year IV, is an expression of Thermidorian balance. These interpretations enable us, therefore, to understand both the Revolution and the festival better. For Daniel Guérin[27] the study of the festivals may suggest a new periodization of the Revolution.

Yet the problems bequeathed by such a view of the festival are enormous. To begin with, it reduces all the Revolutionary festivals to mere artifice. The historians then attribute a strange omnipotence to the organizers' projects and to the commentaries that sustain them. From this point of view, the festival is a docile piece of machinery, ready to be set up or taken down at a stroke, according to the needs of the cause. The day that it pleased Robespierre to describe the cult of the Supreme Being as a better weapon against foreign aggression, Aulard notes, the goddess of Reason fell at once and almost everywhere into discredit. The innumerable local monographs on the festivals owe their unity to the idea that

they were patently the work of a voluntarist rationalism. This is also
borne out by more detailed historical work. Taine sees the Federation as a
scrupulous illustration, according to the rules laid down by the philo
sophes, of the abstract fiction of the eighteenth century. As a result, "the
idyll is played out as in a written program." Even for Mathiez, who, as we
shall see, did not share this interpretation, the cult of Reason could come
about only "when the revolutionaries were all convinced of the need for
substituting a civic cult for the ancient religion." In these deliberately
engineered festivals, therefore, the meaning accorded them by the organizers always triumphed over the meaning experienced by the participants.

One may also wonder whether this interpretation does not overestimate
the diversity of the festivals. Are the spectacular differences it suggests
really to be found in these Revolutionary festivals? One cannot but be
disappointed: after demonstrating the antagonistic intentions of the organizers, the historians go on to describe festivals that turn out to be very
similar. The new festival is always based on the old one that it claims to
replace, and accounts that set out with the intention of drawing contrasts
end up sounding much the same. This is what happened to Aulard. He
began with the intention of showing the extent to which the Festival of
the Supreme Being differed from that of Reason and ended up stressing
above all the influence of the one cult on the other, utterly failing to
individualize them. The great difficulty with the political interpretation
of the festivals, then, is in the relation between a festival's purpose and its
content. How could such different political projects produce such similar
festivals? It might, of course, be maintained that this was due to the
inability of the organizers to imagine festivals that would measure up to
their intentions. But the problem might be posed the other way around:
was it not rather that despite their divergences, there was a profound
consensus among the organizers? Far from revealing opposed policies, the
festival would seem to refer beyond those policies to an identical conceptualization, if not to an identical collective need. Were this the case, the
history of the festivals according to Michelet would be justified.

Actually it is the exact reverse of this interpretation that is illustrated
in the difference between Aulard and Mathiez. The paucity of different
features in festivals that promised to be so varied suggests a certain seeking after identities. Why not then take the festivals as a whole, Mathiez
asks, stressing the uninterrupted chain that links the different Revolutionary cults.[28] Such a view is obviously made more plausible if one con-

siders all the festivals as springing from the wish to replace Catholic worship with a new cult capable of offering its spectators similar satisfactions. This approach produces an abundance of analogies: in the sacred signs, in the civic processions, the patriotic ceremony is a conscious transposition of Catholic ceremony. This is supported by a mass of written documentation. Here is one, picked out for its somewhat crude self-assurance. On 2 Pluviôse, Year VII, at Sucy-en-Brie, the commissioner of the Executive Directory spoke of the statue of Liberty: "Look up higher to that image of our Liberty. I have often heard men and children who have not yet been able to instruct themselves at the springs of Republican morality say: What is that saint? Has she performed many miracles? I shall reply to them in their own language: it is an image before which the corrupt court of Rome, the ignorant court of Sardinia, and no doubt at this very moment the ambitious court of Naples have disappeared. What greater miracles do you want?"

Familiarity with contemporary accounts of the Revolutionary festivals certainly inclines one toward those who see in them a greater degree of similarity than of individuality. Nevertheless, there is a weakness in Mathiez's thesis, namely, that a desire to substitute one cult for another may also have a political motivation. Making this the principal motive force of the festivals does not place Mathiez at as great a distance from Aulard's thesis as he might wish. This substitute for the Civil Constitution of the Clergy, devised to replace the latter when failure became evident, is a "remedy," and Mathiez, who risks the word, has some difficulty distinguishing it from Aulard's "expedient." There is, however, one not inconsiderable difference: for Mathiez, the political, self-conscious imagination is nourished by a less calculated, more authentic source. It was in the great mystical scenes of the Federations, devoid as they were of all artifice, that the men of the Revolution found the idea and the model for the later festivals.[29] The most artificial of the Revolutionary festivals have their roots, therefore, in native spontaneity. The desire for substitution does not spring fully armed from the brains of politicians but from the spectacle or memory of an already embodied substitution, though one unconscious of itself. Each Revolutionary festival may therefore—and Mathiez does not deny this—take on a particular political coloring. In spite of everything, it derives its distant meaning from the great religious drama played out at the dawn of the Revolution by men who did not realize what they were doing. It is here that Mathiez finds himself aligned with Michelet, here that he meets the Durkheimian idea of an analogy between the religious and the social. For the features by which Durkheim recognizes religion also define the festivals: the existence of a celebrating community, unanimity, independence of individuals, a measure of coercion—plus the keeping up of memories. "The Revolution established a whole system of festivals to maintain in a state of perpetual youth the principles that inspired it": this declaration, from *Elementary Forms of Religion,* illustrates the idea, so dear to Durkheim, that religion "involves something eternal, which is destined to survive all the particular symbols in which religious thought has successively been enveloped."

So Mathiez wants to remove the history of the Revolutionary festivals from the history of the sects in which it was trapped. But he frees it only partially; for the theme of substitution, which is the last word of his history, nevertheless marks the interdependence that links him to those who uphold a much narrower political interpretation than his. Like the others, Mathiez plunges into the problem of ends. Whom or what must the festival serve? The men of the Revolution themselves never ceased, in these very same terms, to pose this crucial question. Reflection about the purpose of the festivals is no doubt essential to those who create them, but it may not be enough to understand them. Even in those festivals most closely linked by their authors to a particular pedagogy and so intimately bound up with everyday life that, according to them, one should return home after the festival with more love and esteem for one's fellow man than before, is there not something like a superabundance of meaning?

To discover whether this is so, we must turn in any case to the festival itself, not to what its sectaries intended but to what it actually showed. Here the historians are divided once again. It is difficult to know whether the dominant feeling among them is one of boredom or disgust.

Boredom and Disgust

The motley images that the historians give us of the festival ought, it seems, to be capable of being organized, without too much difficulty, around two models. The first, promulgated by historians favorable to the Revolution, recalls only the impressive movement of the masses, their serene gravity, the peaceable occupation of open space, the invention of liberty. This is how Michelet saw the festivals; it is also how Durkheim conceived them. The second, largely disseminated by historians hostile to the Revolution, is the converse of the first. Here the masses move as on parade, in strictly manipulated battalions; the occupation of space has something forced and illegal about it; the prevailing atmosphere is one of constraint.

It would be overhasty, however, to accept this dichotomy at face value. For, apart from the Federation, and whatever the degree of sympathy shown to the Revolution, the historians are unanimous in concluding that the Revolutionary festival failed. This is very far from the reverent, subtle notion that Michelet has of the phenomenon: even when favorable to the Revolution, they gibe at its festivals. Thus, for Quinet, the lack of imagination of the Latin races seems responsible for the monotony of the festival. The Revolutionary festival is "Roman," in what, for a man so profoundly affected by the sensibility of a Calvinist mother, was the pejorative sense of the term: "The Romans could never free themselves of their old religious forms; they could not even conceive of doing so."[30] The same stubborn formalism imbued the ceremonies of the Revolution; it explained their recourse to a tired mythology, to neoclassical forms, to the figure of Sleep leaning over tombs, Reason standing proudly erect on her altar. Yet even the cult of Reason preserved something homely, something naively popular that was absolutely lacking in the cult of the Supreme Being. This can be seen in David's coercive program, which specifies "the moment when the mothers must smile at their children, the old men at the youths and their grandsons." Quinet sees the succession of festivals as a gradual abandonment of liberty.

In the description of the content of the festivals, the true frontier, therefore, is not between historians sympathetic to the Revolution and those opposed to it, but between two competing images that both belong to an account that is on the whole pejorative. One of the images presents the Revolutionary festival as a gloomy ceremony, rigidly following official directions. The historians who favor it stress the unremitting boredom that emanated from the festival; the festival involved interminable instructions, an endless flow of readings and speeches;[31] the spectacle of the age groups, which all too often was about the only interesting aspect of the festival, was repreated too often not to tire, and the distribution of rewards was itself a feeble expedient. Who can be blamed, Pressensé wonders, if people were yawning by this time?[32] This is because what was lacking was a "divine thought" around which men could unite. The festival, then, sins by omission. This interpretation is supported by innumerable eyewitnesses who remark on the shoddiness of the spectacle, resulting from the lack of money available and the self-consciousness of the

participants. Joseph de Maistre observes with satisfaction that the organizers of the festivals were always in search of a public, whereas each year,
in the name of Saint John, Saint Martin, or Saint Benedict, the people
required no summons to converge in large numbers on "some rustic
temple."[33] Made to order, sustained by exhortation and threats, the Revolutionary festivals were also invariably starved of money. At best, they
reconstituted that "Eden of happy bourgeois amusing themselves in
squads, believing by decree," as Renan sarcastically puts it.[34] At worst,
these formalities were performed by three or four local bigwigs in a
gloomy meeting hall, where, "since nobody has turned up," as the writer
of the account sadly admits, the festival has no sooner begun than it is
brought to an end.

There is a quite different way of describing the Revolutionary festival,
one in which the dominant impression is not one of stiff monotony but,
on the contrary, one of unexpected violence; one in which the festival
involves not edifying readings but indecent farces, suspect travesties,
masquerades stained with wine and blood. It is, writes Lanfrey, who popularized this interpretation, "a permanent orgy purporting to be the cult
of Reason."[35] It is easy enough to show how this description is opposed
point by point to the previous one. Here there are no celebrants walking
as on parade but overexcited organizers; no decent gloom but half-naked
women; no strictly executed program but bloody improvisation, frenetic
licentiousness. What is now seen to produce Revolutionary chaos is not
depressing monotony but transgression; the festival sins not by omission
but by excess.

Each of these models, let me repeat, may come from historians favorable or unfavorable to the Revolution. Each of them may be based on
contemporary statements, accounts, and memoirs: words such as *orgy* and
masquerade were already to be found in the writings of Sébastien Mercier,
Dulaure, or Levasseur, and, even closer to the event itself, in Barère, with
his fear of panic rejoicing. Lastly, each of them is not, paradoxically, exclusive of the other; one is surprised to see them coexisting in the same
author. Take Albert Duruy, summarizing the voluminous correspondence
received by the Committee of Public Instruction, at the end of 1792,
from provinces still preoccupied with erecting statues, planting Liberty
Trees, and organizing funeral ceremonies. The Committee of Public Instruction, Duruy comments, is obviously encouraging this "orgy"—a curious term for such peaceable festivals, overladen with erudite references
and antiquarian reminiscences. Indeed, the whole of Duruy's text betrays

the same hesitation. He describes "a cult of the public square, an orgy of flags, drums, trumpets, horns, firecrackers, singing, and political speeches, a terrible cacophony of instruments, images, and machines, a nameless mixture of the sacred and the profane, of the Supreme Being and the Christian God, of the Virgin and the Goddess of Reason, a confused vortex." Yet, a few lines later, he declares that he can imagine nothing "so cold, so empty, and so dry as all those festivals." He seems unable to make up his mind whether is is describing a fair or a sermon.

What links these two images of the Revolutionary festival in these authors' minds is a sense of the ridiculous. These festivals are laughable for two reasons: they are either boring or they are disgusting. In Pressensé one can see very well the movement from one sensation to the other. Without the slightest sense of surprise, he presents the Festival of Reason as a festival of boredom, dwelling on its artificiality (a "simulacrum" of a mountain), its pettiness (a "cramped" shrine), its coldness (a "glacial anthem"). But his attitude soon turns to one of disgust: "In Paris and in the départements, one tried in vain to arouse the fervor of the crowd by replacing actresses with prostitutes; attempts were made to bring gaiety by introducing debauchery." It would seem that the organizers of the festivals had to resort to disgust in order to overcome boredom. One can sense the forced character of this passage, which makes even derision the execution of a concerted plan.

This inconsistent vacillation between two interpretations is not satisfactory. Let us admit, on the one hand, that the Revolution embodied, as Duruy says, "strange, heteroclite conceptions, antipathetic to the French genius," and that these festivals, full of inebriated women, encumbered with disconcerting symbols, were so opaque that it is well nigh impossible to discover in them the systematic implementation of a philosophical intent. Are we then to say that this failure in execution constitutes the festival's success? Let us also admit, on the other hand, that all festivals are coupled with a desperate monotony: given this flat reproduction, is the success of the execution to be regarded, therefore, as responsible for the festival's failure? Quite obviously, one can only speculate. This brings us back to the question of which is the "truest" of the Revolutionary festivals.

Yet, it is the second of these two images that should concern us. For if the Revolutionary festival is an exercise in monotony, it is only because it lacks the life that convinced participants might give it. The only difference between this image of the festival and Michelet's ideal model lies in the inadequacy of the participants. If, however, the Revolutionary festival is a scandalous transgression, if it allows, even orders, excess, if its whole excitement springs from a violation of prohibitions, then it denies the image that it wishes to give of itself; in that case, what is lacking is not good participants but the very meaning of the celebration.

And yet, in certain historians' eyes, this is the true Revolutionary festival. Daniel Guérin, a champion of this interpretation, sees nothing festive about these official Revolutionary celebrations, so laboriously regulated by David. The "true" festival is one in which the inventiveness of the people is freely and scandalously expressed. The imagination takes power in these festivals, in which "the people in shirtsleeves gave free vent to their fantasy, to their irrepressible spirits. It became a competition as to who could celebrate with the greatest brilliance, the greatest wit, the liberation of mankind. Freed from the age-old weight that oppressed them, they seemed to take wings. They danced on the overturned tabernacles. The scenes that took place throughout France were unique of their kind."[36] These extravagant episodes, in which "so-called relics" were torn to pieces, in which the revolutionaries' red caps were stuck atop the statues of saints, in which carnivallike images were paraded through the streets and theatrical events ridiculing everything that was once held sacred were organized—and which conservative historians see as a caricature, perfectly in keeping with the essence of the Revolutionary phenomenon—Daniel Guérin, on the contrary, praises as the authentic expression of festive joy.

This interpretation has the merit of bringing us to the very heart of the problem: what is a festival? The two major philosophers of the festival provide two diametrically opposed answers to this question. A festival, says Durkheim, is the gathering together of the community, which is alone capable of producing a collective state of excitement; this is why the festival requires unanimous celebrants, but they scarcely need a celebration. This is what Rousseau suggests and what Michelet sees in the Revolutionary festivals. But, says Freud, a festival is not that at all: festive excitement can spring only from the transgression of prohibitions, from the excess authorized by the festival. It is this that Daniel Guérin sees in the festivals of the Revolution.

Must we, then, hand over the festivals of the French Revolution, en bloc, to either the Durkheimian interpretation or the Freudian interpretation? If it proves impossible to arrive at so complete a judgment, we shall be forced to sort out the festivals, decide which correspond to the

Freudian model and which to the Durkheimian model. Such a typology certainly ought to be more fruitful than those, like Dowd's, that classify the festivals according to their apparent object: funerary, religious, military, and so on.[37] Furthermore, it forces us to consider not so much the official program of the festival as the ways in which the people went beyond that program and the improvisations that may have occurred. Lastly, it invites us to examine very specifically whether violence had a necessary part in the Revolutionary festivals and, if so, in which? Where were they celebrated? When? And by whom?

So, as we go through the Revolutionary historiography, we see that it leaves us with three fundamental questions that must be faced before we attempt, as this book proposes to do, to describe the Revolutionary festivals as a whole. The first question, inherited from Michelet, is that of the relation in the festival between unanimity and exclusion: is there a communion of the entire people in the Revolutionary festival? The Festival of the Federation (see Chapter II), a festival acknowledged by all to be unanimous, provides the best opportunity for answering this question. The second question, left open by the controversy between Aulard and Mathiez, concerns the ability of the political history of the Revolution to account for the festivals. It is possible to test it against the example of resolutely antagonistic festivals: those of Châteauvieux and Simonneau, and the festivals that flanked the Thermidorian break (see Chapter III). Lastly, the third question is that of the place given to violence in the Revolutionary festival: the festive episode of the autumn and winter of Year II should provide an answer (see Chapter IV). In an attempt to obtain answers to these questions, we must now examine the actual events of the Revolution.

· II ·

The Festival of the Federation: Model and Reality

WHAT strikes one most about the Festival of the Federation is that it was scarcely an anniversary at all, for it had as much color and presence as the event it claimed and appeared to commemorate—perhaps even more. The idea of a festival emerged almost with the Federation itself, and very soon the festival took on the character of an absolute innovation. As early as July 18, 1789, Charles Villette expressed a wish for a new national festival to celebrate "a revolution without precedent."[1] He saw such a festival as not so much a repetition as the invention of a dramatic representation of unity, the heart of which would be commensalism: a huge civic meal would, for the first time, gather the whole of France around "the great national table."

So the Festival of the Federation was the beginning, rather than a celebration, of something. Images and reminiscences of the Bastille played a very small part in it. Yet the long series of happy days that this fine occasion seemed to promise stood out beyond the festival itself. Louis Blanc was aware of this. It was the future, not the past, that gave the Federation its strength: "A veritable prophecy in action, the most exalted vision of the future that a great people has ever had."[2]

But the exhilarating sense of beginning anew was not the only element in the festival. First, nothing can really begin if the break with what has ended is not made manifest. The festival, intended to mark an entry into a world of light, at the same time dismissed the old world. It even aimed to dismiss the Revolution itself. Although it was the first great Revolutionary festival, and in this it inaugurated a long series, the Festival of the Federation was presented as an end. The speeches delivered on the occasion made this abundantly clear: the festival "completes the edifice of our liberty."[3] It puts "the final seal on the most memorable of revolutions."[4]

But beyond the ancien régime and the upheaval that brought it down, the festival also seemed to be a restoration: this beginning was felt to be a beginning *again*. If the solemnity of the occasion was to have any sacral weight, something in it must go back in the mists of time. This would explain why in the speeches there are so many references to things being "given back" to the French people, to their "rediscovering" their ancient origins, to the rights that mankind is "taking back," and to virtues that will be "reborn."

In such language the Revolutionary consciousness revealed its two complementary needs. It delighted in the notion that a tabula rasa was being made of the past. But the past that was being rejected was not the whole of the past: in destroying history, the men of the Revolution were merely retying a broken thread, either with a primitive history—a mirror that had not yet distorted nature's features—or with Nature herself, in her primal purity. To destroy in order to renew: two operations with which everything becomes possible. It was these two operations that the Festival of the Federation set out to exemplify and that, in turn, gave it its incomparable prestige.

This prestige was apparent, first of all, to the people of the time. The Festival of the Federation seems to have had hardly an indifferent spectator. The testimony of Fortia de Piles, who refutes Mercier's celebrated account of the Federation (he declares that he saw nothing that was not "long, cold, and miserable"),[5] is exceptional. It was met nearly everywhere with enthusiasm, even by those not normally enthusiastic about the Revolution. Madame de Tourzel, for instance, describes "an unimaginable exaltation" springing from a Federation that nevertheless terrified her: her testimony is all the more convincing for that.[6]

A few exceptions aside, the most famous of which is Taine, who remained particularly immune to the intoxicating spirit of innovation embodied in the festival,[7] historians have been enthralled by the novelty of the spectacle. They all seem to agree that it was the finest of the historic Revolutionary "days"—even those observers, such as Jaurès, whose political preoccupations made them sensitive to the inner conflicts of the festival, even those who could not resist seeing the festival as the beginning of the bitter events that followed, and even those who, rejecting the Revolution en bloc, nevertheless gave the Federation the benefit of sincerity in illusion. In the last category is Albert Duruy, very representative in this respect of a certain kind of historiographer, who reproaches the Federation only with its unpleasant posterity: from that great day on, the crowning of a happy year, the process of decline inevitably set in.

A "happy year"? The polemic that arose around that term is well known. In contrast to those who baptized it thus,[8] there are historians who declared that 1790 was no more than a breathing space in the inevitable progress of the Revolution, and one that could deceive only those with a superficial view of the Parisian scene.[9] Thus, the Festival of the Federation is an apotheosis for those who see July 1790 as evidence of a Revolution still in harmony with itself, while for others, it is merely an illusion, as perishable as its plaster decorations. Yet, to begin with, I would like to set aside this recently revived polemic. When one speaks of a happy year, is one really saying that there was still no split within the Revolution? One has only to open the newspapers or listen to the voice of Marat prophesying Varennes in *L'ami du peuple* to know that the Revolution was already under threat. No historian denies that the Assembly was already divided into parties, that the counterrevolution was being planned, or even that there were dark clouds gathering over the Festival of the Federation itself. To say that the year was happy is merely to speak of a Revolution that still recognized itself in the mirror held up to it by events. In fact, by 1790, no fatal gap had yet opened up between principles and reality: perhaps this is what makes the Federation still a happy time.

So, what we must understand is not so much the subjective happiness of the Festival of the Federation as its conformity to the model laid down for it by its spectators, its chroniclers, and its historians. What does this model amount to, apart from the characteristics attributed from the outset to this first festival of the Revolution? First, there was the ceremonial inventiveness so vigorously stressed by Michelet, for whom this festival was quite unprecedented. Second, there was the dazzling demonstration of national unanimity. Third—the most remarkable feature of all, especially if one remembers the immediate background against which it was set, those half-dreamed, half-experienced festivals "granted" by the aristocracy to the people—this was a *spontaneous* festival. According to Louis Blanc, for instance, an entire people, of its own accord, set out spontaneously for Paris. The most famous scene of the Federation is that of the construction works on the Champ-de-Mars, which show all the signs of a successful improvisation.

This ideal image makes the bundle of contemporary accounts of the federations found in the archives disappointing reading.[10] While Michelet imagined that he was reading "love letters,"[11] we find documents heavy with affidavits, complaints, police reports, certificates of presence, bills of expenditure, which reveal more about individuals' financial situations than about their enthusiasm, which is more often left to the reader's imagination than actually described. The mood of rejoicing is noted rather than conveyed: "What you will not see, gentlemen, in these accounts are our transports of joy, which were general."[12] There is a certain reticence, and it becomes almost mechanical to state that "the day passed with many displays of fraternity" without saying what these displays might have been.

The austerity of these accounts explains the coolness toward the Federation on the part of researchers, who have encountered these writings in all their ponderous mass and are therefore more aware of their chronic monotony than of the brilliance of a few isolated descriptions of festivals. Maurice Lambert, the author of an excellent book on the federations of Franche-Comté, resists such conformity. He concedes that "of all the legends of the Revolution, that of the federation is perhaps closest to the truth." But he adds by way of conclusion, "In fact, the Federation was a festival like any other" and its actual result "absolutely negligible."[13]

Let us take from this somewhat surly verdict the two pertinent questions that it implies. Was there *no* result? Apart from the fact that none of the Revolutionary "days" can be said to have had no result, one must still, before deciding, try to discover why this particular festival, supposing that it did not indeed have the results expected of it, served throughout the Revolution as an obligatory reference, a model for the organizers of festivals, and a luminous memory for nineteenth-century historians. And was it a festival like any other? Before reaching a decision, we must in any case abandon the singular. We think rather too readily of the Paris Federation, without regard to the thousands of provincial and even village festivals that took place on the same day throughout the country. We think a great deal too much about July 14, 1790, forgetting that federative festivals preceded it throughout the autumn of 1789 and the winter of 1790. We also ignore the ceremonies of returning the banner or receiving the *fédérés,* those celebrations that took place the day after the festival. Thus, the word *federation* covers and conceals a wide variety of ceremonial. Lastly, we do not think at all about those scarcely organized festivals, still very close to outbreaks of riotous jollity, that accompanied the peasant uprisings of the autumn and winter of 1789–90. In their wild, crude way, they were nevertheless federations too: the gathering of people gave them shape, fear gave them a motive, and all their ceremonies stemmed from an improvised ritual of unity.

Riot and Festival: The "Wild" Federations

In these first festivals (one scarcely dares to call them such, for they were neither announced nor planned and seemed to rise up without warning among the peasant masses themselves) the fundamental feature, against which all the others stand out, was a terrified joy, a mixture of fear and power. It was fear that made the peasants come out of their houses and arm themselves with rifles and sticks, that sent them out onto the road to the next village to seek comfort and help against the brigands from a band of fellow peasants, alerted and armed as they were. These expeditions were the occasion of scenes of fraternization between communities, whose avowed aim was security but from which also was born delight in the feeling, and display, of strength. The mixture of fear and joy, and of the violence and excitement with which they were expressed in action, is clearly visible in these spontaneous festivals.

What exactly took place in one of these turbulent meetings in, say, a village in the Périgord[14] or the Quercy during the winter of 1790? The event would usually begin on a Sunday, after mass or vespers. A village would be invaded by an armed troop from the neighboring village. After somewhat ambiguous scenes in which fraternity and fear fought for the upper hand and threats were never far away, the villagers would make up their minds (or resign themselves) to follow their neighbors' example—the neighboring villages, it seemed, having already taken action. The pews would be brought out from the church, the weathercocks removed, and a Liberty Tree—or rather a maypole, for the term *Liberty Tree* had not yet achieved widespread currency—would be set up in the village. The maypole, traditional symbol of joyful unanimity, would this time be full of menace. Apart from the fact that the setting up of the maypole was accompanied by scenes of violence, some seditious decoration was often attached to it. This might take the form of a sign bearing some slogan such as "Woe to him who pays his rent!" The emblem of public joy became, therefore, an emblem of revolt, so much so that the authorities soon demanded that these "marks of insurrection" be removed.

The maypole was not the only expression of ambivalence. The mixture of joy and violence was found everywhere, and it was the presence of these two elements, blended in unequal proportions, that makes one hesitate to proclaim the true significance of these demonstrations. If the first of these elements dominated, the coming together of the community clearly retained its festive character; but the second was always at the surface, ready to spill over. It needed only some recalcitrant parish priest's refusal to decorate the Blessed Sacrament with the tricolor ribbon for festive exuberance to turn suddenly into riot. Thus it was on July 19, 1789, at Lons-le-Saunier, where a meeting of young people (for it was almost always the young who started and spread such disturbances) took place.[15] They began by decking themselves out with the tricolor cockade; they then made an improvised gift of it to the municipality and "let it be known that the order has gone out to every citizen to accept it." The gift, in this instance, was accompanied with threats, and the whole scene was a mixture of high-spirited spontaneity and provocative blackmail. Another such scene took place in the courtyard of the Château de Manesgre, in the Dordogne, where the demonstrators, whose numbers had been swollen on the way by peasants from Valajouls, with whom they had formed a sort of federation, sat down to an improvised banquet. The peasants' demand—above all, they wanted the lord of the manor to embrace them—was very ambiguous, at once suppliant and provocative. The violence, too, was ambiguous: the shooting that finally broke out was directed only against pigeons and hens. And the celebration was also ambiguous: the peasants, who had come to the end of laborious negotiations to win the weathercock, bread, wine, and the right to feast on the spot, not satisfied with these victories and eager to give them some meaning, insisted on declaring—and this went for the lord of the manor as well as themselves—that "they were all equal."[16]

There are innumerable examples of this interweaving of celebratory and riotous aspects in the event that led up to the official federations. At the Château de la Faurie, near Salignac, a village militia had a complaint to make to the lord of the manor.[17] At the local fair the order was passed around to go to La Faurie the next day and start a bit of trouble. The fifteen or so men who had made up their minds to do this were joined on the way by other peasants. But the violence—for gunfire was exchanged, without, it is true, anyone getting wounded—was interspersed with truces, which provided an opportunity of forming "watches." They made a bonfire that had elements both of destruction and celebration, like those other fires in village squares where church pews were smashed up for firewood. Elsewhere the feasting alternated with threats and blows. In short, there was no riotous scene that did not have its festive aspect and no collective celebration without a groundswell of menace.

But in all these events symbolism reigned supreme. Most of the demands concerned various symbols: the kiss, the weathercock, the cockade. The violence itself was often entirely symbolic, being directed against weathercocks, church pews, coats of arms. Sometimes the symbols were not destroyed but merely subjected to a subversion of their meaning: the weathercock would be taken down from the chateau roof, carried to the Liberty Tree, and turned into a humorous trophy; taken out into the sunlight of the village square, the church pews became seats for Sunday drinkers. Knives were pulled out more often than they were used: the main point was to show what could be done. Perhaps the fact that riotous behavior seemed so dominated by a sense of ceremony can be attributed to exhibitionism. In any case, the peasants waited until the day of the village fair before removing the pews from the church, and they did so to the accompaniment of music. They went off to decorate the mayor with the cockade, but they marched in procession. And if they tramped illegally over a meadow ready for cutting, they were led by the municipal drummer. No sooner did these spontaneous acts of rioting emerge than they took on ritual form.

The Federative Festivals

We are still a long way, it seems, from the Federation, and indeed these half-riotous, half-ceremonial gatherings were never graced with that name. Furthermore, it was often against them, in an attempt to constrain their violence, that the first federative festivals were set up. But we must not forget them: they were the compost—a mixture of fear and gaiety—in which the Federation took root, and all the spontaneity associated with the word *federation* was concentrated in them.

Indeed, that word did not take hold at once. In referring to all those defensive acts that, in the winter of 1790, linked town with town, militia with militia, accompanied by ceremonies that were later called federative festivals,[18] the writers of the contemporary accounts betray a certain terminological hesitancy. "Union," "reconciliation," "social pact," "coalition of towns," "ceremony of fraternity and patriotism," "federation": the last term only gradually took over from its competitors.

Did it owe its success to its youth? The revival of this forgotten four-teenth-century word was in fact quite recent: Richelet's dictionary makes no reference to it, nor does Furetière or the Académie Française. The *Dictionnaire de Trévoux* is also unaware of the existence of the noun but finds room for the adjective *federative:* "M. de Montesquieu used this word, when speaking of the various provinces that make up the republic of Holland and which are united together by treaties." The word first appears as a political term. For Dupont de Nemours, taxation was a "federative knot,"[19] and Mably associated it with the word *republic.*[20] In the years prior to the Revolution, the American example—and sometimes the Swiss example too—popularized the nouns *federation* and *confederation* and gave the verb *to federate* its association with effective action, laced with admiration for those peoples who "confederate." But there is a big gap between political terminology and the everyday spoken language. The word *federation* bridged that gap during the time of the Great Fear. A term had to be found to describe all the leagues, offensive and defensive, that rose up against the nation's enemies. *Union* and *coalition* would have done the job, yet they lacked the solemnity conferred by an institution. So, in the end, *federation* and *confederation* won the day. At first they were used interchangeably; then, it would seem, through the convenience of *federative* (*confederative* was used much less frequently), *federation* finally triumphed.

The federative festivals had a main agent in the National Guard. Against the brigands said to be hiding in the woods nearby, or against those enemies of the Revolution whose presence farther off was so obsessively evoked, the National Guard of a town or village would form a defensive pact with the next nearest National Guard or garrison. The festival was instituted to mark the alliance. It was, therefore, an essentially military festival, with colors unfurled, in which oaths were taken, swords in hand, and in which the heart of the religious ceremony was the blessing of the flag.

The signatures at the foot of the official accounts reflect this military character: they are mainly those of officers in the regular army or National Guard. The others are those of the parish priest, the mayor and other municipal officers, and the notables, themselves often enough officers in the National Guard. Was this always the case? The accounts revealed some hesitation as to the rules governing the choice. The old corporative order, then nearing its demise, sometimes surfaced and dictated an election by guild: one representative from the physicians, another from the tailors, the wig makers, the tilers, and so on. But sometimes, mixed with the old, was a new order trying to make its way. Thus women and children joined the processions in symbolic groups from which all hierarchy was excluded: it seems that women and children could march only "indiscriminately," whereas men were always carefully categorized. Sometimes, too, resort was taken to the rigor of alphabetical order: at Pontivy it was the unambiguous brutality of the alphabet that ordered the procession of the towns.[21] Nevertheless, even in this last case, the democracy was more apparent than real, based as it was on a different order: all the delegates were notables, as also were those "fine men of the National Guard,"[22] for whom such a procession marked one's preference (here an aesthetic choice overlay a social one), who were selected for such processions.

It is difficult to see what was new about these military festivals. What did one usually see in a federative festival? A procession of national guardsmen and regular troops, marching, often outside the town, to attend an open-air mass, stopping for speeches—even the priests' sermons became "harangues" on such occasions—for the blessing of the flags, for the taking of an oath. The procession would then come back to the municipal building to draw up and sign the federative pact that had just been concluded. This was often followed by the lighting of a bonfire and sometimes, in the evening, to finish everything off in style, a ball and fireworks. In this basic scheme the essential element is the expression of a desire for union, which, as we have seen, was nourished by both fear and enthusiasm. The fear was always there; sometimes it is explicitly named, as at Bordeaux, where the official account recalls the genealogy of the terrors conceived there, as in so many other towns, or as at Nancy, where the celebrants, obsessed with the sense of being surrounded by "considerable forests and devastated by whole troops of malefactors," seized the opportunity of the festival to demand weapons. The enthusiasm was always there too, but it was channeled; the shouts and the applause burst out only at certain points. Lastly, what disappeared entirely from these festivals—which, it is true, had been devised to contain violence—was violence itself, with its chain of provocation and parody; apart from a few minor scenes of blackmail occasioned here and there by the resistance of a parish priest or mayor, it was now absent.

Had all spontaneity disappeared, then? Traces of it can still be found in the well-spaced dates of the federative festivals, which reveal the local initiatives and currents of union. These, in turn, may be traced like the currents of fear. Sometimes even the federative oath suddenly emerges from the usual gaiety, as if, on rare occasions, the popular festival felt the need to rise above itself. At Bourges, on June 25, 1790, Saint John's Day,

after the municipal officers had lit the bonfire in the city square, the
citizens dancing around the flames decided to solemnize the gathering by
taking the civic oath.[23] Thus an impromptu Federation was formed.
Sometimes, too, the festival was the occasion of inventing those frontier
rituals by which the inhabitants of villages that had been enemies since
time immemorial were thrown into one another's arms.[24] Such ceremonies
were often very rudimentary, but the symbolism of the act and gesture
was potent: to give added symbolic value to what was taking place, the
commandant of the National Guard of Meljac held the hand of his coun-
terpart from Castelpers while taking the oath.[25] In these spectacles of
unity, youth played a central role: the young were invited to nominate
their own commanders and officers to set up the Federation, to give
expression to the new unanimity. There is a survival here of the notion
that since in each generation it is the young who assume responsibility
for village rivalry, it is therefore the young who must make reparation for
it. These scenes, so moving because they demonstrate the confluence of a
timeless ritual and political innovation, were nevertheless, if the mass of
documentation is to be believed, very rare; the overwhelming impression
is rather one of organization, as is shown by the typically official obsession
with writing up an accurate account of the festival in the municipal records. Who are we historians to complain of this obsession? It is worth all
these archives put together.

Indeed, the archives have another surprise in store for us: although no
official legislation for the Revolutionary festivals existed yet, all the official
accounts reveal the same wave of enthusiasm and have an unquestionable
sameness about them. The same tone, vocabulary, and scenic arrangements are to be found from account to account, and reading them together suggests the existence of a single stereotype of the festival imagined and carried out by the notables. That the model reached Paris is not
the least of the surprises. The movement arose in the depths of the provinces, but it did not stay there for long. Paris soon took it up, trying to
discipline festivals that had already lost much of their sense of parody and
violence but that still eluded the control of the authorities.

The Paris Federation

In Paris, all this commotion was disturbing the authorities. There was
potential danger in the influence that the National Guard was exercising
over the line troops. "The sublime idea of a general Federation, first pro-

posed by the Parisians of the Saint-Eustache district and welcomed enthusiastically by the whole of France, terrified the minister," wrote Camille
Desmoulins.[26] Unable to control the movement, the minister of war de
cided to jump aboard: on June 4, 1790, expounding on the deplorable
situation of the army, he announced that the king had given permission
to the regiments to take part in the patriotic Federations and to renew
the civic oath with the National Guards. In his words, the king "has
recognized in them not a system of private associations, but a gathering
of wills of all the French for common liberty and prosperity."[27] It was
therefore praiseworthy for each regiment to participate in the civic festivals. Next day, Bailly addressed the Assembly in the name of the Commune of Paris: it was high time, he said, for the federations to be feder-
ated, and he proposed a "Great Federation" of all the National Guards
and troops of the kingdom in Paris on the following July 14.[28] In Paris?
Bailly almost apologized for this choice: "We shall go to the ends of the
kingdom to unite with you; but it is within our walls that our legislators
and our king reside." The deputation from the Commune expressed a wish
that at least half the deputies sent to the Federation should be civilians.
The Committee on the Constitution was reluctant to agree. In the end,
the report drawn up by Talleyrand laid down two conditions on participation: one must have deliberated as an active citizen and defended the
Constitution and laws as a soldier. But it was as a soldier that a delegate
was summoned to the national festival: "It is France armed that is going
to gather together, not France as a deliberating body."[29]

It was a controversial, joyless birth, and it prefigured the profoundly
conservative character of the Festival of the Federation. Out of all those
oaths that arose from the federative festivals, uniting village with village
and army corps with battalions of the National Guard, there emerged a
single official oath the terms of which reminded everybody that the purpose of the festival was not to arouse but to protect: to protect persons
and property and the free movement of grain and foodstuffs. The defensive
character of the oath is suggestive of fear, but that fear no longer maintained an organic link with joy and no longer inspired any gesture that
was not predictable. With this official oath, handed down throughout the
kingdom by the municipality of Paris, which insisted that it be spoken
"in concert and at the same moment by all the inhabitants and in every
part of this empire," the spirit of organization triumphed in the festival.
Sometimes, indeed, the festival was seen as no more than an "oath taking"—in other words, as a return to order. At Moulins, the official

account does not breathe a word about a festival but claims to be "an account of the solemn oaths taken at Moulins on July 14, 1790." Furthermore, the choice of deputies emphasized this conservative character still more. The National Guards of each commune had to choose six men out of a hundred. These primary delegates had then to meet in the principal town and in turn choose two men out of a hundred. For its part, the army had no choice to make; the longest-serving officers, noncommissioned officers, and privates were appointed. This was all too fitting a symbol of the progress made since the first federative gatherings, those formless, indeterminate social entities, dominated by youth and imbued with an unmistakable social unanimity.

In the minds of its organizers, then, the "Great Federation" was a way of bringing a turbulent period to a close rather than setting men in motion. They had not foreseen that collective enthusiasm would spill over beyond their joyless projects. The first sign of this was the flood of broadsheets. Proposals for the lodging of the *fédérés,* requests for seats at the festival, concern over food supplies—any subject seemed to be grist to the mill of anyone who could hold a pen. Odes were written and a medallion suggested; printers rushed guidebooks to the capital, "salubrious and patriotic plans of the brothels of Paris," "a price-list of the filles de joie of the Palais-Royal," and "disinterested advice to traveling confederates" in which one can recognize the hand of Restif de la Bretonne.[30] There is, in these feverish texts, a concern to open up to the *fédérés* a city that could be enjoyed without spending a sou. There is, too, an innovative spirit in them that was almost totally absent from the festival itself, one typical example being Madame Mouret's *Annales de l'éducation du sexe,* in which the author proposes that women and young ladies should take part in the festival.[31] This "female federation" was rejected by the Constitution Committee and was to have no other function than that of organizing a tableau representing the confederation, offered to Saint Genevieve by a delegation of five hundred young ladies. But that was to take place on Tuesday, July 20, not at the official festival.

As everyone waited for the great day, excitement and foreboding spread through the Paris population like a contagious disease. Rumor was rife. The aristocrats were terrified at the prospect of a Paris occupied by Revolutionary France, and many fled the city, as did, for instance, Madame Villeneuve-Arifat's mother, who feared "the convergence upon Paris of 100,000 well-armed patriots."[32] Even the patriots themselves were alarmed by the constant rumor that the festival was a trap cleverly set for

them by the aristocrats. Paris, emptied of its inhabitants to the benefit of
the Champ-de-Mars, would, for the whole of a long day, be in their
hands. Their fear had a purpose: against the obscure enemies that it conjured up, it was the strongest cement of national unity.

The most striking image of comradeship in the legendary atmosphere
of unanimity that was then beginning to emerge was that of the construction being carried out in the Champ-de-Mars. There are many versions of
this almost too edifying story of administrative incompetence saved by
the enthusiasm and initiative of the Parisians themselves—men and
women, old and young, rich and poor—who worked together and successfully completed the construction in time. Memoirs, newspapers,
broadsheets, and even witnesses who could hardly be suspected of sympathy, such as the Comte de Fernan Nuñez,[33] agree in regarding that
enterprise as the true festival. This may no doubt be accounted for by the
classic mechanisms of the psychology of expectation, in which Saturday
night becomes the high point of the Sunday holiday, but it may also owe
something to the novelty of the spectacle, which had something in it for
everybody. Those who had returned to Paris after a long absence, disconcerted by "those groups of elegant women" wielding picks and shovels,
remembered the more ridiculous and "piquant" aspects.[34] For those educated enough to regard the scene from the point of view of art historians,
the masses and movements might suggest a Roman crowd scene.[35] The
moralists had no trouble coining maxims from the spectacle of "a quarter
of Paris pushing wheelbarrows." Everybody, indeed, seems to have sensed
the unmistakably festive nature of the proceedings; the unanimity of the
contemporary accounts is too strong to imagine that it was a matter of
chroniclers looking back through rose-tinted spectacles.

By all accounts, the work was carried out not only enthusiastically but
with due regard to grace and ornament. Here is one description, among
many from the *Révolutions de Paris,* in which attention is drawn to that
mixture of the useful and futile that transformed laborious earthworks
into "veritable civic festivals": the tip-cart that arrived at the Champ-de-
Mars full of soil left garlanded with branches, loaded with young men
and pretty girls, taking turns pulling it on its way back. At nightfall
everyone would gather together before leaving the Champ-de-Mars.
When they dispersed, they did so in procession, a tree branch serving as
a standard, led by fife and drum, arm in arm, "both as a friendly gesture
and to move in orderly fashion through the streets."[36] It marked the beginning of a ceremony. There was an element of both exhibitionism (one

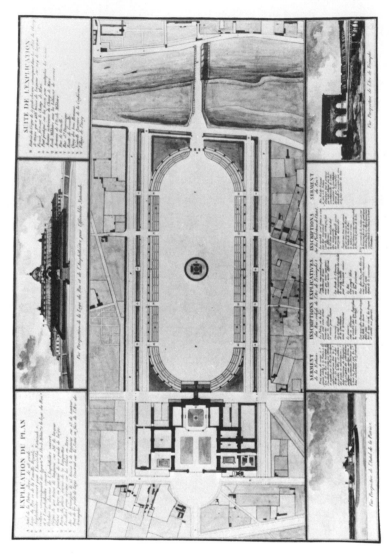

View of the Champ-de-Mars and the Nouveau Cirque. Tinted engraving by Meunier and Gaucher, Musée Carnavalet. © DACS 1987.

had to be seen and made sure that one was) and contained violence. From Louis-Sébastien Mercier and Lindet we know that the butchers' banner was decorated with a knife.[37] One guild thought of turning up at the Champ-de-Mars behind a hearse decorated with toads, vipers, and rats, intended "to represent the ruin of the clergy and aristocracy," accompanied by a troop of old women, their faces painted to look like mourners.[38] The aristocrat remained the hidden witness, the obverse image of those days of unanimity.

Indeed it was his exclusion, if only fictitious, that could alone give the Champ-de-Mars its dimension as a sacred place. For although the amphitheater became a "religious monument" toward which the eyes of the entire nation turned, it was because no aristocratic hand had touched a pick or shovel. Camille Desmoulins sensed this, as always, better than anybody else: created by patriotic hands, the amphitheater became sacred, and in contagious reciprocity the hands became sacred in turn. "I honor no less that multitude of citizens and citizenesses who do not think that they have consecrated those works by their hands, but their hands by those works."[39]

This vision of the Champ-de-Mars and Paris as sacred places is to be found innocently expressed in a great many of the contemporary accounts: the visitors saw Paris, on the horizon of their journey, as a promised land. The General Federation, says the account written for the town of Argent, was to take place "in sight of the walls of the capital on the fourteenth day of this month." The *fédérés* entered Paris, as Quinet puts it very well, as into a holy city. Was it Revolutionary history that made the place sacred? To some extent, certainly. None of the *fédérés* would have considered his journey complete if he had not seen the Bastille. But the Tuileries were just as important a point of attraction. In Paris there was the king, who consecrated the city. He was also the end of the pilgrimage; they would be able to see him, touch him perhaps. There are innumerable instances of this wondrous expectation—to the astonishment of the newspapers, vexed at seeing so many patriotic souls so quickly and so easily dazzled by the royal presence. A national guardsman from Normandy innocently explained why, for him, the festival provided a uniquely wonderful sight: in the middle of the Champ-de-Mars was the enthroned king "whom we could see, quite at ease."[40] The parish priest of Vauvert, who was unable to make the journey, invited his parishioners to transport themselves in heart and mind "into the midst of our brothers in Paris, who at this very moment are enjoying a sight of the face of Louis XVI."[41]

This sense of euphoria, seen also in such offerings to the king as the sword of the Bretons and the ring given by the inhabitants of the Touraine, extended to the smallest things of everyday life. "Just as they gave new souls to all," Quinet observes, "so everything enchanted them."[42] The capital city and its houses were wide open to them; the uniform of the national Guard was an open sesame, an invitation, as a master in surgery at the Collège de La Flèche recounts, to put away one's bourgeois clothes forever.[43]

Could these new souls, in fact, be satisfied by the festival in Paris? The big city could no doubt offer the participants in this organized journey all that it possessed and could put on display: reviews (July 18 at the Champ-de-Mars and the following day at the Étoile), jousts on the Seine, a girandole on the Pont-Neuf. The days leading up to and following the Federation were filled to bursting point with entertainments and spectacles. Some seemed to embody the ideal, simple rustic festival of which the century had always dreamed: at the Bastille, on July 18, the Marquis de Ferrières was delighted by a Rousseauistic festival in which, in a somewhat unreal atmosphere, reminiscent of "the joys of the happy shades in the Elysian Fields," the bourgeois ate his dinner on the grass, "quietly enjoying his life," and in which a few bargemen wearing waistcoats and knickerbockers tried to take the tricolor flag to the top of tall masts made slippery with soap.[44] Others seem to prefigure the ceremonies that were to punctuate the Revolutionary months to come: one such was the carnivallike procession in which, to the accompaniment of the *De Profundis,* a log decked out with a priest's bands and calotte was paraded around the Bastille. But such festivals, of which there were no end, were outside the Federation itself and bore no resemblance to it.

Of all the projects submitted to the organizers of the festival, only the long procession, the mass, and the oath seem to have met with their approval. One is struck by the austerity of such a choice. The procession remained entirely military. Anything that might have given it life and variety, like the confederation of ladies proposed by Madame Mouret, was dismissed. The only ceremonial innovation—one that, it is true, was to enjoy a brilliant future—was to be found in those two battalions, children and old men, "those two extremes of human life that have aroused great interest," between which, on the place de la Concorde, the National Assembly took up its position. For the rest, cavalry and grenadiers of the Paris militia headed and brought up the rear of the procession, encompassing the deputies with regular troops from the départements: a particularly uninventive order. What is more, the motley colors of the delightful district banners[45] and the violet velvet of the king's throne must have been lost to all under the gloomy sky.

The procession itself was interminable: it took two more hours, after it first passed under the triumphal arch, to take up position in the Champ-de-Mars. Lucid as ever, Camille Desmoulins remarked unambiguously, "It was not by the procession that this festival surpassed those of antiquity, for curiosity soon tires of a procession."[46]

This procession, of course, formed the major part of an uninspired, dull, unmoving spectacle. We know why Mirabeau was so profoundly disappointed by it. Lafayette, the man of the provinces, was set up as sole centerpiece of the proceedings, whereas, Mirabeau remarked, "a distinction should have been drawn between the general of the Federation and the monarch, but the king allowed to carry out both functions. After reviewing the troops, the general of the Federation, having again become king, should have resumed his seat on the throne and set out from there once more to take his oath at the altar."[47] The impression that this spectacle might have produced is surely not a product of Mirabeau's imagination: by appropriating the space of the Champ-de-Mars, the king would have made a pact with the nation and solemnized his oath. But we know how lightly the king appeared to take the proceedings, arriving late, permitting his throne to be usurped by another, and generally remaining aloof from the festivities. Certain eyewitnesses, who did not share Mirabeau's political preoccupations, nevertheless deplored the absence of some action capable of animating that huge theatrical space: "We were too small for the spectacle or the spectacle was too great for us. The due proportion between spectacle and spectators was broken."[48]

A New Festival?

Were the historians merely daydreaming? What details, in that austere festival, could have aroused their enthusiasm? Where could they have seen ceremonial innovation and national unanimity in action, the fruits of a creative spontaneity? We must return to these questions.

If we are to seek, let alone find, ceremonial unanimity, we should perhaps leave the Paris stage and visit the provincial federations, which, in any case, provided Michelet with so many of his examples. Indeed, the only constraint imposed on the provinces in commemorating July 14 was that of simultaneity. This is significant in a period when the idea of simultaneity played such a large part in people's imagination, when it was often said that the soul has an invincible repugnance for succession,[49] when Brissot declared that he preferred newspapers to books because, although the latter make their deep imprint over a long period of time, the former "rapidly enlighten" a large mass of men "whose ideas react at the same moment."[50] "At the same moment": this was also the obsession of the organizers of the provincial festivals. The official instructions recommended that the federative oath be taken at noon, "in concert and at the same moment in every part of the empire"; without this simultaneity, the sacredness of the act, it seems, would have vanished. That is why, when the desire for simultaneity came up against real obstacles, so much ingenuity was employed in overcoming them. Sometimes this was done merely with rhetorical tricks, as, for instance, when the men of the mountain regions, conscious of being irremediably imprisoned within "their natural ramparts," protested that they were nonetheless communing, at the same moment, with all the other Frenchmen in their love of country. Sometimes, too, it was done by way of ceremonial arrangements: if bad weather forced the organizers to hold the civic meal indoors when they would have preferred to have had it in the open air, and they had to spread it over several different rooms, care was taken, when a "health" was drunk at the principal table, to announce it at the same time at all the other tables and in all the other rooms "with such speed that everyone drank the same health at the same time."[51] This obsession explains why the festivals were filled with so many *Renommées,* or Fames: armed with their flaming torches, these were allegories of simultaneity, spreading the good news "as a fire in an open space spreads irresistibly."

Although the municipality of Paris sent a circular to all the municipalities of the kingdom insisting on simultaneity, it omitted to send any other instructions. As a result, there was a certain variety in the provincial festivals of the Federation, and although the more primitive of them always found room for the "celebration of the holy mysteries," the opening address, and the taking of the oath, they enjoyed relative autonomy in relation to the Paris model. This autonomy is apparent, to begin with, in the liberties taken with the oath itself. To tamper with the oath was to touch the untouchable, but, in relation to the somewhat constipated Paris text, one finds in the provinces texts in which enthusiasm wins over the rule. In the oath taken at Sabres in the Landes, the *fédérés* swore "to be all inseparably united, to love one another for ever, to bring health to our brothers whenever the need may arise."[52] The language may be defensive, but it is not defensive of institutions.

The relative freedom of the provincial federations is also apparent in the integration of age-old customs: at Béziers, for instance, the General Council invited to the festival all persons who could dance the *treilles,* a dance associated with the wine harvest.[53] As on patronal festivals, each dancer on that day was provided with a pair of shoes and a pair of gloves, together, in accordance with the spirit of the occasion, with a ribbon in the colors of the nation; and they were asked to enliven with their dances all ceremonies, "with the exception of religious services." Similarly, when the local or guild festival fell on the same day as the Federation, the two celebrations were amalgamated without the slightest scruple: thus, on July 13, 1790, the colliers of Montminot celebrated a traditional festival by swearing "to have the axe always raised in order, at the risk of their lives, to defend the finest edifice that ever was, the French Constitution."[54] Sometimes the wearer of some local crown was put at the center of the festival. At Château-Porcien the "queen" of the local girls was given the task of delivering the speech.[55] Sometimes, too, as at Denezé-sous-le-Lude, the bonfire that traditionally brought the festival to an end burned around a maypole.[56] In fact, the organizers used whatever lay to hand. They had no hesitation in incorporating private celebrations into the public celebrations. They were only too happy, for instance, to make the great religious acts of individual lives part of the festival: the contemporary accounts of the provincial festivals are crammed with baptisms, weddings, even endowments for poor marriageable girls![57] The festival took on much of the color of the religious festivals, even to the extent of including the parading of the cross, the Blessed Sacrament, and religious banners. At the altar of the fatherland the priests repeated that this festival was also theirs, and it was often they who, in the absence of a defaulting mayor, pointed out the lessons of the ceremony to its participants.

Already visible in the unrestrained incorporation of traditional ceremonies, and also in the relaxation of the military aspect, the freedom of these festivals is apparent in certain ceremonial innovations. The processions included some unexpected groups: girls, children, old men here and there obtained permission (it is noteworthy, however, that they had to ask for it) to take part in the festival. The citizenesses of Beaufort-en-Vallée planned a surprise for those taking the oath.[58] Eighty-three of them slipped away at one point and returned, to the accompaniment of music, costumed as so many départements. The women of Denezé-sous-le-Lude did even better: after obtaining the reluctant consent of the municipality and their families, they held their own federation, and the picturesqueness of the spectacle attracted to the festival a large audience of armed young men from the townships of Baugé and Le Lude, "eager to lay down their weapons at the feet of the federate women."

Lastly, although the reference to trades was usually excluded from these festivals of unanimity, one of them at least—beyond the mistrust that differences based on guild membership might inspire—acceded to the symbolic dignity of unity: the ploughmen as Rouen respectfully laid their garlanded work tools on the altar of the fatherland. Later it was thought that the Revolutionary festivals could not express national unanimity without merging together participants of "both sexes, all ages, and all conditions." But for the moment the organizers had not yet chosen between this abstract way of representing unanimity and a more colorful spectacle that would by contrast opt for diversity, all the better to shatter unity: at Dole, for instance, the procession included Minims, ladies, Carmelites, girls, Capuchins, wine growers, shoemakers, ploughmen, Benedictines, gardeners, children. It was their motley composition, already under threat, however, that was the distinctive feature of these provincial festivals.

It also marked their visual decoration: a whole symbolism of union was worked out, with much use of Concords, clasped hands, triangles whose points represented, as at Cherbourg, the Law, the King, and the People, arms supporting one another, "one with the colors of the troops of the line, the other with the colors of the National Guard."[59] But it was a symbolism without principles, one that borrowed from everything and everybody. From antiquity—an antiquity that was itself syncretic, in which the solidity of the Doric capital shamelessly surmounted a Corinthian column—it borrowed temples, obelisks, triumphant columns, and, plundering the funerary theme, the pyramids of false marble that flanked the altar of the fatherland. From ancient iconographic motifs, which had recently come back into fashion, it took globes and spheres. From the century's exoticism it borrowed the Chinese pavilion, which inspired the shape of the canopy over the altars of the fatherland, and also the pomegranates and orange trees, with their "odoriferous flowers," which spread their petals over the steps. From Christian legend it took the angels that surmounted the altars and from learned allegory the veiled women bearing branches of bay, compasses, mirrors, feathers, vases, and incense, symbols that had to be deciphered, like so many Concords, Philosophies, Histories, and Religions.

But all these old motifs rehashed by the festival were now painted with the national colors and mingled with the beginnings of a Revolutionary symbolism. Concords and Wisdoms decorated the cap of Liberty. Angels waved tricolor flags. Red caps hung from royal crowns. Broken chains covered the altars. And the aerostats of a scientistic century carried effigies of the Nation up into the heavens.

The spectacles expressed the same blithe lack of consistency. Sometimes the model was the Corpus Christi procession, as in those processions in which an ark of the covenant was paraded around "as supporting figure of religion." But the model could also be the Roman triumph: at Lille there was a procession of chariots "laden with trophies like to the liberty of France," accompanied by the mayor, the king's lieutenant, the general of the National Guard, and the municipality. The centerpiece of the spectacle was the Roman chariot, drawn by an elephant, containing a bust of Louis XVI with all the royal insignia.[60] Elsewhere the festival repeated the ceremonial of the royal entry, as at Aix-en-Provence, where the portrait of Louis XVI entered the city, borne aloft by four national guardsmen, to a roll of drums; to add to the illusion of a true entry, the guardsmen presented arms to it and regaled it with a song.

All these activities must be imagined in the context of the persistence, if not of a certain luxuriance, at least of a sensuality that was later to be absent from the official accounts of the festivals. Here there still reigned, for a little while longer, a sense of color, a taste for fine costumes. The festival was an opportunity for feasts, sometimes described with much self-satisfaction; the accounts are not averse to listing the pâtés, hams, boiled meats, legs of lamb, ducks, and turkeys that covered the civic tables and the barrels of wine draped in garlands and placed on either side of the band. The festival was a pretext for libations and liberality, for the distribution of bread and wine, for the remission of penalties, sometimes for a collective dispensation of summary justice.

It is in this amalgam that we must see the true novelty: not, in all likelihood, the invention of a hitherto unseen ceremonial but the bringing together of disparate elements. Such a verbal and visual syncretism gives the best idea of what the festival was like: the king and liberty, which, Madame de Staël tells us, then seemed to the spectators to be "completely united"; the festival and the Catholic religion, for as the parish priest of the village in the Drôme declared, "It is impossible to be faithful to the nation without being faithful to God, to be faithful to God without being a good Christian and a good Catholic";[61] and lastly, the festival and the finality of the bourgeois Revolution, for the good news that the festival was supposed to spread was, according to the Curé de Saint-Jean at the federative assembly of the National Guards, that "the road to places, honors, and offices was now open. And merit alone will lead there."

The Festival of All the French?

The Federation was readily seen as an absorption of differences. Two images sustain this view. The first was that of the gathering at Champ-de-Mars, which those who, like S. de Girardin, who had beheld "the heights of Passy filled with spectators, the smoke of cannon, the flash of weapons, the variety of uniforms," could never forget.[62] It was not only a matter of aesthetic splendor. The mere fact of coming together seemed at the time to be a prodigious moral conquest: the festival celebrated the passage from the private to the public, extending to all the feeling of each individual "as by a kind of electrical charge." It allowed "that which despotism had never allowed"—that is to say, the mingling of citizens delighting in the spectacle of one another and the perfect accord of hearts. "It should be remembered that under the rule of despotism," Poyet tells us, "men mistrusted one another, having no common interest, hid themselves from one another, and did not know one another, gathering only within their own family, which was the rallying point; the politics of despotism helped to maintain this fatal disunion."[63] The gathering in the Champ-de-Mars seemed to everybody to be the reverse of that partitioned world.

Even more exalting, more demonstrative, was the image of the extraordinary journey that preceded and made possible the gathering; for many of the *fédérés,* it was the first journey that they had ever undertaken in their lives—and it was to remain the only one. A modest delegate from Bordeaux, who reported his impressions of the Federation to his wife, told her of the outings that he thought he should make before he returned home: "Tomorrow I am going to Versailles and Marly . . . I shall then go to Chantilly, Ermenonville, and Saint-Denis; then I shall leave and become a plant for the rest of my life."[64]

This gives some idea of the wrench from everyday existence that the departure for the Federation and, consequently, the dramatization of the journey meant to so many provincials. Moreover, for the sense of the extraordinary to be kept alive, it was necessary that the undertaking should not be easy. The journey had to be long: in fact, the delegates left Avignon on July 5 and Argentan on July 7. The journey had to be exhausting: the newspapers gave the prize to those of the *fédérés* who, like the Bretons, came on foot. ("It was feared that the deputies to the Confederation would not arrive in Paris, since our foppish officers joined their regiments by carriage . . . The Bretons, who have always set such a fine example, overcame fatigue as they had once overcome despotism.") There was talk of "traveling Spartans": as Camille Desmoulins remarked, it was further from Mont Jura to Paris than from Sparta to Delphi. Imagination needed exhausted, sweaty travelers to consecrate the pilgrimage. It needed dangers: Edmond Géraud, a student in Paris, awaited his young brother, traveling to the Federation (their father, an enlightened Bordeaux arms manufacturer, wanted to give his sons the opportunity of seeing the Federation, which he sensed was the grand opening of the nineteenth century). The elder son lavished advice on his younger brother for the journey as if it were some new Odyssey: "Take good care, take care of the knives that the girls will offer you at Chatellerault, at the staging posts. They are drugs, don't buy them. Like another Ulysses, don't be affected by the prayer of the Sirens." [65] There was a need for deeds of valor, even if, in the case of the Brentons, they were carried out with little risk and at the expense only of church pews and symbols of feudalism. [66] Lastly, there was a need for moments of anguish if the journey were to assume epic proportions. The *fédérés* themselves were so well aware of this that they sometimes rejected the warm welcome and comfort offered by townspeople in favor of the sacred austerity of camping out. [67]

In any case, the most important symbol was France itself, crisscrossed from end to end by participants in search of a spectacle or a role and by people rushing up to see them pass, exchanging questions and answers. It was the great national thaw, already sensed by the Marquis de Ségur when he returned to France from Russia in 1790. [68] He found that people spoke freely: in every public square "groups of men were talking in lively fashion." The old fear and circumspection had gone from their eyes: even "individuals of the lower classes" had a proud, direct gaze. Everywhere there was noise and an "extraordinary sense of movement." All this activity was to reach its height with the preparations for the Federation. The Baron de Frénilly, who left Poitou four days before July 14, 1790, had to travel day and night to get to this prodigious spectacle. He thought that he would never arrive on time: "Sometimes there were no horses at the coaching inns; the roads were filled with national guardsmen; we had to go at a snail's pace; every so often we had to pick up one or two exhausted men, give them time to rest, then set them down again." [69]

In this overoccupied France, the trial by distance was a national education. What did the *fédérés* learn on the road? To begin with, as Louis Blanc was well aware, once crossed, rivers and mountains no longer exist as barriers: "Twelve hundred internal barriers disappeared; the mountains seemed to lower their crests; the rivers were now no more than so many moving belts linking together populations that had been separated for too long."[70] In their impatience with boundaries and their delight in crossing them, these men, who could not get over the fact that they had lived for so long caged up, discovered that the old fragmented France was disappearing. Travel leveled the French countryside, as this astonishing account of the return of the federative banner to Angers shows: "The municipality, the département, the district of Angers, other districts and neighboring municipalities could hardly contain their enthusiasm; they dashed out to meet us. The municipality did not consider whether it was moving outside its own territory. Does patriotism recognize today those lines of demarcation that pride and pettiness once laid down?"[71]

It was a tumult that also affected the realm of ideas. Two pieces of conflicting evidence demonstrate this. The first comes from the disapproving Baron de La Tocnaye, who was concerned about the epidemic of rebelliousness that affected the regular troops when they happened to encounter the *fédérés*.[72] His regiment, which set out from Besançon to come to the defense of manufacturers and merchants whose premises in Lyon had been looted, met up on the road with a group of *fédérés* on their way back from a festival. The *fédérés* rushed ahead of the soldiers and warned the inhabitants of the towns on the way to receive them "well"—in other words, to set about converting them to Revolutionary principles, a task in which the good wine of the Arbois played no small part. La Tocnaye was, of course, appalled, but his description of how the evil spread is no less accurate for that. It started when the grenadiers offered their commander a ribbon in the national colors. He refused to carry it, but was forced to give in when his men returned en masse the next day. His acceptance was the signal for almost riotous rejoicing. The soldiers poured out into the streets, danced the farandole, and drove the monks out of their monastery and forced them to dance with the women. The second piece of evidence comes from an amazed Wordsworth, who landed at Calais on the very day of July 14. Throughout his long journey in a France still recovering from its festival, he notes the spread of gaiety that refused to die down as the triumphal arches got tawdrier and the garlands faded. At Chalon, Wordsworth and his companion boarded a boat on the Saône carrying a group of *fédérés* on their way home. Frenchmen and Englishmen warmed to one another; the Cambridge undergraduate and his friend were "welcomed almost as the angels were to Abraham of old." Everywhere, Wordsworth writes, "benevolence and blessedness spread like a fragrance."[73] What struck him most about the Federation—and he was surely right—was that individual joy embodied national joy and was in turn enhanced by it.

Nor is it irrelevant that these two scenes were scenes of homecoming. Paris may have been the glorious end of the journey, but nobody forgot that he would have to go home and tell the tale. The federative pilgrimage—and in this it was original—was a pilgrimage from which one came home; or, to be more precise, one did it only to come home and establish all the more securely, in the movement back and forth between province and Paris, the consacrality of French territory. For in the euphoria of the national gathering, every corner of the country took on value; the ordinary and the extraordinary did not wish to be separated. The Federation owed its unique character to the fact that it was both more and less than a pilgrimage. No doubt every pilgrim comes home a different man, and in this the federative pilgrimage was no exception. The *fédérés* asked to be allowed to keep "some decorative mark" by which they could be recognized: this obsession with relics gave rise to Palloy's commercialization of such devotional mementos and brought him prosperity.[74] So they came home laden with medals and diplomas conferred on them by the municipality of Paris. They offered their hometowns a whole collection of consecrated bric a brac: a reproduction of the Bastille with a piece of stone from the building mounted in a case; a picture of the Declaration of Rights; and assorted likenesses of Louis XVI, Lafayette, Bailly, and so on. These relics were paraded through the towns in interminable processions by the daughters of notables, thus giving authenticity to the extraordinary adventure and salvaging it from the ephemeral. But above all, those much-coveted "marks" were like a baptism given by Paris to the provinces, an affirmation of the homogeneity of a French territory cut out of the same piece of cloth.

The chief relic, the sacral object par excellence, was the federative banner: every evening, at each stage in the journey, it was laid in the senior man's room; miraculous powers were attributed to it; before this "sign of alliance" all rivalry was to disappear, "any idea alien to happiness was to vanish."[75] So much organization went into receiving the delegates in each town or village on the way that the journey home was often—the timetable being less stringent—even longer than the journey to the capital.

The delegates from Nantes left Paris on the morning of July 23 and did not reach their city, despite the impatience of the Nantais, until August 6. From Arpajon, the first stop on their way to Nantes, how often they had to break their journey for "splendid suppers," receptions given by national guardsmen to the accompaniment of music and refreshment, hospitality that was repaid with a few political harangues! How many bunches of flowers had been thrown to them, how many triumphal arches had they passed under, how many oaths taken and taken again, at In-grandes, Lorris, Beaugency, all repeating much the same words as the Paris oath! The flags were paraded back and forth, for the inhabitants of each town came out to meet their banner with its own and, next morning, accompanied the travelers on their way for part of the journey: literally, they could not bear to part. Each town did its best to keep the "homecom-ers" a little longer than the town before. The Nantais travelers judged this competition of balls, dinners, fanfares, and gun salutes; it was Sau-mur's enthusiastic welcome that won it the prize in the triumphal march of that particular banner, "the eternal monument of the oath."[76]

So a story traveled the road whose moral teaching was apparently effec-tive. At Chavignon, a small commune in the Aisne, the rumor spread, without the slightest foundation, that a troop of "ill-intentioned men" was marching toward the commune.[77] On hearing this rumor, all the active citizens in the neighboring villages gathered spontaneously, as they had done two days before for the festival itself. Led by their mayor and parish priest, they marched in procession, arriving during the night, to guard a river crossing and to give assistance to their threatened "brothers." In no time at all the small, peaceful township was transformed into an armed camp. The scene very soon turned into a festival, for once the alarm proved false, the women arrived with wine and victuals. But the reflex worked, and the contemporary account of the scene reads—and this is significant—like the account of a federation. It seems that, once the Federation had been created, any gathering of citizens, for collective de-fense or for any other reason, could not but be a reactivation of the origi-nal Federation.

The true success of the festival lies there. It was a dynamic image of the gathering, rather than the description of an assembled community. There were two parties excluded from the Festival of the Federation, one always named, the other never; and it is not a distortion to maintain that the truly excluded party was not the one most often talked about. The excluded party whose name was on everybody's lips was the aristocrat.

Absent, distant, never seen, never caught, but at the heart of all these accounts, he had no other than a functional reality. His implicit presence was indispensable to the festival: the sense of unity and transparency is never so sharp as when it is won against some mysterious, invisible obstacle. For some, however, he was rather too invisible; for them it was a matter of regret that he did not have a more convincingly physical presence in the festival. Camille Desmoulins, like so many others, comparing the Federation procession to the triumph of Aemilius Paulus, deplored "the absence of what for the Romans had been a particular pleasure: the vision of Perseus, with his wife and children, chained behind the consul's chariot."[78]

The other excluded party, the one that is never mentioned, was the people. It is true that many of the contemporary accounts make a point of saying that in the civic banquets citizens were placed "without distinction of age, sex, or fortune," but is that enough to conclude that everybody participated in the festival? Often the people took part only on the condescending initiative of the notables, or by a series of accidents, or by surprise. At Pont-Saint-Esprit, for example, the festival was first planned as a display of the troops, a spectacle laid on for the benefit of the people but not one in which they took part.[79] After the benediction of the Blessed Sacrament in the afternoon, "the people were also given the pleasure of seeing the troops moving through the streets of the town." A banquet for the soldiers was then laid on in the barrack square by the officers of the Roussillon regiment. At first the people were merely witnesses; then, apparently, they "even took part." This "even" is very telling: something unexpected happened; a barrier was crossed. The same scenario was repeated after the banquet: "the feast was crowned by a regimental *farandole*," led by the commandant and his officers. For the writer of the account, this mingling of officers and soldiers was already sufficient matter for wonder; but the citizens found it hard to hold back as passive spectators of the dance, and "soon afterwards all the inhabitants joined in." But we learn that this mixture of civilians and soldiers took nearly an hour to materialize. From the note of surprise expressed in the account, we can sense that, in this festival, planned and carried out by soldiers, the people joined in only as gatecrashers.

The fact that occasionally the people were invited does not really affect the matter. Sometimes, in the cordiality of the banquet, one of the participants stood up and proposed a motion that "a number of poor people, equal to the number of guests, be given a supper in the evening."[80] In such cases there were two meals held in different parts of the town. The exhibitionistic self-satisfaction with which this good act is stressed is in itself rather telling. So the people had a very precise role in the festival: they provided an illustration of "the advent of the reign of equality"; they were a living demonstration. Some of the accounts say as much quite explicitly: "The guards officers and the municipal officers decided that on so happy an occasion it had to be proved that equality had been achieved by inviting them to the same table."[81] A similar demonstration was given by the municipal officers of Angers on the occasion of the return of the banner: "Each of the municipal officers insisted on taking the arm of one of those women that are called women of the people."[82]

The topographical disposition of the festival stressed this separation still further. Around the altar of the fatherland was a circle of soldiers, around it a circle of notables. Around it were the people: they attended as the oath was taken by the first two groups and sometimes were bold enough to demand that they themselves should take an oath. Nevertheless, they had to demand it.

It was not, therefore, the festival of all the French, but it should be noted that neither of the two exclusions on which it was based was felt as such; neither seemed to be prejudicial to the national spirit that the festival was celebrating. In 1790 the endless elections had thrown up as delegates not only bourgeois notables but also provincial nobles and priests. It was their agreement, or even their fusion, that was being celebrated in the Festival of the Federation. It is now apparent why the double exclusion from the Federation could not be felt as harmful to national unity: the first because it was the mythical foundation of that unity and the second because nobody could yet regard its exclusion as contradictory. The truth of these untruthful accounts derives, therefore, precisely from this consensus. The harmony between the language used in the festival and that used by ordinary people in the towns was no doubt temporary, but for the moment complete.

· III ·

The Festival above the Parties

1792

WHEN the Constituent Assembly broke up, its entire experience of festivals was confined to the two Federations (1790
and 1791), two pantheonizations (of Mirabeau and Voltaire),
and a funeral festival (for the soldiers who died at Nancy). To these should
be added the series of festivals that accompanied the proclamation of the
Constitution in 1791. In the provinces, no doubt, other festivals were
celebrated, according to local circumstances, but without any reference to
orders from Paris. The members of the Constituent Assembly were
acutely aware of this absence of a national character. Thouret had supple-
mentary articles added to the Constitution proposing the establishment
of national festivals "to preserve the memory of the French Revolution, to
maintain fraternity among the citizens, to strengthen their loyalty to the
fatherland and its laws." This pious wish met with unanimous support
from the Constituent Assembly members. Was the desire for such unanimity the reason for the extreme generality of the terms, which left each
party free to imagine its own version of such festivals, its own kind of
psychological action? Or was it, in fact, because the link suggested by
Thouret between the legalized Revolution and the festival embodied the
agreement of all minds? The year 1791–92 brought this question, which
all historiography of the Revolutionary festival has posed, back onto the
agenda.

Yet the legislative Assembly no more succeeded in creating an organized series of festivals than had the Constituent Assembly; it confined
itself to announcing such a series and, in the spring of 1792, instructing
its Committee of Public Education to draw up a bill. At first, however,
the committee was fully occupied with planning the third federative fes-

tival, after which August 10 carried all before it. The inability to reach a conclusion, common to both this assembly and its predecessor, explains why a concern for celebrations of various kinds has usually been attributed to the Convention. This is quite wrong; the first attempts to assess the new experiments in public celebration appeared as early as 1791, when Talleyrand and Mirabeau lent their prestigious names to the first writings in what was to be an enduring genre. Furthermore, 1792 was the year that saw, within a few weeks, the celebration of two great antagonistic festivals, the first organized by the sans-culottes and the second by the Feuillants. The first, the festival of Châteauvieux, was born of the convulsions of a bitter polemic; the second, the festival in commemoration of Simonneau, was specifically planned as a counterblast to the first. If there are two exceptional festivals in the course of the Revolution, festivals that were instruments of a consciously defined policy, they were certainly these two. Their opposition, even more striking on account of their closeness in time, is therefore the first occasion for testing the political interpretation of the Revolutionary festivals. In those turbulent years, in those little-known and often abortive projects, in those festivals intended to be contradictory should we see at work two competing views of the festival? Or, accepting the existence of a consensus resistant to political rivalries, should we perhaps see in all this a unified model of the Revolutionary festival?

The Norm and the Exception

Mirabeau's thoughts on the festivals, found among his papers after his death and edited by Cabanis,[1] can be easily dated. He expressed his views on two actual festivals, the Federation and the funeral festival for the soldiers who died at Nancy.[2] It was therefore between September 1790 and April 1791 that this strange, skeptical, undeluded work was written.

Indeed, it is actually in a passage praising in the usual way the "ever moving and sublime" scenes of these two festivals that a gloomy, almost painful reflection enters. For Mirabeau the memory of the Federation was that of a double defeat: it was first of all a personal defeat, for the man of the Federation was a hated rival, and it was also a political defeat, because the king was not able to take advantage of either the great wave of emotion or the spectacle providentially offered him to demonstrate his reconciliation with the Revolution. Furthermore, Mirabeau caught a glimpse in the Federation, that festival of union between regular troops and national guards, of the threat of contagion, confusion. At the back of his mind was the fear of insubordination, of which the Nancy affair in particular provided a sinister illustration. The funeral festival of Nancy, which was the obverse of the federative festival, had illustrated in a way that reversal of roles that the Federation contained as one of its possible developments: in the dramatic events at Nancy, it was the regular troops who had mutinied and the national guardsmen who had sacrificed their lives in the service of the law—that is to say, at Bouillé's side. This was an unnatural confrontation and one that signaled defeat.

The whole of Mirabeau's project, then, was marked by a negative image of the festival. It was intended to avoid a federative festival that, like the first, would fail to achieve the unity of monarchical government and representative government. Above all, it was intended to avoid another Festival of Nancy. These two intentions give a certain strength to views that, despite their modest form—Mirabeau refrains from adopting a "systematic, regular plan" and declares that he is merely offering "suggestions"— are extremely coherent.

Mirabeau's obsession, born of a fear of mutiny, was to find a means of keeping citizens and soldiers apart, in the name of a structural difference—the regular troops having duties out of all proportion to those of ordinary citizens—that should be reflected in the patriotic ceremonies. Each group should have its own rites; national guardsmen are not soldiers but citizens, and they should not be allowed to mix with the soldiers in festivals. On no occasion whatsoever? No, there would be one exception, a concession to already established custom—the anniversary of the Federation. Now that the Federation had taken place, it would be impossible on that day to prevent the army and the civil population from meeting "under the standards of the Constitution." This is the first time, but also the last, that we see Revolutionary events departing from the ideal conception of the festivals. Resigned to making an exception for the Federation, Mirabeau was less concerned to lay down its ceremonial than to regulate its supervision: it would obey a plan set down in advance in every detail, and it could take place only under the auspices and control of the legislature.

When one stands back and looks at the other eight festivals—four military and four civilian ones, loosely distributed throughout the year, at the solstices and equinoxes, says Mirabeau, though without laying much stress on the exact timing—one finds that they all look very much alike. There is a kind of clumsy stylization in these festivals, whose names, taken straight from a newly invented political vocabulary, recur throughout Mirabeau's text: meeting, declaration, Constitution, coalition, regeneration. In fact, this is not a facile solution; it springs rather from a desire for balance. Of the civilian festivals, one has a quite military character: this is the festival of the taking up of arms. As Mirabeau says, we must "preserve the memory of the admirable accord and heroic courage with which the national guards were suddenly formed to protect the cradle of liberty." In symmetrical fashion, one of the four military festivals, celebrated inside the garrisons by the regiments alone, has a civilian character: the army, which cannot remain indifferent "to the great change that has just taken place," should have its own Festival of the Revolution. Thus, the fact that civilians should have their military festival and soldiers their civilian festival seems to Mirabeau enough to ensure the unity of army and nation. The other three civilian festivals celebrate, unsurprisingly, the "reunion" (that is to say, the night of August 4), the Declaration of Rights, and the Constitution (that is to say, the moment "when the communes were formed into a National Assembly").

Of the three strictly military festivals, two of them also correspond, in an attempt at precise balance. There is one, that of the "coalition," in homage to the conduct of the line troops when, during the summer of 1789, they gathered "around the nation" and responded "to the call of liberty." The euphemism fails to conceal that their action was, in fact, mutinous.[3] So this festival of the military oath is intended to make the soldiers understand that, apart from the exception celebrated by the previous festival, obedience to military law is the norm and brooks no departure. So, despite its pragmatic presentation, the unity of Mirabeau's project is in tatters. This planned celebration may be a commemoration of the Revolution, but it is also an attempt to prevent its spread, to ensure the obedience of the active army and to avoid its contamination by the National Guard. The festival is the instrument of a conservative organization in which, once the law of the Revolution has been laid down, each element—king, legislature, army—must become its obedient servant. Moreover, no single element must dominate the others: there are strict provisions to ensure that the king will never be able to attend the national festivals without being accompanied by the legislature.

Mirabeau's prudence is apparent in other precautions: his wish to separate various elements leads him to exclude the religious apparatus from the national festivals. Was this because the funeral festival of the Champ-de-Mars, such a repulsive model here, had, like the Federation, brought with it those religious sequences attributed to Lafayette's histrionics? Or, at a deeper level, was this a precautionary measure at a time when "a means of activating the mainspring of religion in accordance with a determination concentric with the movement of patriotism and liberty" had clearly not yet been discovered?[4] The reasons why Mirabeau justifies the exclusion of the Christian religion—it is, in his view, too serious, too private a matter to be mixed with public rejoicing[5]—carries less conviction than his desire, once again, to put the festival beyond any risk of contamination. The Revolutionary festival must be a purely civic rite. The repetitive aspect of the names given the festivals by Mirabeau finds an explanation here. Everything in these festivals must always revolve around the concepts of Revolution and Constitution, each allowing the other, each containing the other.

This act of discrimination is still not enough for him. One must also attend to what the festival shows and forestall any improvisation or departure from due form. The men deputed to the festival, the couplets sung, the plays performed, the length and theme of the speeches would first be subjected to scrupulous supervision. The unpredictable element that a festival might harbor is unbearable to Mirabeau, in this an heir to ancestral prudence. Despite all their prestige, even the festivals of antiquity did not entirely elude his mistrust: in the Roman triumph there was something that encouraged "the avid fury of a conquering people," while the saturnalia were in a sense an invitation "to recall in an illusory way the primal equality of men." In short, one could not be absolutely certain of controlling the outcome of a festival. On this point Mirabeau intended to do better than the Romans.

His festivals were to be festivals of containment, in which above all everyone would be reminded of his duties. Talleyrand, aware that such an attitude would cast a pall of gloom over them, was not in favor of regulating the festivals too meticulously; and, the Federation apart, for its greatness protected it from any danger of growing stale, he was against too rigid a frequency.[6] Yet, on the whole, his own project, which actually refers to Mirabeau's views, suggests that, quite apart from individual tastes, there already existed a widely shared view of the Revolutionary festivals. For both Talleyrand and Mirabeau, any attempt to invent festivals must refer to the ceremonies of antiquity: the recital of eulogies, a profound study of national history, competitions of every kind, the handing out of crowns and rewards. Such things made up the scholarly content of the festivals.[7] Talleyrand turns out to be no keener than Mirabeau on

mixing civic and religious ceremonies, with the possible exception of state
funerals. But he felt that it would be unsuitable to do so in festivals of
celebration—that is to say, in the pure cult of liberty.

Above all, neither man doubted "the secret bonds that unite the festivals of free peoples with their political institutions." Each of them saw in
the festival both the product and the instrument of a legalized Revolution. In the case of Mirabeau, there is an additional concern for system-
aticity: his reflections on the matter already betray a desire to mark out
the national territory by a tight network of festivals that would bring the
Paris model to the most modest commune. This, in turn, would encourage men to visit the capital, each commune appointing a deputy to the
canton, each canton to the district, each district to the département; these
comings and goings would be regulated like a ballet, ensuring national
unanimity in the simultaneity and uniformity of ritual.

There was much more than hesitant beginnings, therefore, in these
projects of 1791. Behind them there was already a doctrine, the most
striking feature of which is the caution with which the Revolution, which
the festivals were intended to glorify, is treated, the obsession with and
prevention of any new mutiny. In the harsh confrontation of the two great
political festivals of the spring of 1792, we shall see such caution cast to
the winds.

Two Antagonistic Festivals?

Châteauvieux, Simonneau—the festival of liberty, the festival of the
law—two symbols. The first was intended to honor the Swiss of Châteauvieux, who mutinied in August 1790 and were rescued from the galleys
in which Bouillé had put them: a rehabilitation of rioters, if not a glorification of riots. The second was intended to honor Simonneau, the mayor
of Etampes, killed in a people's riot while upholding the law on foodstuffs:
a glorification, this time, of the victim of riot. One was due to the initiative of "advanced patriots" and the patriotic clubs, the other was born of
an official decision on the part of the authorities. On either side are ranged
great antagonistic names: Condorcet, who pleaded for the first, and André
Chénier, who called for the second. The Festival of Châteauvieux can be
contrasted, term by term, with that of Simonneau, which according to
Brissot, was more like a ceremony than a festival.

The comparison does not end there. The antagonism between the two
festivals was not fabricated after the event but perceived at the time. The
same issue of the *Journal de Paris* that found room for André Chénier's

indignation against the festival of Châteauvieux welcomed the account of a festival given in honor of Simonneau by the municipality of Beaumont-sur-Oise. No sooner had the festival of Châteauvieux taken place than the active citizens and national guardsmen of the Beaubourg section were planning a solemn festival to Simonneau with a great military procession. The festival was conceived as a form of reparation. The patriotic press, for its part, produced an almost inexhaustible list of contrasting features. Here are the two accounts offered by *Révolutions de Paris*:

> The procession [at the festival of Châteauvieux] began late, around noon; it was not that the people were made to wait, as by despots at court festivals. The people turned up at daybreak in large numbers at the Barrière du Trône; but the festival did not wait for the procession before beginning. As soon as people were gathered together, they took pleasure in each other's company; nevertheless the time came to leave . . .
>
> On the site of the Bastille a sort of inauguration of the statue of Liberty was held. We shall omit the details in order to grasp the better this popular festival as a whole, the first of its kind and one that, we hope, will be repeated. Time spent during the first station gave ill-disposed and credulous citizens an opportunity of reassuring themselves and of joining in when the triumphal march resumed, which, it should be added, was favored with all the serenity of a spring day.
>
> There was no excess of pomp; gold did not dazzle the eye or insult the citizens' gentle ordinariness or honorable indigence. There were no soldiers dripping with braid to cast contemptuous eyes, to right and left, on the poorly dressed crowd as they passed. Here actors and witnesses often merged, taking turns in the procession: there was little order, but a good deal of accord; no one indulged the vanity of a haughty gaze; no one set out to be a spectacle; boredom, that son of uniformity, found no foothold among the various groups; at each step the scene changed; the chain of the procession broke many times, but the onlookers soon filled up the gaps: everybody wanted to take part in the festival of liberty.
>
> Luxury was banished; but the commemorative objects that were carried from place to place spoke to the minds and hearts of those present. The procession opened with the Declaration of the Rights of Man, written on two stone tablets as the Decalogue of the Hebrews is represented to us, though it is no match for our Declaration. Four citizens proudly carried this venerable burden on their shoulders; and when they stopped to rest or to await the rest of the procession, a large group of citizens immediately formed around them, each one reading, aloud, with a sense of pride and justice, the first lines of the Declaration: men are born and remain free and equal.
>
> The four busts that followed were met in like manner. Ah! said one,

that is Voltaire, that old rascal who made us laugh so much at the expense of the priests. That other, worried-looking individual [J.-J. Rousseau] loved the nobles even less and never wanted to be obliged to them. What is that third bust? It is of an Englishman [Sydney] who left his head on the block rather than bend the knee to a king. That old man there, the one with the kindly face, we know who he is; it's Franklin, who can more rightly be said to be the liberator of the New World than a certain fop who may not be too far from here.

The two sarcophagi that followed threw a somber coloring over this festival. Seeing them, one could not but recall the massacre at Nancy, the plan of which, drawn up in the *cabinet* of the Tuileries, was sent to Bouillé by the good offices and on the recommendation of his relation, the liberator of the two worlds.

Preceded by their chains, suspended from trophies and borne aloft by young citizenesses dressed in white, marched the forty Swiss soldiers of the regiment of Château-Vieux, merging with several volunteers and soldiers of the line. One could make out our forty martyrs only by their yellow epaulets. They preceded the chariot of Liberty, mounted on the same wheels that served for the chariot in the apotheosis of Voltaire. This little circumstance is worthy of note; let us not forget that it was philosophy that brought us liberty.

The chariot, modeled on the antique, was an imposing construction. On one of its sides, the happy painter of the Revolution, M. David, had sketched the story of Brutus the Elder, himself sentencing to death his conquering sons for disobeying the law. On the other side is depicted William Tell, aiming a javelin, the target of which is an apple on his own son's head; but at his feet we glimpse the tip of another javelin, one that was to bring independence to Switzerland by slaying the Austrian governor. The statue of Liberty, seated on her throne, her hand resting on a bludgeon, commanded respect and would have made a king lower his eyes if he happened to pass her on the way. We should never forget that the scepter of liberty is a bludgeon. It should also be said that the prow at the front of the chariot was formed by six daggers whose tips touched and seemed to threaten any despotism bold enough to impede the triumphal march of liberty.

With steady step twenty democratic horses (if we may be permitted to use the adjective) drew the chariot of the sovereign of the French people; their progress had none of the insolence of those idle coursers fed in the stables of Versailles or Chantilly. They did not hold their heads high; their manes were not plaited with gold, nor adorned with white plumes; their backs were covered in long-hanging scarlet cloth; they walked rather ploddingly, but they kept a steady course.

Behind the chariot, a long-eared courser, mounted by a joker, ridiculously dressed, represented Stupidity, who, having failed to stop this festival, had come to point out its defects, in order to give copy to such scribblers as Dupont and Gauthier, Durosoy and A. Chénier, Parisot and Roucher, etc., etc., etc.

The procession traveled halfway around Paris and made its way through an enormous, ever-thronging crowd, without encountering any obstacle. The gendarmerie on foot and horse had no need to mark out the route; two rows of bayonets were not needed to clear the way before it; the good offices of the minister of the interior were not required; the département had recommended good order to the municipality and the day before a decree was issued concerning carriages and the carrying of weapons, but it was the people themselves who saw to it that it was obeyed and their conduct was a lesson for the magistrates and an example for the National Guard. Four hundred thousand citizens were out in the streets for half a day and all went to the same spot, without the slightest mishap. Words of peace contained this multitude; it fell into line at the sight of an ear of corn presented to it in place of bayonets, from the Bastille to the Champ-de-Mars.

And, six weeks later, this is how *Révolutions de Paris* saw the procession of the "festival of Simonneau":

On Sunday, June 3, there was a free spectacle in Paris; or rather Quatremer and Roucher, Dubu, Dupont, and their ilk wanted to give a lesson to the people and they acquitted themselves with that magisterial, sententious tone that characterizes dreary pedagogues who are themselves uncertain of what they are trying to inculcate in others. Fortunately, the patience of the spectators was equal to the pedanticism of the organizers of the funeral festival in honor of J. G. Simonneau, who was merely its pretext; for, as we have already observed in our first announcement, the shade of the mayor of Etampes was to be appeased by the decree granting him a public monument: but certain individuals had set their hearts on humiliating and subduing the people, supposing that it needed to be constantly recalled to order and to respect for the law and the institutions set up by it . . .

But this pomp was more a review of the National Guards and the soldiers of the line than anything else. The day before, the flags of the regular troops had been blest in haste. This martial spectacle contrasted so strongly with the triumph of the law, which set out to be peaceful, that this mixture of ancient religious ceremony and modern military maneuvers resembled a repetition of those long Corpus Christi processions, which were once put on with more or less the same elements. Let the reader judge for himself . . .

The gendarmerie opened the march under the banner of the law followed by the model of the Bastille.

The colors of the 48 sections came next, represented by shields in quite good taste, surmounted by the red cap of liberty and the motto "Indivisible." This laconic lesson was a useful one to give: may it have its effects! *Messieurs les présidents de section* followed gravely to one side, all wearing their black coats, like so many churchwardens. All they needed was a sprig of orange blossom in their hands. Was it necessary to have a decree concerning the costume of the section presidents, secretaries, and commissioners, as there was for the judges?

They were there apparently to serve as a foil to the white uniform of the troops of the line, who followed in the finest order. Aristocracy was imprinted on the faces of most of the officers, who did not wear the diamond-shaped medal of the French guards.

When M. de Penthièvre takes his blest bread to Saint-Eustache, we see a mass of tiny flags fluttering overhead that are then distributed to the children of the parish: they were taken as the model for the banners representing the 83 départements of the empire.

The most curious item in the procession as a whole was a kind of shark raised aloft on the end of a pikestaff; the sea animal had its mouth open and was showing its teeth; on its body was written, "Respect for the law." It is said that the pikestaff represented the law and the shark the people. It is our opinion, on the contrary, that the pikestaff is the people and the shark what you will—despotism, aristocracy, or religious fanaticism. The département should have taken care in its program to forestall the spectator's uncertainty in this respect. We missed any such indication. The king of the Chinese, it is true, has a fish as his arms; but we are not in Peking. M. Quartremer owes us a few words of explanation, for he was the master of ceremonies.

Large numbers of national guardsmen seemed to support the marine monster, who frightened nobody, but made everybody laugh. This was not the case with the sword of the law, which bore that truly fine inscription: "It strikes to defend."

But why cover the plinth that supported it with gold gauze? Why identify the sight of this metal with the idea of justice? Great severity in the decoration was required here or none at all. The organizers of the festival used the Latin word *lectisternium* at this point; but since they insist on proving their erudition, they ought at least to explain the word to the people . . .

After them came Simonneau's sash, entwined with a mourning veil, a palm, and a crown, then his bust, followed by his family in mourning; then the pyramid that will perpetuate his memory; all was borne by men dressed in the antique mode, but in so mean, so dirty a manner that it was enough to disgust everyone with the Greeks and Romans forever.

On a gilt curule chair, surmounted by a small silver statue of Saint Minerva, was offered to all eyes a representation of the book of the law, open. It was expected that this spectacle would make a bigger impression, but it was altogether too reminiscent of missals and saints' shrines, especially as those who bore these objects were dressed in priestly fancy dress such as is used in our Corpus Christi processions. The good women of the parish were there—all that was missing was their priest. The illusion would have been complete if there had been censers; for there were several baskets held by small boys who differed only from choirboys in that they were not tonsured. One looked in vain for those venerable old men announced on the prospectus, those good, white-haired village patriarchs in their holiday garb.

A group of women followed, presided over by the Dame de Gouges, whose bearing recalled rather too much that of drum majors at the head of their noisy troops. When the Constituent Assembly handed over the book of laws to the guard formed of mothers, it probably did not imagine that it was putting on a theatrical performance. This troop of ladies in white, crowned with oak, did not have the desired success. Whatever one may say, women seemed out of place on the great day.

The colossal statue of the law brought up the rear; it was represented by a seated woman, leaning on the tablets of the rights of man, which she seemed to be trying to cover under her cloak. She was given a scepter as attribute; a brake, the attribute of law among the ancients, might have been more appropriate; in any case, the people must not be accustomed to confusing law and monarchy.

Much might be said of the inscription placed under the pedestal of this figure: "Truly free men are the slaves of the law."

We prefer the three words written around the throne of the law: "liberty, equality, property."

Immediately in front of the legislative body was carried the civic crown intended for Simonneau's bust; but it was carried, as it was the custom not so long ago to carry what were called the honors, that is to say, the crowns of counts or marquises, at the burials of our forebears.

The administrators of the département and the king's ministers preceded the representatives of the nation, who, almost without exception, made sure that they attended this procession. The Festival of Liberty on May 15 was not met with the same favor.

When it reached the Champ-de-Mars, the calumniating picture of Simonneau's death was hung from a great palm tree, around which the other items of the triumph were arranged in picturesque fashion. But one thing worth observing, and one may interpret it as one will, is that the organizers chose precisely the front of the altar of the fatherland, which faces the entrance of the field of the Federation, by which, on July 17, Bailly and Lafayette came and, in the name of martial law, shot down the patriots gathered on the altar.

There were three artillery salvos; an anthem, in the manner of Roucher, who is no Ossian, was sung; incense was burned; the book of the law was displayed; Simonneau's bust was crowned; but all this took place out of sight of the crowd of citizens ranged on the terraces, who saw the entire ceremony only with the eyes of faith, thanks to a cordon of the soldiers of the line and national volunteers, disposed as far as possible from the center. Only men in uniform and a few women in white enjoyed the privilege of coming closer. The people, or, if you prefer, the nation, for whom all this was being done, paid the cost of it, but saw nothing. The Festival of Liberty on May 15 was at least national, in that the people were both actors and spectators in it, though, of course, there were no bayonets on that day.

If we had chosen to compare two accounts of the festivals in Feuillant newspapers, the overall impression would be little different. No doubt we would have to reverse the terms, but the opposition—in both senses, political and aesthetic—of the two festivals would remain intact.

It seems impossible to deny a political antagonism so consciously expressed. It was in an atmosphere of struggle, constitutional party against patriotic party, that the two festivals were planned. At Châteauvieux, from late March to mid-April, the Jacobin Club echoed with fearful prophecies: what if the festival gave the signal for a massacre of the sansculottes? (The Feuillant side symmetrically expected a signal for an attack on the monarchy.) That was why Robespierre[8] rushed it forward, despite Tallien, who, in view of the delays taken by its organizers, wanted to postpone it. Was everything not ready? It hardly matters. The mottos are less important than the idea, and the presence of the victims would be more eloquent than David's brush—in any case, the great painter would find many another occasion for expressing himself. Robespierre displayed all the impatience of someone who saw the festival as a purely political demonstration, a declaration of distrust in a deceiving court incapable of applying the Constitution. This was also the view of the Constitutionals, who saw the homage paid to the galley prisoners as a call to insubordination. No one expressed it better than André Chénier:

It is said that in all the public squares where this procession will pass the statues will be veiled. And without pausing to ask by what right private individuals giving a festival for their friends take it upon themselves to veil the public monuments, I will say that if indeed this wretched orgy takes place, it is not the images of the despots that will have to be covered with a mourning veil, but the face of all good men, all those law-abiding Frenchmen, insulted by the successes of soldiers who take up arms against the decrees of the state.

A few weeks later, the festival changed sides, the organizers their intentions, the detractors their identity. This time it was Robespierre who tore the Simonneau festival to pieces: "This was no national festival, it was a festival for the public servants . . . How that procession of municipal bodies, administrative bodies, and juridical bodies brought back the image of the Old Order! Bayonets, swords, uniforms, what ornaments for the festival of a free people!"[9]

No one was ever to forget that clash of opinion: it gave birth to a whole new literature that was to mark the entire Revolutionary decade. The anti-Jacobins clung to the theme, never to be abandoned, of the saturnalia, the masquerade, the festival bristling with pikestaffs and adorned with prostitutes.[10] That is what, according to them, Châteauvieux amounted to. The patriots, by contrast, saw the festival for Simonneau as stiff, solemn, official, an event offered as a spectacle to the people, who observed it without taking part in it. Opposing political prejudices seem to have produced entirely opposite festivals, even to the extent of what was actually described: in fact, this is the most interesting thing about them.

Yet it should be said from the outset that the political antagonism between the two festivals was not carried by their organizers to extremes. The organizers of the Festival of Châteauvieux did not dare to perch the galley prisoners on the triumphal chariot prepared for them, and, in the end, they merely joined the procession. The festival took on another meaning. It was now not so much a festival offered to the soldiers of Châteauvieux as a festival of liberty, attended by the soldiers. Sometimes even, when the announcement was made, as in *Le moniteur,* that each year at the same time the festival would be repeated in the same way, as a "spring festival," it took on quite different implications. This moderation, which pleased Madame Jullien,[11] was practiced not only by the organizers but also by the participants, who behaved well on both occasions. Indeed, this behavior suggests the profound consensus between the two groups— over and above what separated them—as to what a festival should be. Everyone described the festival in which he took part as a triumph of

Soldiers' festival at Châteauvieux. (Tableaux historiques de la Révolution française.) Engraving by Berthault, after Prieur, Musée Carnavalet. Photo: Bulloz.

Funeral in honor of Simonneau. (Tableaux historiques de la Révolution française.) Engraving by Berthault, after Prieur, Musée Carnavalet. © DACS 1987.

order: "A gathering of over 300,000 men, restrained and directed solely by their respect for law and order, is a spectacle well worthy of the philosophical observer," wrote Le Coz of the Simonneau festival.[12] And here is Madame Jullien on Châteauvieux: "The vast crowd stood like a wall in miraculous order and precision, so that the policing of a crowd was never carried out so well and so gently."[13]

According to *Révolutions de Paris,* the political struggle, muted though it might have been, nevertheless produced two entirely different festivals belonging to two rival aesthetics. At the Festival of Châteauvieux, no weapons, no cannon were to be seen; there were no drum rolls, no rhythmic marching.[14] At the Simonneau festival, however, there were cavalry, trumpets, national grenadiers, flags—a martial spectacle, in contradiction, according to the anonymous reporter, with the peaceful character of the law. On the one hand, simple, bare ornaments; on the other, ostentatious luxury—the gold of the curule chair, the silver of Minerva. What both explains and epitomizes the different parties is an aesthetic opposition between David and Quatremère de Quincy. David, organizer of the festival of Châteauvieux, was a proponent of realism; Quatremère, organizer of the Simonneau festival, favored abstraction. The Revolution, according to R. Schneider, gave everybody a push in the direction of his own inclinations, stimulating in David a taste for realism and in Quatremère a desire for escapism.[15] The naturalism of the first festival forms a sharp contrast, therefore, with the allegories of the second, which explains why the two festivals were not equally understood by the people. Those who attended the June festival were at a loss as to the meaning of all the symbols, while those who attended the April festival had no difficulty in interpreting what they saw. This was because, according to Dowd, who supports Schneider's hypothesis, David, who had nothing of the pedantic scholar about him, never lost contact with the reality of ordinary everyday life.[16] In short, David succeeded where Quatremère failed. Proof of this may be found in the reluctant homage paid to David's skill by his adversaries; if David had been able to practice his talents in the interest of the monarchy, said the *Journal de la cour et de la ville,* "we would have been reconciled soon enough with the head of the French school."

Yet the newspapers lost no time in attributing to identical groups opposed aesthetics: take, for instance, the group of women dressed in white to be found in both festivals. *Révolutions de Paris* saw them simply as young citizenesses when they walked in the Châteauvieux procession. Six weeks later, in the Simonneau procession, the same group was greeted with the ill-tempered words, "Whatever one may say, women seemed out of place on the great day." Let us leave the newspapers for a moment and put ourselves in the place of those who attended the processions. Before them passed the emblems with which the Revolution had already been identified: the Bastille, the eighty-three départements, the cap of liberty (also present at the Festival of the Law), and the tables of the law (also present at the Festival of Liberty). They waited for the centerpiece of the festival, the two statues, which, despite their different attributes (the bludgeon and the scepter), were both on a colossal scale, both seated on triumphal chariots. If they followed the procession, after a more or less identical itinerary through Paris, they would arrive at the Champ-de-Mars for an identical ceremonial. In each case, the objects carried in the procession— the two statues—were laid on the altar of the fatherland, the same incense was burned, the same music commissioned from Gossec was played. Was it surprising if the spectators then began to shout, as is reported, "Long live Pétion!"[17] or "Long live the Nation and Liberty," even at the festival for Simonneau? Some commentators see these shouts as proof that the people wanted to add something to the somewhat dreary Feuillant festival.[18] But it would probably be truer that any colossal figure carried in a procession was perceived as Liberty. When Quatremère, in his note of 1819 on Roland, the creator of that Law with its extremities of plaster and clay, remarked sadly that "this emblematic prediction had no more consistency than his emblems," he was perhaps simply forgetting that the emblem itself was not perceived as that of the law.

Moreover, one may also wonder whether the opposition between David and Quatremère, though so vigorously drawn, is actually valid.[19] For the two men, linked by the same taste for the frieze—the equivalent of which in the festival was the procession[20]—both convinced that a composition ought "to rise in a pyramid," do not seem to have belonged to opposing schools. The gold and silver for which Quatremère was so criticized for lavishing on the Simonneau festival reveals nothing more than a taste for the polychromy of antiquity, which he used willingly enough in the Panthéon and which David himself used for the statue of Rome on which Brutus' austere meditation rests. Lastly, these two men had already collaborated on various festivals (almost certainly on the funeral celebrations for Voltaire, for which David designed the chariot that was to be used again for Châteauvieux, a masterpiece that Quatremère admired, jealously preserved under the Panthéon peristyle, and lent out much against his will), and were to collaborate again (for the Lapelletier festival, Quatremère was given the commission for the monumental pediment). They may not actually have worked together on these two festivals, though the picture representing the dying mayor of Etampes is often attributed to David, significantly if wrongly, as is clear from David's letter to the *Courrier de Gorsas,* which is fairly explicit on the bad taste that allowed the ancients (in tunics and togas) and the moderns (in the uniform of the National Guard) to coexist in the Simonneau festival.[21] It might be added that David's pupils, wearing Greek-style tunics, had been given the task of bearing the bas-relief of the mayor of Etampes, and that David himself, suspected at the time of "aristocracy," had every interest in exaggerating his disagreement with the organizers of the Simonneau festival.

Yet we should examine a little more closely Schneider's hypothesis that there is a profound contradiction here between a realistic festival and an allegorical one. The Festival of Châteauvieux was realistic, one might say, on account of the presence of the galley prisoners, of the clanking of real chains in the hands of citizenesses dressed in white. But we also know of the efforts made to blunt the shock of this presence and to allegorize it: the galley prisoners were no longer mutineers but "representatives of the emancipation of mankind"; the galley itself was not used but instead a "model," whose impact was weakened by miniaturization, and of which only the oars were life-size, while the warning that the festival ought to have contained amounted to no more than those javelin tips at the prow directed against "despotism bold enough to impede the triumphal march of Liberty." But who detected a threat in that allegory? Conversely, the Simonneau festival, which was supposed to be allegorical, did not eschew the realistic effect of scars on the chest and forehead of the victim's bust. So allegory and realism were not altogether mutually exclusive. Above all, how can one fail to notice that the realism spoken of here concerns only the details: scars on a bust and a toy galley. In fact what was colossal in both festivals and likely to strike the imagination were the enormous allegories.

Furthermore, was there, for the men of this time, an absolute incompatibility between realistic features and the use of allegory? It is true that David criticized Quatremère for displaying ancient and modern costumes side by side, but did he do so in the name of realism? It might equally well have been in the name of the classical doctrine of allegory, which required purity. Yet the gaping wound in Lepelletier's side could appear in David's picture, along with the crowd that immortalizes him, thus denying it and embodying it at one and the same time. This is because the wound was intended to be not so much convincing in its rendering as exemplary in its meaning: it is not a representation but an incitement to deserve the crown, a theme offered to voluntary action rather than to contemplation. It is this aspect of incitement that links the realistic details to the allegorical emblems in the anticipatory function of the heroic motif; it also explains why recourse to ancient forms, in circumstances so new, appeared neither old-fashioned nor unfitting: the antique repertory is a collection of lessons even more than a treasury of forms and images.

In short, the two festivals are very close to one another. We must also reject the last word in political interpretation, that of Dulaure, who, subtle as ever, interprets the difficulty of the two festivals' establishing their individuality as the consequence of a conscious, meticulous decision.[22] If the Festival of the Law accepts the emblems of liberty and the Festival of Liberty the emblems of the law, it is because "one party tacitly made concessions to the other." Yet the wish to accommodate the other party was of much less account than the inability to imagine anything else. The men who planned the two festivals shared the same memories and drew on a stock of ideas and images absolutely common to both parties. In fact, there were not two festivals, one the creation of David and the other of Quatremère: rather, the artists saw every festival as an opportunity for deploying a talent trained in the same school. Whether or not they sat on the right, whether the festival on which they were working was organized by the moderates or by the sans-culottes, they were incapable of imagining anything other than the deployment of neo-classical symbolism in the service of the myth of unanimity.

The Unity of Tragedy

This is clearly shown by the fact that during that year of conflict, certain features emerged that the great festival of Year II, and even those of the Directoire, were not to disown. The most obvious of these was the emancipation from religious influence.[23] These festivals marked a clean break with the Federation and seemed to implement Mirabeau's dictum: no priests, no mass in civic celebrations.[24] The pantheonization of Voltaire was a dress rehearsal for this secularization, and even the Simonneau festival itself was "copied entirely from those of paganism,"[25] greatly to the regret of the man's admirers. At about the same time, the Commune issued decrees hostile to religious processions. Thus began the process by which religious themes were to be occluded, a process begun under cover of a necessary separation of genres: religion was banished to the obscurity of private life, while the civic spirit was publicly exalted. The religion of all was now the civic celebration. There was no going back.

But, this great civic festival had not entirely broken with the religious model, whose processional form it tirelessly copied. The procession not only marked the festival day; it practically was the festival. For the triumph of Voltaire or the festival of Châteauvieux, the traffic holdups were so bad that people arrived at the Panthéon or at the Champ-de-Mars at night. There was hardly any time left to dramatize their arrival, which, in any case, was ill-conceived. The final scene—the removal of the veil that covered the national standard over the altar of the fatherland, the burning of incense, and even the careful arrangement of busts and banners on the altar—mattered far less than the "translation" of the sacred objects. It was this, broken by "stations" to change bearers, that defined the Revolutionary festival.[26] Was this an indication of a failing imagination, reduced to imitation? Not entirely, for it was part of the very logic of a festival that was intended to take place in the open air, involved thousands of participants, and rejected theatrical spectacle to take the form of a procession, a form that embodies the sanctifying act of occupying space and requires the connivance, perhaps even the identification, of actors and spectators.

To the prophets of doom who went to the Jacobins complaining that the decorations planned for Châteauvieux would never be ready in time, Robespierre replied proudly, "We shall not be short of triumphs to atone for the misfortunes of the oppressed." There he touched on another unifying feature: the presence in the Revolutionary festivals, past and to come, of a tragic, somber theme. Seventeen ninety-two was the year of danger for the fatherland, the proclamation of which inspired in Paris a ceremonial of somber effectiveness: two processions, one on the Right Bank, one on the Left, crossed the city, pausing on the way in the squares. There, one found amphitheaters, which Madame de Tourzel saw as "sorry looking scaffolding provided with a small tent,"[27] tables placed on a couple of drum cases, and, around the amphitheater, a circle not of carefree spectators but of volunteers, who in turn surrounded not a Liberty Tree or the altar of the fatherland but a cannon. This was also the year of that battle song of the army of the Rhine, whose refrain so directly expressed its powerful emotion and laid claim to the emotive contagion of the proclamation. It spread throughout the national territory like lightning, having been sung for the first time on April 25 in the mayor of

Strasbourg's private drawing room[28] and on October 17 was baptized the "hymn of the Revolution," henceforth inseparable from that Revolution, spontaneously chosen by a whole people who, in doing so, seemed rather to have created it than to have adopted it. Lastly, 1792 was the year when death held center stage in the Revolutionary festival. Already, a year before, two funeral festivals—those of Mirabeau and Voltaire—had quite eclipsed the second Festival of the Federation. And now, at the Festival of Châteauvieux, the living galley prisoners, mingling with the marchers in the procession, were much less visible than the two sarcophagi symbolizing the dead, while the bust of the victim was the heart of the Simonneau festival. No doubt the organizers were drawing on the antique repertory, retransmitted through the Masonic repertory,[29] expecting to dull the memory of those dead with the embellishing, immortalizing forms of the pyramid—masked mourners, the crown, the cypress, equally suited to a Feuillant death as to a Jacobin death. But, as we have seen, they did not carry allegorization to its limits: the scar and the wound were still there, and they too were premonitory.

For it was in the funeral festivals that the most determined expressionism of the Revolutionary festival was to survive. It was in the mimed obsequies around dummy tombs that the organizers, breaking with the wish, inherited from antique art, to banish the image of death, were to set out to appeal to the imagination of the spectators. For the Lepelletier festival the elegiac Marie-Joseph Chénier himself wanted "the body of our virtuous colleague, exposed to all eyes, to reveal the mortal wound that he received fighting for the people's cause." For the abortive festival of Bara and Viala, David planned an equally expressive spectacle: "You, the incorruptible Marat, show the passage opened up to your soul by the murdering dagger; you, Pelletier, expose that flank, ripped open by a satellite of the last of our tyrants; you, Beauvais, show the wounds that brought you slowly to the gates of the tomb." Even François de Neufchâteau, so measured in his instructions, was to suggest "bloody figures, with dagger wounds, wandering around the public squares." This tragic simulacrum thought up for the commemoration of Rastadt was to arouse indignation and anger. And it was not only in Paris but also throughout the provinces that, on the occasion of funeral festivals, bloodied shirts would be exhibited, the poplars surrounding the altar of the fatherland broken and smeared with red, and "ornaments imitating the natural" would be shown.[30] In short, there was a return to a mood and style that some would have preferred to avoid.

For, according to the original intention of the master of ceremonies, death could not be an occasion for rejoicing. When, on November 9, 1792, the Convention learned of the victory at Jemmapes and thought of celebrating it, many voices were raised (including those of Barère and Lasource)[31] against organizing public celebrations of this occasion: the festival must be universal or nothing at all. And how could one celebrate when men had died? By an ironic reversal, however, it was the funeral festivals that were to mark the various stages of the Revolution—for Mirabeau, Lazowski, Lepelletier, Marat, Féraud, Hoche, Joubert, Bonnier, and Roberjot. Despite the wish to exclude tragedy, it constantly reappeared: in the bloody draperies of Lepelletier's processions; in Roberjot's costume, decorated with a funeral veil, which henceforth occupied the place left vacant at the Council of the Five Hundred; and in the mausoleum, the true monumental symbol of the Revolution, erected in dramatic isolation and around which moved the crowds of the processions, cypress in hand, and marching troops, bayonets reversed, a mourning veil on their standards, while the drums, veiled in black, rolled and the smoke of odoriferous woods and incense burned on the altars. A whole pre-Romantic sensibility is expressed in these "gloomy festivals, worthy of Ancient Rome";[32] they dispensed an emotion irreconcilable with the regular display of utopian joy, and they were freed from the desire to please; they occupied a place midway between fascination and repulsion. This was precisely the definition that Kant gave of the sublime (and in 1790, at that). By making room for "this negative pleasure,"[33] the Revolutionary festival, in the early forms adopted in 1792, was unfaithful to its purpose.

Before proceeding, let me make this fundamental point in my argument quite clear. The year 1792, which saw the creation of two great antagonistic festivals, and their polemical use by the parties, produced not two ideas of the festival but one. This is a criticism of the inadequacy of an interpretation confined to the political rivalries expressed by the festivals. We must come back to this theme. Further consideration of the supposed antagonism between the festivals of Reason and the Supreme Being, and still more of the presumed break created by Thermidor, will provide this opportunity.

· IV ·
Mockery and Revolution
1793–1794

THERE was still no organized expression of the overall purpose that we have attributed to the festivals of the French Revolution. There was no system of festivals, though there were plenty of people calling for one. Vergniaud and Jean Debry proposed a festival to celebrate Jemmapes; the Committee of Public Instruction gave it some thought.[1] Yet the festival did not take place. Everybody was too preoccupied with the trial of the king and the political battles of the spring. It took the elimination of the Girondins for people's minds to turn once more to festivals. In June, Lakanal submitted to the Convention a project of national instruction that included Sieyès's reflections on festivals; and on May 31 the decree for a "general, Republican Federation of the French people" was ordered for the following August 10.

The final project, the work of Lakanal, took the form of a summoning to Paris of National Guards and regular troops.[2] Its only claim to originality is that it substituted for the word *federation* that of *reunion*, which was less compromising at a time when federalism served as a banner for those départements that had risen up against the Convention. There was to be, then, a Festival of Reunion; yet what the organizers had in mind was certainly a new Federation.[3] Like that of 1790, the festival set out to embody an imaginary unanimity;[4] like it, too, it was linked to the feeling, or illusion, that everything was starting afresh. Lakanal chose the eve of August 10 to confide in the Convention his reasons for making that day a fraternal "jubilee," a time of general reconciliation for the whole French nation.

The festival of August 10 was conceived as a representation of birth, a festival of the Constitution, in which the "tables" were read, in which the constitutional act was laid on the altar (sometimes at the same time as newborn children). No doubt, here and there, funeral pyres were erected on which symbols of the ancien régime were burned. Yet is was the water of regeneration that was at the center of the rituals, rather than the fire of destruction. In Paris, on the place de la Bastille, a colossal Egyptian-style statue of Nature was depicted clasping breasts from which water gushed forth, and the commissioners of the primary assemblies each drank a gobletful. In the provinces, in the public squares, the fountains were incorporated into the temporary festive decor, as at Crest, where, beneath the garlands, could be read the inscription "Fountain of Regeneration."[5]

But the gap between the reality and the images of the festival had widened considerably in three years. It had become very difficult to believe in the innocence of this baptism. Much of the old Federation was conspicuous by its absence from the new festival. Where was any reference to the great drama of the summer of 1793? To a nation in danger? To revolts in the provinces? The festival of August 10, 1793, celebrated a triumph. It had nothing to say about dangers, ignored outcasts and victims, was silent on violence. Even that incongruous donkey, behind the antique-style chariot, intended, with the "fool" riding it, to represent stupidity, was no longer to be seen as in the Festival of Châteauvieux. This time the festival had become entirely what Edmund Leach has called a "formality."[6] It rejected, it goes without saying, role reversal; but it also rejected the masquerade, that intermediary form in which the formal rules of life are only temporarily eclipsed. The festival of August 10, 1793, with all its hypocritical seemliness, thoroughly contradicts, therefore, the image, so dear to conservative historians, of the drunken, scandalous festivals thought up by the Revolution. But were the historians dreaming? Was there never, anywhere, a festival that went beyond the official program, that turned ugly, that revealed the deep wounds within the Revolution? We must now approach this question, also bequeathed to us by historiography.

The "Other" Festival

The talented Sébastien Mercier, who provided the model for that "other" festival, makes little distinction between the Revolutionary festival and the Revolutionary *journée*. Of the thirteen descriptions of festivals in *Le nouveau Paris,* seven actually concern *journées*. This merging of the two allows an amalgam of festive and riotous episodes. (Mercier never lost his

Fountain of Regeneration. Pen drawing and watercolor by Tassy. Musée Carnavalet. © DACS 1987.

love of picturesque details—the pie sellers plying their wares around the scaffold, brandy being drunk out of chalices—even when being imprisoned in the Bastille made it difficult for him to work from life.)[7] Nourished by Roger Caillois and Georges Bataille, our modern sensibility is used to this amalgam; it understands that the Revolutionary *journées* are to be treated as festivals; it even expects them to be accorded the privilege of being festivals. Yet we must resist going down that particular path— not only out of historical scruple about keeping strictly to what contemporaries themselves called festivals, but above all because the violence that could exist within the festival is not at all the same as the violence found in a riot. The latter is an uncontrolled explosion, and we know precisely where and when it will end; the former remains in some sense under institutional restraint. The latter is experienced without the slightest sense of distance; the former is always more or less a representation of violence, which never gets entirely out of control.

When we read the official accounts stating with such self-satisfaction that the festival took place in order and decency ("there was no sign of those indecent forms familiar from the ancien régime, madness did not brandish its flaming torch"),[8] so inclined to fall back on the language of police orders and pastoral letters, at least we learn, by contradistinction, how the organizers saw that "other" festival. For them, as it had already been throughout the century for the civic and religious authorities, this was, of course, the ill-planned festival, the secret, nocturnal festival, the noisy festival, the revelry, the mingling of age groups, classes, and sexes, the orgy. Did the festival of the French Revolution really manage to avoid completely that image of revolt?

Of the many festivals celebrated in the Revolutionary decade, we find a number of improvised festivals happening outside the official programs: they occurred when messengers arrived at the political clubs with news— true or false, it did not matter, providing it was good news. The news of the taking of Toulon is a good example: at Creyssac the crowd rushed out into the streets, a joyful avalanche that followed no fixed itinerary but dashed to the Liberty Tree.[9] The report was greeted with an act of pure exuberance, with unorganized din, firecrackers, drums, and snatches of songs that were not automatically taken up and repeated in chorus. Above all, there was a great desire to communicate the excitement to others: representatives were sent off to the neighboring clubs, whose members arrived to the accompaniment of pipe and drum.[10] These primitive festivals, which one hesitates to call such, except in a very syncretic way, were the "réjouissances des sans-culottes."[11]

If one looks hard enough, one also finds nocturnal festivals, in which the torches that accompanied the coffin of monarchy were used to full dramatic effect, in which the bonfire came into its own, in which the dancing lasted until two o'clock in the morning; festivals in which the crowd crossed spatial boundaries, embarked on outings outside the commune itself, and took over a church for their dancing and feasting. In those austere times, there were few accounts of such revelry; the menus that adorned the official accounts of the Federation have disappeared from these festivals, and the "spartan meal" mentioned by the writers is more a harsh reality than a model. But at least everybody drank out of the same bowl, "like true sans-culottes"; and at least everybody really did mix with everybody else, which was very different from the "egalitarian disorder" referred to by the village potentates when they quietly marched the villagers out four by four.[12] This "disorder" meant an absence of hierarchy; it did not have the monstrous self-consciousness of the "mixture" imagined by Barère, standing before the throng with all the stiff approval of a bishop. In that festival the women, whose place in the Revolutionary festival was usually so reluctantly accorded and whose role was so limited, forced through the circle of national guardsmen to snatch the last thread of cloth from the papal or royal effigy. The young men of the commune refused to be dismissed when the official festivities came to an end at nightfall, and there were several border incidents. There was a constant danger of brawls, which sometimes broke out, thus illustrating the classic presentation of a festival as "all too often a source of quarrels, disputes, and assault."

There is, then, another festival. It is quite different from the ideal model propagated by the organizers; it differs from it above all by the place it gives to mockery. Thus the people's club of Pau met to consider a serious question: how could they "present the ridiculous side of the judges, barristers, priests, clerks of the court, and procurators?"[13] Unfortunately, we have no detailed accounts of these discussions (which is all the more disappointing in that some of the speakers, according to the official report of the meeting, had "good ideas"), but the fact that such meetings were held is highly significant in itself. Anyway, if we follow the festival in detail, it soon becomes clear how the people's clubs set about ridiculing their lords and masters. This took the form of exaggerating some distinctive feature or bringing out some physical deformity: the noses of the Feuillants and the ears of aristocrats were made longer; the portliness of the royal effigy was accentuated. Some of the effigies, like those representing Fanaticism and Monarchy, were made several times larger than life, like those that so much surprised Boullainvilliers in the Flemish festivals; others, like that of the pope were represented as costumed dwarfs. At Montignac, the members of the people's club chose a citizen who, "in mature years, was at most three feet six inches tall" to represent Ferdinand of Spain; his arms were bound with a chain; he was preceded by two children carrying marmots and followed by musicians playing Savoyard airs. The group was then perched on a hillock, where it was exposed to the mockery of onlookers.[14] Sometimes the burlesque effect was achieved simply by deforming the costume: the royal cloak was torn to shreds, the procurator was given only half his robes, Marie Antoinette was dressed in rags. Sometimes it was achieved by some degrading allusion: the statues of saints might be surrounded by nettles and dandelions; a woman representing the city of Toulon, the "whore of kings,"[15] might be given the makeup and clothes of a prostitute; or royal papers might be thrown pell-mell onto the dung cart, for mud, manure, and excrement had a part to play in the humiliation. Sometimes, too, there was a resort to the emphatic, mechanical repetition of gestures: the bishop endlessly giving his blessing, the penitents endlessly swinging their censers, like drunken marionettes. Thus the festival depicted an endless procession of scarecrows turned into figures of ridicule.

The sense of burlesque was also achieved—and in this the festivals continued both traditions—by means of animal representation. If the Revolutionary sensibility saw its ideal expression in vegetal exuberance, it regarded the animal figure as a form of malediction or at least grotesque debasement. Would Freud, who suggests that the displacement of the figure of the father toward the animal figure is one of the themes of infantile neurosis, agree that the expression of the royal or papal image by the animal figure may be a theme of collective neurosis? The horse that jibs under its stole, the pig decked out in sumptuous clothes, the monkey with a bishop's miter on its head are, in any case, the pitiful heroes of these atypical festivals. We are certainly very far from the hydra of federalism, an animal with a purely metaphorical existence. These all too real animals are supposed to convey their abasement to the objects they carry (chalices clinking around their necks, crucifixes, Bibles, gospel books tied to their tails) and to the figures (kings, popes, the great powers of the coalition) mounted on them. In several different places, donkeys were harnessed with episcopal ornaments.[16] Feudal insignia were pulled along by goats; pigs secured to pikestaffs were crowned; a calf's heart was paraded around the festival bearing an inscription to the effect that this was an aristocrat's heart. The organizers often depended on antiphrasis to suggest the normal representation and sometimes too, in a caricatural play of appearance and reality, on some plastic allusion: the king's portliness might be suggested by the pig, while his "execrable companion" would be recognized in a nanny goat.[17] In seeking these parodic correspondences, the Revolutionary inventors often resorted to old popular motifs. Some communes exhibited kings and bishops mounted backwards on donkeys, as the cuckolded and defeated were once represented in the village: in the festival at Dormans, the figure of William Pitt, perched on a donkey, his face toward the tail, was exhibited throughout the town.[18]

Those festivals that included such figures were certainly carnivalesque, especially when taken as part of celebrations that legalized not what was illegal but what was already permissible. Objects that in ordinary life were distinct were here joyfully amalgamated, the formal rules of daily life suspended, roles exchanged. We see children handling matches for the auto-da-fé of the unclean remains of aristocracy and, duly encouraged, spit throughout the procession on the cart overflowing with parchment and bearing a sign reading, "Relics of our brothers."[19] We see women flogging saints' statues. Priests' soutanes drop to reveal the dress of the sans-culottes; nuns dance the carmagnole. A cardinal and a whore walk on either side of the coffin of Despotism; the celebrants shamelessly dress up in dalmatics, chasubles, and copes stolen from the church, as in that celebrated procession imagined by the Unity section, which, in Frimaire, Year II, marched before the Convention. The greater the gap between appearance and reality, the more successful was the effect. When a carter wore the most elegant chasuble to be found in the sacristy,[20] or when, as at Sainte-Enimie, the priestly ornaments were covered with dragons,[21] success was assured.

In these atypical festivals, the general repugnance felt by the men of the Revolution for disguise, the mistrust that tended to see any costume, including that of the sans-culottes, as a mask concealing the enemies of the Revolution, seems to have been overcome. Citizens did not hesitate to sport the red or blue ribbons of the aristocrats, the livery of the police lieutenant fleeing before the Rights of Man, and even to perform some abhorred role: the people's club at Auch set out to find a citizeness capable of taking on the role of Charlotte Corday.[22] Disgust for mimicry also declined: sometimes fictitious masses were said at the high altar, concluding with a noisy *Ite missa est,* or the Office of the Dead was sung around a condemned Fanaticism; the trial of the king, and even his execution, were reenacted in public, at the very place where a real guillotine was set up.

In these festivals, under cover of masks, one could abandon over-restrained language, in which memories of the schoolroom so inevitably served to avoid the tragic charge of the Revolution, for brutal parody: one no longer spoke of "the last king of the French" but of "Louis the Shortened" or "Louis the Guillotined." He was exhorted in one song to "get down off the throne, Capet, France orders you to." The "pope," who, at Bourg served in a mock abdication, ended up in the flames, bearing the inscription, "I'm done for, no more prejudices."[23] The pitiful effigy, here as in the carnivallike festivals, was at the center of the celebrations—so much so, indeed, that the festival sometimes abandoned its solemn designation ("festival in memory of the martyrs of liberty," for instance) for the sharper, more expressive "burning of the effigies."[24]

All this parodic dramatization was accompanied by scenes of menace, as if recourse to theatricality could not but be provocative, as if all that had been burlesqued, banished, stoned, drowned, burned, like some sacrificial victim, could call forth others to replace them. The public decapitation of effigies was quite explicit when those effigies proclaimed their identity—aristocrat, federalist, fanatic—in large letters across their chests.[25] In a mock execution at Conches, the onlookers sang to the melody of the Visitant order of nuns words that were clearly intended for other kings: "A vous qui ignorez la fête / De Capet mort sur l'échafaud / Rois craignez qu'un jour votre tête / Ne fasse aussi le même saut" (To you who do not know of the festival of Capet / who died on the scaffold / you kings, take care lest one day / your head drops off like his).[26] Here the festival is addressed to the excluded party, not like so many respectable festivals that hypocritically deplored the fact that they had to keep him away (those festivals for husbands, for instance, which were soon to declare that they could not admit the "cold bachelor"), but in order to summon him, to promise him the punishment that would be his, and to administer it to him in symbolic fashion. Thus, too, religious bigots were dragged to the festival, where religious ornaments were burned, and they were mockingly but firmly invited to worship liberty. Sometimes even blood was shed, as in that somewhat expressionistic festival at Mauze, to which an effigy representing the English minister Pitt was brought, "and so that the representation should be all the more natural, a bladder filled with blood was placed in the neck so that when the blade cut off the head all the spectators were sprayed with it."[27]

At Tulle, there was a festival that displayed all these features. It took the form of a farandole organized by the people's club. In fact, it was a burlesque procession, glittering with ornaments removed from the cathedral. The centerpiece was a mock burial: on the coffin, which was supposed to contain the remains of Superstition, there was a square cap, a pair of ass's ears, and a missal. There was mimed violence, too, in the form of a flogging of saints' statues. The whole of this farandole was really an act of intimidation: the people's club had thought it up on the occasion of an exchange of political prisoners with the Jacobins of Limoges. It was a festival of welcome in reverse, a threatening, dishonoring reception, during which the "real" guillotine was displayed.

With the festivals of this type, we see a movement toward a different model. They were the only ones in which the Revolution was not represented as a group of maidens dressed in white or a group of virtuous mothers. At Montaigut-en-Combraille the people's club planned a procession in which citizens and citizenesses, armed with pitchforks and sticks, would represent "the Revolution taking the tyrants to the scaffold."[28] There is an attempt at identification here, which, nevertheless, should not lead us to conclude that the festival was being identified with riot, since the representation introduced an element of distance. But certainly there was a possibility that one could spill over into the other. For, from the "guillotine in effigy" (often set up, moreover, in the same place) to the real one was but a step.

Where, When, with Whom?

We must now consider these festivals in terms of where and when they took place, and for whom and by whom they were organized. The geographical distribution of these festivals of mockery is not easy to determine. What is certain, however, is that the festivals using burlesque effigies were more frequent in those places where a carnival tradition already existed—in the southwest for example. What also seems to confirm this is the recrudescence of scenes of dramatized mockery when the festival coincided with the carnival period: this happened when the Festival of the King's Death had to be postponed, either on account of bad weather or because the instructions were slow in arriving from Paris, and happened to coincide with the carnival. It would seem that in certain regions and at certain times, cultural archaism was stronger than Revolutionary innovation.

Who organized these festivals? It may be said that the farther removed a festival was from the authorities in Paris, the more likely it was to find room for improvisation. The festivals of the Paris sections were very con-

ventional, those of the provincial sections somewhat less so. Yet it was the
people's clubs that were largely responsible for the freest, most disturbing
festivals. This was because when they presented their programs, they were
unaware of what was being done in Paris (while the municipal authorities
copied the Paris model very faithfully). It was also because the extreme
formalization of their activities, the rituals of their meetings, the repetition of certain songs and poems, the presentation of placards and ornaments, the regulation of precedence, and certain set turns of phrase made
them very aware of ceremonial problems. Lastly, one must take into account the degree to which the presence of the Revolutionary army gave
them an incitement to action. The festivals in which effigies of the pope
were burned and kings threatened were also those that welcomed soldiers:
as Richard Cobb saw very clearly, such an encounter stressed the political
alliance between the army and the clubs and gave those festivals their
aggressive tone.[29]

When, then, did they take place? This question is all the more important in that it involves another of our concerns. Indeed, if we must assign
those festivals with violent episodes to precise dates in the history of the
Revolution, we are bound to ask why they belong to that brief history
and are inevitably brought back to this political periodization of the festivals, whose relevance has not so far seemed entirely convincing. Yet we
are tempted, when considering the Revolutionary festivals as a whole, to
give a very precise answer to this question. When did the parodic, violent
festivals take place? Between Vendémiaire and Ventôse in Year II. Not
that outside these two dates one cannot find festivals in which parody and
burlesque played their ambiguous roles, but they are relatively rare. In
the six months of the autumn and winter of Year II, however, there are
a great many examples. Before Vendémiaire, the utopian model of the
David-type festival of August 10 was followed almost universally. By Germinal, the element of parody had gone. The great wind of mockery in the
Revolutionary festival blew for only six months.

But in the meantime, ordered, well-regulated festivals, without any
trace of compensatory inversion, continued to be celebrated. In most of
the communes, and contrary to the tradition established by L. S. Mercier,
neither the Festival of the Retaking of Toulon nor the Festival of Reason
necessarily included parodic simulacra or transgressive dramatizations.
Nevertheless, this did sometimes happen. In fact, the carnivallike scenes
might or might not, depending on local circumstances, be included in
the three great festivals of those six months: Reason (Brumaire), Toulon

(Nivôse), and the Death of the King (Pluviôse). They were even more common on those "festivals inaugurating the busts," which occurred throughout the autumn and winter as the busts ordered from Paris arrived, probably because here the program, unlike that of the other three festivals, was not laid down from above and therefore permitted transgression more easily.

Lastly, it should be remembered that the other elements of the festival had not disappeared: it would be quite false to imagine purely carnivallike festivals existing side by side with the festivals that I have described. We must imagine festivals that included elements of mockery along with other elements. One striking example occurred at Morteau.[30] This festival, marking the burial of the monarchy, was remarkable for the presence in the procession of very different types of spectacle: simulacra without any parodic implications (Voltaire and Rousseau), simulacra with parodic implications (the royal effigy, the queen between two learned doctors of the Sorbonne, "Cardinal Collier and the Dame Valois-Lamothe," a "large group of aristocrats with long ears"). But also, in the middle of all that, were representations of Time, Destiny, and Mercury. In the processions, the virtuous mothers followed the mitered donkeys. And "Mirth and the Graces" accompanied the dung cart into which the effigy of Capet slowly sank.

Why at this time? Was it the danger to the nation that accentuated the obsession with oaths and set alight that lust for vengeance on the traitors for which the scenes of mockery might have been either a dress rehearsal or an exorcism? If so, it is difficult to see why the summer months, which were even more anxious, did not give rise to festivals of this type. Must we, then, resort to another hypothesis suggested by the coincidence between the date when the contemporary accounts begin to describe parodic scenes and the beginning of the great campaign of de-Christianization? Did not the people's clubs become accustomed to transgression during those months of struggle against "superstition?" Burning pastoral letters, drinking the health of the Republic in the bishop's chalice, sticking red caps on statues of the evangelists or setting to work on them with hammer and saw, or pulverizing "so-called relics"—such acts were accompanied, even among the village thugs, by an obscure sense of defying the heavens, which emerges in the comments of innumerable eyewitnesses. The people's clubs, then, echoed with expressions of self-satisfaction: nothing had happened! The heads of the profaners had not been struck by lightning! God had not performed a miracle in defense of the statues pulled off their pediments! In this noisy self-satisfaction one senses the ambiguity of blasphemy that conceals within it, like a distant call, the fear behind all the bravado, a very acute sense of scandalous transgression. In such an atmosphere, is it surprising that some of these scenes got into the festival and sometimes were even at its center? Furthermore, scenes of de-Christianization often turned into festivals: the parish priest of Caussens, for example, attended a procession that culminated in the burning of the crucifix and holy images.[31] And when Monestier, on 3 Germinal, Year II, listed the various operations used in de-Christianization, he suggested that "all such ceremonies should be embellished with carmagnoles, in which the good citizens of both sexes and every age gave themselves up to a desire to dance."[32]

A certain practice had caught on, therefore, in those autumn and winter months of Year II. Need one go any further than to point out this quasi-mechanical kinship between the gestures of de-Christianization and those of the festival? Daniel Guérin thinks not. According to him, the people rushed into the breach opened up by the instigators of the anti-religious diversion. They did not take the initiative themselves, but when the possibility was offered them, they embraced it enthusiastically and found in it an opportunity of giving free vent to their imagination. Once the campaign of de-Christianization had begun, "the sans-culottes had the sense that a great burden had been removed from their shoulders. There was an explosion of joy, a cry of deliverance. That 'torrent' referred to by Robespierre, Danton, and Dartigoeyte gave the dances on the over-turned tabernacles and other 'unprecedented' scenes an absolutely unique flavor."

It is an ingenious interpretation. Guérin is well aware of the difference between the festivals of parodic inversion and the "Revolutionary celebrations laboriously mounted and regulated by David." But his wish to contrast the festivals of the bourgeoisie (stiff, correct, colorless) with the "festivals of the people" (imaginative and joyfully scandalous) leads him to overstate his case. Is he not looking at the *bras-nus* through rose-tinted spectacles? Certainly, in the people's clubs of the Year II one no longer found only those "patriotic bourgeois" among whom the clubs of the Friends of the Constitution were mainly recruited and which had excluded, either de jure (by their statutes) or de facto (by excessively high membership fees), workers, artisans, and peasants of modest or poor means. These groups now joined the people's clubs in overwhelming numbers. It should be said, however, that the poor peasant class was still underrepresented, and that even when it was in the majority, the leaders were always bourgeois or petty bourgeois—close to the people, perhaps, but already a cut above them—and it was they who organized the festivals, composed the programs and instructions, wrote couplets, made the speeches.

So it is difficult to speak of "festivals of the *bras-nus,*" especially when the carnivallike scenarios may also be, in a way, simply the expression in individual form of the vocabulary of the Revolutionary bourgeoisie. It was this group that poured their sarcasm on the priests' "baubles," their "mummeries," their "tricks," their "dressing up": a repertoire of religious theatricality was called upon to establish the practice of the Revolutionary festival. This view was sometimes stated with a great deal of ingenuity. The account of the Festival of Reason at Pau is almost apologetic about allowing into the procession donkeys covered with red robes, black robes, soutanes, and cassocks, and "imitating by their slow walk the grave manner of the former presiding judges." [33] This festival had to show "attributes and caricatures that represent in the eyes of the people the triumph of liberty over slavery." Here mockery takes the form of an applied illustration. In fact, when the orators speak of "breaking the bishop's crook and miter across the rocks of the Sainte-Montagne," [34] this is not the language of the *bras-nus* but the rhetoric of middle-class schoolboys, which may remain merely verbal or, in favorable circumstances, become the program for a spectacle, in which case there is no reason to believe that uneducated men, with memories of popular rejoicings, would not have taken part in the action. But the main point is that both kinds of men participated.

Lastly, one hesitates, when reading these accounts, to conclude that the imagination really had seized power in Year II, especially as Guérin bases his interpretation on only a few well-known texts, usually describing such Parisian scenes as the processions before the Convention, whose parodic charge is obvious enough, but which were not, strictly speaking, festivals. Nor does he see the contamination that existed between the two types of festival, the "popular" and the "bourgeois," the amalgam that they formed of ceremonial elements, the difficulty of deciding which were or were not popular: after all, the throwing away of official papers—pastoral letters but also charters and title deeds—and the dance around the flames that consumed them were not confined to the "popular" festivals alone. These "patriotic hearths" were not necessarily blasphemous; on the contrary, throughout the ten Revolutionary years, like the compulsory politeness of the festivals, they constitute the very mark of a lack of inventiveness.

Moreover, this is confirmed by the fact that the presence of the carnivalesque element seems quite independent not, perhaps, of the educational level of the organizers but of the political intentions that dominated their creations. For the burlesque simulacra could appear in very different political contexts. In the festivals of the royalist-federalist sections, effigies were also burned, this time on piles of paper emanating from the people's club rather than on piles of royal charters; still, we are a long way here from "Hébertism," even in the somewhat vague sense given the term by Guérin. The threatening parody, once the somber savagery of the winter of Year III had passed, reappeared in places where one might not have expected it. At Vic-le-Comte, in Year III, as in so many other communes, the Jacobins were chased through the streets. This chase was given the name of "festival": "Every evening there is a joyful festival; we tie up a Jacobin and parade him through the streets to the accompaniment of fife and drum; we sing and dance; we stop for a moment in front of the Jacobins' house and frighten them; it's their turn to be strung up."

After Thermidor, the burlesque effigies returned: in Pluviôse, Year III, troops of young men (during this period the very official Festival of the King's Death took place), who had set out to burn an effigy "in the shape of a Jacobin," gathered up the ashes—in a degrading, carnivalesque ritual—in a chamberpot and threw the lot into the drain at Montmartre. The newspapers speak of "a pitiful effigy," proof that it was burlesqued.[35] At Beaumont-de-Périgord, on 26 Thermidor, Year V, a public holiday— a somewhat ambiguous festival, it is true, since, although it was the day of the votive festival, there were also plans to plant a Liberty Tree—the young people made, flogged, and burned a "straw man, to which they gave the infamous name of Robespierre."[36] At Blois, at the festival of August 10 in the Year VI, there was a mock execution: "We gave ourselves the pleasure of burning Robespierre in the form of a distorted effigy and this caricature was found highly amusing."[37] This is also a scene very close to the Jacobin—and, for that matter, reactionary—parodies referred to by Gastin on 29 Floréal, Year VII, at the Council of the Five Hundred: "I have seen in a commune all too famous for the many murders that have been committed in the course of the various reactions, the national cockade tied to the tail of the vilest animals, which a huge crowd led through the streets addressing it as citizen."

What does this resurgence show? On the one hand—once more, and this was not the last time—it shows that the burlesque simulacrum, despite the fact that it seems to belong to the brief history of the Revolution, does not express a particular political view. Violence and mockery are neither "Hébertist" nor "extremist." They are not even, since both revolutionaries and counterrevolutionaries may use them just as easily, bound up with the cause of the Revolution. On the other hand, it shows that the parodic episodes have less to do with innovations introduced by the masses in revolt than with the ritual forms of the carnival: in fact, they are a way of saying farewell to the old world and of declaring, in a provocative or threatening manner, the law of the new world. The "victim," whether burned or drowned, whether it resembled Robespierre or Capet, the two leading roles in the Revolutionary drama, represented the past. But there was no longer any question, as in the official festivals, of representing the character in question with any respect for verisimilitude or for pedagogical ends. It was rather an act of deliverance, embroidered in an anticipatory ritual. The young men—for it was usually the young who were behind the scenes, linking the Revolutionary festival with its traditional role—were concerned not so much with acting out the symbolic installation of youth in a utopian society as with rushing violently ahead in the direction of the future. The sense of the simulacrum is not backward looking here but forward looking.

Reasonable Reason

We should pause here and briefly examine the Festival of Reason, which, for historians, has epitomized all the seditious features to be found in the various Revolutionary festivals. I do not wish to consider it at the moment from the point of view of violence and mockery, which certainly show their grimacing faces in the festivals of Reason, as they did in the festivals of the autumn and winter of Year II, but no more and no less. There were very few festivals in which, as Reason was being installed on the altar, the crucifix that had been there was thrown to the ground.[38] We are bound to ask ourselves, therefore, why such a negative view has developed whereby the Festival of Reason has been regarded, even by advocates of Revolutionary celebrations, as the "least laudable" of them.[39]

To begin with, its very name is redolent of militant atheism. Yet we know how very ambiguous the birth of the Festival of Reason was. On 20 Brumaire, Year II, there were proposals for a civic festival of Liberty to be held at the Palais-Royal. A civic festival? Rather an open-air concert at which the musicians of the National Guard were to play. The proposed festival was unequivocally dedicated to Liberty, since there were plans to perform there, for the first time, *L'hymne à la liberté,* words by Chénier, music by Gossec. If the idea was abandoned only three days before the *décadi,* it was because the previous ten days had been marked by the procession of those renouncing the Convention. In the atmosphere of emulation that followed, the département and Commune decreed, on the very day that Gobel recanted,[40] that the festival would be transferred from the Palais-Royal to Notre-Dame, but, it should be noted, without any changes being made in the arrangements for the patriotic festival. As before, the musicians of the National Guard, combined with those of the Opéra, were to perform hymns to Liberty, before the image of "that deity of the French." Why the musicians of the Opéra? Because they were used to giving a patriotic entertainment, conceived by Gardel at the time when the national enthusiasm of 1792 brought thousands of soldiers to the frontiers. By cutting out the call to arms, the cannon, the movements of armed men, it was an easy matter to adapt this little spectacle—whose name, "an offering to Liberty," is significant. And no doubt the anthems sung could equally well be adapted "to celebrating the triumph that Reason has gained in this season over the prejudices of eighteen centuries." Nevertheless, the deity of the French, here as in so many festivals, was still Liberty, not Reason.

The arrangements for the festival do nothing to remove the equivocal aspect of the project. Chénier's anthem opened the presentation with this invocation: "Descend, O Liberty, Daughter of Nature." At the summit of the mountain, at the entrance to the small round temple dedicated to Philosophy, "the faithful image of Beauty that appears" was certainly meant to represent Liberty.[41] There was no goddess of Reason, but halfway down, on the Greek altar, her flame was burning.

If we leave Paris and turn to the provinces, we find the same uncertainties in the scenic arrangements. Sometimes, as in Paris, the female figure at the center of the festival is certainly Liberty: at Saint-Sever she is identified by her "imposing attitude,"[42] and at Meyssac she is depicted pouring wine into a vessel, a flaming cap on her head.[43] Sometimes, however, she is Reason, as at Besançon, where the procession led a female Reason to the cathedral,[44] or, as at Thiron, where a curly-haired Reason, clutching a huge bouquet of myrtle, was carried in procession.[45] But even more often her attributes are left vague:[46] like Equality she carries a level, like Liberty a cap and a pike, or, like Death, a guillotine. It is far from being the case that she is always given the flame—according to the *annales patriotiques et littéraires* the only correct attribute for Reason—and a book. At Confolens she is represented as a shepherdess, carrying a crook decked out with tricolor ribbons, in the midst of a "swarm" of companions. At Corbeil she is a beautiful, virtuous woman, decorated with warlike attributes, surrounded by wounded men,[47] and, although the song dedicated to her may theoretically be addressed to Reason, she is actually Victory.[48] Elsewhere, crowned with oak, vine leaves, and ears of corn, she could be Nature. Or again, as at Saint-Gatien-de-Tours, she is a winged figure, certainly more like Fame than Reason.[49]

The "deity," in all simplicity, the president of the regenerated people's club of Port-Brieuc pronounced her, and he was right. The main point was that this was a tutelary female figure.[50] What facilitated this syncretism was, in the case of the statue, the possible reuse of another image. Thus the people's club of Rodez suggested keeping the colossal Virgin that crowned the bell tower (the four evangelists surrounding her could, no doubt, be turned into Pelletier, Marat, Chénier and . . . Bayle!), and turning her into "the only deity that will soon be recognized on earth." Reason? No, Liberty again. So we should not see all these female figures as emblems of a de-Christianizing policy. Sometimes the figure was chosen simply to suggest the beauty of the canton. At Montévrain, elected by the "brilliant troop of girls in white," the beauty was represented by nothing more than a local beauty queen. The municipal records state that a girl came up "in the name of her corps" to offer homage to the goddess.

We do not, then, get any sense of a highly individualized festival. According to the official accounts, it actually went by different names: at one place it might be the Festival of Morals, at another the Festival of Virtue. It is also clear why it is difficult to distinguish it from the Festival of the Supreme Being, to which, logically, it is opposed. I don't need to repeat here what was demonstrated so well by both Aulard and Mathiez: the two cults were not clearly differentiated in the minds of the organizers, using as they did the same decorations, the same speeches, the same invocations, and the same actors. In the Festival of Reason there were sometimes invocations to the Supreme Being,[51] and the Supreme Being might be worshipped in the Festival of Reason without anyone thinking it necessary to erase the inscription. An orator at Chartres declared, "Yes, citizens, there are religious ideas of which any wise, true man bears the belief and conviction in his soul; those ideas are true." That was on 9 Frimaire, Year II, and he had certainly listened to and remembered Robespierre's speech of 1 Frimaire. The same language was used for the inauguration of a temple of Reason. In short, it was the France of 1905, not that of 1794, that saw the cult of Reason as the triumph of freethinking.

What, then, is left to account for the exceptionally scandalous place the Festival of Reason holds among the festivals of the French Revolution? A recent brilliant interpretation attributes this reputation to the profoundly theatrical character of the festival, which was remarkable in a ceremonial ensemble that rejected theatrical representation. Judith Schlanger provides a great many arguments in support of her reading.[52] The festival, like a play, might be given several performances: it might be performed at Notre-Dame in the morning and repeated in the afternoon in other settings—the Convention, for instance. Like a theatrical production, it called on professional help, and, again as in the theater, it could close down. Schlanger might also have noted the theatrical origin of the spectacle, which was copied from an opera libretto. These arguments must be examined one by one. The theatrical character of the spectacle is obvious enough, and more so in certain of the provincial festivals, which called upon complex theatrical machinery, than in Paris, where the procession of girls before the flame of Reason was an uninspired invention. At Chartres, where a spectacle entitled "Reason Victorious over Fanaticism" was performed in the church, a woman wearing a tricolor helmet and carrying a spear in her hand—a Republic—set fire to "the pomp of Fanaticism," then rose, borne aloft by a machine representing a thick cloud, to a statue of Reason. As the cloud rose upward, the spectators discovered a "new world," composed of "a huge group of young citizenesses dressed in white and young citizens dressed as National Guards." It is quite obvious that this ambitious spectacle required the collaboration of an architect and local artists.

However elaborate the theatrical spectacle may have been, was it so very far removed from other Revolutionary festivals? Perhaps the haste with which it was organized made it more necessary than usual to resort to professional help. But the dramatic device chosen, as in all the Revolutionary festivals, was that of appearance and disappearance.[53] Everywhere the cardboard throne concealed the altar of the fatherland, which was then revealed by fire; or a huge tent, whose folds bore the attributes of monarchy, went up in flames after the explosion of a flare; all the decorations collapsed, and "in the middle of a perfectly lit drawing room, one saw an altar of the fatherland on which was placed the statue of Liberty." Such transformation scenes were tirelessly repeated from one festival to another, and the main theme, far more than that of purification or destruction, was that of the confrontation between darkness and light. What was banished here by an idealized flame become light was darkness, everything that "intercepts the beams of liberty," everything embodied, in turn, by the "lair" on which the throne seemed to be built, the veils in which the statue of Liberty was swaddled, the caverns hollowed out in the flanks of artificial mountains, in which the enemies of Liberty were supposed to hide. All these accessories were present in the Festival of Reason, of course, but not only in that festival: they belonged to the common repertory of all the Revolutionary festivals.

There are still two features that gave the Festival of Reason an additional theatricality. First, as in the theater, there was the presence of living actors, in this case women. Was it not, perhaps, in some obscure way, this triumph of the feminine that was found so shocking in the Festival of Reason? From the beginning of the Revolution women had aspired to take part in the festivals, as their partial successes in the Federation show. But there were also more ambitious projects, such as the harangue, wrongly, but significantly, attributed to Olympe de Gouges, which revealed a desire to create new "priestesses," worthy *at least* of directing festivals and weddings." This aspiration, which was so often rejected, sometimes found adequate expression. (At Pau, for example, where the women wanted to take part in the "festival of the graces and of patriotism," the administrators rejected their request; but, despite their supposed frivolity, the women stood at the town hall, ready to march, "for fear of some event," with the watch, made up of twelve invalids armed to the teeth.) Was this the case with that living Reason, chosen from among the local beauties in a competition that was often judged by women? The appearance of women in the forefront of the Revolutionary ceremonies caused such surprise, but sometimes, too, such enthusiasm, that one could still find after 9 Thermidor "reactionaries" who regretted the festivals of the Terror on account of "the goddess's cool charms." And David's enthusiasm was undimmed when he remembered those days from his exile in Brussels: "Reason and Liberty were enthroned on antique chariots; superb women, Monsieur; the Greek line in all its purity, beautiful young girls in chlamys throwing flowers; and then, throughout, anthems by Lebrun, Méhul, Rouget de Lisle."

It is nevertheless by no means certain that this spectacle, even if greeted with admiration by the aesthetes, was always well received by the public at large—not only by those who pretended to see in those goddesses of Reason whores rather than innocent maidens, but also by those who found female representations inappropriate in such circumstances. One reader of the *Annales patriotiques et littéraires* was astonished to learn that Reason was a woman and felt sure that the author of the article must have made a mistake. The figure, he said, must not have been Reason but Liberty: "For the senses and the philosophical imagination are both equally shocked at the idea of a woman—especially a youthful woman—representing Reason. In women, this pure faculty is identified so to speak with weakness, prejudice, with the very attractions of that enchanting sex; with men, its empire is removed from all error: strength, energy, severity come in its wake. But above all Reason is mature, serious, austere, qualities that would ill suit a young woman." It is therefore quite likely that the unbearable oddness of the Festival of Reason was partly due to the role played in it by women: by introducing an element of illusion, not to say of subversion, their presence in the festivals seemed to harbor a danger.[54]

The second feature is that the festival of Reason was held indoors, which seemed to break with the Revolutionary dogma of the open-air festival. Yet it should be pointed out that this was not quite as original as was often claimed. In the provincial festivals there had often been a long, open-air procession, probably ending in the church, since its purpose was the inauguration of a temple of Reason. This circumstance, and also the season, probably imposed an ecclesiastical setting. But this was often at the cost of a radical transformation. The darkness had been expelled from the church, by means of such lighting as Brongniart prided himself on at Bordeaux.[55] The mystery had been fought by closing off the chapels with a curtain of elms entwined with ivy; intimacy had been denied by turning the church, as at Cognac, into a "meadow," by means of a "paving" of grass, which covered it to the door, by erecting inside "mountains" with waterfalls, where mothers could come and sit on the moss and give suck to their children, while young sans-culottes made a fire. In this pastoral setting, could one still have a sense of profanation? The citizens could come and picnic there, "eat in common like brothers," and dance there without there being the slightest sense of transgression. Such a sense, as in other things, was thought of a posteriori.

Violence and the Festival

We must now return to the general problem of violence in the Revolutionary festival. We find, of course, that the festivals did not usually dare to represent violence: it was not often a theater of cruelty. From a statistical point of view, then, Freud's interpretation is certainly not borne out;

Durkheim's view, however, finds greater validation. The festivals were dedramatized: they set out to be transparent and often succeeded in being so, though at the cost of a certain utopian platitudinousness: they were parentheses in an existence that, in other respects, the Revolution dramatized in an extreme form.

Sometimes, no doubt, there was a meeting of Revolutionary violence and the festival, as in the first anniversary of the king's death, when, at the instigation of the Jacobin Club, the Convention set out from the place de la Révolution for an impromptu commemoration, and arrived there precisely at the same moment as a cartload of four prisoners due for execution, a sinister addition to the proceedings that had not been envisaged in the program. Certain secret agents of the minister of the interior declared that during the execution—they referred to it, in fact, as a "ceremony"—the people danced, sang, and were very pleased with everything: "If the guillotine had not been working, the festival would not have been so good." But if the women to whom these sentiments were attributed seemed to rejoice at the entry of violence into the ritual of the festival, the Convention felt that its authority had been undermined. Its members believed that behind this apparent coincidence lay a wish to demean the representatives of the nation. Had not the tragic cart, whose progress was usually so slow, appeared at the gallop in order to arrive at exactly the same moment as the Convention? In the session held on the following day, Bourdon de l'Oise took up the insinuation and asked that the Convention no longer attend festivals that it had not itself planned and policed. The proposition was adopted without much opposition. The organizers of the festivals were themselves quite convinced that there was an essential incompatibility between the festival and violence, an impossibility for the festival not only to mimic violence but even to coexist with it.

So we still have to find an interpretation for those festivals in which violence did erupt, since, in the course of the Revolution, there were certain festivals—very much in the minority, of course—in which violence was an integral part of the spectacle. It is clear what a Freudian interpretation, as in René Girard's recent thesis,[56] might make of them: the festival uses violent parody only to deliver the celebrants from it; the function of this well-regulated transgression is to prevent it from spilling over into social violence; the festival plays at violence in order to contain it all the better. The enactment of mimed violence—and therefore violence that can be terminated—is a way of bringing to an end violence that is acted out and therefore not terminable.

According to this hypothesis, moreover, the two types of festivals associated with the French Revolution would seem, in some obscure way, to have had the same function—that is, of negating violence either by denying it in a world in which it must not even be named or by using it, as in vaccination or exorcism. The earliest festivals rejected the theater, sometimes going so far as to prohibit any form of representation; the later festivals accepted a primitive form of theater using carnivalesque techniques. We have, then, two types of festival, very different in form and efficaciousness, but both ultimately having the same purpose.

Yet it is difficult to accept that this interpretation accounts fully for the parodic festivals of the French Revolution. This key may be valid for well-tried rituals but is ill suited to the still-hesitant ceremonies of a period still searching for its ritual. Indeed, what strikes us here is the fact that the parodic simulacrum was used as a threatening provocation, as a call to violence. "Our correspondent at Chartres writes," reported the *Annales patriotiques et littéraires,* "that while awaiting the original they guillotined the bust of the traitor Pétion."[57] The violent simulacrum heralded and triggered off events that were also violent. At Quimper, on the occasion of an ordinary *fête décadaire,* the holiday at the end of a decade of days, the inhabitants indulged in a mock assault on the prison with a view to frightening the inmates.[58] Sometimes even the simulated violence was associated with real violence. On the place de la Fraternité at Eymoutiers, a mock execution was linked with a real one: "We saw Lady Guillotine ready to expedite a fanatical priest."[59] Recourse to simulation here was in no sense intended to obviate recourse to violence; on the contrary, it heralded a Revolutionary violence that could erupt at any time.

Indeed, is that not how it was seen? In this instance, one wonders whether the simulacrum reproduced reality and, if so, to what degree. Yet, it seems, the more caricatured the simulacrum, the more emancipated from any concern with verisimilitude, the clearer it was. What was essential to it—the threat and, beyond that, the affirmation that the Revolution had still not completed its work—was clear for all to see. During the king's trial the Convention was turned into a theater, with the comings and goings of petitioners, waving torn bits of clothing, blood-stained scraps of shirt or sheet. According to Barère's memory of this masquerade, social fear and aesthetic repugnance were inseparable: "The Assembly seemed terror stricken and indignant, so revolting such scenes, which were more suited to an English theater, seemed to them."[60] But the members of the Assembly did not need to have the implications of such scenes for the fate of Capet explained to them.

The appearance of parodic scenes in the festival cannot, therefore, be linked to some specific mode of expression of the Revolutionary masses. Nor were they associated with a particular political event. They were rather the result of the fact that the Revolution was seen as not having finished its task. Whenever the Revolution seemed to be stalling or to have run out of steam—and this applies as much to Year III as to Year II—the same scenes reappeared.[61] The mock violence was accompanied by an invitation to go further. It was a display of unused energy, a dress rehearsal. By the same token, we can see why the organizers of the official festival were so determined to exclude mock violence, or at least to limit its extent: indeed, one never knew where it might lead. In any case, it goes without saying that it frightened those who were trying, through the festival, "to create harmony in the moral and political world,"[62] that is to say, to bring the Revolution to an end.

· V ·

Return to the Enlightenment
1794–1799

FROM Germinal, Year II, onwards one might be forgiven for thinking that it was all over. The parodic vein had worked itself out:
there were no more masks, no more travesties, no more grimacing
simulacra. At the same time, the people's clubs had lost direction; their
membership was scattered, their meetings less frequent, their numbers
reduced to a handful of ringleaders, and everywhere the initiative had
been lost to the all-powerful model disseminated from Paris.

This very period saw the triumph at last of the attempt, which had
constantly been thwarted from the earliest days of the Revolution, to
produce a coherent system of festivals. From the provinces came demands,
all the more vociferous since the introduction of the Republican calendar,
to put some kind of order into local practices, to work out some acceptable arrangement between the *décadi* (every tenth day in the calendar) and
Sunday, and, in general, to fill up with new ceremonies the gaps left by
the abandonment of the old. By the end of Frimaire, the Convention had
asked the Committee of Public Instruction to present an overall plan for
establishing civic festivals, games, and national exercises. In Nivôse, Mathiez, who had been given responsibility for the report, was heard by the
Committee. The discussion of the plans continued intermittently until
11 Germinal, at which date the Committee of Public Safety took over the
matter.[1] This was the origin of Robespierre's report on Revolutionary
principles,[2] which, in Floréal, ordered, as Mathiez had done in Nivôse,
the distribution throughout the entire year of regenerated festivals, but
this time supported the plan with a long preamble. It was hastily adopted
by a Convention now completely under the orator's thrall. The new system of festivals, now officially established, opened with the Festival of the

Supreme Being, which was so closely associated with Robespierre's personality that it was said to be entirely his own work, for it seems that he conceived it, arranged every detail of its implementation, and played the star role in it.

So we cannot avoid the issue of what precisely the Festival of the Supreme Being represented in the mind of its creator. This is an old question that recurs whenever Robespierre is discussed. Was the Festival of the Supreme Being an ingenious brainwave, an ill-intentioned trick meant to establish the fortune of the possessors (as suggested by Daniel Guérin), or a well-meaning plot to reconcile patriotic Catholicism with the Revolution (as suggested by Mathiez)? Or was it, on the contrary, the culmination of a religious project, the effusion of a naturally religious soul (as suggested by Aulard)? In short, by establishing this festival, did Robespierre show himself to be a clever politician or a truly devout man? A strategist or a pontiff?

None of these interpretations is short of supporting evidence. If one chooses to opt for Robespierre the politician, one may obviously argue, as Mathiez does, that the Revolution, which had just recovered from defeating the double opposition of the Hébertists and the Dantonists, was now eager above all to avoid new divisions and saw the ability of the festival to promote social integration. One may also, like Dommanget, see the Festival of the Supreme Being as Robespierre's greatest—and almost only—political project, planned and implemented by a consistent series of actions.[3] On November 21, 1791, it is true, Robespierre assured the Jacobins that it would be better not to risk a head-on collision with "the religious prejudices so adored of the people." In March 1792, in opposition to Guadet, he repeated that one should be careful not to confuse the cult of the deity with that of the priesthood. From this position one passes, without the slightest contradiction, to the blows delivered in Frimaire, Year II, to the policy of de-Christianization, to the theory of Floréal, and to the practice of Prairial.

If we are determined to reveal the extent to which Robespierre's beliefs were deeply held, there is no shortage of arguments either. What we find is the classic portrait of a man in whom character and persona coincide absolutely, in whom the reflections of Rousseau nourished a spontaneously religious outlook. The coherence of Robespierre's thinking serves to show once again, as Aulard was so keen to demonstrate, that "from 1792 he had a concerted design where religious matters were concerned, a strong determination to resist popular enthusiasm, a remarkable firmness in confronting almost the whole of Paris, whose philosophical unbelief was amused by Hébert's childish pranks."[4]

Indeed, the two interpretations are not mutually exclusive. It is perfectly possible at one and the same time to see the Festival of the Supreme Being as a political maneuver and as a serious belief, the latter justifying the former. This is all the easier since neither belief nor maneuver was original at the time. If one wishes to interpret the Festival of the Supreme Being as an instance of the cunning of reason, it is clear that Robespierre expected it to complete the closure of the Revolution, for it is possible to reread the Floréal report with a view to seeking, and finding, at least as obsessive a presence of the vocabulary of established power as that of the "divine names."[5] It is simply a question of "securing" (morality to eternal bases), of "fixing" (faith and happiness), of "establishing" (on the immutable foundations of justice). But that is precisely what all the successive leaders of the Revolution tried to accomplish, one after another. Neither the purpose pursued nor the means adopted—the festival as a force for conservation—are therefore peculiar to Robespierre. Whether Robespierre is admired or cursed, he did develop the most widely held of the Revolutionary ideas, and this conformity almost dispenses with the always thorny question of sincerity.

As much might be said if one wanted to see the Festival of the Supreme Being as the culmination of a wave of religious enthusiasm. There is nothing about that faceless God imagined by Robespierre, that "Great Being," that "Being of Beings," that "Supreme Being," that is peculiarly his. There is nothing there that was not repeated endlessly in the catechism of a deistic century. It might even be said, if we follow Jean Deprun on this point, that the terms used by Robespierre, which he borrowed from both the Christians and the philosophes, at the meeting point of "the traditions of Bérulle, Rousseau, and Voltaire," were even more ecumenical than is usually supposed. All the intellectual and moral authorities of the century, then, are to be found around the cradle of Floréal, with the exception of the Encyclopedists,[6] who are indeed singled out for opprobrium. Only those "ambitious charlatans" are chased from the temple for their militant radicalism, their particular mistrust of deistic talk, and surely, too, for their "persecution" of Jean-Jacques. It scarcely needs to be added that this exclusion functioned, as one might expect, as the condition for a general reconciliation. Once the "sect" was set aside, the Floréal report and the two speeches made by Robespierre at the festival itself would have no trouble bringing together the elites on the basis of a Rousseauist proposition that "atheism is a naturally distressing system." For the rejection of original sin, a view that atheism is a perversion symmetrical with superstition, the demand for a cult liberated from the narrowness of the sanctuary and the rigidity of dogma, the distance placed between God and the priest, the supposed closeness of God to men, the abandonment of the historical religions to the benefit of natural religion, and lastly and above all, the transfer of religious feeling from the sphere of individual existence to that of social existence—all this, which is developed with admirable rhetorical flair in the Floréal speech, is, beyond individual divergences, the true ground of understanding of the eighteenth-century philosophes. Boissy d'Anglas, commenting enthusiastically on Robespierre's text, was even to find a means of reintegrating the Encyclopedists into his domestic circle: it was enough to conceive of their atheism as a necessary tactic, dictated by a terrified awareness of the "innumerable calamities" brought about by superstition.[7]

Here, as elsewhere, Robespierre is no more than an echo. But the strength and beauty of the Floréal speech prevent one from seeing it as simply a work of plagiarism. The intellectual consensus of the century found in Robespierre emotional conviction. If there is a constant in his sinuous, manipulative interventions in the Jacobin debates, it is a hatred of display, whether of the sword brandished by Isnard or of the red caps that seemed to give credence to the claims of the section representatives. In short, he had a horror of signs and "effigies." The festival of the winter of Year II shocked him on three counts, by combining darkness, masquerade, and violence.[8] None of that could be tolerated by the cautious conformist who described himself as "one of the most defiant and most melancholy patriots to appear since the Revolution."[9] One may be sure that this Alceste did not have to consult only *raisons d'état* to combat the old sans-culottes God, the somewhat incongruous praise of which still arrived on occasion from the provinces, but also the instinct of respectability that sustained the political choice of "purified religion."

There is, therefore, in the report of Floréal, Year II, a combination of an existential disposition and a circumstantial politics, both—and this is the secret of its strength—working for the embodiment of a century-long dream: for if all enlightened opinion could accept the project of Floréal, if so many enthusiastic men believed that 20 Prairial would see the end of the Revolution, it is because they found in the festivals the consecrating image of the "new Philadelphias," the "happy nations" that had haunted their dreams.

Moreover, if we are to deny Robespierre the genius, whether good or evil, depending on one's point of view, of innovation, one has only to go back to Mathieu's project, which seems to have gotten bogged down in the quicksands of Germinal, but on which in fact Robespierre's plan depended heavily. Mathieu may not actually have conceived of a Festival of the Supreme Being, but all his festivals were placed under the auspices of the Supreme Being. Mathieu envisaged five festivals: July 14, August 10, Janaury 21, May 31, and October 6. Robespierre's scheme excluded (perhaps for its barbarous splendor) October 6. Then there were the twenty-three *fêtes décadaires,* identical in both projects. Can one read anything into the very minor alterations brought by Robespierre? He linked the age-group festivals less closely to the seasons, eliminated certain of the redundancies introduced by Mathieu, who overcelebrated the family from both an institutional and a biological point of view, abandoned the Festival of Marriage and Fraternal Love, extended Mathieu's list of virtues, adding justice, modesty, stoicism, frugality, and, incorruptible as ever, disinterestedness. He gave up celebrating the allied peoples to the advantage of the French people, abandoned the Constitution for the Republic. There was nothing very radical in all this. The most important change, perhaps, was that Reason, still honored by Mathieu, had disappeared from Robespierre's list of festivals. This is hardly surprising.[10] The project of Floréal does have one touch of militant defiance: it makes provision for "a festival to the hatred of tyrants and traitors," the only allusion to the redoubled work of the guillotine, a fleeting admission that nothing was over yet. But at the time, nobody noticed it in the joy of the rediscovered utopian festival.

The "Happy Nation"

Old enough, on 20 Prairial, Year II, to remember precisely the festival on that day, but young enough too not to have taken very much notice of the "terrible impressions" of the period, Charles Nodier, thirty-nine years later, still praised it for the break it made with the sickening orgies of the previous winter. He tried to convey his enthusiasm:

> Never did a summer's day rise more pure on our horizon. Only much later, at noon or sunrise in Europe, did I find that same transparency in the firmament, through which the gaze seems to penetrate to other heavens. The people saw it as a miracle and imagined that the unaccustomed splendor of the sky and sun was a certain sign of God's reconciliation with

France. The tortures had ceased. The instrument of death had disappeared behind the hangings and banks of flowers. There was not a single crossroads in the city that was not draped with its flag, not a skiff on the river that was not bedecked with streamers; the smallest dwelling had its own decoration of draperies and garlands, the meanest street was strewn with flowers and, in the general intoxication, the cries of hatred and death had died away.[11]

Many other accounts in a similar vein sometimes lead historians to give a quite exceptional place to the Festival of the Supreme Being, "the most brilliant" festival of the Revolution, according to Mathieu, and also "the most popular."

Popular? Compared with the festivals that preceded it, it was the least improvised. It was the first festival of a series, the harbinger of a lifetime of festivals (and sometimes so well understood as such that it included thirty-six maidens dressed as *fêtes décadaires,* like so many festivals within the festival); every attempt was made to regulate it down to the smallest detail. In Paris endless instructions were issued, appointing the organizers who would place the groups, hand out the ears of corn and baskets of flowers, and order the movements; even the costumes of the representatives gave rise to a long discussion, which, according to Barère, was merely frivolous in the eyes of lightweight men "who have never calculated the effects of legislation for the senses." In the provinces the municipal accessor of Brest wrote to "Citizeness Louise Baptiste, schoolmistress: Please announce to the citizens and citizenesses hereinafter referred to that they have been chosen to represent innocence and wisdom."[12] Instructions were issued on how the little girls' hair was to be arranged, what bouquets of flowers were to be given them, where the rosette was to be tied; nothing eluded his vigilant eye. The musical side of the festival was planned with the same meticulous care: in Paris the Institut National de Musique was given the task of supervising the feverish rehearsals of the singers of the sections in the anthems chosen for the occasion.[13] And there were less joyful texts, in which lists of those who were to pay for the festival were drawn up, and punishment specified for those who sabotaged it; a whole coercive apparatus was in place. Innumerable precautions were taken to ensure its smooth running, for, at the Festival of the Supreme Being, the population was there en masse: in this at least the festival was popular.

Was it also popular in its scenic arrangements? This is by no means certain, for what the festival was trying to demonstrate is not at all clear. Neither religious fanaticism nor atheism: the Festival of the Supreme

Being, which in this foreshadows those of the Thermidorian Convention and the Directoire, stretched between denunciation of monarch and rejection of anarchy, is always saying, like Marx's petty bourgeois, on the one hand this, on the other that. This balance was relatively easy to convey in the speeches, which invariably took the form of attacking "superstition" and the priests while paying homage to the Orderer of the universe, in laborious demonstrations of the existence of God that owe everything to the argument from final causes. But the figurative part of the program was less easy to fulfill, even when a great deal of ingenuity went into it. Citizen Toulouset, at Auch, ordered the procession moving toward the altar of the Supreme Being to stop before a lugubrious cypress from which was to hang the following inscription: "Seeing me as you pass, remember the ills that the priests have done you." The main thing was to establish "the essential difference between the God of nature and the artificial, bizarre God of the priests," and thus to accustom the French people to symbolic language.[14] Such a wish was expressly formulated, but it could not but remain a pious one.

There were, it is true, here and there, in imitation of the Tuileries group in which False Simplicity, Selfishness, and Ambition formed a twisted pediment at the feet of Atheism, a few "hideous figures" being dispatched by executioners. But there were few cities in which, as at Le Mans, not Atheism but *an* atheist was represented, threatening the heavens with a life-size arrow, and most of these monsters lacked any direct expressiveness.[15] When real soutanes, real calottes, and piles of parchment were burned, it was quite a different matter, as Boissy d'Anglas tells us.[16] More important, however, the patriotic burning of Atheism was no longer the center of the ceremony, and its dramatic character was to that extent diminished. The separation in space of the two scenes—that of destruction and that of the offerings to the Supreme Being—make this clear. As in Paris, where the ceremony at the Champ-de-Mars, unlike that at the Tuileries, was purely lyrical and religious, with orchestral music, the presentation of children to heaven, and the oath, this separation was respected almost everywhere. At Angers, where a Fanaticism had been erected near an obelisk (note that it was a Fanaticism and not an Atheism, the latter being less threatening at Angers at that time), brought low by a Liberty, there were endless discussions about the meaning of the procession.[17] Should it go from the Temple of the Eternal to the obelisk or from the obelisk to the Temple of the Eternal? In the end it was the second route that was adopted, after one of the organizers pointed out that it was more fitting to bring down Fanaticism *before* paying homage to the

View of the Mountain erected in the champ de la Réunion. Anonymous colored engraving, Musée Carnavalet. Photo: Bulloz. © DACS 1987.

Supreme Being. Nothing shows better that the burning of a detested symbol was no longer the centerpiece of the ceremony: it was now an earlier stage, one that certainly should be completed before the celebration proper, with its positive implications, began. Indeed, it could easily be dispensed with: in many of the provincial festivals, this symbolic violence had disappeared of its own accord.

By the same token, it was a respectable festival: the official accounts noted with satisfaction the "grave decency" and restrained behavior demanded by the organizers. The children were to be "clean and ready at five o'clock in the morning"; the young ladies were to use powder with restraint, "if they are determined to wear it"; their eyes should be lowered, their skirts bunched up in the Roman style and suitably secured; and on the young ladies' banners such reassuring mottos as "We are being reared according to principles" should be displayed. It was a peaceful festival, too, in which no trace of mockery, profanation, or calls to revenge were to be found. There would probably be a few gunners and a few fireworks experts. There would be the flash of weapons, but they would be entrusted not to men but to youths; they would therefore be dissuasive rather than aggressive, a force held in reserve by the Republic. In fact, allusions to the Revolution were reduced to a minimum: the "busts" had disappeared almost everywhere; only rather crude, ill-educated orators would declare, as at Château-Porcien, that "the Revolution is a boiling pot of which the guillotine is the skimming ladle." [18] Here and there the funeral model still survived, as at Calais, where the festival was conceived as a long procession between five cenotaphs. [19] The general spirit of the ceremony was nonetheless antiheroic. There is no hero when all are heroes. The Festival of the Supreme Being was a heroicization of the everyday, almost of the biological, and had no time for Revolutionary heroism.

What had replaced such heroism was the representation of the abolition of differences. If one has any doubts that the Festival of the Supreme Being represented a fantasy return to the equality of origins, one has only to compare two processions: at Poligny, on July 14, 1790, the procession consisted of "the administrators of the district directory, the tribunal judges, the king's commissioner, the members of the office of conciliation, the justice of the peace and his assessors, the national gendarmes, the ecclesiastics of the town, and the officers and soldiers of the infantry regiment." [20] Four years later these gentlemen had disappeared from Poligny. The procession now consisted of young citizens and citizenesses, fathers and mothers. Yet we must be careful what conclusions we draw from this. The festival was in no way intended—and this is certainly the case here—

to illustrate the eternal unity of the social body, or to demonstrate the equality produced by the Revolution. One member of the people's club of Compiègne wanted to include in the festival a simple village girl in a petticoat, side by side with an elegant citizeness; but this was too clearly a reference to the social divisions that people wanted, above all, to ignore.[21] The people's clubs acceded to instructions: here, as elsewhere, they would stick to maidens holding baskets of flowers. So, by the skilful distribution of roles, the festival achieved the equality of harmony. By what miracle did the inhabitants of Angers, "from the hapless resident of the charity home to the landowner," all call themselves brothers?[22] Everyone had an indispensable part to play in the festival, "whether as father or husband, daughter or mother, rich or poor, young or old." Even the cripple was useful by providing a living image of "honored misfortune," and he was given one or two verses to sing in this lyrical festival.

Reducing social man to biological man is a utopian feature. Anyone who is familiar with the utopias of the century sees that the Festival of the Supreme Being created the unexpected delight of an Arcadia incarnate. This procession of villagers—mothers "each carrying in her arms a child at the breast," maidens offering on a porcelain dish a pair of turtledoves, shepherds "each with his lamb tied with a pink ribbon," those light troops that looked as if they had come straight from Astraea with their quivers and their crooks—here they were at last, out of the pages of books and combining their grace with the robustness of the fine names of the land of France. How delightful when Galatea was none other than Marie Fenouillet! At Theys in the Isère, three ploughmen bearing a harrow were to be followed by six harvesters, who would be "Marie Guichard Lacroix, Madeleine Blanchard Pierraz, Marie Fenouillet living with the Bravoz, Anne Ponchot Rouge, Louis de Carret's daughter, Louise Bouverot living with Connaz, all of whom will hold a sickle in one hand, a small bunch of cornflowers under the other, tied with mixed fresh herbs and they will have straw hats tied to their backs."[23] The last group would be composed of citizens of every trade, carrying the tools of their craft: these citizens would be "Etienne Papet *père* carrying a shuttle, Louis Bouchet Fouillet a comb, Pierre David Guignot an axe, and Barthélemy Jenard a rip saw. Georges, a blacksmith, wearing his apron and carrying the tools of his trade . . ."

Like the pastorals, the Festival of the Supreme Being was also intended to be a festival of abundance: frugal, perhaps, but unctuous and calming, a festival of dairy products, fruit, and bread. The chariots carried cornucopias; the bread, crowned with ears of corn, consecrated by virtue of

being laid on the altar of the fatherland, was broken among the participants. And it was a festival of fecundity: the maidens' banderoles—
"When we are mothers"—declared their destiny, while mothers gave suck
to their infants, "especially males." Pregnant women, in themselves allegories of the permanence of the Revolution, were summoned imperiously:
"The General Council of the commune requests each of you to appear at
six o'clock in the morning at the place de la Liberté, with your husband,
who, given the condition of pregnancy in which you find yourself, must
perform his duty of accompanying you and holding your arm; you will be
able to hold a child by the hand."[24] To illustrate this legitimate plenitude,
there were also tableaux, based on pictures by Greuze, which the organizers tried to reconstruct, as at Nancy, with the chariot of the "Good Family": a woman busying herself with a bassinet, a father teaching a child
perched on his knee to read, another child embracing them, a fourth
crowning them.[25] This "tableau vivant of morality and patriotism" was
held as often as possible in the countryside, so much so that the festival
might be called, and sometimes quite simply was called, a spring festival.
More often than any other, this festival emptied the city streets, was held
in the public gardens (as at Saint-Malo),[26] in meadows (as at Caen),[27] or,
in the villages, at the precise spot where the houses ended. The obligation
laid upon the communes—or, in any case, the pressing invitation contained in David's program—to erect a mountain on which mothers, children, maidens, and ploughmen might sit at ease contributed to this exo-
dus. The miniature mountain of the Festival of Reason was now to be
sought outdoors, on a hill, a "natural hillock," which then became the
sacred place. If there was no such mound or hill, a portable wooden framework could be covered with juniper, ferns, and shrubs, with "paths" dot-
ted with thatched cottages. The utopian cottage, as at Le Bugue,[28] which
appeared behind a chateau reduced to ashes, full of virtuous Republicans,
was the true victor of the festival, far more than deistic belief.

In this vegetal exuberance the animal had disappeared except in its
more useful (oxen, lambs) or emotive (doves) forms. The decoration made
wide use of violets, myrtle, vine leaves, olive, and oak, as recommended
by David, which the municipal authorities, depending on what was available in local hedgerows in June, replaced with eglantine and honeysuckle.
At Sceaux the festival organizers advised the local inhabitants to ban the
hangings and cushions of the ancien régime at the crossroads and to use
flowers and foliage instead. It was a question not only of the best kind of
ornament, of course, but of the very essence of the liturgy: the crowning
with palms, the rose leaves trodden underfoot by old men, the flowers

kept in large bunches by the mothers and thrown to the heavens in homage to the Great Orderer—such actions were an essential part of the ritual. It is true that, in addition to the Festival of the Supreme Being, there was also a Festival of Nature. The festival was for early risers, who, as at Tarbes, gathered on the bridge across the Adour, awaited the rising of the sun: this was also an act of gratitude toward the Architect, as the following verses by Léonard Bourdon make clear:

> Incredules qui voudriez
> Voir l'Etre Suprême et l'entendre
> Avec des moeurs vous le pourriez
> Mais aux champs il faudrait vous rendre
> Tête à tête avec une fleur
> C'est là qu'au bord d'une onde pure
> On entend un Dieu dans son coeur
> Comme on le voit dans la Nature.[29]

This is the secret of the enthusiasm felt by those who took part in this festival, as innumerable reports by village schoolmasters, municipal officials, and organizers testify. The festival, of course, reflected the enthusiasm of a quite small, enlightened section of the population, but it is significant, nevertheless, for it represented the Revolution. And this was not, as we have seen, the enthusiasm of improvisation. Nor did the festival celebrate the value given to human life by the threats that that terrible month of Prairial had laid upon it, a fear for life that gives it value and is able, according to Jaurès, to make a problem like the immortality of the soul, which had hitherto remained little more than a vague daydream, of passionate interest.[30] This is to attribute too much metaphysical depth to a festival whose happiness was essentially about social unity. The Festival of the Supreme Being, based on a huge lie, in fact celebrated the rediscovery by the Revolution of the principle in whose name it was carried out, of the image of itself that it strove to maintain, as R. Palmer saw very clearly.[31]

At Troyes, the municipal authorities invited the citizens to take their meals in front of the city gates, to remind them of the "good days of our ancestors and of the golden age." Never mind, as Maggiolo notes bitterly, if, ten days later, there was only enough food at Troyes for the next thirty-six hours![32] The essence of the matter was not to be found there but in those wondering letters written to the Convention by its representatives: "I have been given a crown of flowers at the hands of innocence," writes Trévoux Méaulle. "The ploughmen have offered me a few mature ears of wheat [in Prairial? in the Ain?]. Little girls and boys recited alternately the articles of the Rights of Man. The joy was pure, the enthusiasm great, the Revolution there."[33]

The Revolution was there, indeed, so close to its dream that people forgot the artificiality of its representation and the distress that followed it.[34] Is more proof needed? It will not be found in the processions, which were nevertheless so conformist, of all the happy nations of the century. No, it is to be found in a modest utopia of Year IX, conceived by a Bordeaux barrister and a former member of the Constituent Assembly, Joseph Saige, whose bitter indignation on the subject of the Terror is clear enough.[35] In the New Philadelphia, which he conceived as a revenge on the disorders of Year II, it was nevertheless the cult of the Supreme Being that seemed to him to be the necessary cement of the community, and it was the Festival of Prairial that inspired his plans for the great festival of the year, with its vases of incense and perfumes, its shepherds' music, the procession of innocent-faced boys and girls, crowns on their heads, baskets of flowers in their hands, celebrating in a colorful and harmonious way the benefits of the God of the Seasons. There is no more telling instance of the power exerted by a model.

This festival, homogeneous with the discourse of the Revolution and homogeneous too with the whole of France, from one end to the other—an important feature for men fascinated by the potential for unity to be found in the festival and determined "to leave no heterogeneous body within the Republic"[36]—is often regarded as the last of the Revolutionary festivals to be worthy of serious attention. The break formed by 9 Thermidor seems to separate two completely unassimilable series. Thereafter one "falls" into Thermidorian or Directorial festivals. This is the ultimate argument of the political interpretation of the Revolutionary festivals, or at any rate its least disputed one. Is it a paradox to consider that it is disputable, that the Festival of the Supreme Being, more in harmony than previous festivals with the hopes of the Revolution, is the exemplary Revolutionary festival after which one can imagine nothing but repetitions?

The System of Brumaire, Year IV

Between the commotion caused by Thermidor and the last days of the Convention, the commemorations actually celebrated were marked by the malaise from which the regime was suffering. The first two were a legacy from the Mountain. On the last day of Year II, implementing a decree of

26 Brumaire, Marat's body was brought to the Panthéon. Was this really Marat's festival? Reading Léonard Bourdon's report on the festival, and despite the fact that the procession employed emblems perfectly appropriate for Marat's life, one may doubt it, for Marat's festival was also the festival of national victories, of the armies of the Republic, of fraternity. The overdetermination of the festival made it very difficult to remind a somewhat thin audience of the memory of Marat, especially when the Convention, suddenly recalling some half-forgotten session, was conspicuous by its absence. Twenty days later it was Rousseau's turn: this festival was also a Robespierrist legacy. Indeed, the presence of the village soothsayer, botanists, and mothers in the procession recalls the atmosphere of the Festival of the Supreme Being. And this time the Convention was there! Ten days later, on 30 Vendémiaire, there was the Festival of Victories. This was a thoroughly Thermidorian festival. Three days earlier the Convention had heard Marie-Joseph Chénier announce, in opposition to David's dictatorship, a new system of national festivals; in fact, 30 Vendémiaire saw military exercises and an attack on a fortress by the pupils of the Ecole de Mars instead of the artistic exercises laid down by David.

But the new system was slow in coming. The Convention had scarcely worked out a policy on the national festivals. The long discussion of Nivôse and Pluviôse, Year II, which was more concerned with the *fêtes décadaires* than with the national festivals, shows this very clearly: there were many speakers who still demanded, in a vocabulary that was nonetheless very devalued, that the first of the festivals be devoted to the Supreme Being. These hesitations were perfectly understandable. Marie-Joseph Chénier was to say as much in the first days of the Directoire. The Convention was constantly stopped in its tracks by seditious movements. It was forced to improvise festivals in haste: the funeral for the representative Féraud, of sad memory, for instance! It had to be content with perpetuating certain celebrations (July 14, August 10) and adding its own festival, 9 Thermidor. All this was decided after endless debates. It was not until the great law of 3 Brumaire, Year IV, on public instruction that we find clear inspiration and a proper plan for the organization of the festivals.

With the law of Brumaire, Year IV, the decree of Floréal, Year II, lapsed: there would now be not four national festivals but seven. Five of them, it is true, were moral festivals: Youth, Old Age, Spouses, Thanksgiving, and Agriculture. Of the commemorative festivals of Year II, one had been transferred without difficulty from the Montagnard decree to the

Thermidorian law: this was the one that, on 1 Vendémiaire, celebrated the foundation of the Republic. The others fell by the wayside—oddly, of course, in the case of the festival of May 31, whose official disappearance in Year IV served to reinforce the clandestine effacement of Year III. Meanwhile, a ceremony celebrated in the Salle des Séances on 11 Vendémiaire, Year IV, attempted, by paying moral reparation to the "martyrs of liberty," to wipe out forever the unpleasant memories of May 31. What now replaced May 31, in a symbolic substitution, was the festival of the regime itself, that of 9 Thermidor. Very soon this arrangement was to be extended by the law of 23 Nivôse, Year IV, which reestablished the celebration of the execution of Louis XVI, and by the decree of 10 Thermidor, Year IV, which gave definitive form to the commemoration of July 14 and August 10. There were, then, throughout the Directoire, five great national commemorations: July 14, August 10, 1 Vendémiaire, January 21, and 9 Thermidor. Sometimes were added one-time-only celebrations necessitated by events such as the funerals of Hoche and Joubert, or the triumphal festivals like that of 20 Nivôse, Year VI, which celebrated peace in Europe. Sometimes, too, they were combined with other celebrations: the most striking example was the long procesion that, on 10 Thermidor, Year VI, brought before the Parisians the objects of science and art collected in Italy. This review of the "curiosities" of the century was also intended to illustrate, for good or ill, the themes of 9 Thermidor.[37] Lastly, the Festival of the Sovereignty of the People, which the law of 13 Pluviôse, Year VI, cynically fixed on the day prior to the elections as a prelude to the day of "right choices," and the festival of 18 Fructidor complete the whole set.

In the speeches that accompanied the drawing up of this new series of festivals, what emerges most strongly is a desire for system.[38] Barailon, who opened the discussion on the *fêtes décadaires* in the Thermidorian Convention, criticized the decree of 18 Floréal for its lack of system. What Robespierre had done was "irregular"; it failed to distinguish between the effects achieved, repeating several times throughout the year the same festival under different names. He had ignored the natural accord between festival and season,[39] and had taken little care to link the historical festival with the cardinal virtue represented in it. He had created a series of festivals—those devoted to disinterestedness, good faith, courage, frugality, and friendship—with no apparent sense of progress or order. None of these festivals was "linked to what followed and what preceded it." Barailon's criticism ended with a wish: "Let it be impossible to alter a single festival without there seeming to be a break, a gap." Sometimes even, referring to this necessary linking of one festival with another, the Thermidorian Convention paid homage to the authority of Condillac. It was striving to create a series of festivals that would form a "well-made language." When Merlin de Thionville presented his *Opinion sur les fêtes nationales* on 9 Vendémiaire, he declared: "Ah! If the resolution of which I have just spoken may be accompanied by that whose necessity Condillac has so well demonstrated, which l'Epée and Sicard have so well prepared, and with which Singlin seems to be concerning himself so successfully; if one day the perfect clarity and precision of language [*langage*] may be combined with the dignity, brilliance, and harmony of the language [*langue*]; in a word, if the art of reasoning is ever reduced to the art of speaking a well-made language . . . , soon the French people, more easily enlightened by its orators and more easily enlightening itself, will attain the highest point of wisdom and true greatness."[40]

How is one to recognize a well-made language? To begin with, by the fact that its terms do not ramify interminably: there should not, then, be too many festivals. A precise nostalgia imbues even these reflections: if the Revolution could have been carried out in a single movement, if it had not been impeded by clumsiness, hesitation, or perfidy, there need only have been a single commemorative festival to celebrate—for example, one festival per month, which might have been called quite simply the Republican festival, as Durand de Meillane wished,[41] or again every four years, a great commemorative festival that would assume the whole Revolutionary past, a "festival of the Revolution," as Mathieu de l'Oise demanded in Year II.[42] But, since this was not the case, it was necessary to have several festivals. This being so, care should be taken to limit them to a small number and to declare this once and for all. Furthermore, a well-made language was expected to distinguish scrupulously between its terms. Orators were constantly trying to decide, in some imaginary experiment, whether it was possible to amalgamate festivals with different commemorations. For, if there was some obstacle to their shared celebration, was it not a sign that, as in a successful axiomatics, the festivals maintained were properly independent of one another? Yet, however independent they may be, it was also important that one could perceive a family resemblance among them, deriving from the inspiration of the Revolution: for any system manifests the compatibility of actions situated in very different times and places. Lastly, they must be beyond dispute and present to everybody the same mirror. In this the commemorative festivals reveal their claim to a unanimist pedagogy: whereas, under tyranny, the "annals of the whole people were effaced by the history of one family, condemning the nation to seek in that history the causes of its happiness and the annual occurrences of its public celebrations, the citizens of free countries celebrate and consecrate only the immortal events of the national family."[43]

Do the commemorations maintained by the law of Brumaire, Year IV, actually correspond to this list of requirements? When one considers the actual celebrations, with all their gaps and, still more, their repetitions, one may often doubt it.[44] So, throughout the Directoire, attempts were made to justify the order adopted, both by trying to bring out the original physiognomy of each of the festivals and by demonstrating the place that it held in a "philosophical and inspiring series." This, during his two ministries, was the favorite activity of François de Neufchâteau, who tirelessly busied himself with a retrospective systematization. If, for example, the Festival of Spouses succeeded that of Youth, it was "to indicate, by this proximity, to a youth that has all too often wandered from the sources of true voluptuousness, the sacred bond that, on the basis of virtue, links the body with love."[45] At the same time, François de Neufchâteau was trying to compose a handbook of the national festivals by going through the enormous mass of official accounts kept at the Ministry of the Interior and selecting what he regarded as the best examples for an "exquisite volume," which was then to be proposed for emulation by the humblest of the Republic's communes. Thus, to the end of the Revolutionary decade, we find the same dream of unanimity: each citizen should recognize everywhere the same plan, the same object, the same rites, the same songs. In fact, this determination to make uniform is a boon to the researcher.[46]

Is this, compared with Robespierre's series, a new set of festivals? The organizers intended it to be so; after Thermidor, they constantly presented their work as representing a break with the inspiration of Year II. Bourdon de l'Oise urged the Convention to abandon its mania for processions, Merlin de Thionville urged it to abandon coercive instruction, while Marie-Joseph Chénier was feverishly occupied in reconstructing a political virginity. Should we take their protestations literally? Are we to see between the Robespierrists and the Thermidorians, as Henri Grange tries to do,[47] an abyss separating two theories of the festival and two distinct species of theoretician, the second alone wishing to subject the popular masses to the fatherland, possibly with the help of religion, and alone guilty of an attempted conditioning of the crowds, almost a rape—an ordered, mechanical rape, of course, based on conditioned reflexes?

Indeed, we may be willing to conceive of the festival as a manipulation. But how can any contradiction be seen between the end and the means imagined by La Révellière-Lépeaux, on the one hand, and by Robespierre, on the other? One would be hard put to find one, since Robespierre too was depending on unanimity to exert his power over men's souls and on the religious sense to console and contain the populace; furthermore, this festival, like that of Révellière, was decent and grave.[48] But the Rousseau-ist legacy, so visible in Robespierre, cannot be freed from the accusation of wanting to manipulate men as much as Henri Grance would wish. Of course, La Révellière wanted to alter the substance of mankind in such a way as "to identify him with the form of government and to make love of liberty his dominant passion."[49] But where, if not in Rousseau, did he get the idea for such an identification? "I would like to have lived and to have died free," says the *Discours sur l'inégalité,* "that is to say, so subjected to the laws that neither I nor anyone would be able to shake off its honorable yoke." La Révellière finds in Rousseau, just as Robespierre does, the idea of "good conditioning," the whole trick of which consists in the fact that those conditioned are unaware of it. Once the conditioning is complete, everything will proceed with the blind facility of instinct. Who said, "Then all we have to do is to allow things to take their natural course"? La Révellière. And who thought it essential to give at an early stage "an impress of obedience and docility that will seem second nature when the time comes"? Rousseau, in his project for the education of M. de Sainte-Marie. When what is at issue is not a child but a people, Rousseau and La Révellière would once again be in full agreement. It is useless for a people to be aware of the meaning of the games and festivals to which it is summoned; It is enough that they become imbued with the spirit of the festival and are capable of carrying out its movements, without asking themselves about its ultimate purpose.[50]

From the festivals of Year II to the festivals of the Thermidorian Convention we find the same theory, therefore, embodied and flourishing, under Rousseau's *dirigiste* authority. One also finds the same invocations (the ceremonies continued to be held in the presence of the Supreme Being) and the same emblems. Even in Thermidor, Year VII, at Clermont, the ceremonial of August 10 used David's scenic arrangements with a Nature endowed with two rows of breasts from which milk trickled.[51] Nevertheless, since there were new festivals, new arrangements had to be made. But for the Festival of Agriculture, the organizers quite simply borrowed from Mirabeau's old project the ceremonial of the furrow traced by public authority and removed the procession to the fields; for the Festival of the Sovereignty of the People, a "metaphysical festival" par excellence, the organizers remembered the bundle of white sticks that the Federation had used to represent the *départements*. The greatest imaginative effort was made, however, for 9–10 Thermidor, the festival of the regime itself. This festival was spread over two days, as if to illustrate the Thermidorian balance between monarchy and anarchy. On the first day, the whole commune, divided into age groups, overthrew and destroyed a gilded throne, decked out with crown and fleur-de-lys, and bearing the inscription "Constitution of 1791." By the second day, nothing remained of the throne but debris, on which was erected another throne, masked, veiled in black, "cadaverous," bristling with daggers and masks, crowned with the inscription "Constitution of 1793." This throne was in turn subjected to organized destruction, this time by fire. Then, once all trace of the two thrones had been removed, the statue of Liberty was erected in the cleared space. However interesting this ceremonial may be—especially in the difference between the two modes of destruction used[52]—one can hardly regard it as an example of great inventiveness: the destruction of the throne and its replacement by the statue had already been used in the festivals of Year II. Lastly, how can one fail to note the use, to designate and confound the Robespierrist faction, of images—masks and daggers—with which it was itself so obsessed?

What we have here, then, is a repetition: the organizers of the Thermidorian and Directorial festivals eliminated from their creations only those elements that were suspect in Robespierre's eyes; in fact, whenever the Thermidorians had to defend the national festivals against their detractors, they had recourse to Robespierre's arguments. When Daunou bases the system of Brumaire, Year IV, on the "universally felt need for benevolence and agreement," when François de Neufchâteau sees all festivals as bearing within them "a religious character, a philosophy of sentiment, a moral eloquence that speaks to all hearts," when La Révellière considers that his ideas and maxims "will displease priests and philosophers equally," it is always the voice of Floréal, Year II, that one hears. Furthermore, when the second Directoire set out, after Fructidor, to stir up the embers of the festivals and to revive the *fêtes décadaires*,[53] they still went back to Robespierre's project or to Mathieu's even older one for the names of the *décadis*.

No further proofs of coherence are required, therefore. The astonishing continuity that we have discovered in the festivals of the French Revolution lead one to believe that, if the Revolution is an indissoluble whole, that certainly is reflected in its festivals. From now on let us speak not of the festivals but of the festival of the French Revolution.

· VI ·
The Festival
and Space

THERE is no end to the list of spatial metaphors associated with the Republic or with Revolutionary France: from the beginning of the Revolution a native connivance linked rediscovered liberty with reconquered space. The beating down of gates, the crossing of castle moats, walking at one's ease in places where one was once forbidden to enter: the appropriation of a certain space, which had to be opened and broken into, was the first delight of the Revolution.

It was a new experience but one that, for the men of the Revolution, was supported by the legacy of a whole century concerned with showing the influence of spatial configuration on public happiness. Belief in the educative potential of space derives directly from the idea of utopia: it was popularized by a mass of writings from reformists, urbanists, hygienists, and architects. This doctrine was so unquestioned that very little attempt was made to reveal the connections by which space might exert its educative influence over people's minds: it seemed to impose its power in a direct, unmediated way. Thus, a new political arrangement seemed to involve a new arrangement of urban space: when Julius Caesar, the Abbé Brotier remarks, wanted to change the form of government, "he began with changes in the circus."[1] Similarly, an ingenious disposition of space was thought, in and of itself, to be capable of containing individual crime: placing a civic altar near an assembly hall was enough to prevent a legislator from betraying his duty.[2]

There was, therefore, a self-confident spatial voluntarism: in the eyes of those men, a whole conscious, transparent, utterly illegible geography must replace an unconscious geography. There was to be a rational program of spatial occupation that included the renaming of squares and streets and the numbering of houses, as well as effecting the disaffection of churches and the destruction of the symbols of the ancien régime. This was an immense undertaking, in which the festival was to play an essential part. For the feeling of the festival seemed to emerge from the judicious arrangement of space; just as all conflict disappeared from a well-designed utopian city, all surprise and all dissonance must be avoided in a festival that had successfully marked out its own space. That space must be found: sometimes invented, sometimes reshaped, both marked out and emptied, figures drawn upon it, ways made through it. This was not such an easy matter, as we shall see.

Space without Qualities

In seeking a location for the festival, the organizers never lost sight of this imperative: public enjoyment must be able to extend regularly and without obstacle. What was needed was a festive space that could contain an endless, irrepressible, and peaceful movement like the rise of tidal waters. In this, indeed, the space of the festival was the exact equivalent of the Revolutionary space itself, as described by Fichte in his *Considerations:* "While the luminous flood irresistibly spreads, the obscure islets grow smaller and break up, abandoned to the bats and owls."[3] For Fichte, the dazzling flood was that of Revolutionary truth; for the festival organizers, it was that of Revolutionary joy. But both sensed an identical expansion: "Democracy is the happy, unimpeded extension of happiness"; "holy equality hovers over the whole earth," said the official reports. There was, therefore, no trace of transgression, no suspicion of violence. The places conquered by the Revolution have been promised to it from all eternity: the space chosen by the festival was to manifest this.

Ideally, at least. Little by little, the representatives of Revolutionary history were to make one compromise after another with this requirement. Let us consider this history, then, at its birth, at the time of those federative festivals that express it with a liberty that was still unimpeded and intact.

The festivals' first requirement was the open air. The Federations were to be celebrated outside the towns, "under the walls," "on the open road," "on the heath," "in the plain." When possible, the organizers preferred the wildness and fresh air of open spaces to the familiar intimacies of the village square, in the shadow of the church. As a result, the municipalities often became a theater for interminable conflicts with the priests, who would have preferred to celebrate mass in their own chapels, at their own altars. Their resistance shows the extent to which the choice of the open air disconcerted many people and was seen as both a liberation and a provocation. This could not be better expressed than in Vergniaud's letter of January 16, 1790: "In a village of the Périgord, the peasants forced their priest to place a cockade on the Blessed Sacrament; furthermore they insisted that the priest leave the door of the tabernacle open; for they wanted their Good God to be free."[4]

This passion for the open air had very ancient roots. It is just as apparent in the urbanism of the century as in the daydreams of its utopians. For the men of the Revolution, it drew additional energy from the negative model of the aristocratic festival, which enclosed, divided, and isolated. Partitioning very soon became the emblem of counterrevolutionary thought.[5] It may be remembered that in July and August 1789, during the first disturbances, barriers and tollgates were knocked down, and the abolition of the barriers around Paris (Charles Villette, always a sensitive witness, saw them as "six leagues of circular walls penning in a million men like a flock of sheep")[6] was experienced as a festival, punctuated by symbolic gestures: the people of Paris danced around the gatehouses, which had always been described as smoky lairs, under the triple curse of enclosure, secrecy, and darkness. The ladies of Les Halles went out, beyond the destroyed gates, to cut a young tree, which they set up in the Louvre, in the middle of the place du Carrousel, under the king's windows, thus symbolically abolishing the frontiers between town and country. The riotous opening up of space was spontaneously expressed in festive terms.

It is true that the scenic arrangements required by the Federation could be achieved only in the open air: the dramaturgy of national unity required it. In the open, in the healthy neutrality of a free space, all distinctions seemed to fall away. This theme is to be found, in innumerable variations, in the speeches of the federative festivals. At Pontivy, during "the Great Federation of the 120 towns and townships of Brittany," the speakers gave the following warning: "Let us above all be on our guard against any weakening of those feelings by a consideration of distances, by those ancient denominations of countries, states, provinces, conquered or not conquered, of great and small towns, of town and country, of canton and hamlet, which seemed to divide us from ourselves."[7] And at Montélimar the speaker declared, "In gathering here, good neighbors, you have broken down the barrier that, under the name of province, divided the children of a great family."[8]

In the spatial arrangement of the ideal festival there was, therefore, to be no sense of limit or of occupation: "The national festivals can have no other boundary than the vault of heaven, since the sovereign, that is to say, the people, can never be enclosed in a circumscribed and covered space and because it is alone its own object and greatest ornament."[9] It was right that the crowd should take its oath facing the sky, like those *fédérés* at Nancy, who, "free as the air they breathe," climbed a mountain in order to be closer to it.[10] The dome of heaven was clearly a theocentric space, ordered by the radiating gaze of an architect God.[11] This invisible dome manifested the only transcendence that the Revolutionary festival acknowledged, and this explains the condemnation of the ceremonial use of the canopy; the canopy arbitrarily deifies whoever is protected by it, and furthermore, it sets up an unbearable screen between the Supreme Being and his worshippers.[12] It is in every sense a usurpation.

Lastly, the open air had the enormous advantage of being a space without memory and was therefore able to symbolize entry into a new world. When the three columns of the National Guards of the Meurthe, the Moselle, and the Haute-Marne left the all too historical settings of the squares of Nancy to reassemble outside the city, on a "precipitous" mountain, ground that has "hitherto been uninhabited," the official account of the ceremony shows very clearly the reasons for this choice: first, the altar that crowned the mountain was the only piece of man's work in sight, and second, however much one scrutinized the space around, "one can glimpse in the wild desert no trace of servitude."[13] These happy circumstances were not always found together; sometimes the location of the festival had to be established in a fractured space, and the participants had to travel from the altar of the fatherland along winding paths, through ramparts, past ruined towers, and across drawbridges.[14] It may have been very unusual for the feudal settings to have such an insistent presence. But did it? The official accounts are eager to avoid the issue by reducing it to aesthetic curiosity: "One object contrasted even more with the prevailing atmosphere of the civic festival: this was the picturesque prospect of the crumbling ruins of an ancient castle."[15]

The ideal place in which to install the Revolutionary festival was therefore one that provided an uninterrupted view, in which every movement was immediately visible, in which everyone could encompass at a glance the intentions of its organizers. Unimpeded vision and the festive spirit seem to have been indissolubly linked. At Rouen, on the "bruyères Saint-Julien," there was no obstacle to the progress of the four columns converging on the altar of the fatherland and synchronizing their march in such a way that they entered the camp simultaneously at the first cannon shot. At Nancy, three columns, approaching from different points on the horizon, converged at the top of the Sainte-Geneviève hill, thus offering the eye an image of men's progress toward their necessary reunion. Only so bare an aspect could make possible "the interesting spectacle of several thousand armed men who, ranged under different banners and scarcely knowing one another, went off to form a people of brothers." [16] Only such a place could make visible to all the unique moment of meeting: "In an instant, all animosities, all prejudices disappeared; they embraced one another like good brothers." [17] Such a spectacle inspired something like a rational, spontaneously educating joy. Malouet recognized this when he grumbled, "What is served by transporting men to the top of a mountain and showing them the whole domain of their rights, since we are forced to bring them down again, assign them limits, and throw them back into the real world, where they will find obstacles at every step?" [18] Malouet was no doubt contrasting harsh, obstacle-ridden reality with the utopian happiness of panoramic vision; he suspected the inconsistency of such a euphoria but did not question its reality.

So we can understand the importance that the festival organizers attached to the choice of site. [19] This is also borne out by the example of the Paris Federation. The flood of architectural projects, and the peevish fury with which each architect set about denigrating the solutions of his rivals, should not make us forget that an astonishing consensus existed. In the end it hardly matters that some proposed the Neuilly road or the Grenelle plain or Clichy, or that the choice of the Champ-de-Mars was a difficult one. What all the discussions about the ideal location of the festival show is widespread agreement that the place chosen should be large enough for a demonstration of fraternity and easy of access, according to the norms long since laid down by Boullée. [20] What the architects wanted was an enormous open space, easy to approach, in which nature would not have to be distorted too much to attain a theatrical effect. The obsession with the amphitheater, an architectural model that the century's daydreams had always associated with the virtue of the communal gathering, [21] and which enabled the spectators to share their emotions equally and to see one another in perfect reciprocity, [22] imbues all these texts. When Linguet was looking for the ideal location for a fireworks display, it seemed to him that the Pont-Neuf—the five parallel bridges, the quayside stretching as far as the Grève, like so many ready-made amphitheaters—was an obvious choice. [23] For Thiémet, the sidewalks of the grassy banks beyond the old gates of Chaillot were like "so many amphitheaters arranged with the sole purpose of celebrating Liberty."[24] This was also the direction of the fundamental criticism Blondel leveled at Cellerier's plan: by digging up the site of the Champ-de-Mars, he had abolished the uninterrupted view afforded by the natural amphitheater.[25]

There was another preoccupation too: since it was all too clear that this space should not be confined, how could the crowd be contained without enclosing it? There emerges from all the proposed arrangements a wish to make the outer boundary of the ceremony as inconspicuous as possible: if such a demarcation is absolutely necessary, then let it be represented by a tricolor ribbon; better still, let the boundary of the festival be the outermost circle of spectators, a moving boundary that may always theoretically expand with the addition of more people. It was this image that made the circular figure the perfect one for the festival site. The circle was an emblem of national unanimity, as Mouillefarine fils was well aware, when he apologized for "the proliferation of round forms in this project." "Not," he adds, "that I am more an advocate of circular forms than of other forms, but, in my view, the circle is more symbolic of the facts to be immortalized, its solidity deriving from reunion and unanimous accord."[26] It was also this image that argued so vigorously in favor of the choice of the Sablons plain: the Bois de Boulogne could take any overspill of spectators, extending the festival while retaining universal fraternity and avoiding too abrupt a boundary. There were very few indeed—Escherny was one of those isolated voices[27]—who criticized the arrangements of the Paris Federation for diluting the emotion of its participants in too great a space. So the festival seemed to have nothing to lose from the sheer size of its proportions; the emotional unity still seemed to be strong enough to prevent any fragmentation.

Whatever the facts of the situation may have been, one senses that it did not matter very much that these projects should have been imagined for Paris; for it was in a place lacking such peculiarities that the festival was most at home. When Servandoni justified his choice of erecting the place Louis XV "in some isolated spot outside Paris," he presented his project as being consistent with the necessities of festivals. In its search for a transparent, legible space, in which the emotion that it aroused would be diffused in a regular manner, the Revolutionary festival chose a site for its abstract suitability, not for its historical associations or its aesthetic charms. In this it revealed its kinship with utopia. All places are equally suitable for the utopian festival; it has no need of the picturesque, may reject the facilities of "character," may take place anywhere: utopia is isotopia.

Is it surprising, then, that the heart of the Revolutionary festival was so often the ascent of an aerostat into the heavens? The aerostatic festival was the utopian festival endowed at last with its own incarnation, for the aerostat drew all eyes at once toward the sky, where the only transcendence of the festival resided. It achieved the perfect convergence of individual emotions. It accomplished that simultaneity denied by processions,[28] which allow only a fragmentary view. It managed to overcome all obstacles; and the relations of the festivals, which manipulate suspense, emphasize the uncertain flight of a machine still in its early stages, in order to stress the final triumph all the more. The aerostat that was launched on 19 Thermidor, Year VI, to receive the objects of science and art collected in Italy, had at first enormous difficulties in "piercing" the obstacles. "But suddenly the superb machine took on a sublime momentum, plunged into the air . . . That fortuitous, but faithful emblem of the destinies of the Republic struck all the spectators."[29] The man who ascended embodied symbolically, for all those staring up at him, the magic of the festival promised by David: "The drums roll, everything takes on a new form."[30] The aeronaut who set out on September 10, 1791, to receive the Constitution described very well the intoxication that the flight of the gondola gave him. His was the overwhelming excitement of someone crossing the city without having to follow a complicated network of narrow streets: "Standing, uncovered, holding the Constitution in my hand, I passed in a straight line over the Champs-Elysées, the Tuileries, the Louvre, the rue and faubourg Saint-Antoine."[31] It was the sheer ease of the crossing, the ability to take in "the whole of assembled Paris." The rider of the clouds was an embodiment of Vauvenargue's dream, which was also that of the century as a whole; he himself became that "extended" mind that "considers things in their mutual relations; he grasps at a glance all the roots of things; he gathers them together at their source and in a common center; lastly, he spreads light over great objects and over a vast surface." From the great, ordered, necessary deployment, made possible by a space without qualities, derived the true happiness of the festival.

The Symbolic Mapping-Out

Is that all that needs to be said, then, when a festival has found a bare space, made all the more eloquent by its very bareness?[32] Not entirely. As

François de Neufchâteau says, when reflecting on the spaces where the festival might take place, one may "solemnize" wherever a Liberty Tree is erected, "wherever grass covers an altar of the fatherland."[33] Although the location is not important, the place must be marked out; the festival must eliminate all ancient traces and establish its own symbolic map. There is no festival without a monument: ever since the Federation, in this too exemplary, their necessary coexistence had often been stressed.[34] For only the monument gives eternity. In order to make this privilege more self-evident, Gois considered it judicious to lay "the great work of the Constitution" within the monument.[35] And that is also why the material used should be indestructible marble, a requirement ironically contradicted by the perishable constructions erected in the feverish haste of the Federation (the rest of the Revolutionary decade was to be no more successful in overcoming the ravages of time).[36] In the absence of the immediate eloquence of the material, one must count on the language of forms: here a square base on which the statue of the king, crowned by France, would sit heavily; there a twenty-foot-square platform; there again pyramids "in the bend of the Neuilly road"—all so many allegories of stability.

In all these projects, two motifs recur insistently. The first is the colossal column, which was the most commonly used of all these fictitious monuments; for, beyond its antiquarian connotations, it has the advantage of being seen from all sides. According to Gatteaux, it should have the effect of astonishing strangers visiting the capital for the first time and raise questions in their minds [37] (This is a proper utopian style: the column sums up the city and the city is summed up by the founding event.) The second motif is the square central altar, sometimes associated with the column, an anchorage point for the festival, dramatized by the oath, which focused but suggested no separation: not only did nothing separate the altar from the vault of heaven (here, obviously, there was not the slightest canopy), but nothing must isolate it from the rest of the universe. The four side poles pointed "toward the four corners of the world."[38] It also had to be able to serve as "steps for a whole people."[39] Solidity, sobriety, practicality: did Cellerier's project, which was accepted for the Champ-de-Mars, better embody these requirements than Blondel's? The question must remain without a definite answer, but it is true that the winning project did not betray what was expected of an altar of the fatherland. Indeed, the square stylobate suggested solidity, and, at least for the imagination, the giant staircases could accommodate a large crowd.

Lastly, the architects of the Federation wanted to mark out the festival space with a regular pattern of statues. Everybody stressed the educative value of the statue, erected in all its anthropomorphic exemplariness. By the same token, statuary could have a negative effect, which explains why it seemed so urgent, before the *fédérés* entered Paris, to purge the urban space of the infamous statue in the place des Victoires,[40] and why it was against the statues—much more than against painted images—that Revolutionary vandalism was later unleashed. But since the teaching promulgated by the statue seemed indisputable at the time,[41] there was nothing to prevent its being diverted to the good. One has only to reel off the list of the "instructive" statues: depending on the places and locations, the twin figures of the king and the Nation were surrounded by an instructive army (the Law, Philosophy, Abundance, Religion), all subjected to the dominating, unifying figure of Liberty. According to Linguet, it was Liberty that had to rise out of the ruins of the Bastille, like Minerva rising already armed from the head of the people.[42] In the statue planned by Sobre,[43] Liberty, lit up at night by a luminous pediment, dominated from its height of twelve feet; Liberty in Gatteaux's project too, a palm in her left hand and in her right a pikestaff topped by a cap, would seem "to take possession of this great kingdom."[44] The Chevalier de Mopinot rejoiced in the fact that the Revolution thus seemed to be promised.[45] This patterning of the public space with heroic statues, all endowed with a lesson to be delivered and now offered to all in the public squares, was a wish in which the memory of antiquity and the utopian dream come together.[46]

Statues, columns, obelisks, pyramids, and soon Liberty Trees drew the mind to the spontaneous axiomatics of the high and low: a surprising feature for a space so obviously devoted to horizontality. But there are several verticalities. Unlike the Gothic building, the column, the statue, and still less the tree do not really arrest the eye. They provide it with a motif of elevation but without limiting it: they are moral themes, not visual constraints. Can the same be said of the pyramid or the mountain, which was later so often to take its place?[47] It may be remembered that texts written well before the Montagnard episode express quite unambiguously the purpose of this ceremonial arrangement: the proximity of the sky. Yet, despite their familiar presence and despite the real proliferation of mountains, one senses the unease felt by the Revolutionary sensibility when confronted by the "obfuscating" mass of this architectural motif. When political opportunism was to suggest the removal of the mountains, no doubt all the good reasons derived from present circumstances were brought up again. Of the mountain erected by the Robespierrist ceremonial on the esplanade des Invalides, the anti-Robespierrist motion proposed by the Halle au Blé section retained above all the ornaments: the marsh, the reptiles, the vague bestiary, all the murky associations of federalism. But in the discussions that then began—it was 1 Ventôse, Year II—the levelers of mountains found it quite natural to resort to a language that went beyond politics. "What is a mountain," cried Mathieu, "if not an eternal protest against Equality?" There was a sense that one was returning to the certainty that underpinned the whole of this spatial organization—namely, that verticality is scandalous. When, on 22 Brumaire, Year II, the Commune issued an invitation to destroy the bell towers, it was in part because "their domination over other forms of building seems to have contradicted the true principles of equality." Aulard declared such notions to be utterly stupid, but he nevertheless expressed the essential feature of the spatial arrangement of the Revolutionary festivals in the privilege given to horizontality.

Moreover, how can one fail to be struck by the fact that these buildings, erected to mark the various festivals, are not dwellings? Indeed, the theme of the dwelling is particularly rare in the architectural projects of the Revolution. Only the wish to house the deputies aroused the sustained interest of architects. For the most part, the buildings erected on the occasion of festivals never lent themselves to evoking a hollow space, even when they were required to house something (in any case, more often archives than men). The massive volume of the pyramids, columns, and obelisks was imposed not by convenience but by the requirements of symbolism. It was both a sign—covered as they were with inscriptions, these monuments were veritable "books"—and a signal. In Sobre's project, the statue of Liberty surmounting the column is seated on a "luminous recipient," itself endowed with a double function: to carry for miles around a view of "that flaming symbol" and, if need be, to give the signal that liberty was being celebrated or that the fatherland was in danger.[48]

The Revolutionary festival, then, completely ignored the distribution of interior space and seemed unaware of its emotional resources. What complaints there were when circumstances or the weather made it necessary to celebrate a festival indoors! The interior space of a church, in which a festival was sometimes forced to take shelter, had lost all meaning: the pillars were an obstruction to the view, the vault spread its false sky over the celebrants, the architecture seemed to rival the ceremony. The church was a badly planned, inconvenient theater, an artistic illusion that did not even achieve its object. It held secrets and surprises in reserve; one could discover it only gradually; it was more like a poem than a building. This repugnance was not at all new; it was shared by the century as a whole. When Morellet visited Saint Peter's in Rome,[49] he was astonished that the huge building forced him to develop his impressions in several stages, but he was surprised and aware that in this he was in disagreement with the artists and metaphysicians of his time.[50] For them, as for the organizers of festivals, the ceremonial space should be entirely visible at a glance. So what was most important in the conversion of churches into *temples décadaires* was not the ingenuity[51] employed in transforming a former Eternal Father into Father Time armed with his scythe or a Saint Cecilia into a goddess of Equality by turning her triangle into a level. The essence of such conversions was to be found in those abolished side chapels, those truncated transepts, that re-creation within the church—by means of flags, hangings, foliage—of a place that could be taken in at a glance and almost held in one's power: a necessary guarantee of security.

When the monumental will of the men of the Revolution was exerted upon an already existing building, these requirements became fully evident. When an anonymous engineer of the department of bridges and roads wanted to convert the Jeu de Paume into a commemorative monument, what concerned him was not in the least the problem of what to do with the interior volume of the Jeu de Paume, which, in any case, was reduced in his description to "four walls and an open view of the sky," but how to achieve, for reasons that combine security with aesthetics, the isolation of the monument, according to the norms of his century's town planning.[52] In order to facilitate access for processions, the way would have to be cleared for a street, with broad, suitably large flights of steps. The view would have to be made more dramatic by erecting, at one end of the temple, "a portico, all the better to suggest its object." But the engineer-architect's inspiration faltered before the interior space. His ideas seem to amount to no more than a suggestion to reproduce in cast iron "the sad, respectable furniture of that august assembly." What would the pilgrims do there? He doesn't tell us. As in so many programs for Revolutionary festivals, once the procession has reached its goal, there is no additional indication to the celebrants as to what they should do next.[53] It is as if the monument and even the temple itself provided sufficient emotional satisfaction simply by virtue of being seen. What, then, was the point of going inside?

The Renovation of a Ceremonial Space: The Example of Caen

At least in a town one had to enter and move about. The passion for open space, which was well satisfied by the federative festivals, seldom found such favorable circumstances. Nor could the other festivals, which did not give rise to such military display, depend on the extraordinary numbers that marked the festivals of those early days. They had no alternative but to accommodate themselves to urban space. And a town could not be treated as easily as a horizontal space, penetrable on every side and without memories. It was not as easy, in built-up areas, to arrange for processions to converge at a single point, and unconscious memories could never be avoided. So one finds in the routes actually adopted by the processions in urban space traces of the resistance of the towns to the despotism of reason. Such resistance no doubt varied greatly, according to the requirements of the organizers, the (highly variable) degree of attention given to the commemoration of the Revolutionary event, and the very structure of the towns.

The village was a special case: there, the journey from the municipal buildings to the *temple décadaire* was usually quite short. There one could not so easily free oneself from the presence of the past—and, indeed, there was perhaps little wish to do so. Moreover, the traces of the Revolutionary events could not amount to very much in a village. There was less to commemorate and, no doubt, less to forget.

Take an average-sized city, Caen,[34] where the ceremonial routes were pretty well known—well enough for a map to have been published on which, with a few exceptions,[35] all the Revolutionary ceremonies celebrated at Caen involving a procession were marked. There were in all thirty-four routes, almost all of which involved return journeys and very few of which did not follow the same route both ways. At Caen, as elsewhere, there was no attempt to make a tour of the city: not that the Revolutionary ceremonial ignored the therapeutic value of the "tour"—surrounding the altar of the fatherland or the Liberty Tree was always felt to be beneficial—but urban space was seldom enclosed in a consecrating figure. In the smaller towns, however, the "tour" did exist, but it was not at all a common ceremonial arrangement.

At Caen, then, the routes of the processions followed two basic figures. The first connected the old mercantile city with the classical city—in other words, the church of Saint-Pierre with the place Royale. There were a few variations on the first model: a northern route skirted the popular,

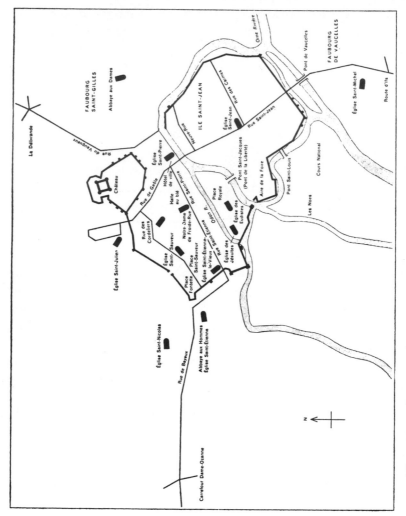

The various places passed by the processions during the ten years of festivals at Caen.

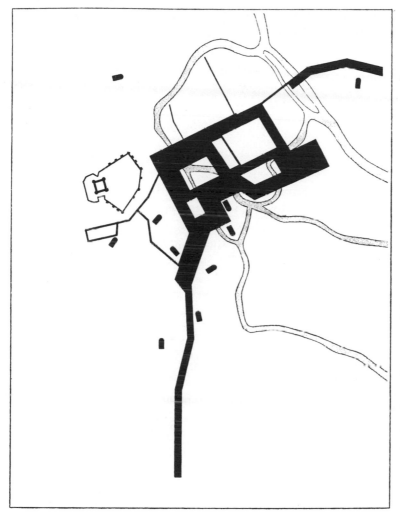

An imaginary itinerary of the various routes taken over the ten years of the Revolution by the processions at Caen.

commercial quarters, which, of course, were heavily imbued with sacral traditions. But, whether by the south or by the north, the old mercantile city, where in 1789 armed bands from the suburbs converged on the Hôtel au Blé, the Corn Exchange, demanding a lowering of the price of grain, hardly figured in the festival at all. The procession gave far more importance to the classical city, a choice that was much influenced by those endless "visits" to the great men of the Ile Saint-Jean, to the bishop's palace or to the Hôtel d'Harcourt, which, over the centuries, had also linked the ancient heart of the city to the houses of the notables.[56]

The second model, which triumphed more and more as the Revolutionary decade advanced, completely abandoned the old town and set out from the place Royale toward the cours National, with variations all caused by the urban development of recent decades. A good example of these routes is the one taken for the Festival of the Supreme Being, which, at Caen, as in many other cities, resolutely turned its back on the traditional urban routes and adopted the most decentralized itinerary. This was a completely new route made possible by the construction of new roads, but it had a fine future. The reasons for its adoption probably had to do with convenience: even by just skirting the old city via the Saint-Etienne–Saint-Pierre (by now Descartes-Lepelletier) axis, one had to take a route that, despite the road widenings of the latter half of the century, remained very narrow. This would be sufficient to explain the neglect of an itinerary that had often been used during the ancien régime, especially by the great civic procession that took place on Whitsunday. But psychological reasons, concerned with associations with "decency," the official account tells us, coincided in this instance with reasons of physical practicality: by crossing the old city, one might come up against signs of popular resistance to the Revolutionary ceremony. In Year VII, the civic procession of Youth, which adopted a traditional itinerary, passed on its way, as the director of the département indignantly complained to the municipality, shops that were not shut, merchants and workmen on the public highway, and streets obstructed by carts laden with goods.[57] We can only guess the extent to which this physical obstruction was linked to a moral obstruction.

A third type of route combined the other two, linking the old city to the new districts. An example of this was the procession on 1 Vendémaire, Year VI: an ambitious itinerary, since it linked the place Fontette with the cours National (two recent urban spaces, one of them brand new),[58] between which it took in some of the old quarters. To some extent circumstances dictated the itinerary,[59] but its length probably had a different significance: 1 Vendémaire, the festival of the foundation of the Republic, was a festival of unanimity that sought to occupy as large a portion of the city as possible. This would seem to be confirmed by the setting up, on that day, in all the districts, of civic banquets organized by the National Guard, in a democratic determination to "invest" the entire city.

In any case, all these routes stress the overwhelming ceremonial privilege enjoyed by the southwest quarter. Quite unambiguously, the Revolutionary procession chose one city against the other, a low city against a high city, the marsh against the citadel, the meadows against the steep, narrow streets around the abbeys (the marchers were never to know the exhaustion that sanctified the climb up to the church of Saint-Nicolas, which played so great a role in the Whitsunday procession), a lazy city against an active city, turning its back on the docks and streets of the small tradesmen, a spacious, silent city of gardens and monasteries, now leased out, against the noisy, crowded, cut-up city. This choice almost completely precluded any crossing of the city by the north-south axis, which had been the traditional one under the ancien régime: it had been the route taken on the second Sunday in Lent by the procession from Notre-Dame to Saint-Sauveur and that of the octave of Corpus Christi, when the entire city climbed the slopes of the Vaugueux to accompany the pilgrims from the Délivrande, and in the opposite direction, to inaugurate the place Royale, on September 5, 1685. It never occurred to anybody to do other than set out from the Cordeliers and descend to the statue that, said the orator, "should speak for all time": symbolic homage paid by the old city to the new. Very little of this tradition remained in the Revolutionary processions, which in any case showed little interest in venturing into the suburbs: of the thirty-four routes, only ten went beyond the strictly urban boundaries.

To go outside the city was no longer a matter of crossing the fortifications.[60] Although these were related to the ramparts—which, it is true, were crumbling throughout the century and whose dismantling continued throughout the Revolutionary decade[61]—the processions treated the city as an open city. One had to pass the line of the ramparts to go to the cours National: either by taking the recent pont Saint-Louis, which had been opened in the city walls to provide a new entry, or by one of the temporary bridges set up over the ditch and the Orne. There was one crossing that seemed so natural that it was marked by no station, acknowledged by no dramaturgy: at the lowest point in the city, that uncertain Holland where grass and waters merged, was an invitation to a dream of extension, not to a drama of crossing; the consciousness of the city was certainly that of a wide-open town whose defenses had crumbled, even in the imagination.

Yet to go to the cours National, a place of leisure and commerce, was in no way to testify in favor of the inclusion of the suburbs in the festival or for the burgeoning awareness of the urban center. On the contrary, very few processions followed the development of the city along the new roads. Of all the routes it was the most atypical: the only route of the whole series to follow the north-south axis; the only one to skirt the castle; the only one to venture into the narrow streets, the citadel quarter, the kingdom of the "ordinary people"; the only one to cross the old fortifications of the Saint-Julien market; the only one to stop at the place du Civisme— the place Saint-Sauveur—in order to erect a Liberty Tree on the spot formerly occupied by the pillory, and which was also and was still to be the site of the guillotine;[62] again, the only one to make clever use of the space of the place du Civisme, now grafted onto the place Fontette and thus given new depth, for a spectacular scenic ensemble. But many of the topographical oddities of the itinerary are explained if one knows that it was thought up by that *section du Civisme* that comprised the parishes of Saint-Julien, Saint-Sauveur, and Saint-Etienne-le-Vieux. This absolutely unprecedented route, which ignored the contours of the old parishes (they had, it is true, already become rather blurred),[63] was destined to give reality to the arbitrary administrative surgery to which the section owed its existence: a local patriotism that made itself heard, if we are to believe the official reports, which are all unanimous in saying that no procession at Caen had a more festive air than this one.

Apart from this route—and the civic procession of Representative Laplanche, which was affected by the circumstances[64]—there were, in fact, two regular excursions into the suburbs. The first was occasioned by the military festivals: the three Federations of 1790, 1791, and 1792, the Festival of Thanksgiving, and the Festival of Victories of Year IV. All involved the movement of the National Guard, estimated at about five thousand men. All needed space; so the procession left the city, crossed the Orne at its widest point, over the four arches of the pont de Vaucelles, and spread out over the plain of Ifs so that the troops of the battalion could form a square. The military character of the festival, which was evident in its ornamental arrangements,[65] is also apparent in the itinerary chosen: the place de la Révolution, which the procession crossed, was also the site of the barracks, which had recently been given iron railings by a municipality as anxious to exile its soldiers as its sick or mad.[66] But although these festivals certainly had to cross into the suburbs, they did indeed cross them rather than incorporate them: not a single stop was anticipated in Vaucelles. But the authorities could depend on the deployment of troops to contain any suburban hotheads.

The second occasion in which the suburbs were crossed was for the Festival of Agriculture. In Year V the procession took the route of the Federations toward Vaucelles. In Years IV, VI, and VII the organizers of this festival chose an east-west axis, a choice that may be explained by the ease of contact between town and country afforded in that direction. So it was toward the end of the rue de Bayeux, around the carrefour Dame Ozenne, that the celebrants moved in order to reach the fields of Saint-Michel, the traditional site of the September onion fair. This excursion outside the urban space seems to have been necessitated by the very arrangement of the ceremony, which made it incumbent upon the chairman of the local administration and the general commanding the troops to trace a real furrow, with a real plough, observed by real ploughmen. But since the town itself was not lacking in gardens and even fields where such a scene might be mounted, we may conclude that there was some other reason for crossing the ambiguous space of the suburbs. The important thing was precisely to cross the *octroi* barrier, the point at which dues were levied on goods entering the city: it was this point that really seemed to separate town from country. The crossing of the *octroi,* which led out into the open ground of the flat country, was felt as the true city boundary: this "boundary" festival demonstrated this better than any other.

But the existence of these escapades outside the urban space are not enough to convince us that any real importance was attached to the *faubourgs.* Indeed, the outer suburbs had been no better treated under the ancien régime.[67] During the great Caen procession of Whitsunday, the municipal council stopped at Saint-Etienne to get its breath back and did not follow the procession into the hilly suburb of Saint-Nicolas; from 1762 onward, certain of the politically rebellious guilds also refused to go any farther. But, theoretically, one might have expected the Revolutionary processions to show more gratitude to the enthusiastic inhabitants of Saint-Julien and Vaucelles (especially as the first days of the Revolution had aroused them to festive exuberance: on June 28, 1789, the whole of Vaucelles set about decorating a triangular pyramid erected in Necker's honor with garlands of oak, roses, and cornflowers).

This lack of concern for the outskirts and this definite preference for the southwest quarter of the urban space marks out a clear pattern of choices and rejections, of sacred and profane. Among the places most obviously neglected by the festival was the castle, which throughout the century had been the terminus of those New Year's processions in which the city presented its compliments to the Hôtel de Ville and to the castle, with, from 1760 onward, a detour via the Hôtel de l'Intendance. Perhaps the castle no longer enjoyed such an imperious presence in this eighteenth-century city, where even the military engineers were constantly battling to repair its walls, and where a flood of heterogeneous constructions were laying siege to its moat. Yet the castle still dominated the urban space: wherever one looked, wherever one walked, one could not be unaware of its presence. And it still had the force of a symbol, as was seen during the disturbances of July–August 1789 and November 1791, when the festival took an ugly turn and troops from the suburbs set out to storm the citadel in search of arms and blood. Despite this (or perhaps because of it), it was ignored by the ceremonial itineraries: nothing in the festival reminded one of the castle, except the sound of artillery salvos fired from its walls to announce a holiday. This apart, the Revolutionary procession deliberately turned its back on the seat of public power.

Other well-known landmarks were also ignored, such as the abbeys, especially the Abbaye aux Dames, which had been turned into a hay barn and which no procession ever came near, though, it is true, the Saint-Gilles suburb was not easily linked to the city. The Abbaye aux Hommes had its brief moment of glory when, in June and July of Year II, it was chosen as the Temple of the Supreme Being. It was obviously for the spacious proportions of its eleventh-century nave that it was chosen for the final stage of ceremonies, for which a large crowd of people was expected—the funeral service for Mirabeau, when the congregation even spilled over into the square in front of the church, or the celebrations of Campo-Formio, when the high altar was camouflaged behind a battery of tricolor flags—and the festive crowd probably had little sense of the religious character of the place.

Lastly, the procession ignored most of the churches, including, it goes without saying, those of the suburbs, but also Saint-Julien, which was merely skirted by the sectional processions, and Saint-Nicolas, where the now abandoned Whitsunday procession used to end. Many of the processions passed the leaning tower and portal of Saint-Jean, situated on the only street in the city that could boast a width of eight meters. But the processions never stopped there. Yet, under the ancien régime, the parvis Saint-Jean had been the assembly point of the militia, and in the city it played a symbolic role almost equivalent to that of the castle. In November 1791 it was attacked by the people of Vaucelles, indignant that a priest who had refused to take the oath of allegiance was allowed to say mass at Saint-Jean, and was subjected to a symbolic occupation.

In fact, the Revolutionary procession made use of only two of the city's holy places. First, there was the church of Saint-Pierre, with its thirty-meter-wide parvis, which throughout the century had been increasingly cleared of the buildings that encumbered it, and whose convenience had already been pointed out by Huet.[68] There the funeral service for Louis XV took place and the festivities for the coronation of Louis XVI (not, interestingly, in the place Royale). There, throughout the century, bonfires were lighted;[69] there the most senior of the magistrates lighted a hundred faggots. The Revolution preserved the ceremonial function of the parvis: there it set up all its bonfires, which now burned not only faggots but also royal regalia and saints' statues, and it brought into the church, remodeled with a copious supply of obelisks and antique medallions, its most solemn processions, such as that marking the king's death. The second holy place to be used by the Revolutionary festivals was the Jesuit church, in the then still-rural district on the banks of the Odon. There, for topographical and aesthetic reasons—it offered "views" on all sides— the people's club chose to meet. In the opinion of the commune council, it was "one of the finest monuments in the city." There, in that architecture of Catholic reconquest, under the wooden baldachin, dripping with angels and cherubs, the people's club sat and issued its decrees, and from there the processions that marked Year II set off.

On the whole, therefore, the festival erased the religious symbols from the city. This was not entirely an innovation; it had simply radicalized an undertaking that had begun with the urbanism of the Enlightenment. In the name of practicality, the city lost the Belle-Croix in the rue Ecuyère, despite the protests of the parish priest of Saint-Etienne. These motives had not disappeared from Revolutionary ambitions but had been given the extra support of ideological reasons. Hence, that vast undertaking of erasure, which was not made up for by any building, by the Revolution, of its own symbolic objects: the artificial mountain that concealed Saint-Sauveur, the Liberty Tree put in the place of the pillory, the enribboned mast that, in the place Royale, replaced the statue. Not that the symbolic marking-out was not thorough: in all, the squares and crossroads of Caen were decorated with thirty-one Liberty Trees during the Revolutionary decade. But of all those trees, and apart from the two already mentioned, only the poplar at the pont de la Liberté and the holm oak in the place des Casernes seemed worthy stations for the processions or even for the simplest dramatization. As so often happened, once the Revolutionary imagination had brought forth its monuments, it was not very sure what to do with them.

Those places where the Revolutionary procession did see fit to halt were all new: the place Fontette, which, when the Revolution broke out, had only just assumed its present appearance, with the construction of a brand new Palais de Justice, made the more expressive by a square pedestal supporting columns in the neoclassical manner.[70] The place Royale had been ignored by the traditional processions, in part on account of its distance from the main thoroughfares, but perhaps also because it was rather unimpressive.[71] (This fact aided its appropriation by the Revolution: once the statue of the king had been removed, on July 3, 1791, and replaced by the tricolor mast and the altar of the fatherland—or given an even more dramatic focal point in the form of a pyramid containing a tomb, as for the funeral celebration of a wax effigy of Hoche—the space lost all monarchical character.)[72] Lastly, there was the cours National, which was particularly well suited to festivities.[73] True, the place was traditionally given over to recreation and leisure: according to Huet, the nobility "strolled up and down there in summer."[74] And it was there, for instance, that in September 1725 the fireworks display was held to celebrate the marriage of Marie of Poland. But to these reasons, deriving from custom, one must add those that sprang from the immediately spectacular character of the place. It was the most highly praised spot in Caen, with, beyond the Orne, the verdant island caught in the arms of the river between the city and the pont de Vaucelles. It was the point beyond which the engineers of the Ponts et Chaussées dreamed of expanding the city, and it was there that the festival exploited the obviously aquatic character of the urban site, the division of the Orne into three arms and the serpentine course of the "Noés," the tributaries of the Odon, into the meadowland: for August 10 and 1 Vendémiaire, those fine-weather festivals, mock naval combats, jousting on the longboats, and swimming competitions gave the spectacle an additional dimension.

In the cours National the privileged spot was the angle formed by the *petit cours* and the *grand cours*. Sometimes this was the spot to which the eye was drawn. There was erected the altar of the Festival of the Supreme Being, where mothers held their babies up to heaven; there too, for the Festival of Liberty in Year IV, the royal throne, then the triumviral throne on which an effigy of Robespierre was seated, attracted all eyes. In Year V this theatrical prop was moved, for the sake of both the view and the institutionalization of the ceremony. The thrones were then placed in the meadow, and the angle of the two *cours* became the focal point. It became the fulcrum for the temporary amphitheater that supported the authorities: a place for spectacle, made official in Year VII by the setting up of a permanent circus supporting an altar, for which the debris from the military stores, which had been kept at the other side of the river, was used.

It is easy enough to see why the cours National arranged in this way was increasingly used as the arrival point for processions and even as the place where everybody would go to watch the spectacle—a mock battle or a fireworks display—without joining any procession. In doing so, one obviously lost the sacral charge of the procession, but what was gained was the specialization of a district as a leisure district, defined in terms of aesthetics and convenience. It was more a question of the festival's carving out a new space for itself than one of trying to transform an old space.

At Caen, the urban voluntarism of the men of the Revolution was successfully implemented in the festivals. Old Caen may still have had those itineraries: the place du Pilori could still be glimpsed beneath the guillotine. The parvis Saint-Pierre was still lit up by the flames of bonfires. But if the celebrations took the old routes, it was only out of inertia. In fact, the organizers made an effort not to use the old routes, and for the most part they succeeded. The festival that they invented erased memories, including those of the Revolutionary decade. So the itineraries ignored the castle, which had held Prieur and Romme, the market, and the church parvis, where riots had once erupted, the more salubrious part of the Ile Saint-Jean, which had sheltered the Girondins during the federalist episode. They took little notice of the suburbs, where discontent was always rumbling just below the surface. The festival had succeeded in putting Revolutionary history in parentheses and in providing itself with those *dégagements,* those "open" spaces, so often dreamed of by town dwellers. This is a word that may be understood in many different ways.

The Resistance of Paris

Was it so easy everywhere to avoid the old associations of places? Was it easy in Paris, where the Revolutionary festival intersected at every moment with Revolutionary history itself?

It was, of course, as at Caen, the firm intention of the organizers that it should be. They wanted to treat Paris, like Caen, as an open space, penetrable on every side, so the processions usually took the routes made possible by the urban development of the classical period: the cours de Vincennes, the cours la Reine, the new bridges (the pont de la Concorde, an essential link between the itineraries on the Left Bank and those on the Right Bank, had only just been completed), the new boulevards, which until recently had been no more than ramparts, were now, with their tall trees, promoted to quite different purposes. Some festivals kept to this open space, which had hardly been touched by urbanization: in Thermidor, Year VI, pictures and statues from Italy, bears from Berne, and dromedaries proceeded through the English-style gardens and past tasteful houses that adorned the southern boulevards and did not venture beyond. Some festivals, such as the funeral celebrations for Lazowski, organized by the Commune, set out from the Hôtel-de-Ville or plunged, for circumstantial reasons, such as in the pantheonization of Mirabeau, which included a mass at Saint-Eustache, into the narrow streets around Les Halles. Yet, generally speaking, the organizers had no wish to go over the itineraries of the old historic Paris, or the new itineraries associated with riot.

This is clear from the fact that, except for the pantheonizations, which necessitated a different route, the geographical locus of the procession was the place Louis XV; but the place Louis XV was then felt, even by those who were fond of its architecture, to be outside Paris. When the Chevalier de Mopinot was looking for the most convenient place for the monument that was "to convey to future races the time of the happy Revolution," he preferred the place des Victoires, the true center of commercial and residential Paris, on the boundary between the old quarters and the new. Indeed, the festivals of the ancien régime, especially the aerostatic ones, had often chosen it as their starting point. The Revolutionary processions—except for two[75]—ignored the place des Victoires. This was because they were concerned less with a geographical than with a metaphysical center, one that, despite its eccentricity, included the Champ-de-Mars, which, thanks to the Federation, had become the true national center.

This classic place for the termination of the procession was almost unknown to the Parisians, who had only recently learned how to get there. For them it was "country" and lent itself so well to ceremonial requirements only because it was precisely a "desert," susceptible to any transfiguration. Michelet, who saw the Champ-de-Mars as the Revolution's true legacy to Parisian urbanism, was well aware of this: "Whereas the empire has its column and the monarchy the Louvre, the Revolution has as its monument . . . a void. Its monument is sand, as flat as Arabia . . . A tumulus on the right and a tumulus on the left, like those that Gaul erected, obscure and dubious witnesses of the memory of heroes."[76]

Yet the processions did skirt the great architectural setting of the classical city. The funeral for Lazowski passed the Louvre. The Republican Reunion and the Festival of the Supreme Being set up their plaster architecture in front of Mansart's and Gabriel's palaces. But in doing so, they ignored them. The works of the great architects were never integrated into the ephemeral constructions of the festival. They were never themselves subjected to a transfiguration that might bring them, by metamorphosing them, into the festival. Sometimes the arrangements of the festival tended even to reduce awareness of the monarchical city: for the Festival of the Supreme Being, the amphitheater at the center of which the monster Atheism would go up in flames was backed by the Pavilion of Unity, which concealed it; and groups of trees masked the buildings of the courtyard of the National Palace. For the festival given in honor of the citizens who had died at the siege of Nancy, Gabriel's facade was hidden by a gallery erected in front of it, so that the spectators had their backs to it as they observed the altar of the fatherland, the pyramids, and the triumphal arch placed at the other end of the field. Since the festival could not compete with the great architectural style of the city, it set out to efface it.

It did so not by trying to rival its creations but by negating them to the advantage of the countryside. Even the Bastille, converted by Palloy into a ballroom beneath the trees and on the site of which, after innumerable projects had been submitted, any attempt to erect another building was abandoned (again the consolation offered was that an empty space was more eloquent), lost its capacity to evoke any other images than those associated with the countryside. For the triumph of Voltaire, it becomes Julie's Elysium: "From beneath the stones emerged laurels, rose, myrtles, and various shrubs."[77] Not only the Bastille but the entire city attempted a vegetal metamorphosis for the festival. Festoons, garlands, and branches were set up in front of every door and completed the effacement of the urban: "It was as if Paris had been turned into a huge, beautiful orchard." This simulated countryside had the advantage over the real countryside of excluding mystery: the forest, hastily erected on the Champ-de-Mars for the funeral and in which Bonnier and Roberjot were buried, completely banished the image of the labyrinth. It presented no shady mass: opened up by paths, penetrable on every side, it could be walked through in perfect safety. But such a setting could be imagined anywhere; any town could erect one. Again one senses that such projects were in no way peculiar to Paris.

Yet Paris resisted. Against an ideally abstract space, the city opposed the meanness of definite proportions,[78] the narrowness of the streets,[79] the suspect reputation of certain places,[80] all had associations bequeathed by history. It also deprived the festival of the crowds without which one was left with thin processions of officials and a mere sprinkling of spectators, forced by the nature of things to take less ambitious routes, sometimes even to be lost from sight. Lastly, whatever the organizers did, the festive city had been overthrown by the Revolution. There was something about it that militated against the reasonable, considered initiative of human wills; whatever route was taken, one now came up against an unconscious memory of riot. The route from the Champ-de-Mars has been tried by the people of July 13, 1789, but with a certain timidity: on that day, the crowd did not dare to cross the moats. Next day, they set out again with greater assurance and did so. A year later, at the Federation, that route was taken, symbolically, by the whole of France. Streets and squares were peopled with ghosts, saturated with images. How could one avoid translating that history into images, brilliant or gloomy, in the programs? Could Voltaire's chariot not stop in the square where the prison that once held him stood? Where was Lazowski to be buried if not on the place du Carrousel, where the cannon of August 10 had been set up? Even those places that the maps of the festivals describe so often as empty or treat ideally as deserts resist this neutralization. Yet the Champ-de-Mars, a pure artifact of the Revolution, was less vacant than the arrangements of the festivals suggest, as Michelet saw clearly. "Even here," declared Robespierre, "on this altar, our feet cannot tread a spot that is not soiled with innocent blood."[81] And on 26 Thermidor, Year VII, Sieyès still remembered it: "It was here, it was on this very spot that hoardes of barbarians, wild, bloodthirsty strangers, met."[82] The Revolution had turned this Arcadian field into a "field of death." So, whether its organizers liked it or not, the festival encountered the tragic side of the Revolution and had to purge itself of it.

Hence the hesitation noticeable in so many projects. Was following in the footsteps of the gloom-ridden Revolution necessarily to efface it? Was it not, on the contrary, to deepen its imprint still further? Sometimes that is what one expected, and it was certainly what Portiez understood when, on 20 Messidor, Year III, he maintained that the festival ought to be celebrated "on this very spot"—on the very spot, that is to say, of the tribune of the Convention, "red with blood," and on the place du Carrousel, where the discontents of Germinal and Prairial had congregated. But sometimes, too, giving in to the frantic desire to forget that imbued the programs (even the most ambitious, like Robespierre's, in Year II), the organizers tried to keep the processions away from the dark places of Revolutionary history, so that the festival would emerge as the obverse of riot. Desired, sometimes even embodied, as in the Festival of the Supreme Being, this spatial solution could not fail, in a city overdetermined by the Revolution, to lack clarity. On 9 Thermidor, Year IV, the route of the Festival of Liberty, following a still very classic path (it began at the Bastille and ended at the Champ-de-Mars), avoided the place de la Révolution but not the place du Carrousel, where the guillotine was eventually set up.

Was this not to admit that there were certain places that could not be purged of their past? This, in any case, was how the place de la Révolution was regarded. The two illustrious heads that fell there fell also, as we know, into the amnesia that followed Thermidor. The Thermidorian conformists certainly wanted to remember the monarchy (whose emblems were to be burned at the place du Carrousel), but not Louis (and therefore they avoided the place de la Révolution); the "decemviral tyranny" (whose emblems were to be burned at the Champ-de-Mars, in the places associated with Robespierre's triumph), but not Maximilien Robespierre. Indeed, this was no more than the culmination of a retreat that had been begun much earlier. The meeting between the festive Convention and the guillotine occurred once, by chance, on January 21, 1794. The repugnance expressed the next day in the speech of Bourdon de l'Oise—as we know, he forced through a decision, that the Convention should never go to festivals whose organization and policing it had not itself ordered— was a sign of the times; it heralded the divorce between the festival and violence. Whereas the guillotine moved eastward (though it returned to the place de la Révolution for the exemplary execution of Robespierre) and was set up first at the place Saint-Antoine, then at the place du Trône Renversé (the present place de la Nation), the festival continued to move westward. Even the great Montagnard festivals, with the exception of the Festival of Republican Reunion, abandoned the Bastille and set out from the Tuileries for the Champ-de-Mars. Thus began the superstitious taboo that was soon to affect the place de la Révolution, and which so many orators tried to exorcise in an interminable series of questions: What could be done to wash away this stain? Are we to set up on the square a monument to Concord, which would be both expiatory and reconciling and which would attract peaceful citizens? Should it be left as an open space? The act of exorcism was sometimes entrusted to a few solemn words: Portiez suggested that a statement be read in the square declaring that it would never again be a place of execution. In fact, the Convention ordered this to be done but never actually did it: it postponed the proclamation. Nevertheless, the place de la Révolution lost its name shortly afterward. All these discussions show, in any case, that the city remembered at the festival that the square was a place of gloomy fascination and avoided it.

What all this illustrates is the unexpected eruption of history into the utopian dream. Utopia acknowledges history only in its mythical form—the founding event, whose meaning is periodically taken up in the celebrations. The Revolutionary celebration would soon no longer be felt as the founding event as such: the time of the Revolution passed very quickly, leaving, as Balzac was very well aware, huge gaps between the events.[83] Seen through the events that followed and disfigured it, the Revolutionary baptism seemed so far off! In speeches, of course, it is easy enough to get around the difficulty caused by the density of history: one can pretend that the meaning of August 10 was simply to fulfill July 14. One may even baptize the Tuileries "Bastille"—the "Bastille of August 10" or the "Bastille of '92"—thus homogenizing both time and space. But this trick is much more difficult to implement in festival programs. A decision must be made whether to celebrate the festival here or there, and certain places are constantly shifting meaning: the arcades of the Louvre; the place du Carrousel, where Commune and Convention fought for power; the Palais-Royal, which, because it had become the chosen meeting place of the Royalists, had lost its associations with the first glorious Revolutionary summer; the Invalides, where a crushed federalism made even the word *federation* suspect;[84] and, of course, the place de la Révolution.

The Space-Time of the Revolution

There is an obvious failure here, for as good sons of the Enlightenment, the festival organizers saw space and time as an occasion of the same discovery. The festival of their dreams ought to make the ceremonial space the equivalent of the time of the Revolution. But, despite all their efforts, things turned out differently.

The procession is an art of time as well as space: it denies simultaneity;[85] sometimes it was expected to transform history into space. Take, for instance, the views of Citizen Gence on the Marat festival.[86] It was an unhappy project, but one whose arrangements are all the more interesting in that, going beyond a particular festival, they are offered as a theory of festivals in general and processions in particular. The whole text is a plea for mobility. Convinced, like his century as a whole, that "one should strike the soul above all through the eyes, the most powerful of our organs," Citizen Gence considered that one should "present, throughout the course of the procession, as in a tableau vivant, all the principal events in the life of a famous man, retracing them by means of inscriptions and characteristic emblems in the various, successive groups." The technical and pedagogical considerations proliferate, all stemming from the doctrine of sensualism and intended to turn the procession into a well-made visual language. Each group, insofar as it expresses a different idea, insofar as it should be grasped separately, must be carefully isolated. But it should not be too isolated either, if the sense of the whole is not to be dissipated. The ideal would be "neither to disperse objects nor to merge them together," "neither to isolate nor to cross the sensations and ideas of the various groups." Lastly, it is a good thing that the movement of the procession should be "uniform and slow rather than hasty," so that the eye has time to "take in the tableaus" and, consequently, to be imbued with them and to retain the lessons that they have to give.

But, concerning the arrangements for the Marat festival, it is doubtful whether this movement would be able to bring out a sense of development and avoid mere succession. What the procession distributes in space is not at all, contrary to what Gence expects, the events of Marat's life, unfolded according to the order of a genesis, but legendary events in isolation, a mere carving-up that conveys no sense of depth. What the spectator of the "apotheosis" was to see before him was a "group depicting Marat's public virtues." On the chariot supporting them would be shown, in a gesture prudently duplicated by a maxim, Marat attacking the despot's throne, denouncing the perfidious generals, or devoting himself to study. Then would follow "the group of private Virtues," demonstrating the acts of piety and generosity of the Friend of the People in everyday life. Then came the chariot of Rewards, bearing the crowns and tributes that Marat's virtues merited. Last came the chariot of Examples: these consisted of age groups, each taking an example from Marat's life and adapting it to its role and capacities. In case one were still in any doubt, this closing of the procession with age groups, which, in their sempiternal litany, embodied a repetitive time, would finally convince one that the Marat procession was merely a legendary, exemplary inventory, in which the relationship between the various groups was merely one of contiguity. It was an architect's eye, not that of a theatrical director, that presided over the conception of what was a frieze rather than a procession. The time that was integrated into it was a time of pedagogy: indispensable if one were to grasp the various fragments of the representation, but without any relation to what was being represented. The successive order is at most that of a reading.

Things become even more complicated when, instead of the man, who, especially after his death, may always be grasped and fixed in a lengendary inscription, the subject of the festival is the Revolution itself. Of all the programs, the one in which may be seen the greatest concern to cross the space of Paris and the time of the Revolution is David's proposal for the festival of August 10, 1793.[87] Indeed, this is precisely how Michelet describes that festival: "A history in five acts of the Revolution," recounted to the Parisians in five successive places: the Bastille, the Poissonnière crossroads, the place de la Révolution, the Invalides, and the Champ-de-Mars.

The beginning and end of the story are obligatory borrowings from Revolutionary rhetoric. The procession set out from the Bastille, then returned to a state of nature, a choice that served both to conceal and to embody the meaning of the event: it concealed the event because nothing remained of the historical July 14 except those inscriptions that "at intervals" mentioned it; but it symbolically embodied the event because the vacant place, whose "wealth will be drawn from nature," served for the enactment of the great Revolutionary baptism. The water that flowed from the "fecund breasts" of the colossal statue, drunk from the same goblet by the envoys of the primary assemblies, promised regeneration. The return to origins was made quite explicit on the day of the festival in the speech delivered by Hérault de Séchelles, who took up David's words: "The eternal will see men once more equal and brothers, as they were when they left his divine hands." Symmetrically, the Champ-de-Mars, the terminus of the procession, also indicated the terminus of the Revolution. The arrival of the groups represented the arrival of the Revolution in harbor. Quite unequivocal arrangements confirm this voluntarist negation of time, which deliberately ignored the ability of the Revolution to engender new events: the offerings on the altar, the oath, the link of the "bundle" representing the départements, the laying of the ark of the Constitution under the safeguard of the people. The various groups had to pass under a portico, to which, again, "Nature alone will contribute": concealed behind thick foliage, linked by a tricolor garland supporting a level, they were precisely two "termini."

But between this conventional beginning and end, with which many of the programs contented themselves, David's project at least had the originality and interest of attempting to use Revolutionary history. With three significant episodes, three stations to embody them, and different scenic means to express them, it was an abridged version of the history of the Revolution, and a very revealing one. After the dateless baptism celebrated at the Bastille, David kept October 5 and 6, 1789—a very odd choice, and the only one, it seems, in the history of the festivals of the Revolution. But where? At the Poissonnière crossroads, where the heroines of October 5 and 6 were never seen. The alteration in space reveals the arbitrary nature of all the scenic arrangements, and this lack of realism was so strongly felt by contemporaries that there was an endless flow of requests to move the triumphal arch that had been set up there to a more appropriate place, on the grounds that the site did not call for it and that the choice of a monument lacked originality. Yet David's project was not entirely devoid of realism: the heroines of October 5 and 6 were to be "seated on cannon, as they were at the time." But could the spectators see them, despite the branches that they held and the trophies, which David regarded as "unequivocal," as those brought back by the king from Versailles? Judging from the newspapers of the time, one may doubt it. On the very day of the celebration, even the speech of Hérault de Séchelles at the Poissonnière crossroads did nothing to remove the uncertainty: it consisted of an invocation to liberty and some utopian verses on the role of women in giving birth to heroes. The task of recounting the story was left to the inscriptions on the triumphal arch: the spectacle, empty of history, yet again relegated it to writing.

From the boulevard Poissonnière to the place de la Révolution, where August 10 was to be celebrated, the procession crossed a space that symbolized three years of history. The new event was very clearly marked by David in terms that stressed the effort in linking the date to the place. "Citizens, here we are at the immortal and imperishable day of August

10." The place where the procession had in fact arrived was the place de la Révolution. It too was an arbitrary choice; the place du Carrousel would have been more suitable. But this was merely because August 10, in Revolutionary memory, was at one with January 21. The physical disappearance of the king was alone capable of effecting his social disappearance, and this gives some impression of the emotional wrench of January 21. Moreover, this is precisely how David justifies his spatial choice: "It is at the place where the tyrant died that it should be celebrated." On the day of the festival, Hérault de Séchelles, exposing the memory of the tyrant to public execration, as David's program intended, went further: "Here the ax of the Law struck the tyrant." Yet here nothing of the king was to be seen, and in his place, or, to be more precise, in the place occupied by the statue of Louis XV, was a Liberty, already peacefully installed among her foliage. Thus there reappeared, opposite Gabriel's palace, the "wood" that Diderot would have liked to have kept if "it had fallen to him to redesign the place Louis XV on the same spot." The vegetal exuberance canceled out the memories of the scaffold, and the king, or rather monarchy, had to be sought elsewhere, namely in those regalia by now so well used by the festivals of the Revolution: scepters, parchments, crowns, which, according to the now established dramaturgy, were burned in "expiatory sacrifice," as thousands of birds rose up in a great flight of streamers bearing to the heavens "a few articles from the Rights of Man," a happy sight that deflected the spectator's eyes from the gloomy center of Revolutionary history.

At the Invalides we come to another space and time abandoned by David to insignificance. It was this place that had been chosen, quite arbitrarily, to celebrate the final high point of the Revolution, the last convulsion before it could celebrate its closure: the defeat of federalism. It was in this last reference that, not without obvious reasons, the largest gap appears between the festival arrangements and historical reality. What did one see at the Invalides? A colossal plaster Hercules (the French people) trampling underfoot a Hydra (ambitious federalism), emerging from the marsh. How did contemporaries decipher this allegory? (The *Journal de la Société républicaine des arts* relates their mocking incomprehension.) Hérault de Séchelles went no further than to say: "French people, this giant, whose powerful hand gathers together the départements and holds them in a single bundle, is you. This monster is federalism." Nothing, however, was said about May 31.

Of all the festival programs, this one was probably most careful to find room for the time of the Revolution. But the means used show what was made of it: the choice of an arbitrary place, in most instances; the allegorical character of the scenic arrangements;[88] the absence of detail about events (there was scarcely any mention of what was being commemorated and why); an indifference to the reputation of the event chosen; the statism of everything (the procession filed past the powerful but frozen gesture of Hercules destroying Federalism); the recourse, in those places where something did happen, to the crude dramaturgy of disappearance and appearance. Between the stations of the processions, any link between the events represented was lost. Furthermore, what the stations did represent were events that were scarcely new and surprising, thus preventing the distance between the stations from suggesting a genealogy. David reduced history to chronology and in doing so abandoned the intelligibility of a genesis. Indeed, he was so well aware of this that he wanted to build "a vast theater in which the principal events of the Revolution would be represented in pantomime." This proposal was almost entirely abandoned by the actual festival,[89] but it shows the extent to which David's procession had abandoned any attempt to explain what was happening: this program bears the signs of the time, but not its meanings.

To what may we attribute this failure? Not so much to the treatment of space—where the Revolutionary festival, as we have seen, often shows high audacity—as to the difficulty of making this space say something about the Revolution itself. What the organizers did not manage to imagine were episodes with a causal connection. For them these events were never more than repetitions of the founding event and were powerless to alter the Great Invariable figure of the Revolution. It was Revolutionary time that was the obstacle. Ideally, the Revolution should proliferate; it could not be transformed.

· VII ·

The Festival and Time

TIME was not only the formal framework within which the Revolution took place; it was also the raw material on which it obstinately worked. One has only to consider those overflowing boxes of documents expatiating on the question of the arrangement of time. Always described as "great," this Republican undertaking was indeed so if the effort that it must have cost to produce these documents is anything to go by. It was necessary to imagine a new apportionment of leisure and work, to discover the resistance of men for whom the old week continued to distribute work and the days as before (hence a flood of police documents—charges, prosecutions, penalties—on two linked offenses: the refusal to work on Sunday and the refusal to celebrate the *décadi*).[1] The traditional festivals, the "times found in holy Scripture," had to be abolished; hence, interminable controversies arose with those who stuck to them, those whose job it was to date documents—lawyers, notaries, and printers, who could not sell their almanacs unless they included those solemnities beloved of the "base multitude."[2] The new time had to be marked by the rhythm of the Republican festivals; hence the carping correspondence of commissioners with municipal officers, who, lacking men, money, and sometimes conviction, fell short of what was expected of them. To the flood of documents produced by this determination to create a Republican time, should be added the inexhaustible, troublesome literature born of the thorny problem of coordinating the calendars and the variations in local practice, for some priests resigned themselves to moving their own ceremonies to the *décadi,* while those in neighboring cantons were determined not to do so. This distortion was an endless source of quarrels and was all the more ironic in that the changes in the calendar were presented as, and felt to be, a simplification.

Is this evidence of a defeat? Certainly. But it is also, on the part of the men of the Revolution, evidence of a coherent determination. So, for the moment, let us examine not the results of the undertaking but its powerful motives. Those men were very well aware of the irrational hold that the calendar had over people's minds; for them, the calendar was a sort of talisman. In this sense, as Joseph de Maistre saw very clearly, the new calendar was a "conjuration." Both Romme and Fabre d'Eglantine, convinced that inclusion in the calendar "consecrated," wanted to oppose one talisman with another. They were anxious reformers for whom everything still remained to be done. The first thing to be done was to manifest the discontinuity brought about by the Revolution in the flow of time, to signify, quite unequivocally, that the era of the Republic was no longer the era of kings, and to mark this absolute beginning. The next stage was to divide time up with new festivals: this required choosing objects or events worthy of being celebrated. Lastly, they had to invent a guarantee against unforeseeable change and therefore to find a means, against time, of making the Revolution eternal. The festival lay at the heart of all these enterprises: it began, divided up, commemorated, and closed. It did so with unequal success.

Beginning

The legislator's first task was to begin the Republican era with a festival, thus placing the new time beyond dispute and showing that history derived from a founding act. It was necessary to have "a fixed point to which all other events might henceforth be related."[3] There was hardly any dispute as to the need for this. Of course, in the Committee of Public Instruction, there was a moment when good reasons were presented why no new beginning should be made: by making all the calculations backwards, by changing all the names, one might make the old era accord with the rhythm of Republican time. But however attractive this recovery of the past might have seemed to men anxious to make evil serve good, "retrograde computation" did not prevail against the magic virtue of a fresh beginning, against the imperious need to stress a break, against the conviction that one was living through an exceptional history: the time opened up by the Revolution seemed new, not only in the way it was broken up but almost in its very texture. In such circumstances, how could one imagine that one could move at a steady pace from old time to new time? The Convention thought that this was hardly worth arguing over, especially as a particular circumstance dictated the date and the celebration. As Romme reminded the Convention, there are two ways of beginning the year: it may begin either with a season or with a historical event.[4] But the Republican reformers were spared this uncertainty, for it was their own history that had named the season. There was no need to argue for very long over the respective merits of equinox and solstice: the Republic had been declared on the precise day of the autumnal equinox. Romme's report stresses this miraculous simultaneity over and over again: "on that very day," the sun illuminated both poles at once and the flame of liberty illuminated the French nation.[5] "On that very day," the sun moved from one hemisphere to the other and the people from monarchical government to Republican government. Romme lists the significant co-incidences that emerged from this encounter between the history of men and that of the stars. Furthermore, autumn is the season of blessed abundance; even the Egyptians celebrated the emergence of the earth out of chaos at that time.[6] In short, the argument was so overwhelming that Romme believed that the future was assured: this inaugural festival would be one of the most widely celebrated by future generations.

Indeed, this explains the particular place occupied in the system of Republican festivals by that of 1 Vendémiaire. For the legislators, 1 Vendémiaire was, like July 14, a beginning. But whereas July 14 opened up a stormy history, 1 Vendémiaire inaugurated a natural history.[7] It was the day in the Republican year to which no one doubted that the customs of the old January 1 would be transferred; it consecrated the social regeneration of the French people, but also promised the peaceful regularity of the movements of the stars in the course of the Republic. This hope is apparent in the details of the celebration. The symbolism of 1 Vendémiaire was purposely "celestial": in the processions, the chariots of the sun followed the chariots of the seasons, while the aerostats rose into the air as the sun entered the sign of Libra.

The municipal administration at Aurillac, in the Cantal, imagined the following astonishing procession:

> Then will appear a superb, shining chariot drawn by twelve horses; this will be the chariot of the sun; before it will be the signs of the zodiac and the hours according to their new division; beside it will walk young citizenesses, dressed in white, who will represent the hours of the day, while young citizenesses dressed in white and veiled in black will represent the hours of the night; on the chariot will be seen the still slumbering genius of France covered with a veil covered with fleur-de-lys and making simple movements from time to time; the people's magistrates will lead

the march, as a sign of their vigilance; they will be divided into sections like the city; sexes and age groups will be separated; children and women will be veiled as a sign of their still imperfect awakening.

That morning of pacified history brought together, therefore, two legalities, one natural, the other historical, even juridical. To the latter were added the commemorations of the Directoire, which linked the festival of 1 Vendémiaire not only with the establishment of the Republic but also with the acceptance of the Constitution of Year III, a new beginning that overlay the old and redoubled the sacred nature of the Republican birth. Stress was laid on "the perfect agreement existing in the history of the French Revolution between the time of the foundation of the Republic and that of the acceptance of the Constitution[8]—and the possibility, therefore, of celebrating on 1 Vendémiaire two anniversaries in one.[9] Is it possible to read into these precautions, this piling up of reasons, a desperate sense that the beginning can never be justified too much? How can one fail to think this when one reads all these declarations, in which nature is summoned to the aid of history? Certainly the Revolutionary calendar would be the work of men, but of enlightened men, men following "the natural course of things." This, no doubt, tended to efface the artificiality of what they were doing, conceal the hand of reformers caught up in too specific a history. What could not be done for the Revolution as a whole! This, as we shall see, was one of the assurances that, against all hope, the Revolutionary celebration tried to implement.

Dividing Up

The calendar and the creation of festivals cannot be separated: there can be no calendar that is not also a calendar of festivals. But the series of festivals, as presented by the traditional calendar, is pure chaos. This observation was not born with the Revolution, as endless complaints throughout the century show. It had long been thought that beneath this disorder was concealed an organizing principle, which had been forgotten in spite of its obvious simplicity: originally the festivals were tied up with the return of solar and lunar phases and were intended to mark the renewal of the seasons. In N. A. Boulanger's book *L'antiquité dévoilée par ses usages,* which was then something of a Bible, the men of the Revolution learned that if, in imagining festivals, they had gone no further than that,

then nothing would have equaled their sober nobility. But according to
Boulanger, that "primitive plan" had long ago been corrupted: "Generally
speaking, it may be said that, for close on two thousand years, the distribution of festivals among every people in the world had been carried out
without taste, without order, without motive, without legislative intention and has been merely a series of encounters between an infinity of
chances and false principles." [10] Of what value is an accumulation of customs that cannot be explained? They must be replaced by more equally
distributed festivals with properly understood motives. These are the high
points that give meaning to ordinary time; they create a sense of time and
order it by regulating the rhythm of social life. It was not, therefore,
simply a narrow, antireligious sentiment that lay behind the new arrangement of the festivals in the calendar. It was rather a desire to clear away
the undergrowth in the forest of customs, for reasons stemming from a
sense of order. *Antiquité dévoilée* condemned Gregory XIII, as severely as
Romme was to do, for a scandalously confused piece of work; was he not
weak enough to accept movable feasts, with their inevitable train of "disordered variations that dishonor our calendar"? What Romme demands,
as firmly as Boulanger, is the establishment of a system of festivals on
simple, constant principles: a clear "ritology."

So, ideally, the important festivals ought to divide the year into equal
portions: natural regularity should be the model for calendar makers. The
Republican planners condemned the week, which "does not divide up
exactly either the month or the year," and the traditional festivals,
whether religious or popular, which jostle one another at certain times of
the year for no apparent reason, then leave long stretches without any
ceremonials. In short, the traditional calendar belonged to the realm of
the bizarre, with all its endless complications for anyone wanting to
decipher it. Nobody believed that it could give man the means of
"recognizing himself distinctly in the course of his life." In the Republican calendar, by contrast, everything—the ternary termination, which
individualized the season, the name that gave the month its particular
color, the ten-part division and regular distribution of festivals throughout the web already laid down—ought to contribute to such an end. [11]

No doubt the tenfold division left unsolved the problem of intercalary
days, which are sometimes five and sometimes six and make the masterpiece look decidedly rickety. No matter; these periods would be stuffed
with festivals. Romme, like Robespierre, resorted to this means to make
that strange, irritating, irregular period stand out from ordinary time.

Fabre d'Eglantine went farther than Romme's project, which he regarded as "cold." And what was he afraid of? That Romme had not sufficiently erased the arbitrary character of that "remnant," that "balance of account." For those days left on account, which indeed spoiled the sense of equality, even more dazzling solemnities were required; hence the search for a collective name and the invention of the rather graceless term *sans-culottides;* hence the idea, with a view to making the end of the year more conspicuous, of devoting that period of festivities to the Republican balance sheet. There would be not more than five days to determine the wealth of the nation. An accumulating wisdom could be expressed in that time by enumerating all that the Republic owed to intelligence[12] (a rather peevish amendment from Robespierre replaced intelligence, that suspect gift, with something more equally distributed—virtue), labor, and noble actions (these did not include, it should be noted, political or military exploits). These five days were to be devoted to distributing awards, which made judgment finally public in this curious Festival of Opinion, which was both "gay and terrible," in which mouths opened and public servants were judged.[13] (In the calendar's opening festivals these five days were represented by the very oldest members of the community, champions who distributed crowns and received the oaths.)[14] So the year came to an end with the judgment that at last brought before the common level those who had been elevated by their functions, created a tabula rasa, and allowed everything to begin again. The complementary days, unsatisfactory as they were, also contributed therefore to a serene "equalization." Is any further proof required? When leap year came around, the sixth day, a surplus of a surplus, was to be devoted to national games. This was to be the festival of festivals. It was to close the four-year period as surely as the year was closed.

The same ambition for order presided, theoretically, over the distribution of the festivals throughout the year. They were expected to form regular knots in the calendar web, to leave between them equal periods of profane time—good periods, not too short.[15] The calendar reform provided an embodiment of that eighteenth-century commonplace—among innumerable examples one might take that of Rouillé d'Orfeuil[16]—that there were too many festivals and that they should be spaced out more evenly. Something of this demand remained in the calendar of Republican festivals that were actually celebrated: 10 Germinal, Youth; 10 Floréal, Spouses; 10 Prairial, Thanksgiving and Victories; 10 Messidor, Agriculture; 10 Fructidor, the Old. All the first-*décadi* festivals—apart from the

Festival of Thanksgiving and Victories, which could be celebrated other than in Prairial—reveal an accord of season and celebration. They all embody an attempt to achieve an annual distribution of festivals that was satisfying and simple.

Why did the system remain incomplete? From spring to autumn, the solemnities did indeed occur regularly: the blank of Thermidor was to be quickly filled by the commemoration, on the ninth and tenth, of the Festival of Liberty. But, on the one hand, the autumn and winter were left fairly empty: there was a long ceremonial dead season. And on the other hand, to the well-distributed fine-weather festivals were added other celebrations, those of July 14, August 10, and 1 Vendémiaire. It was impossible not to celebrate such festivals and was difficult to move them, for a historical festival, as M.-J. Chénier remarked, "cannot reasonably be amalgamated with another and celebrated at a different time from its own."[17] As a result, there was a superabundance of festivals in the summer, and this revived the old complaints of the ancien régime against festivities that emptied the fields of plowmen. The Revolutionary festivals did not succeed in achieving the regular distribution of work and leisure that they had promised.

What impeded, or even prohibited, the fulfilment of this promise was the commemoration of Revolutionary time, which intercepted the festivals of age or season. Nothing shows this better than the text, taken from Romme's project, which claims to relate the entirely new order of the months to a continuous narrative of the Revolution (see Table 1).

Everything in this astonishing comparison is derived from the Revolution, Romme assures us. In order to establish this coherence, Romme is nevertheless forced into incoherence: he begins the year at the seventh month, in the spring, in order to evoke that spring of 1789 when the French felt "the need of regeneration." He keeps the whole story of the Revolution within a single year, which forces him to take some dizzying shortcuts, like that which, from July 14, 1789, rushes on to August 10, 1792: "Wherever one wants to be free, the Bastille falls under the blows of a *Sovereign People.*" In the commentary that Romme adds to his tableau, "The People," a title given to the month between July 19 and August 17, certainly refers to the people of August 10, 1792: three years are therefore being spanned here, and the same people seem, in a single upsurge, to have brought down the Bastille and the king, whose fall seems to belong to July 17, 1789, itself. There is another oddity: the *Réunion,* during the month between April 20 and May 19, was so called because it was then

Table 1. The order of the Republican months, adapted from Romme's project.

Month	Event commemorated
Germinal (March 21–April 19)	The French, exhausted by fourteen centuries of oppression and alarmed by the frightful progress of corruption, of which a court that had for long been criminal was setting the example, felt the need of *Regeneration*.
Floréal (April 20–May 19)	The resources of the court were exhausted. It summoned the French people, but their *Reunion* was their salvation. They appointed representatives, whose courage irritated the tyrant.
Prairial (May 20–June 18)	They were threatened; but they assembled at the *Jeu de Paume*, and under the protection of the people, they swore to save the people from tyranny or perish. This oath echoed throughout France.
Messidor (June 19–July 18)	Everywhere people took up arms; everywhere people wanted to be free. *The Bastille*
Thermidor (July 19–August 17)	fell under the assault of a sovereign and angry *People*. Enemies multiplied, treason flourished, the court plotted, perjured representatives sacrificed the interests of the nation to sordid ends.
Fructidor (August 18–September 21)	But *The Mountain*, ever faithful, became the Olympus of France.
Vendémiaire (September 22–October 21)	Surrounded by the nation, and in its name, the National Convention proclaimed the rights of the people, the Constitution, and the *Republic*.
Brumaire (October 22–November 20)	*Unity*
Frimaire (November 21–December 20)	and *Fraternity*
Nivôse (December 21–January 19)	are the strength of the French; and *Liberty*, by a sovereign act,
Pluviôse (January 20–February 18)	and national *Justice*, which brought down the tyrant's head,
Ventôse (February 19–March 20)	are forever united with holy *Equality*.

that "the French people appoint representatives whose courage irritates the tyrant": this allusion to the States General also becomes, in Romme's commentary, the month "devoted by the Constitutional Act to the primary assemblies." Throughout this work one senses the need for overdetermination: every choice must be capable of being justified several times over, either by a return, in the history of the Revolution, of encounters and coincidences or by harmony with nature. For if Romme tried above all to present "the principal events of the Revolution, either in its end or in its means," he nevertheless did not abandon natural motives. Does not the seventh month, the one that strangely opens this tableau, owe its place to the fact that it is the "first" of the spring and therefore particularly suitable to evoking regeneration? And similarly, the end of the tableau, which is crowded with allegories, shows in "Unity" and "Fraternity" the months when men, "after gathering in the fields all the fruits of the earth, retire under their roofs." It is therefore the peace of late autumn that gives its pictorial equivalent to the establishment of the Republic. What follows in Romme's commentary comfirms this correspondence. In September, people will be able "to enjoy together in brotherhood the benefits of nature and of a good social organization."

One glimpses, therefore, a hesitation in Romme's project. So easy in the ceremonial utopias, the division of time by the Revolutionary festivals—and on this point Romme, Robespierre, and Marie-Joseph Chénier are all the same—always staggers between arithmetical division (theoretically preferable) and a less regular division that takes the great events of the Revolution into account. Consequently, the Revolutionary almanac of the festivals, itself overburdened and unequal, would not be, as Romme dreamed—despite the bucolic connotations with which Fabre d'Eglantine was to endow it, despite the ferns, columbine, and pimpernel—truly suited to "the man of the fields." Was it better suited to the man of the Revolution?

Commemorating

THE REASONS FOR THE COMMEMORATION

One satisfaction was accorded the man of the Revolution from the outset: all the organizers of calendars and festivals agreed on the need to sustain the festival with the memory of the Revolution. Their speeches outdid one another in expounding on the good reasons for the celebration. To commemorate is, to begin with, to overcome ignorance. The festivals would unfold for the children of the Revolution the whole history of the Revolution.[18] Even the adult would find a source of instruction in the commemorative rites.[19] Because it came so soon after the Revolutionary events themselves, this repetition might seem superfluous. But when one looks back, one always discovers with astonishment the incredible proliferation of those few years when memorable events seem to have been telescoped into a brief moment, when "revolutions, the experience and glory of three centuries,"[20] crowded in upon one another. It was not a bad thing, then, to order this proliferation of memories by the festival. Furthermore, the festival was a tangible guarantee against unreality. Throughout the eighteenth century, thinkers from Locke to Hume had maintained that belief must be constantly given new impetus by the force of present impressions; by linking the memory of the great events of the Revolution to periodic spectacles, it was believed that those events could be saved from gradually lapsing into unbelief. Furthermore, by dint of repetition, the sacred, beneficent atmosphere of mythical times could be resuscitated. Through contemplation, recitation, or, better, by a miming of the glorious days that were the Revolution's age of innocence, faith would be rekindled through contact with heroism.[21] By transporting the past into the present, the historical rite conferred the virtues of the former upon the latter. Up until the events known as Brumaire, people constantly expected miracles simply from the evocation of July 14, as if the return to origins was necessarily a new baptism for the citizen.

These reasons provide some explanations while concealing others. If we examine the vocabulary of the commemoration, the purpose of the festival seems purely conservative: to maintain, to perpetuate, to preserve. Yet any memory that is not sustained by a project dies of asphyxiation. The appeal to memory must here too be governed by a representation to come. And in fact, the organizers of the festival were certainly thinking of the future, but only on condition that it was to be an exclusively repetitive future. The purpose of the festival was to fulfil that great hope of bringing the Revolution to an end.[22] One has only to examine some of the reasons for consecrating 9 Thermidor with a festival. "What a useful lesson [9 Thermidor] gives! It constitutes the finish line of the Revolution!"[23] There is a double lesson here: to the general lesson of political science (revolutions come to an end) is added a unique diagnosis (9 Thermidor embodies that end).

But the certainty that 9 Thermidor constituted the last link in the Revolutionary chain did not seem equally necessary to all—especially when first Germinal, then Prairial showed that the *faubourgs* were quite capable of producing new *journées*. No matter! The festival would provide the missing evidence: it would be made the last Revolutionary event. It was this willed, arbitrary closure that the commemorative festival was specifically intended to embody. For, in order to leave social disturbance behind (this obsessive theme is common to all the writings on the festivals) two conditions must be met. First, the Revolution's past must be taken in hand and declared to be irreversible. The historical festival that legalizes illegality is a guarantee: it prevents any sliding back; it banishes the debilitating notion that the heroes' sacrifices might have been in vain.[24] It offered its guarantee to all those men who had irrevocably tied their fate to that of the Revolution and who were listed by the president of the Conseil des Anciens for the festival of 1 Vendémiaire: in other words, those who had acquired national wealth and "all those who are attached to the soil of France by ownership or agriculture—a numerous, useful, respectable class, which was fortunate enough to traverse the Revolution with prudence."[25] But second, if, in order to reassure those men, the past had to be saved, they also had to be promised a future in which there would be no new convulsion or any new event that, by completing the Revolution, might, in fact, threaten to unbalance it.

In order to bring the Revolution to an end and remove from the future its threatening uncertainty, the most urgent task was, therefore, to decide on the narrative of the Revolutionary events. If the festival made it possible to extract from so "eminently unstable"[26] a nation a shared interpretation of its past, then the festival would have achieved its purpose.[27] Removed from the whims of time, projected into the eternity of discourse, the Revolution would discourage men both from challenging it and from wishing to continue it. And perhaps, in the mimed recitation of its "great days," it would be possible to recreate a lost unanimity. This, in any case, was the intention of the organizers of the commemorative festival. Not that they were unaware of its potential dangers: "Revolutionary times are of such a nature that it is very difficult to control the storm and to build for a more peaceful time."[28]

Deciding on the narrative involves choice: how and what is one to choose from among the mass of events of the Revolution? History must be left to tell all, for it contains everything likely to arouse human curiosity. But the festivals are the history of sensibility alone. If they said everything, they would fail in their purpose, for, whereas the ancien régime had already receded so far into the past that it no longer displayed "its contrasts, its incoherences" to memory, the immediate past of the Revolution was, as Michelet showed so clearly in his *History of the Nineteenth Century,* "a world of ruins." The festivals, then, must select those events that, by suggesting that the Revolution has come to an end, will reinforce national reconciliation.[29]

This means, of course, that there were gaps in the narratives proposed. Certain of the *journées* were to be lost in those gaps: 12 Germinal and 1 Prairial of Year III, whose demoralizing evocation would frustrate any wish to make 9 Thermidor the end of the Revolution; May 31 of Year I, which would revive unbearable memories for the Convention; September 2, 1792, which would tarnish the brilliance of August 10. Between the commemorations, then, were long stretches of oblivion. Sometimes, even, whole sequences of events disappeared. Dubois-Dubais compared himself to the painter who, representing the sacrifice of Iphigenia, places a veil over Agamemnon's head; he felt forced to abandon "an account too harrowing for sensitive souls and also to throw a veil over so many indescribable scenes of horror that covered France with graves and ruins, from the frightful day of May 31 to the memorable one of 9 Thermidor."[30] Many speeches elaborate on this theme: the "multitude of victims"[31] must be removed from the collective memory, for misfortune must not be made eternal but merely sufficiently evoked to provide true lessons, just as "a people celebrated for its exalted wisdom and its ardent love of liberty preserved the ruins of its houses and temples in order to stir itself up against the Persians."[32]

In the commemorative festivals, censorship was as apparent, therefore, as memory, and a discussion of uncertain outcome opened up between the advocates of oblivion and the advocates of memory. Sometimes the latter even regretted taking that stand. One must commemorate because one is legislating for the present century. But "if we had entirely left behind us all the storms of our Revolution; if French liberty had no more enemies, either within or without . . . then I would say to you: convey to future generations nothing that may remind them of our past mistrusts and ferments."[33] This desire for effacement was sometimes geographical. In the frightful days following Germinal, Year III, the image that obsessed the orators was that of "an inviolable altar,"[34] which they wanted to erect in the middle of the place de la Révolution, as if, in the gloomy center of Revolutionary history, the mass of a monument was needed to erase the image of the scaffold; it was even solemnly declared that the place de la Révolution would never again be used as a place of execution.[35] Sometimes it was thought that oblivion would be aided by a linguistic purge: as early as Fructidor, Year II, M. E. Petit, a deputy from the Aisne, proposed punishing with imprisonment speakers who used those words that the Revolution had brought into currency but that revealed its divisions, "the words *Mountain, Plain, Marsh, Moderates, Feuillants, Jacobins, Federalists, Muscadins, Alarmists.*" Sometimes, even, there was an attempt to cover the roots of the Republic with general amnesia: "Far from reproducing gloomy memories, I would wish that the generation that will follow us could be entirely ignorant that France was governed by kings, and above all that the Republic had parricidal children."[36] Ignorance of the origins of the Revolution was, in this pessimistic view, the best guarantee of its security.

Is there, then, a single event that may be marked by the festival and the memory of which presents no danger? The most determined advocates of collective oblivion were in no doubt that there should be commemorations; no reticence was needed to celebrate the triumphs over the despotic coalition or to honor the memory of the victorious generals. In celebrating Hoche or Joubert, their contemporaries were simply drawing up an accurate account of posterity's debt to them. These, however, are circumstantial commemorations, excised from the brutality of events. These are not festivals about the foundation of a people. If one confined oneself to commemorating military exploits, it would seem that the French were intended only for war.[37] The festival would then betray its purpose. If one wanted it to provide "that rest after long torments,"[38] which both individuals and political bodies irresistibly seek, then a perpetual festival must be created, one that can truly last forever.

It was important, then, to find unequivocal solemnities, festivals that recalled no mixed memories. July 14 or August 10? Even in these privileged examples, the arrangement of the narrative would make no small contribution to the purity of the memories. For, if all the expected benefits were to be drawn from the commemoration, it would have to comply with a great many requirements: it would have to stylize the leading figures, which amounts, "by abandoning to history the passions and prejudices of the heroes that are no more,"[39] to adopting an epic simplification; it would have to avoid any contamination of one memory with another and therefore separate the Revolutionary days from their consequences. If, indeed, they were reintegrated into the chain of events, it would be necessary to draw up a balance sheet of the good and ill that they did, the result of which, to say the least, would be dubious. Here, again, remembering would have to be hedged in with a mass of precautions. "In evoking July 14 and August 10, our aim is not to celebrate bloodshed and the punishment of the guilty. On the contrary, we are trying to remove them from our memory in order not to poison the pure joy that the triumphs of Liberty inspire in us."[40] "Let us not poison this festival"—August 10—"by remembering the times that followed it, all too closely. The victors of August 10 had no part in the murders of September. True Frenchmen know how to fight and win; they never murder."[41] And, in a general way, "let us not mingle with the Liberty Tree and the laurel of victory the cypresses of the Revolution."[42] There is no innocence in this commemoration; its prelude is a meticulous scissors-and-paste job, which isolates the celebrated days from the tissue of events in which it occurred. The insularity of the festival, a fortunate island in the monotony of laborious days,[43] also corresponds to the insularity of the days that it commemorates, the double condition of the euphoric memory.

It is understandable, then, if the Revolutionary festival presents to the public a series of "tableaux," each distinct from the other, rather than a coherent story. The attempt to present each festival as the embodiment of a virtue reinforced this effect. In a project for reorganizing the national festivals, Lequinio proposed to link each commemoration with the praise of a virtue. Thus, August 10 depicts Liberty and January 21 Equality, while 9 Thermidor represents Courage.[44] Thus, by means of a sovereign nominalism, each historical festival becomes the depository of a stable value. Even the story of 9 Thermidor, which is in itself so dramatic, may be reduced to a conflict between two eternal values, whose confrontation produces two opposed tableaux. What the "burin of history" etches is, on the one hand, "the tableau of the heinous crimes, hitherto unheard of, of Robespierre, Couthon, and their sectaries," and, on the other, that of "the courage, devotion, constancy, and wisdom of the National Convention."[45] Between the Robespierrists on the one hand and the Convention on the other, what exactly took place? We are not told; history has evaporated, leaving a typology of virtues and vices. The festival has become the tableau vivant of morality.

THE CHOICE OF THE COMMEMORATION

Providing one respected these precautions, there were certain commemorations that were beyond dispute. Three of them seem also to have been above suspicion: the respectable 1 Vendémiaire, for the reasons already explained, to which one might add the peculiarity that no drop of blood was shed on that day; July 14, of course; and, already with rather less than total certainty, August 10.

July 14 represented the youth of the Revolution. In so many of the projects of the festivals and commemorative speeches devoted to July 14, one finds no trace of struggle or even of effort. July 14 was a dance, a masterpiece of pure activity in which the movements of a unanimous people were miraculously ordered in the figures of a gracious, gratuitous ballet.[46] It was while dancing that "the French nation, drunk with liberty, shining with liberal ideas, trod underfoot the baubles of the throne."[47] If they were not dancing, they were singing: "In the fine days of the Revolution, brilliant, animated song served as a prelude, in the public squares, to the overthrow of the throne."[48] The consequences were added to the act almost as an afterthought. It was without premeditation, in a pure expenditure of spontaneous energy, that the towers came crumbling down and the gates were forced open, both, it might have seemed, as insubstantial as the Bastille of the commemorations.[49] The virtue of this festival was that it only had to repeat what had already been a festival. So July 14 is never described other than in effusive language: "How beautiful they were, those first moments of liberty! What simultaneity of courage, what delicious outpourings of trust, what union of feelings!"[50] But then it was the Revolution's birth certificate: a *cogito* of Liberty to which the whole chain of Revolutionary "days" was fastened. Baudin, in the speech that he devoted to the anniversary of July 14, shows quite clearly that for him the privileges of logical and chronological priority were confused. Indeed, the Constitution of Year III dates "the origin of the political crime of those Frenchmen who abandoned their country and for whom all hope of return is forever lost"[51] from July 15, 1789. From that split between two eras, which consecrated the social pact itself, stems the primacy of July 14. Since it had to be paid for by an exclusion, did this not have the effect of robbing the festival of some of its exuberance? Not at all, for it was the very existence of the Revolution that made the exile of the "enemies of liberty" necessary; national unanimity emerged from it, therefore, all the more dazzling.[52] The festival was for the whole of France, "minus an imperceptible, rebellious minority."[53] There was, however, a slight shadow over the tableau: July 14 did not complete the job; it did not bring to birth the whole of the Revolution at once. The inexperience of the novice revolutionaries who propped up a worm-eaten throne with a badly conceived constitution was enough to explain, of course, that new struggles had to be embarked on. The fact remains that the lesson inflicted on the kings by August 10 was also valid for the legislators, for it was to their inexperience that one owed the separation in time of the two events that, from the standpoint of the Directoire, basked in an ideal contemporaneity.[54]

So August 10 completed the inaugural event of July 14. It purified the work undertaken by "removing from the constitutive elements of the Republic those heterogeneous parts out of which the *réunion* had formed an impure alloy to the benefit of tyranny"[55] and fulfilled the meaning of July 14. But it was July 14 that lent it its vivifying energy. Those who marched on the chateau with the *fédérés* on August 10 were the inhabitants of the Antoine and Marceau *faubourgs,* the very same men of July 14. We know with what youthful pride the label "patriots of 1789" was borne throughout the Revolution. Among the men of the *faubourgs* that one sometimes had to resign oneself to recruiting, it was so reassuring or so politic, to see only victors of the Bastille! In any case, it was they who, in collaborating with August 10, transferred to it the magical properties of July 14; for in August 10 there is, at first sight, something enormous and terrible,[56] which contrasts with the blithe spirit of July 14 and gives rise to more austere thoughts. But, as in the case of July 14, everything happened so quickly! The victors over monarchy were amazed that their victory was so easily won; and what the people discovered through them was something that had hitherto been kept secret, namely, the weakness of the tyrants. The accounts of the day agree with those celebrations, at which, as soon as the alarm bell rang and the call to arms sounded, scepters and crowns went up in flames on a pyre while a veil was rent in two to reveal the statue of Liberty, rising on a cloud of birds.[57]

The newspapers were right to some extent, in the days following August 10, to write that this epiphany betrayed the nature of the event.[58] But this was because, in the light of memory, it had lost all opacity; it had become the mere fulfillment of "the fine conceptions of the Mablys, Rousseaus, Raynals, and other modern philosophers."[59] Yet to be delighted with it, one must not look too closely at its consequences: if we follow the course of events, do we not see emerging a September 2 or a May 31? "When, turning to the time of August 10, one follows the thread of the country's fortunes, over three years, one seems to be pursuing two careers at once."[60] The first, of course, was an entirely triumphal one, that of the Republican armies; but the second was that of tyranny, born nevertheless out of the luminous August 10 itself. In order to reach this astonishing result, the people had to exaggerate their enthusiasm, exceed their real energy: "In bringing about the fall of the throne, one had to go well beyond the limits of liberty: one had done much too much damage to the rigorous principle that alone can maintain, in a great state, the respect due to the public laws."[61] If we are to give August 10 its true meaning, then, we would do well to say as little as possible about its consequences.

So we have 1 Vendémiaire, July 14, and perhaps August 10; the list of commemorations that were beyond dispute is certainly a very short one. Apart from these three great dates, there were few historic days of the Revolution that did not arouse fear or revive conflict. There were even anniversaries, such as January 21, that it would have been almost impossible to celebrate. And there were those, if one wished to celebrate them, that would open the door to an interminable rearrangement of the celebrations. That of 18 Fructidor is a good example.

THE IMPOSSIBLE COMMEMORATION

Of all the festivals of the Revolution, the one in which the historical event had every chance of becoming more obsessive—like the *journées* that contained it, and unlike so many of the Revolutionary "days," it seemed to be lacking in any vagueness—was the festival of January 21,[62] or, to be more precise, the festival that, in a cascade of genitives heavy with several meanings at once, was called "the festival of the just punishment of the last king of the French." To speak of "just punishment" is no doubt to claim acquittal in a trial that is not really over; but it is also to take a euphemistic detour that keeps certain overbrutal images at a distance, and to designate that king as the "last" may be a mere statement of fact (in the neutral order of succession, he was indeed the last), but it may also be a wish, and better still, a program: the blade of the ordinal designation guarantees that he really will be the last.

What precisely did the festival show of the event that was being celebrated? In a sense, the event defied representation. What was proposed by the Committee of Public Instruction showed very little inventiveness: the fires that, in Thirion's plan, might, while warming the celebrants at this winter festival, also serve to burn the symbols of monarchy and feudalism had been much used in the Republican festivals. Indeed, this rather hackneyed allegory had been subjected to some acerbic criticism. "What meaning is intended," Lecomte asked sarcastically, "by the fires that, it is proposed, would consume before the eyes of the people what remains of the symbols of feudalism?" One can't have it both ways: either these symbols are still in existence and it would be better to have a mock burning, or they no longer exist and the ceremony is superfluous. The question asked by Lecomte is at the very heart of the general debate about the festivals of the Revolution: can a festival that is ideally conceived as a festival of Enlightenment represent gloom and horror? The superstitious fear of embodying what one wishes to deny, always present in the festival, is even more strongly felt in the case of January 21. Hence, the laconic nature of the official arrangements and, in the festival itself, the poverty of the representation. On January 21, in the public squares, parchments and scepters were burned on the bonfires. And the processions marched on, lost among the Brutuses, Liberties, Rousseaus, Franklins, and a few rare Monarchies. And were there any actual Louis XVIs? Even fewer. And if there were, the representation was often unrecognizable as the royal figure: at Bordeaux, on 2 Pluviôse, Year VII, between two "temple doors" arose a figure of the Perjurer. No doubt the well-placed spectator could have read on the crown around the head of this allegorical image "Louis XVI." But the official accounts and the descriptions in the newspapers had eyes, it seems, only for the ceremonial of abstract exemplariness: what they remembered was the punishment of the perjurer.

Even the anniversaries of Year II, which were improvised before the administration took over the celebrations and were therefore given over to a more unbridled invention, reveal a certain unease amid the joyful inversion, with its almost carnivalesque echoes. At Conches, on 20 Ventôse, Year II, the unfortunate object of public ridicule, drawn around on a cart, was not Louis XVI but—was it some statue removed from its pedestal in a church?—a Saint Louis in a royal cloak. It was an overderermined image, for it was in fact supposed to represent Louis XVI. It was "the head of Monsieur Capet the saint representing the fat Veto, his great-great-great etc. grandson." Does not the parodic charge become defused and the character of comic vengeance become neutralized in this amalgam? Carnivalesque insult, it is true, dethrones a king securely established on his throne: this is because it makes one feel good to insult him or to beat him and unthrone him for a day. But the dramatization of the festival dethroned a king already dethroned; it was devoted to flatly duplicating an event whose tragic emotions or scandalous force it could in no way equal. Furthermore, it in no way wished to do so and showed as little as possible. And what did one hear? Even in this less explicit domain, one can sense the unease in the celebration. At the festival of Year

III in Paris, the first great official model, the funeral march played by the Institut National de Musique was regarded as too gentle. Might it not seem that one wished to deplore the tyrant's death? Gossec tried to save his world: "One would abandon oneself only to the gentle emotions inspired in sensitive souls by the happiness of being delivered from a tyrant."

The effacement of the event was obtained, therefore, by an intentionally incomplete symbolism, in which the image was there only in order to give way very quickly to language: either to the words brandished atop poles by the sententious banner bearers in the processions or to the speeches, obviously much richer in rhetorical devices and euphemistic turns of phrase, delivered on the altars of the fatherland by the municipal officers. Sometimes, no doubt, these orators confronted the event head on or, at other times, made no mention of it. Yet more interesting is the category, actually in the majority, of speakers who managed to speak of January 21 only to ignore it the better. Two features strike the reader in those speeches in which the memory becomes clouded: the effacement of the person of the king and even—a notable fact in a festival with such a title—the effacement of punishment. Various rhetorical effects served to dismiss the image of the executed man. There was very little mention of Louis XVI or of Capet. At various points in the speeches references were made to "the perjurer-king," a "perfidious king," the "last crowned tyrant," the "plaything of a shameless, evil woman," or again—and this no doubt is the expression in which, in the temporal institution, the sacred king of the Capetian monarchy is most effaced—the "first of the functionaries." The argument also contributed to blurring the king's features: the question was not so much one of him personally as of the monarchy that he embodied, by chance and almost by mischance. His personal crimes, in the context of the succession of crimes committed by kings, so self-righteously catalogued, began to fade and almost to merge into the background, for the orators' favorite theme was that France had punished in the last of its kings the excesses of his predecessors, no less guilty than he was himself: "a terrible example of justice that has at last been done in one century or another to usurped authority." "In one century or another." This historical indifference had a precise function: in the compact succession of time then evoked, it was not so much history that was being deciphered as a second, diverted nature; and collective responsibility holds the images of too personal a punishment at a distance.

Indeed, the royal execution brings on a mass of euphemisms: there is no trace of the scaffold in those speeches in which the "national sword" is the most brutal image of the guillotine to be found. There is scarcely a mention of death: the orators preferred to speak of it as "the price of all crimes," a "terrible event," or again, by a long detour in which we can decipher the embarrassed wish to deflect guilt from oneself, "that consequence so true, so just, so natural, which was so precisely of its time." In that immense neutralization and naturalization of the inadmissible, what became of January 21, the day when the throne of Liberty was erected, the anniversary of the Republic? It might just as easily have been August 10 or 1 Vendémiaire. The anniversary had disappeared. In this sense, but in this sense only, that festival of forgetting was a second capital punishment.

Who, in fact, punished whom? We can read through those speeches without finding an answer. They are silent on the trial, on the divisions within the Convention; and they attribute the punishment to Providence or to the allegorical triumph of some virtue (either beneficent Liberty or Wisdom, or again, when the orators were concerned with stressing the originality of that stage of the Revolution in relation to others, Justice). A privileged dramatization of an immobile virtue, which seemed to have no other motive than to provide it with adequate expression, January 21 required no other expressly designated action.

Images and speeches, however, belong to the ornamental, and all this would amount to very little if the ceremonial had not also chosen to base itself on a suppressed history. The instructions of Nivôse, Year III, gave the festival the specific physiognomy that it was to preserve to the end, that of the festival of "the Republic's employees," of which the declaration of hatred for royalty was to form the heart. From Year III to Year VII, the place of the oath, which, from the beginning, gave the festival its coherence, continued to grow. Somewhat hastily devised in the ceremonies of Year IV, the ceremonial of the oath had become longer and more complicated by Year VII. From then on, an invocation to the Supreme Being was an obligatory adjunct to it, as if to signify all the more forcefully to the oath-taking group the presence of a transcendence. Then there were the "imprecations against perjurers," an occasion for scholarly purple passages delivered by university professors, who described in lurid terms the eternal wandering and the pangs of remorse that would be the deserved consequence of perjury. It becomes clear enough what associations of ideas the festival was intended to set in motion. Describing in advance the punishments meted out to perjurers, a sanction of the law that the jurors had just accepted, the festival was a national enterprise of intimidation. And everyone could, on 2 Pluviôse, appreciate its seriousness: the punishment meted out to a perjurer-king was there to support the general lesson handed out by a pedagogy of fear.

Indeed, the courses do not have to expatiate sententiously on that fear for us to be convinced that it was the real basis of the festival. Everything concurred in confirming this: the sacramental formula, written in capital letters on the altar of the fatherland; the steps that had to be mounted to reach the platform on which the oath would be taken; the Constitution of Year III, on which one had to place one's left hand; and the heroic pose that one tried to adopt as best one could. Furthermore, there was the silent coercion of the onlookers' eyes. This inflexible ceremonial of sworn death was likely to arouse a terror that one can sense in many of the official accounts, despite the yoke of their official language. Many men slipped away when the time came to take the oath. Some tried to rob the oath of its force by introducing minute alterations into it, which they saw as annulling it. Again, there were many who, at the moment of declaring or signing, were petrified, as if by some mysterious paralysis: in that "sudden illness" can we not recognize the sincere simulation proper to hysteria?

But the oath was so frightening only because fear itself was the compost in which it was rooted. Such determination to force people to swear their hatred of monarchy and their attachment to the Republic can be explained only by the growing fear of a future that might contain monarchy and exclude the Republic. The purpose of the oath was to prevent any going back on the Revolution; it dramatized not only the impossibility, consented to by each individual, or going back but also the impossibility of any future other than a repetition of the present. Are not all takers of oaths, as Sartre so brilliantly described, swearing to perpetuate an unfruitful present? What the swearer denies is time, in its corrupting dimension. The conservative purpose of the festival belonged quite happily to the pedagogy that sustained the oath. A right of life and death over each and every person, the oath was a collective guarantee against individual weakness and, at the same time, against the danger of history's drifting out of control.

THE INTERMINABLE COMMEMORATION

And yet it was precisely such a drifting that, after Thermidor, can be glimpsed in the interminable revision of the commemorations. This is evident in the example of the last anniversary proposed as a date for a festival, 18 Fructidor.

It is rather difficult, despite Michelet, to raise the events of 18 Fructidor to the dignity of one of the historic days of the Revolution: troops occupied Paris in the morning without resistance or disturbance; three of the members of the Directoire deprived the other two of their functions; deputies sadly acceded to their purging. Much is missing in that bitter victory: the vivacity of a moving crowd, the groundswell of the people, even the pathos of the scaffold. The "dry guillotine" was preferred by a plan that suddenly intended to repress opposition while keeping up appearances. Yet this muffled way of going about things did not mean that everything had changed. Again it was improvisation and adventure that disappeared in the breach opened up by 18 Fructidor. This is clearly apparent in the new reading of the past that the event made immediately necessary.

The commemoration of 18 Fructidor resuscitated the questions that followed 9 Thermidor: How can the Republic be made to take root in people's hearts? And how, since religious persecution was being revived at the same time, could one give the people the compensation of another cult? After 19 Fructidor, Audoin asked the Five Hundred to form a commission to prepare an overall project for the Republic's institutions. Silent on the festivals up to 29 Fructidor, the Ancients also started making commemorative speeches. From then on, a cascade of interventions took place in both assemblies: the choice of emblems, the ordering of the *fêtes décadaires,* the suitability of the commemorations—everything was open to discussion. One senses that 18 Fructidor awoke the anxiety that smouldered beneath the contrived coherence of the festivals of Year IV.

In the long debate that then opened up, what place was found for reflection on the commemorative festival? That was the tender nerve. Indeed, as far as the *fêtes décadaires* were concerned, there was nothing to fear in undoing what had already been achieved; in this matter, everything was to be done anew. But for the already established commemorative festivals, 18 Fructidor was the new event that meant that everything had to be rearranged. To begin with, did it not bring into disrepute the Thermidorian conformism that endlessly repeated that "the Revolution came to a halt on the day when the Constitution of the Year III was established"?[63] The theme of the discussion that opened in the Council is highly significant: was it "fitting" to consecrate the anniversary of 18 Fructidor with a national festival? The question had never been openly asked of any other festival; this shows clearly enough that the newcomer could expect a rough ride. In fact, those who were determined to believe that the Revolution had ended long before would have liked to have been able to forget 18 Fructidor, which ridiculed their hopes. For the others, sustained by an equal determination to have done with it, 18 Fructidor now embodied, together with 9 Thermidor, the end of the Revolution.

One must pay attention to these discordant voices, which stirred up the whole Revolutionary past. There were those who found this new commemoration repugnant. What shocked them, first of all, was the bad taste attaching to self-glorification: "Is it to those members of the Directoire still in office that we are to erect monuments? I wish to speak to you with due Republican severity. Be fearful of setting an example, against the spirit of the Republican laws, of consecrating events and actions by those very individuals who took part in them."[64] But how was 18 Fructidor to be integrated harmoniously into the language of the other festivals? Whereas in various ways all the others express the enthusiasm of a great people for liberty, this festival dispenses only gloomy lessons. All the others have grandeur. But to celebrate 18 Fructidor would be to consecrate mediocrity. What, indeed, does it show? "A general perfidy, French accomplices"; and anyway, does one celebrate one's misfortunes? "What events," declared Luminais, "would you consecrate today in making 18 Fructidor an anniversary and perpetual festival? You would celebrate the powerlessness of a few conspirators, the thousandth success of patriots over the friends of royalism, the victory of our brave defenders over a handful of seditious men. Victory has crowned them a thousand times more gloriously on the banks of the Rhine, the Po, or the Adige, on the frontiers of Spain and in the marshes of the Vendée."[65] This indictment in the days following the coup d'état can hardly give way, even euphemistically, to the illegality of 18 Fructidor. The adversaries of the project insisted, then, on the divisions that the festival incongruously revealed[66] and recalled the lassitude felt by the public: were there not already far too many festivals? If it is absolutely necessary to commemorate 18 Fructidor, however, why not merge it with the commemoration of 9 Thermidor? For "on 8 Thermidor of Year II, as on 17 Fructidor, Year V, we were in the midst of a counterrevolution."[67] One can see very clearly what this proposed amalgamation was expected to achieve: by reviving the image of the twin perils engendered one by the other in a ceaseless circular causality, one gives the impression that 18 Fructidor eludes history and has changed nothing at all.

But for the advocates of the new festival, 18 Fructidor was not at all the same thing as 9 Thermidor. Of the two defeated conspiracies, the second was the more to be feared because less open.[68] Not that 18 Fructidor was an absolutely unprecedented event; but must one, because all the Revolutionary events seem to share a certain kinship, give up any attempt to distinguish between them? Furthermore, if it were absolutely necessary to carry out the amalgamation, should it not be rather with August 10, which struck the same enemy?

Indeed, the actual celebration of the festival resorted to a symbolism not very different from that of August 10. In it the genius of Liberty also trod underfoot the "baubles of monarchy," and a statue of "Political Hypocrisy" had the book of the Constitution, which it was pretending to worship, snatched away from it by the president of the Directoire, "by an arm impelled by vigorous indignation." If there was an innovation in the festival, it was the representation of the deportation of the conspirators: "On a pedestal were the figures of Justice and Clemency; the first held a raised sword; the second was stopping the sword with one hand and pointing to the West with the other; the inscription read: 'They conspired against France, they will no longer live within her bosom.'"[69] There, said its defenders, lay the originality of 18 Fructidor: it was an allegory of political moderation. It did not cost a drop of blood. In that sense, by bringing the Revolution to an end, which 9 Thermidor failed to do, it too was an advent: it marked the period when moderation began to emerge in political disputes.

In this it was also a festival of regeneration. This theme had the support of the Institut: Daunou, at the first anniversary, on 18 Fructidor, Year VI, regaled his colleagues with the "marvels" that the festival had made possible: it had given back to the Republic "its genius and its destinies."[70] If proof were required, it might be said that it had restored brilliance to the other festivals, which had been growing stale for some time, and whose decline before the coup d'état had been described by Leclerc, in the great report of Frimaire, Year VI, on the institutions:

No more national festivals; a gloomy silence would have made August 10 and July 14 look like the most ordinary days if a few faithful Republicans had not made sure that a commemoration was held. The foundation of the Republic itself was doomed to lack all gaiety. Like the others, that memorable time, which 400,000 individuals had celebrated with so much pomp and enthusiasm in the Champ-de-Mars, had been reduced to the confines of a tiny courtyard in which scarcely five or six hundred individuals could

stand, packed and hidden, one might say, between four walls: a locality too
worthy indeed of the circumstances.[71]

By restoring the Republican celebrations, 18 Fructidor gave proof, therefore, of its conservative character. Why not turn it into a festival of the
elections? On that day one would show the people "Liberty enclosed in a
ballot box."[72] Garnier de Saintes proposed that this be done every five
years. In the end it was to be done every year.

So there were now six historic festivals, and, it seems, only a modest
addition had been made to the total number of commemorations. Yet it
was seen very quickly that the new festival necessitated profound changes,
for it revived certain events that had once met with censure. The date 13
Vendémiaire, which had hitherto been so constantly obliterated in the
commemorations, became an indispensable link in the intelligibility of
the history that led to 18 Fructidor: it was the "fatal indulgence" shown
to the guilty, after 9 Thermidor, that made 13 Vendémiaire unavoidable;
and it was the "half-measures" after 13 Vendémiaire that made 18 Fructidor so urgent. So new figures were added to the celebration of the Revolution. The "redoubtable legion of Vendémiaire" would now join the
great family of Revolutionary heroes who stormed the Bastille on July 14,
broke into the chateau on August 10, and rallied to the Convention on 9
Thermidor. Heroic unanimity now encompassed 13 Vendémiaire, which
was now, without the slightest effort, recounted in the same manner as
the great, miraculous *journées*.[73]

But 18 Fructidor put the celebration of 9 Thermidor in the shade, for
9 Thermidor had not turned out as promised. Not only had it not completed the Revolution; it had condemned it to new convulsions. From the
vantage point of 18 Fructidor, 9 Thermidor was now bound up with what
followed; it had become an ordinary historical event. Nevertheless, the
festival remained, though hedged in with all manner of precautions. Reference to 9 Thermidor contracted so much that it now coincided only
with the historic days of 9 and 10 Thermidor. It was still possible, while
trying not to go beyond this very reduced period, to tell a heartwarming
account of 9 Thermidor. But, as soon as one went beyond that, one could
see the beginning of "that bloody reaction that devoured so many Republicans under the baleful domination of Robespierre's agents, Jacobins, ter-
rorists, and anarchists."[74] Even the guilty faction itself was now confined
to a handful of conspirators, "a few heterogeneous elements,"[75] while the
Montagnard Convention pursued its entirely honorable course.

So care had to be taken about which memories were retained in the festival; care even had to be taken in choosing the men to be entrusted with the task of celebrating it; only "the true friends of 9 Thermidor" should be admitted.[76] A whole new art of celebrating 9 Thermidor began to emerge. It was an art of allusion: "Revolting excesses produced contrary effects, and we had to weep over civic disturbances."[77] It was an art of euphemism: "Blessed 9 Thermidor! You recall to us the triumph of virtue over crime."[78] It was an art of preterition: "Do not expect me, fellow citizens, to recall here those days of grief and tears . . . To try to reopen deep wounds, still hardly healed, by showing you Robespierre seated on the dictatorial throne, giving the signal for murder and fire in every corner of the Republic, to awaken passions that are still scarcely calmed, resentments still too bitter, by drawing the frightful portrait of civil war."[79] It had become very difficult indeed to speak disinterestedly of 9 Thermidor. Bad conscience was countered by the evocation of present happiness. Fortunately, the political swing of the pendulum that 9 Thermidor had set off and that made its commemoration so delicate a matter was now contained. Images of harbor and safety, which had already been widely used, now served again, without difficulty, to refer euphemistically to 18 Fructidor.

Obviously, things were far from over. There is no trace in the projects for festivals of the "correction" brought about by the elections in Floréal, Year VI. This time the purge was an anti-Jacobin one; however, it did not stop the erosion of memories of 9 Thermidor. Yet the revenge taken by the councils on 30 Prairial, Year VII, introduced a new rearrangement into the system of celebrations. It would have been difficult, however, to celebrate the coup d'état of Prairial, so an attempt was made to bring out the resemblance between it and July 14, which provided a magical justification for any Revolutionary event.[80] But the defeat of the executive foreshadowed the decline of 18 Fructidor: that festival was its festival. And the revival of the Jacobin climate helped to efface the memory of Thermidor still further.

Contrary to all expectations, there was still a festival of 18 Fructidor. But now the illegality of the *journée,* hitherto concealed, rose to the surface of public statements like a necessary but very obvious stain: "It should not be concealed; it was a violent, extraordinary event; it dealt a cruel blow to the Constitution, to the men of the judiciary, and even to the men of the Directoire." It could be tolerated only if "one moaned over that blow."[81] The firm unanimity attributed to 18 Fructidor was breaking up: "Private passions had too great an influence on that day and on its consequences."[82] By the same token, the illegality had given rise to others: "We must bewail the abuse that a few men and particularly the former Directoire made of it."[83] Far from having been the closure that it was hailed as being, 18 Fructidor made new historic days—30 Prairial, for instance—necessary. The incompatibility between 18 Fructidor and the great festivals of unanimity burst forth in speeches, therefore, as a little earlier the inassimilable character of 9 Thermidor had burst forth.

The challenge to the festival of 9 Thermidor, in particular, increased. Yet that day was still a festival. But had the festival kept its meaning? It lay at the heart of the great debate of Thermidor, Year VII, on the civic oath taken by those citizens who formed the National Guard. Up till then, they had been required to swear their hatred of monarchy and anarchy. In the Jacobin atmosphere that 30 Prairial resuscitated, the balance that had been the philosophy of the regime no longer seemed tolerable; furthermore, the discussion revealed the degree of anxiety now associated with commemorations. Was not tampering with the oath an attempt to revoke the irrevocable?

In order to regard the image of the twin perils as unacceptable, one must look anew at what preceded and followed 9 Thermidor. The period following 9 Thermidor had become one of sheer counterrevolution: "Citizen representatives, you will not endure this retrograde, disastrous march into which you are being driven: you will remember that the system you are being asked to keep, even after 30 Prairial, Year VII, is the work of counterrevolution itself."[84] Was not the eve of 9 Thermidor, under a different face, also counterrevolution? Not entirely. What had broken down in these discussions was the Thermidorian consensus: seen from Prairial, Year VII, the regime of 1793, far from being that "unfortunate deviation" deplored by Thibaudeau, had become "the perhaps inevitable effect of the Revolutionary torrent."[85] Hitherto banished from the Revolutionary memory, the Montagnard episode was brought back into the fold. By the same token, one could no longer record without a sense of scandal the memory of La Révellière, who, according to reliable witnesses, declared anathema on anarchy at the Festival of the King's Death, "when he ought to have spoken of monarchy, when the institution of the festival was directed against it."[86]

In that new system of accounting "times and crimes,"[87] the hope of a neutral party disappeared: 30 Prairial had killed it. "All our ills," said Français, on the even of the festival of 18 Fructidor, Year VII, stem from the fact that we extinguished, instead of regulating, the spirit of the Revolution before the Revolution was entirely over. Second, from the lack of skill of all the governments that have followed since 9 Thermidor, and which have adopted an attitude of hostility toward both the royalist faction and the terrorist faction, instead of concentrating all their forces against the first, and mitigating, neutralizing, and directing the second, which was and will be again, when it is so wished, a powerful auxiliary against the royalist faction . . . I know that much has been said about a neutral, average party, equally the enemy of all extremes and destined, by its wisdom, always to keep the balance; but this party is lifeless, colorless, motionless; it is made up, throughout France, of a few disguised royalists and a great many weak souls ready to turn their coats; in any trouble, the balance falls from their timid hands.[88]

One was then called upon to define anarchy, "the ardent passing fever of revolutions and frightful interregnum of laws."[89] For, once one had given up the very convenient fixation abscess of the Montagnard dictatorship, anarchy threatened with gangrene all the memories of the Revolution. Limited hitherto to Robespierre's government, it now spread to the first few hours of the Revolution; what was being celebrated on July 14 and August 10, it seemed, was anarchy.[90] If it were anarchy that had animated the fine days of burgeoning liberty, how could one celebrate its defeat on 9 Thermidor? Furthermore, in an inverse contagion, anarchy reached as far as 30 Prairial itself. This was the most astonishing fact of all, for up to 30 Prairial, whenever a new event was added to the sequence of Revolutionary events, it altered the preceding commemorations but passed itself off as untouchable. This time that was not the case: "Perhaps we ourselves need a great deal of wisdom and courage to be sure of the natural movement that leads us to be hard on the Directoire as it was hard on the legislative body."[91] Thus, 30 Prairial itself was seen to contain the seeds of anarchy. One was now faced with a vertiginous alternative, for if one could show that anarchy really did exist in the Directoire, "if the monster could be surprised *en flagrant délit* on the directorial seat,"[92] then Prairial was exempt from anarchy. But if the Directoire were innocent of it, then "the representatives of the people must be termed anarchists and sent to the scaffold." These speculations, which their author calls subtleties, nevertheless give us some idea of the measure of the problem. No one dared say any longer that the Revolution had ended on 30 Prairial.

What emerges as the dominant feeling here is one of lassitude. Many speakers demanded that the festivals be left alone, that their sacramental content be preserved: "Otherwise, with every change of system, we are condemned to see a sudden revolution taking place in words, in things, in places, in men, in laws, in institutions. Thus we are exposed to being perpetually governed by factions, which, by their very nature, are forever mobile and forever excited, rather than by laws that are firm and unshakable. Thus, sooner or later, if the disorder continues, the mass of the people will be like soil that, by being overworked, begins to lack consistency and is eventually washed away."[93] The prospect, then, had been precisely reversed. If one failed to commemorate, it was not because the Revolution was interminable; on the contrary, it was the interminable proliferation of festivals that condemned the Revolution to continuing forever. In that exhausting pursuit, events were now reputed to be innocent; it was their recital that had become guilty.[94]

Ending

Ending was therefore both the ambition of the Revolutionary festival and its evident failure. Of all rituals, the ritual of ending proved to be the most difficult to invent. This is so even if one considers the limited time of the single day of the festival. Take David's program for August 10: once the celebrants had laid on the altar of the fatherland the objects that they had carried throughout the procession, they were at a loss as to what to do. The festival, lacking some culminating point, circled around an uninventable closure. How could the festival be brought to an end and be extricated from the influence of corrupting eyes? An answer to this endlessly repeated question may be glimpsed in the festivals' ever-more frequent recourse to the ceremonial of the age groups.

As the Revolutionary decade advanced, whatever variety was left in the ceremonies was due to representation of the age groups. The motley vitality of the guilds, which had animated the traditional festivals, as well as the festivals of the early years of the Revolution, had gradually faded away. At the beginning of the Revolution, certain festivals were still close to the Corpus Christi processions. Thus, at Strasbourg, for the Federation, one could see in turn the fishermen with their "Rhine carps carried in a small boat," the farmers with their plows, and the gardeners scattering bunches of flowers on the altar of the fatherland. With the guilds died the picturesque elements introduced into the spectacle by what we now call the socio-occupational order. Representation of the trades, however, had not entirely disappeared from the festivals. But sometimes it was received with suspicion, and attempts were made to iron out its oddities: at Metz, on 10 Messidor, Year VI, it was reported that "if the bakers are invited, they must dress decently and not display the sort of nudity of their arms and chests that they sport at the kneading trough." Sometimes the distinguishing marks declined from year to year: at Moulins, on 30 Ventôse, Year VIII, there was a procession of groups representing "Industry, Agriculture, Commerce, the Arts, and the Sciences," but this was very far from the allegorical representation of a trade.

Such traditional groups were gradually replaced by the age groups. The extraordinary extension of the ceremonial of the ages may be followed from year to year in festivals where one might not expect them and with which they really had nothing to do. Nowhere is this clearer than in the ceremonial for the festival of the king's death, whose subject, it would seem, would exclude any representation of the ages. For Year IV and Year VII, we have parallel bundles of official accounts;[95] the spread and development of the ritual from one year to the other is quite clear. In Year IV, the ages had a very small part in the official accounts. The festival preserved a certain terrible character, perhaps because "Louis's massive, bloody shadow," as the orator at Reims put it, still stretched over it. In Year VII, the festival had become pedagogical. It was no longer any different from the festival of youth: it was given up to singing and recitation competitions, and to sporting events. The commissioners of the Directoire took advantage of the spectacle to invite parents and children to attend schools and expatiated on a theme that was to be much exploited in the future, namely, that ignorance is the mother of tyranny. The terrible festival had gradually become a reassuring, solemn prize distribution.

But there were festivals that took on the ceremonial of the ages. Among them, of course, were the three festivals expressly devoted to the age groups: those of Youth, Spouses, and the Old. This shows the extent to which the ceremonial of the age groups quickly became widespread.

Of this ceremonial the most striking feature—especially as, thanks to Philippe Ariès, we have become familiar with the representation of a traditional society in which all the circumstances of life are experienced without distinction by the various age groups together—was the separation of the age groups. This was manifested, in the first instance, by space: the gaps left between the processions were an objective correlative of a discontinuity in life. But beyond the processions, the separation ex-

tended to the dances (the children were allowed to weave their own farandole around the Liberty Tree after those of the elderly and the young
people), the banquets (the civic meal of the old people was often duplicated by that of the young),[96] the games (at Aurillac, on 10 Prairial, Year
IV, the games for the Festival of Thanksgiving and Victories were meticulously distributed between various age groups: prisoners' base, target
shooting, and fencing for the young, firearms for the mature men), and
the speeches (the commissioners of the executive directory often divided
their speeches into four addresses to the four age groups). Furthermore,
the authors of the projects for festivals declared their approval of this
separation.[97] In the great debate of Nivôse, Year III, on the *fêtes décadaires*,
Lanthenas demanded distinct places for the various age groups; moreover,
he did not want readings to be entrusted indiscriminately to any one
group: were there not "things that would be suitable for an old man to
read . . . others that would come better from the mouth of a mature
man," and some "that would interest, coming from young people and
even sometimes from children"?

There was nothing original, it seems, in the groups proposed: the four-
part division that he outlined—childhood, youth, adulthood, old age—
was highly traditional. Yet this apparently indisputable division into
broad categories did not exclude a proliferation of subcategories. Furthermore, the terminology of these official accounts is often very imprecise:
sometimes terms like *jeune homme* or *jeune fille* are used to refer to nine-
year-old children. Conversely, the use of the term *child* is extended: "All
children who have not yet reached the age of fifteen are placed before the
administrators in processions," say the instructions. Between the group of
jeunes filles and that of the *petites filles*, room is sometimes found for *grandes
filles*.[98]

Apart from these uncertainties, there are nevertheless commonly accepted thresholds in the periodization. Nine is unquestionably the end of
childhood. From nine, one was allowed to take part in the physical competitions; at nine—or sometimes at twelve—one could belong to the
battalion of Hope; at nine, one had the right to support the elderly in the
processions. Other divisions concern the importance of the nine-year
threshold; it was the age below which physicians recommended that the
doses for remedies be halved[99] and at which teachers fixed the beginning
of elementary education or military training.[100] And despite the power
exercised by the figure 7 on attitudes and age divisions in the eighteenth
century (Buffon, Linnaeus, and Cabanis each illustrated it) there were also

authors who consecrated the figure 9 as the key to the rhythm of life,[101] at least for the male sex.

Youth (or adolescence, or again "adolescent youth"—the vocabulary was far from clear) occupied the period between nine and twenty-one, but there were at least three stages within this age group. The first ended at twelve. It was from this nine-to-twelve category that the boys were recruited who led the elderly from their houses to the altar of the fatherland; this suggested that the very youngest boys would not be strong enough to guide the old people's movements. Twelve was also an educational threshold, the age at which Michel Lepeletier and Durand-Maillane mark the end of elementary education and entry into a new stage that lasted until sixteen.

The official accounts of the festival agree in stressing the solemnity of the age of sixteen. Before sixteen, they sometimes note, one is only a *petit jeune homme;* after that one becomes a *jeune homme.* It was at sixteen that one could claim the privileged ceremonial functions exercised by young men in the commune: sometimes the sixteen-year-old boys were called upon to carry the Constitution. Lastly, and above all, sixteen was the age of one's first initiation into the Festival of Youth, the age at which one could bear arms.[102] It was, of course, the age of puberty, according to Buffon, for boys at least, but it is clear in any case that the periodization of the Revolutionary festivals was essentially male.

Did eighteen, as certain writings suggest, constitute another break? There were projects for festivals that preferred eighteen to sixteen as the age at which one could bear arms. Nevertheless, eighteen seems more often to have been the average age of this third stage of youth rather than the age of entry into any particular functions. At twenty-one, though, one was unquestionably at the end of immaturity. This was the age at which one entered into political reflection: it was the voting age, the age that the Constitution of Year III, in this unlike the Constitution of 1791, laid down for citizenship; it was the time when adult society received the young men.[103]

After this period, so rich in events bound up with the ages, one came to the great plain of maturity, whose monotony, it seemed, nothing could break. Apparently the festivals said nothing about the stages that might, from twenty-one to sixty, break up the even time of maturity. Looking more closely, however, one can distinguish between two groups: the newly married and parents with children, a division that excluded the unmarried, the missing category of the Revolutionary festivals. The newly married were defined negatively as those who did not yet have children and, to be more precise, as the spouses of the year: they enjoyed a special role in the Festival of Spouses, were given the task of making the offerings in the Festival of the Old, and still had links with the young. But it was the fathers and mothers who provided the orators with an inexhaustible theme; surrounded by their children, they formed a solid group in the processions. When they had married off their last child, they then entered a new category, one with very imprecise boundaries, but which the official accounts sometimes take the trouble to define: they were now "fathers and mothers of an advanced age."[104]

Then came the age whose boundaries were the least controversial, the upper boundary on account of the uncertainty of death, the lower boundary on account of a very broad consensus. It was the favorite age in comedies, in which the amorous old graybeard is always sixty; medical treatises considered old age to begin at this point, and it was an important age in rural tradition.[105] This category had very few distinctions, though sometimes, in a rather vague way, the authors of the projects distinguished a particular subgroup, the "sages." But usually mention was made only of particularly brilliant performances in this category; the official accounts of the festivals refer to the ages of the elderly when they seem to belong to the realm of the marvelous—that is to say, from seventy onward.

The very fact of assigning boundaries to the age groups was an argument in favor of discontinuing this periodization. The divisions were not always made with the same precision, however. The gradual character of the passage from childhood to old age was never absolutely in doubt. No special ceremony was envisaged to stress such breaks, and, no doubt, one had to have reached sixty before one could have hoped to be the hero of the Festival of Old Age, but no particular ritual marked the passage. By contrast, the Festival of Youth involved real initiation rites, and, again, the real celebration lagged far behind the projects, which are striking in the meticulous detail of the arrangements envisaged. In his proposal Leclerc goes so far as to advocate a separation—temporary but complete—between the adolescents and their familiar world.[106] Those young people chosen by the municipal administration for candidature would set out for the principal town in the département armed with a *livret de famille*, national dress, and a complete set of arms. They would choose a leader—a memory, perhaps, of childhood priests—for the duration of the journey, which would be made in stages. On arrival, they would be received by the departmental administration. It is clear that only removal from the

Festival dedicated to Old Age. Etching by Duplessis-Bertaux, after a drawing by P. A. Wille, Bibliothèque nationale, Cabinet des estampes. Photo: Bulloz.

narrow horizons of the village seemed to Leclerc capable of convincing the young man that he had entered upon a "new career," that he was leaving his family to be "adopted by the fatherland."

Of course, poverty prevented such a plan from being put into practice. Nevertheless, the real festival preserved a very clear initiatory character, in which the abandonment of the practices and signs of childhood was symbolically marked: the sixteen-year-old youth had to cross the circle formed, around the altar of the fatherland, by the gathered assembly. Sometimes he had to bow before entering, as in the Festival of Youth at Moulins, where the youths had to pass two by two beneath a level suspended from a garland of flowers. Those who entered the circle holding a flower (a link with childhood) emerged bearing a weapon (a link with maturity). The taking of arms (when a commune did not possess any, the instructions, at least, had to be given "by way of pretense") constituted the material trace of the break with the past. So too could be the cockade, which many speakers in the great debate of Year VII wanted to make a symbol of adulthood. "I would not want children to be able to bear the cockade while still young," said Bonnaire. "It should be made a matter of sentiment. You would achieve this perhaps if you allowed the wearing of the cockade to begin only at the age when one begins to serve society: one registers with the National Guard at the age of sixteen; only then does one enter the great family and should carry the colors." [107] So Bonnaire advocates reserving the solemn handing over of the cockades to a certain age group and lays great stress on the purpose of the act: "In the past, we have paid scant regard to giving young men a noble idea of the moment when they are welcomed by society." Weapons, or the cockade, or an oak branch, which in the absence of weapons symbolized strength, marked entry into adulthood. The profound emotional significance of this initiation was increased by rejecting those who disdained to appear: such were neither youths nor men; they were nothing.

The dramatization of the ceremony also took the form of trials that, under proper supervision, the young men had to confront. Here again, reality lagged far behind the projects. Leclerc wanted young men to be accepted by the National Guard only if they could prove that they could read, write, practice a mechanical trade, and handle arms: there would therefore be four types of tests during the festival, duly supervised by the presidents and crowned with a display of the results on the altar of the fatherland. J.-M. Collot dreamed of a form of scouting: "From time to time I would like the young men to go away to camp and spend a few nights in a wood or in some difficult terrain, with precautions indicated by nature in such a case . . . I would like there to be surprises and unexpected difficulties. For example, I would leave the young men on the edge of a ravine or small river and leave them to find their way of crossing without danger, by means of a bridge, or a small, hastily constructed raft." [108] In practice one often had to be content with a brief period of military training or even some symbolic gesture: the speaker addressed the young men, who drew their sabers. They decorated the barrels of their guns with oak leaves and sang the *Marseillaise*. The return procession symbolized what had just taken place: the young men now marched with the company into which they had been incorporated. [109]

All these ceremonies concerned the young men of sixteen. The rites began a period of training that was to end at twenty-one, when their names were written in a civic register, a ceremony that, in the Festival of Youth, had to be given all due solemnity. [110] A thing written down still had all its sacral force, and many of those who fainted during the festival did so at the moment of signing. Finally, the festival ended with the taking of the oath, the obligatory dramaturgy of the Revolution, which here conferred its irreversibility on the rite of passage. The speeches stressed the solemnity of the occasion: "Young men, who have acquired the right of citizenship," the president of the municipal administration of Saint-Flour began his address to them. So it was above all the Festival of Youth [111]—in this, the Revolutionary festival made few innovations— that, dramatizing the passage from the land of birth to the land of social membership, enacted the meeting of the generations.

Apart from this dramatization, the central figure of the ceremonial of the ages was the gift. This consisted of figs and grapes, which were distributed by the old men to the young, or the young spouses presented the elderly with baskets of fruit, bread, and even a small glass of liqueur. Sometimes—and here the reciprocity of the age categories was stressed even more—the same objects circulated from hand to hand: the municipal officers gave civic palms to the elderly, who handed them on to the young. As formerly in the country and guild festivals, these exchanges culminated in a meal eaten in common. In the civic banquets, from the old people's table to that of the young, various acts of politeness were performed and presents were exchanged, or in the public square, each of the age groups paid homage to the cider barrels, which were finally taken under the Liberty tree and drunk from in common. [112]

It was hoped that these exchanges would be accompanied by the exchange of virtues. The old men who leaned on young citizenesses in the processions should acquire their strength and enthusiasm; and the girls, in turn, should acquire the experience and seriousness that they lacked by a sort of contagion.[113] The Festival of the Sovereignty of the People provided the most striking illustration of this exchange of objects and meanings. This festival, created in Year VI by the law of 13 Pluviôse, and whose explicit purpose was to guarantee good elections, was supposed to be the most abstract of all. But it was assiduously celebrated nonetheless, and its whole ceremonial consisted of a precise exchange of the roles assigned to the elderly and the young, the former carrying the book of the Constitution on the outward journey, the latter on the return. The elderly carried a bundle of white sticks on the outward journey and then entrusted it to the young men for the return journey to the commune's administrative headquarters.

To exchange was in no way to invert, however: here, once again, we see the particular character of the Revolutionary festival, so poor in compensatory inversion, and where the exchanges of activities are always so meticulously regulated. Perhaps there was no festival where this was not so: even when a degree of liberating excess was allowed, the reversal of roles inevitably came to an end with the evening of the festival. But liberating excess is precisely what was missing here. The exchange of roles implied no revenge; it was simply a circular figure.

This helps to explain why the Revolutionary festival, forever torn between being and seeming, the ordinary and the extraordinary, resorted so often to the order of the age groups. If the ceremonial of the ages could be substituted so easily for other imaginable orders, and for the occupational order in particular (it had even been suggested, it seems, that there should be a mutual exclusion),[114] it was first of all because it was better equipped than others to deny the inequality of roles and conditions.[115] The representation of society, a partial expression of human existence, would destroy the ideal unanimity of the Revolutionary festival; but the order of the ages extends to all individuals in the community. The segmentation that it imposes allows of no exception of class or caste. The hierarchy that it sets up is dismantled and rearranged, without society taking part in it. Only nature distributes the task here, in a regular neutrality that seems to guarantee equity. Nobody put this more firmly than Esparron, in his *Traité des âges:* "Take a look at the tottering theater of life, with all its multiplicity and variety of scenes. What strikes one first is that a new actor always seems to be making his appearance: in one sense, this is an illusion, in another a reality. It is always the same man, but man successively: child, youth, adult, old man. Only Nature is in on the secret; only she is entrusted with the task of bringing on and disguising the characters."[116]

Lastly, and above all, the order of the ages, in its sempiternal litany, represents a sacred time that is always identical with itself, an indefinitely recoverable eternal present: the time of myth, the succession of eternities. Thus, the ceremonial of the ages helped to remove history from the Revolutionary festivals a little more, even in the commemorative festivals in which history ought nevertheless to triumph. The children who burned the symbols of a monarchy that they had never known or who carried the book of the Constitution stood for a time when the Revolution would no longer have to be defended. To entrust to them this sacred depository was to believe in a future when it would no longer have to be displayed. Historical evolution is subjected here to biological maturation. The history of Mankind is reduced—this was already a Saint-Simonesque metaphor—to the maturing of a collective being. Thus, what is expressed is the certainty—or hope—that the Revolution was not an ever-open history but an order that could no longer be disturbed by anything. The ceremonial of the ages seemed the best way of carrying out the impossible task of bringing the festival—and through it the Revolution—to an end.

So the organization of festive time was in the grip of an obsession with security. In all the animated debates concerning the new Revolutionary calendar and the choice of its festivals, there were very few voices pleading for an open Revolution, very few minds capable of conceiving that the Revolution had not yet "come to the end marked by philosophy." This opinion, which Duhem defended in the session of October 5, 1793, in the Convention, found no support. Yet Duhem persisted: he demanded that the Convention should abstain even from commemorating those undisputed times that Republicans "hold so dear to their hearts." How, indeed, could one legislate for posterity? How could one know if what one had chosen to include in the calendar was really "the greatest achievement of the Revolution"? This uncertainty as to history's verdict, and also the danger of idolatry that he detected in any solemn inclusion, led Duhem to demand a calendar that had the equitable neutrality of numerical order. But Romme, with the consensus of the Assembly behind him, victoriously defended his work. To adopt the dryness of numerical order would be to renounce "the moral and Revolutionary cachet" that results from a commemorative calendar. And, worse still, there would be nothing left to convey the Revolutionary message to future generations. This was the fundamental aim; this was the obsession with this whole organization of time. Its purpose was to instruct: the festival had to have a future in its own image.

· VIII ·
The Future of the Festival:
Festival and Pedagogy

HERE, indeed, was the essential point, the identical element in all these festivals: none of the men who organized the Revolutionary festivals was resigned to its insularity or to its gratuitousness. Utility—for Hegel the very atmosphere of the Enlightenment—dominated all their projects. At the end of the festival, men should go home happier and more enlightened: indeed, these were the same thing.

This is as much as to say that the festival was never over—not so much because one looked forward to it or because one remembered it, as through the discipline that it set up, the moral habits that it instilled, the system of rewards and penalties that it gave rise to. In the organizers' minds this resulted in an equalization, a flattening out, almost, of time; a contamination ought to occur between the high points and ordinary time. At Montignac, the citizens of the people's club who took part in the roadworks campaign ordered by Lakanal began and ended their labors with a drumroll and a march to the Liberty Tree, all flags unfurled; they named those virtuous, laborious days the Festival of Labor. The whole of life should be caught up in the festival if one accepts that the festival is a lesson in everyday morals, the impregnation of every citizen by the spirit of the Republic.

This presupposes trust in men's ability to be educated: like the pedagogy of the Enlightenment, the organizers of the festivals inherited a fervent belief in the ability to train minds, and their projects, even more clearly than their pedagogical treatises, reveal the poisonous consequences of their faith in human plasticity. One consequence was the moral *dirigisme:* "Since it is a good thing to know how to use men as they are, it is even better to make them in the way one needs them to be." This forceful formula comes from Rousseau's *Discours d'économie politique,*[1] which was repeated, if with less verbal felicity, by everyone. Another consequence was censorship, for if man is that soft, infinitely pliable wax, any counterteaching may undo everything that good teaching has achieved. An uncontrolled man may fall into the thrall of anyone or anything. Hence that proliferation of caution, precaution, and surveillance: this was the weak spot of all revolutions, which the organization of the festivals makes particularly apparent.

"The Schools of the Mature Man"

In the course of the Revolution, there was no debate on education in which the question of the festivals did not arise and no debate on the festivals in which it was not said that the festivals ought to be educative.[2] This was because it seemed aberrant to devote so much care to the education of children only to abandon them later to the hazards of adult life. The question was, how could the words of master and book be extended beyond the walls of the school? More particularly, what was to replace those words for the generations that were not educated and would never go to school? This gave rise to a new, even more difficult problem, for those generations deprived of Republican education had learned what they knew from other sources. The festival was a response to this concern. Without the festivals, the present generation was uneducable; without them, public education was condemned to be like Penelope's weaving, unstitched with each new generation. Without festivals, there was no hope of "throwing the nation into the mold."[3]

So the festivals were a supplement, even a substitute, for education.[4] Indeed, they were even better, for they did not provide exactly the teaching expected of the schools. The schools set out to train minds. Consequently, only a few schools, or schools for the few, might be needed (here we see the reservations felt by the elite about popular education). The festivals, by contrast, were addressed not to the intelligence but to the man as a whole and involved the entire community. Schools were for public education; the festivals were a form of national upbringing. This was a sufficient reason to make the festival a priority, as Sherlock explains in a tract that takes up a celebrated distinction made by Rabaut Saint-Etienne:

The Declaration of the Rights of Man. Engraving by Niquet. Photo: Giraudon/Art Resource, New York.

Public education is the privilege of a few; the upbringing of the nation
provides necessary nourishment for all. They are sisters, but the upbringing
of the nation is the elder. Nay, she is rather the mother of all citizens, who
gives them all the same milk, who brings them up and treats them as
brothers and who, by the care that she lavishes equally upon all, gives them
that air of family resemblance that distinguishes a people brought up in
this way from all the other peoples of the earth; its whole doctrine consists
therefore in seizing hold of man in the cradle and, even before his birth,
for the child who is not yet born already belongs to the fatherland. She
takes hold of the man and never leaves him, so that the upbringing of the
nation is an institution not only for childhood, but for the whole life.[5]

How could it be claimed that the festivals carried out this permanent
moral training? How could they act on man and by what means? In the
first instance, it was the regularity of the festivals—that equitable distribution throughout the year, so desired but so seldom achieved—that was
to sustain the individual life. The festival required assiduous attendance,
which was also a condition for the efficacity of the teaching dispensed in
the schools. So the fundamental problem of the festival, as in the schools,
was that of "attendance."

The festivals were also schools, simply by virtue of gathering men together: for a festival, as for a school, one must first decide on a place as
"the meeting point for the exercise of the social virtues,"[6] a place capable
of being at one and the same time, as Jean Guineau wished,[7] a Champ-
de-Mars, a museum, a meeting place for families, a theater, a circus, and
a marketplace. In that privileged, overdetermined center, mere contact
between people was an education in civics.[8] The men of the Revolution
accorded an immediate virtue to the *réunion* or gathering, very different
from the riotous assembly or even the crowd. Almost always they saw
men's isolation as a cause of the decline of public opinion, and a whole
political geography was born from this observation. For them, land divided up by hedge, fence, or wall produced enemies of the Republic, as if
the physical fragmentation were a federalism of nature all too likely to
produce another. Open land, meanwhile, which allowed the eye to move
freely, strengthened the Republican spirit. Was this because it made Revolutionary surveillance easier? Apart from this somewhat cynical reason,
it was also because the movement of eyes, the exchange of feelings and
ideas, seemed to carry with them an immediate teaching: the city, the
place of commercial exchange, was also the place of cultural exchange.
The festival, the occasion when people come together, must therefore be

a source of enlightenment: "a numerous, and therefore less superstitious people," one commissioner for the département of the Rhône wrote with eloquent succinctness.[9]

In the festive gathering, under the eye of a community from which he cannot be separated, the mature man becomes once again pupil and child, tightly reined, closely watched. The Republican festival, like the school, was "severely ordered, religiously observed," quite the reverse of that panicky rejoicing described by Barère as the evil, nocturnal, secret obverse of the civic festivals.[10] The festival, like the school, seized upon the private life and publicized it irretrievably. This is quite clear in the discussion of Year VI on institutions concerning the civil state. Leclerc, the author of the project, wanted to extend festive solemnity to the whole of life and to persuade each citizen to celebrate everyday acts and the principal "events" in his life.[11] To achieve this, it would be necessary to have in each family the sacralizing presence of a book and to make citizens keep a journal in it of the various events that marked their lives: using this practice, the father would note down prizes won, good days and bad days, the day he was a witness at a friend's wedding, or the day when he lost such and such a friend. It was to invite citizens to a salutary act of recording, to the solemnization of the whole of life. Furthermore, it was to create a convergence between private and public rejoicing; for, with each birth, marriage, adoption, grief the private act of writing would duplicate the official records. It would simply give a more psychological, more intimate version. In keeping the family book, said Leclerc, one would be stressing the moral side. But the family book and the official book, authenticated, moreover, by the same signatures, were like two sides of the same reality. Both guaranteed that family festivals would be contained within a closed circle; everyone could enjoy them, draw useful emotions from them for their own moral betterment. The private festival would gain by being a public festival; and the public festival would recover the charm of private celebrations. Some organizers were well aware of what the Republican festivals had to gain by drawing on the spontaneous theatricality of the family festivals.[12] Where else but at a wedding, for example, could one find "more likable objects, detached troups of actors who conduct themselves better"?

All the arguments were for the convergence, therefore, in the festival of individual emotions and general fervor. When in Year VI a great debate opened in the councils as to whether or not weddings should be confined to the *décadis,* those who maintained that weddings should coincide with the (tenth) day of rest had difficulty demonstrating that the "lesson" of marriage would thereby be infinitely enlarged, extended, better understood, and better assimilated, and that marriage would thereby gain in strength. It would not be easy to break undertakings accepted before so many witnesses, with so much pomp, and on the day that was being solemnized at the same moment throughout the Republic. Creuzé-Latouche returns to this argument constantly: the meeting of private celebration and public celebration removed any opportunity for the man who claimed to live outside the laws.[13] Where would he go to flee from the "cry of general indignation"? How would he extricate himself from the obligation of preparing himself for the festival, of wearing better clothes than usual, of sweeping the doorstep, decorating streets and houses? The festival was also a school by virtue of the image that it sent back to the people of itself—the best possible image. It was a model to be followed, which, at the same time, suggested a gap to be filled.

The festival was a school by virtue of its regularity, its public character, the tension that it required, and, obviously, by its content, what it "showed" and "explained," expressions whose obsessive use makes clear enough what was hoped of it. The festive episode most slavishly based on the school model was the *bulletin*—the heart of the *fête décadaire*—which had to be read, with distinction if not eloquence, and in which it was hoped to condense the maximum amount of information possible. Apart from the summary that it was supposed to give of the affairs of the Republic, it was hoped that it would describe "government patents for new inventions, or new methods of manufacture,"[14] or the implementation of new irrigation methods from Italy.[15] But beyond this didactic purpose— often, it is true, felt to be caricatural[16]—the festival was a place of challenge, combat, competition, reward, triumph (one notes here the hold over people's minds of memories of a schoolroom Greece, "where the gods themselves crown one another and submit themselves to the judgment of men").[17] This explains why the Republican festivals, even those dedicated to very different celebrations, all ended up looking much alike, like so many speech days buzzing with praise and criticism. This resemblance is sometimes explicitly underlined, as at Chelles, where, for the festival of August 10, Year II (even though it was celebrating an event that had nothing to do with school), the boys of the village paraded with their teacher, a book in his right hand, a cane in his left; then came the girls with their teacher, armed with a book and a crown, a striking visual summary of the system of sanctions with which the festival was intended to be identified.

Yet, however much one wanted the festival to be a school, it had to be something more. We also have to attract people, sighed the administrator of the commune of Bischwiller,[18] aware that some account had to be taken of the pleasure that ought, as Grégoire suggested in his report on vandalism, to be its mainspring. Education through the festivals was "without labor and without expense."[19] The festival could be a school, therefore, only if that school were a festival,[20] a circle that forced the useful to comply with the agreeable, "to speak to the senses," and therefore to entrust the whole education of men to the attraction of images.

The Power of Images

To believe that the festival could seize the whole man, as the school seized the whole child, was, it is said, to have a pretty poor idea of the autonomy of thought. In this sense the men of the Revolution—one has only to think of Mirabeau—had perfectly assimilated the empiricism of a century that had constantly eroded the independence that Locke still accorded human reflection. For them, reflection never freed itself from sensation; and man defined by his quality of being, a being of sense, is led not by principles but by objects, spectacles, images. The festival organizers, who were never in any doubt about this commonplace of empiricist psychology, also borrowed its vocabulary: "soft wax" and "clay" provided them with ready metaphors,[21] as did the "seal," the "stamp," or the "imprint" with which the school, the festival, or the institution seemed to them necessarily to mark men. The empiricist references were also reinforced by a return to the Revolutionary events themselves and by an act of collective psychology: unstable, fickle, impressionable as the French nation was, it was also more sensitive than any other to the power of images.[22]

This was both an admission of humility and a sign of power. It was an admission of humility because the realm of wishing, thinking, and believing did not seem to be in any way independent of the realm of the senses; because no intellectual operation was anything more than an extended or transformed sensation; because no faith derived its vitality except from the impression with which it was associated. When, at the Council of the Five Hundred, the question of the organization of primary schools was raised, Joubert, reciting Helvetius, noted that we are not so much pupils of our masters as of "the circumstances that have surrounded us, the objects that have frequently attracted our eyes and captured our attention."[23] This disillusioned way of considering man's faculties was also an affirmation of power: it placed human destiny in the hands of the good

legislator-pedagogue. Since every sensation is tinted with pleasant or unpleasant aspects, whoever could think up a system in which pleasure im-
pels to virtue and displeasure is the price of vice would get to the heart of
the political and moral problem. This leitmotif of the Revolutionary assemblies is entirely in line with the thinking of the century; it was precisely what Holbach had said.

At first sight, the application of these principles to the festivals is very
simple. In order to produce that "dilation of the spirits," that "lively
agitation," that "striking awakening" that indicated that a festival had
succeeded, it had to act upon all the senses at once, multiply impressions
and emotions, lavish profusely "living and religious images." The idea of
the fatherland, and of the Republic, was always to be linked with that of
superabundant wealth.[24] The resulting imaginative connection would
produce an irresistible political belief and an invincible heroism.

And that would be all; there was nothing else to be done. No one
concerned himself with the various stages by which images exert their
power. The only circumstance that strengthened their grip was impregnation; and even that was not always necessary. Painting, sculpture, music, and sometimes even reading often seemed to possess an immediately
persuasive power. The anthem of the *Marseillaise* "created" battalions,[25]
an engraving popularized great examples, the reading of the *bulletin décadaire* inflamed in the mind as quickly and surely as Diderot had imagined,[26] astonished that one could allow the reading of subversive texts and
then, ten years later, be surprised to find oneself surrounded by different
men. This action of signs on ideas and ideas on morals was linear; it was
conceived according to the model of contagion.

Yet here, the self-confidence of these men faltered a little. If there were
festivals that, in their eyes, corresponded to this ideal model, they were
the religious festivals. The liking of mature men for spectacles had already
been satisfied by the religious ceremonies and processions; their eyes were
still filled with the gold of chasubles and the glow of candles; and the
priests knew how to use terror as well as pleasure. In the church there was
silence, darkness, mystery; if one raised one's eyes, "a young, naked man,
attached with nails, through his feet and through his hands, to a cross
bespattered with blood, his head leaning to one side and crowned by sharp
thorns, expiring in the most horrible torments, this was the spectacle that
first struck one."[27] Michel-Edme Petit, who drew this picture during the
period of the Convention, even doubted whether the shock thus produced
could be offset by the teaching of the Constitution. The problem, then,

was to substitute[28] for these images other images of equivalent force, but different content, by borrowing from "the liturgy, which brought representation to perfection," and by studying the formalization of its most successful gestures and movements.[29]

But even in this substitution there is a note of anxiety. If the priests were so successful at using images, it is because paintings, sculpture, and music are two-sided arts, capable of drawing toward evil as well as good, toward superstition as well as enlightenment. Even a man as confident in the education dispensed by music as Leclerc did not belive that one could accord blind protection to this art, which could also lead to vice. The problem faced by these festival organizers, therefore, was this: they must strike the imagination yet avoid the disgust that might be aroused by the overfacile, exaggerated effect or the overexpressive image. Secure in their belief in the power of images, they had to use them, while remaining obstinately convinced, according to a scheme inherited from classical thought, that everything that is figurative is false. When presenting the Constitution of Year III to the Councils of the Ancients, Bosquillon was indignant that, in the public festivals, the "sacred book," the Constitution, exposed to the veneration of the citizens, was merely a mock book, a cover over an empty book, or, worse still, the "horrors of fanaticism," a disguised missal.[30] So a very meticulous selection was made of pedagogical methods; but contradictions recurred, and an invincible malaise remained.

The Correct Use of Images

Visual representation, then, was at the center of the organizers' concerns, as it had been throughout the century. Certainly they also recognized the stirring power of auditory images, and some became theoreticians of their use in the festivals.[31] Nevertheless, the eyes seemed to them "the most powerful of all the organs" and sight the very sense by which man is educated, by virtue, no doubt, of the immediate character of the information gathered in the eyes. Of all the arts, therefore, those involving sight were thought to be the least deceiving: "What the painter shows," wrote Diderot, "is the thing itself; the expressions of the musician and poet are merely hieroglyphs of it." A mass of works[32] from this time illustrate the pedagogical privilege accorded sight.[33] This status is confirmed by the question set at the competition for the painting section of the Institut: "What was and what can still be the influence of painting on morals and the government of a free people?" Visual representation dominated almost exclusively, therefore, the debate that revolved around two major questions: Which visual images are the most convincing; that is to say, which of the arts is best adapted to the purpose of the festival? And what credence can be given to spectacle in general?

The first issue was soon exhausted: unanimity was easily reached in favor of sculpture. This was because in painting the image is made smaller; within the limitations of its setting, it irresistibly attracts the attention of the detached, somewhat frivolous spectator, precisely the type that the Revolution sought to exclude. Even when a painting is the occasion of a fairly realistic dramatization (as in that curious festival at Evreux, in which the executioner cut off the head of a portrait of Louis XVI, showed to the people the fragment of painted canvas, and threw it into a wastepaper basket),[34] it cannot really claim to have the verisimilitude of a statue. "The productions of sculpture," wrote G.-M. Raymond, "are infinitely closer to nature than pictures."[35] The picture scatters the spectator's attention, whereas sculpture concentrates it into an energetic laconism: "Sculpture," according to Falconet, "has only one word to say, and that word must be sublime."[36] Furthermore, deprived of anthropomorphic exemplariness, painting cannot lay claim to the spontaneous sacrality of the statue. Thus, if the communes had the means of realizing their ambitions, they resorted to sculpture much more than to painting, and to statues rather than to busts, for "the honor of statues" is infinitely superior to that of busts,[37] preferably the colossal male statues adopting some heroic pose—in contrast with the female figures of the Republic or Nature, which sit in maternal peace—in which the Revolution saw its most successful embodiment.

The second question was a much thornier one. Led by their sensualism to trust spectacle, the men of the Revolution dreamed not so much of the austere transparency of a festival, where, in a sense, there would be nothing to see: it was the mode bequeathed to them by Rousseau and which was beyond dispute. Each of the political generations that the Revolution brought to maturity claimed conformity with the model for itself and for the festivals that it had invented (and each accused the other, the preceding one, of encumbering its festivals with an unbearable mass of visual bric-a-brac). Instead, everyone dreamed of the Revolutionary festival as a village festival without spectacle, enlarged to the dimensions of the entire nation. This was to believe in the need for a divorce between theater and festival,[38] in the possibility of a completely detheatricalized festival.

It goes without saying that the organizers were using very old arguments, such as the one that brings out the ephemeral character of thetrical communion. Even the advocates of the theater—Diderot, for example—wondered how, once the curtain came down, the ephemeral cohesion created by the theater could be maintained. In other words, the spectacle usually has no tomorrow, and this is fatal to a festival that is intended to be rich in lessons for the future.

Furthermore, the festival organizers were sensitive to the aesthetic and social fragmentation brought about by the theater. This was an old argument: the theater separates auditorium and stage, erecting the boundary of the footlights between actors and sepctators;[39] it divides up space to an absurd degree, marking off as many "private groups"[40] as there are boxes and leaving a dark area backstage, which the Revolutionary imagination tended to people with traitors and aristocrats; it abolishes the fluidity of space, holding back communal exaltation between its walls, preventing it from irradiating freely throughout the participating throng. Where, precisely, could the people find their place in the theater? If represented on the stage, they kept banging clumsily up against the mean limitations of that small space and breaking into groups, which, manipulated somewhere as if on parade by some invisible authority, lost their genial liberty. In the auditorium, the people were reduced to the status of an audience: this explains Rousseau's fondness for a festival without object, so close to the deliberating assembly of the social contract. To gather men together for "nothing," without the help of the slightest mediation, was to transform an audience into a people.

Above all, the organizers of the Revolutionary festivals rejected that which constitutes the reality of the spectacle—masks, makeup, and machinery, "loaded" events, counterfeit characters—all amounting to one huge lie. For these seekers after pure presence, the slightest scenographic artifice or the most fleeting image was already *de trop,* and mimicry always had something of the grimace about it: at the horizon of their dreams, there was that mythical Greek religion in which "no image represented the goddess and in which she inhabited people's hearts."[41] This pursuit of a purifying austerity explains the refusal of a request from the Section des Quinze-Vingts to burn a fire in perpetuity on the altar of the church of Saint-Antoine. The answer came back from the offended commune: "No material sign in the temples." Indignation was all the stronger in that the theater claimed to represent not an insignificant event but the object of the festival itself. When, in Prairial, Year II, some astute spectacle organizers wanted to take advantage of the success of the Festival of the Supreme Being to make it an excuse for theatrical representation, a decree from the Committee of Public Instruction soon put an end to their plans. And Payan, the *rapporteur,* had nothing but sarcasm for the odd notion of caging up "the sublime tableau of Prairial . . . within the tiny proportions of the stage." The whole text should be quoted, so revealing is it of the suspicion of the theater felt by the Revolutionary sensibility: "What stage, with its cardboard rocks and trees, its sky or rags, could claim to equal the magnificence of 1 Prairial or to efface its memory?"[42]

Lastly, in the spectacle, the spectator is in the grip of an invincible passivity: he has nothing to do but listen and look. Such unbearable inertia was almost insulting for a revolutionary people steeled to struggle. The festival ought to involve the celebrant.[43] This certainty, argued at length by Merlin de Thionville, is even capable of producing what is least expected: a highly critical retrospective look at the Federation itself, that festival in which nothing was offered the people except the role of "worshippers, with their feet in the mud and their heads in the clouds," and three objects of worship: a miterd head on an altar, a crowned body on another altar, and a horse bearing yet another altar."

To the wish, tirelessly expressed, for a festival that would break with all spectacle and therefore with all falseness, the real festivals provided only an imperfect response. This was because, to begin with, the organizers saw very quickly that festivals in which there was nothing to see would be boring and also because their puritanical criticism of theatrical illusion was opposed by a psychology that had remained obstinately sensuous. Was one to renounce the incalculable power over youth possessed by those things that move the soul? Was one to deprive oneself of those things that had given the priests such power?[44] In fact, a collaboration was therefore worked out between the theater and the festival. Sometimes the stage took over the images and themes of the festival. At Bordeaux, in the summer of 1790, the theater put on a "festival of liberty" and paraded the battalion of costumed children that had been the centerpiece of so many Federations.[44] Conversely, the festival sometimes availed itself of the resources of the theater. It might occasionally call on the theater for help and set up in the public square,[46] linked by processions, stages in which a Revolution cut up into episodes was played out. It might also become indistinguishable from the theater: this, it was said, occurred with the Paris Festival of Reason, whose ceremonial, so wrongly reputed to be original, was slavishly copied from an opera libretto.

But these exchanges, these borrowings, these services lent and rendered were not made without regret or precaution. When they called up simulation, symbol, and allegory for their own instructive purposes, the fesival organizers also laid down under what conditions and within what limits these could be used without danger. A whole pedagogical art of the image may be deduced from their projects and their productions.

Take, for example, mime (the attack on the fortress, a battle, the crossing of a bridge) and simulacrum (the portraits, busts, and statues carried during the processions). Both involved mock figures, made necessary by the absence of the event or individuals represented. They therefore involved deception for Rousseauist sensibilities that already suspected an element of betrayal in any kind of duplication. How, then, could they be used correctly?

What should be aimed at was a certain verisimilitude, a minimal realism, in which there would be no illusion. In miming a battle, one should rattle "bayonets, rifles, sabers, hatchets, forks, and other weapons."[47] There was also some attempt to introduce an element of hesitation, of suspense, into the action. The verisimilitude of mime requires that the outcome should not seem to be determined in advance. Not, of course, that the ending was ever a problem; but it was right that a mock siege should not be over too quickly. It was better still if the whole commune could be involved in it, a great collective game, which would exorcise the evil temptations of separation that the theater encouraged and that strengthened belief. At Charmes, for the festival celebrating the retaking of Toulon, the citizens were invited to gather at night, in open countryside, around "lighted fires in the shape of a bivouac"; then, when the alarm sounded, an assault would be launched on two mock cities—Lyon and Toulon—which would go up in flames in the night.

The same concern for verisimilitude applied to the materials used and the forms chosen. A decent simulacrum had to be of a certain size: the tiny mahogany guillotine coquettishly borne on a white silk cushion by an actress symbolizing "Woman Liberty," as at Langres, may have been meticulously executed, but no one would have found it the least bit intimidating. Similarly, the miniature castle burned in the public square of Thiviers was too mean for anyone to believe that it could shelter "the enemies of public felicity." Miniaturization destroys any attempt at illusion. Attention must be paid, therefore, to proportion. Just as important, however, was the material: cardboard, canvas, or paper stretched on canvas, in which Stendhal as a child saw on the place Grenette at Grenoble "scepters, crowns, and other symbols," are too perishable. The hut made of yellow paper paraded around at Viroflay for the Toulon festival was severely criticized by the national agent, who failed to recognize it as a fortress. The people's club of Montignac, sick at possessing only improbable dummies of Marat and Lepelletier, sent commissioners to Paris in search of a faithful engraving. The people's club at Castres strove hard to achieve realism: the dummy of Saint-Fargeau was decked out in "his ordinary clothes" in such a way as to show the bloody shirt and the "gaping wound and the parricidal blade still stained with blood." It required a great deal of work if the simulacrum was to earn the title of sacred, a magical adjective, which absolved it of its suspect kinship with the idol.

What was needed was enough illusion for the lesson to be conveyed but not so much as to cause confusion; a certain distance was still required. In the case of mime, there were obvious limits to imitation, since actions and emotions had to be condensed. In the case of a simulacrum, there was a desire to avoid the fragility of cardboard and canvas; but if bronze were used, it would verge on the monumental. Between the extremes of paper and bronze, plaster seemed to possess precisely the right consistency. Similarly, it should not be thought that the living form—the "living statue," as the accounts put it—carried out the pedagogical function best. It might well be superior to a statue, however. A young boy lying on the front of a chariot, motionless beside his drum, seemed more likely to recall Marat's memory than a clumsy statue. Yet the superiority of the tableau vivant was not universally accepted. There is a famous article in which Momoro justifies the choice of the actress for the Paris Festival of Reason: an "inanimate simulacrum" might more easily have aroused contempt in vulgar minds and therefore threatened them with idolatry.[48] A living woman, by contrast, would discourage identification: such a representation would not run the risk of being sacralized in the place of what was being represented. Again, what was being sought was an allegory, not a simulacrum. When one wanted to evoke real individuals, it was even less certain that a living man—who, as everyone in the commune knew, was merely taking on the features of Marat or Lepelletier for the duration of the procession—could generate more intense emotion than a statue. Momoro was well aware that, apart from the reification involved in all idolatry, the living representation is closer to the theater and paradoxically reduces verisimilitude. The most realistic mode of representation is not necessarily the most convincing.

So we must pause at this point in a very uncomfortable situation. The organizers often preferred to be free of the model to be imitated, free of the need to make a figurative realism convey a message. Thus, at the Festival of 9 and 10 Thermidor at Beauvais, Thermidorian conformists wished to express the power of the "triumvirs" with a mock throne. Here there was no real throne to be reproduced. The throne exhibited at the festival was "a tribune of blood, represented by a pediment painted in red, to which were tied garlands of oak mixed with hawthorn, with crossed scythes." No attempt at verisimilitude here, but a whole symbolism of cruelty is suggested in the garish color and the blades: here the lesson is appealing to an emotional, intuitive form of knowledge.

The Revolutionary festival, however, was also suspicious of symbols. This was because, in the depths of the symbol, as in the realism of the simulacrum, there sometimes lay an uncontrolled element that could well be an invitation to the very violence that the Revolutionary festival was seeking to extirpate. The cruelty recalled by the symbol must be recognized as such, but must in no way lead to another act of cruelty. The simulacrum hesitates to show the relationship between executioner and victim, to dramatize the punishment itself. One suddenly wanted to show the people the effigies of "the traitor Capet and his whore Marie Antoinette," but one hesitated to guillotine them again in the festival: the pedagogy of terror was not often entrusted to representations.

A certain conjuration of violence was at work, then, which explains why allegory was the favorite form of representation in the Revolutionary festival. Unlike the simulacrum and the symbol, allegory is, according to Quatremère de Quincy, "an imitation that is to a certain extent nonimitative," an admirable definition of a representation that is concerned more with substitution than with reproduction.[49] Allegory, therefore, does not try to sustain illusion. What it cultivates particularly is allusion. It has only to indicate; representation, which, in the simulacrum, has to maintain at least a minimum of fidelity, is abandoned. The forms, even if they are the graceful forms of the goddesses of Liberty, are important only for the idea that they envelop. When, in Pluviôse, Year VII, the minister of the interior wanted to play down the manner in which the Festival of the Sovereignty of the People would be celebrated, he invited artists to suggest "images"—or rather, he corrected himself, "ideas." The allegorical concern to keep a certain distance from reality is such that one of the rules of the treatises on taste, inherited from Du Bos, is never to mix in a single work historical characters and allegorical characters, for the latter "stretch over the former the veil of fiction and in both cases the tableau becomes an unsustainable lie."

This distance, this austerity of allegory may be seen as one of the main reasons why the Revolutionary festival made such use of it. Allegory is seemly. One of its advantages, writes Jacques Lacombe, "is to hide itself under a borrowed veil."[50] As a result, it tones down whatever features might otherwise be too vivid; it has the decency of indirect speech; it protects from the threat that excessive imitation carries.

And that is also why it served to defuse the invitation to brutality that can go with spectacles. Reading the official accounts, we should not believe too readily that popes to be whipped, Pitts to be insulted, and Capets to be guillotined were dragged out into the public squares. A more attentive reading tells us that the dummy did not often bear much resemblance to Capet, and that a royal headband, or sometimes an even less explicit emblem, served. In short, it was not so much a pope that was being thrashed as Fanaticism, and not so much Louis XVI as Monarchy. Fanaticism and Monarchy, but also Abundance, Liberty, Justice—the lesson of the Revolution was conveyed by a swarm of allegorical figures. Many of these figures were female, a fact that widens still further the gap between the Revolutionary events and the forms that symbolized them. This did not pass without protest: "Women everywhere, when what we need is a vigorous, severe regeneration!"[51]

There was another side to the decency of allegory, namely, the fact that it often looked like a puzzle. This difficulty has been stressed by all those who have written about allegory (from Winckelmann to Addison, from Sulzer to Jansen) and tried to decipher what is often like a code. This code may well have given great pleasure to the festival organizers, experienced as they were from the schoolroom at deciphering it, but it ran the risk of boring the public, which did not possess the necessary keys, and for whom, after all, those figures were intended. This was an occasion for indignation and easy sarcasm,[52] but sometimes it was also a genuine worry for educators. By trying to keep the emotional charge of the images presented at a distance, the Revolutionary festival lost any power to persuade. Half-aware of this failure, the organizers then put all their hopes in speeches.

Nothing Goes without Saying

The Revolutionary festival was certainly verbose: that was the unanimous verdict of its detractors. One has to agree. The festival of the Revolution said more than it showed:[53] it was full of gloomy readings and endless speeches. At the most ordinary festival in the smallest municipality in the canton, one had to listen first to the commissioner of the executive directory, then to the president of the municipality, and one was lucky if some village schoolmaster did not feel obliged to give his own interpretation of the facts or to declaim some appropriate stanzas. The schoolchildren would be there, hoisted up onto an improvised stage, stumbling through the Rights of Man, with the audience only pretending to listen. In short, the festival offered very little more than a sermon. There was probably music; but generally it took the form of anthems, and therefore words again, which had to be learned by heart or read from boring librettos. The festival must have seemed endless, though, paradoxically, dedicated to the praise of sober laconism.

But this was nothing. Even more striking was the proliferation of placards and banners that accompanied the groups in the processions, duplicating the images, statues, or busts. Sometimes these were quite simply explanatory: how would one have known that the evil candles carried at Cognac in the festival of August 10 were those of Reason, or Philosophy, if the notice had not read, "May the flame of Reason always be your guide"?[54] But even in the case of a more easily interpreted symbol, such as the sheaf of wheat or the vine branches carried by the plowman, it was never thought unnecessary to add a few words to the effect that these were "Nature's gifts to her children." This was because the descriptive function of this language was far less important than its hortatory function; it was, in any case, a crude language that in the limited space allocated to it urged people to action, like the repeated chanting of "They shall be avenged, they shall be avenged" during the funeral march of Rastadt. But language could be interpretive: at Bourg, in a festival of the people's club, three donkeys were paraded around wearing a royal crown, a biretta, and a tiara. The inscriptions, not content to name the characters suggested by this polemical bestiary, made it quite clear what one should think of them. "I am more useful than a king," said the first, "more respectable than a priest," said the second, and "more chaste than a pope," said the third.

What is the significance of this determination to overlay the visual with the verbal? Quite obviously, it had an antiquarian connotation: the image of the festivals of antiquity remained the more or less explicit model. Indeed, in certain festivals—that for Simonneau, for example—the inscriptions were written in Roman capitals and brandished by men dressed in Roman costume. Here again, one finds that fantasy of ancient cities, with their streets and squares full of messages to the citizen, that so marked the thought of the century, and of which Bernardin Saint-Pierre had set forth the modern version.[55]

Can we also see it as a sort of Revolutionary romanticism? It might be thought that this trust placed in the power of the word was hardly surprising at a time when no one separated speech from action, since a bad speech in the Convention or some injudicious remark might lead to the scaffold. The men of the Revolution themselves dwelled on this hypothesis, convinced, like Cabanis, that the Revolutionary upheavals had given the language an incomparable energy and that, "in Republics, a word, a mere mention on a public rostrum, a decree of three lines urges men on from exploit to exploit."[56] The Revolutionary sensibility expected words to have an immediate contagious effect: in how many pamphlets do we read that the enemy armies should be flooded, by means of aerostats, with the Declaration of the Rights of Man, the best weapon of dissuasion?[57]

In spite of this, recourse to words seems above all to have followed the logic of empiricism (the myth of the tabula rasa or of soft wax obviously involves the use of simplified speech, the rhythmic repetition of the aphorism and slogan, since redundancy is the essence of teaching by imprint). It also stems from a lack of confidence in the educative power of images. Images seem to be so threatened by ambiguity that they need the reassurance of commentary. It was the task of this commentary to provide a fixed translation, capable of restraining the uncontrolled movement of meaning and of limiting severely the room for interpretation.[58] Nothing goes without saying: that might be the slogan of Revolutionary aesthetics. In this regard, David's presentation to the National Convention of his picture of Michel Lepelletier on his deathbed is a fascinating example of the reading of a painting by its author.[59] To the father wishing to show the picture to his children—a situation that, in itself, reveals the painter's pedagogical ambitions—David suggests four steps, accompanied by four lessons. First, the children should observe the hero's "serene features." These they will read as meaning that one has nothing to reproach oneself for "when one dies for one's country." They will then pass to the sword: this will teach them of the courage that Lepelletier needed in daring to commit the regicide. Then to the wound, which might be the occasion for a negative lesson, inspired by repulsion: "You will weep, my children, you will avert your eyes." But this moment is soon saved by contemplation of the crown, which can be deciphered as the immortality that "the fatherland holds in reserve for its children." Thus the whole picture becomes translated into a series of statements. It is an invitation to that methodical journey suggested so insistently by the ordered sequences of compositions such as *Brutus* or *Socrates,* but which is also possible in the case of a very spare painting. In his very full explanation, nothing is left to chance interpretation: there is room for no unformulated reserve.

With his usual perspicacity Péguy sees commentary that exhausts the meaning of images as the distinctive feature of Revolutionary pedagogy, the mark of its caution and wariness.[60] What deprived *La mère coupable,* the play in which Beaumarchais repaints Rosine and Almaviva in the colors of the time, of the freshness of *Le barbier de Séville* and *Le mariage de Figaro?* This only: in *Barbier* and *Mariage,* the characters come onstage without ceremony, and we have to wait until the dénouement of the play to find out what they were really like, what they felt, what was happening to them. Here everything is said in the program, before the play even begins. Count Almaviva is "a great Spanish lord, of a noble pride, but without arrogance." The knight, Léon, is "a young man in love with liberty, like all young, ardent souls." All that is left for the play to do is to develop, as expected, the indications in the program: all sense of spontaneity has gone.

Nevertheless, contemporaries believed that something else had been gained. In fact, the use of commentary alone seemed able to bring a solution to the great contradictions that we have discovered between the projects of the festivals and the festivals themselves, between the need to show and horror at the exhibition. When Isnard, in the Convention, brandished a sword to lend emphasis to his speech on Girondin policies, Robespierre was indignant and begged the Assembly to abolish all such movements of "material eloquence" likely to create "an emotive contagion."[61] But if what one shows is carefully defined, enclosed within a particular mode, and tied to a particular usage, the exhibition loses its threatening character and is turned into code. This explains Rousseau's recourse to costume, despite his loathing of ostentation: exhibition is forgotten in the safety of a signalization.[62] This is also what the Société de Philanthropes had in mind when, in its *Calendrier du peuple franc pour servir à l'instruction publique,* it recommended that each father select a name for his son associated with the trade that he himself practiced and wished to perpetuate in his family (Agricola, for example, for a farmer's son). At twenty-one the young man would add to his name that of some famous man whose memory he particularly venerated—Brutus, for example. In this way, one would know precisely what sort of man one was dealing with; each person, each object, commented the Philanthropists, "requires an application that may make known the nature and properties of that person or thing."

Words, therefore, brought the festival to an end. The people's club of Condom, which met in 1794 to celebrate the destruction of images—pieces of wood, metal, and marble in the church—greeted this abolition of the visual with the cry: "May words be henceforth instruments!" An instrument for what? Judith Schlanger is well aware of this question when she points to the timeless present that David's programs presuppose when they say not at what moment in the spectacle tears should flow but that they will flow, even before the festival has taken place.[63] This, therefore, is neither an observation or a prescription, but a normative description that includes the movements of the soul as well as the scenic arrangements: an incantatory truth that is the truth of desire achieved in the imaginary, and in which Revolutionary pedagogy finds its exemplary culmination.

BUT whom will it teach? As in all pedagogical fanaticism, the question is never posed. The organizers seem to be quite unaware of those "fickle or dull natural rebels," whom even Holbach opposes to Helvetius' pedagogical optimism. Those festival-schools are addressed to adult-children, who, it seems, are without past, memory, or habits. Very few thinkers realized that it was a question not so much of "instructing the people" as "replacing for it one education by another."[64] There were very few thinkers who, like Just Rameau, suggested basing their festivals on the present generation's "habits, corruption in customs,"[65] and advised philosophers to go out into the provinces. In the 44,000 communes referred to by J. Terral, "morals seem to present as many subtle differences as there are degrees of enlightenment, opinions, and divisions."[66] There men already had festivals; there the Revolutionary festival met, to the surprise of its organizers, the tenacious exuberance of old customs.

· IX ·
Popular Life and the Revolutionary Festival

S EEING so many Brutuses and Sidneys paraded not only in the streets
of towns but even in the most isolated villages, hearing so many
anthems sung by people who could not possibly have understood
their meaning—for, despite all the good reasons advanced to explain the
success of the *Marseillaise*,[1] one is still perplexed as to what the crowds of
peasants at Sault de Vaucluse or Locquirec could have understood by "May
an impure blood water our furrows"—one is convinced easily enough of
how weak the links must have been between the Revolutionary festival
and popular life. The almost unanimous verdict on the Revolutionary
festival was that it was an improbable, absurd grafting, which explained
and merited the failure that so many of the official accounts attribute to
it. Whether appointed representatives or commissioners of the executive
directory—it hardly mattered—the officials were parachuted into a provincial life of which they knew nothing. They neither could nor did they
wish to see traditional life; they fought relentlessly against popular customs and imposed against local feeling a festival without roots, destined
to disappear when they themselves had gone.

A few timid voices were raised against this commonly received idea.
A. Varagnac, for example, suggests that if the Revolutionary festival
failed to be truly popular, it was because it was not given time to take
root; ten years were really not long enough.[2] With time, says Varagnac,
a whole "authentically archaic" folklore of Liberty Trees and Festivals of
Youth would, no doubt, have become established.

"No doubt": the uncertainty is worth noting. It is not easy to know
whether the men of the Revolution would have succeeded in their undertaking. Do we even know what, in fact, they wanted to accomplish? Did

they consciously set about to exterminate popular life? Or were they merely guilty of blind haste? Were they so unaware of the ceremonial aspect of traditional life that they never had recourse to it in their own festivals? It is this enormous problem that I would now like to take up in detail.

A Shameful Ethnology

Although they saw nothing of popular practices, these officials were nevertheless invited to observe them and to report their observations. Statistical investigation was an important matter in Revolutionary France,[3] and traditional practices came within its purview. It was intended to include popular customs side by side with information concerning roads, forests, and epizootic diseases.[4] There were informants who were asked for precise observations and even practical field research. These investigations, which were carried out throughout the Revolution by different men and at different rates,[5] yielded a rich treasury of information.

To examine these documents is to go less far away from these festivals than one might think, for the men who were officially entrusted with these investigations were also those who organized the Revolutionary ceremonies in their départements or cantons. It was they who wrote the speeches and arranged the processions. For them the festival was a constant preoccupation (and even a busy one, when one remembers the well-filled calendar of Revolutionary celebrations). It is all the more interesting, then, to wonder how they perceived the festive aspects of popular life and what they kept of them.

It will be impossible to analyze here all the available documents,[6] so let us confine our attention to those produced under the Directoire. There are many reasons for this choice,[7] the main one being the personality of François de Neufchâteau, who was so passionately interested in the problem of the festival and so aware of the overall character of statistical research. The opportunity it afforded him for surveillance was probably not unconnected with his work, but for him it blended with belief in the necessary connection between the various elements of human life: the material life, the social life, and the ceremonial life were merely aspects of a single reality. This totalizing, quasi-aesthetic ambition required scope ("We must embrace the universality of France") and precision ("The work must produce the effect of a mirror that faithfully renders the object that it reflects").[8] This already Stendhalian demand, which seems to promise a harvest of true but insignificant data, was tirelessly repeated in the admonitions of the central commissioners to the municipal commissioners: "You will be like a pure, faithful mirror."[9]

The men who were sent out onto the roads of France in the hope that they would see clearly were also expected to be "patriotic" and "enlightened." These two conditions seemed so essential to success in the undertaking that they turn up again, some years later, in Chaptal's demand that the prefects entrusted with a similar task should possess "patriotism and enlightenment." This was a highly ambiguous requirement, for what equipped these ethnologists in the countryside was what perhaps also left them ill equipped for their task: how could the France of patriotism and Enlightenment see another France that was neither?

All these men—although it was truer of the central commissioners[10] than of the municipal commissioners—really belonged nowhere. A commissioner of the executive directory belonged, and yet at the same time did not belong, to the regional world. He belonged to it because he had to live there, but the residential obligation of a central commissioner was a year at most. This was a very short time in which to become naturalized to provincial ways, and there are many other signs to remind us that, even if the commissioner were a local man, he was not quite of the region. He was appointed, not elected; his salary came from Paris; lastly, his "enlightenment" led him to look at regional reality from a certain distance and prevented him from getting involved in it.

There was another factor that made his situation worse: his instructions from the minister were not at all clear. Of course, he was asked to observe communal life. He therefore had to note whether "the bells were still rung," whether "the signs of a particular cult obstruct the highway," whether "the national festivals arouse interest or not." But such concerns were more inducive to carrying out a diagnosis of public opinion[11] than an observation of popular life.

Public opinion, of course, is not at all the same thing as popular life: the latter is marked by its prolific variety, whereas the former is ideally one. There were very few commissioners who dared to write that public opinion was excellent at Moissac, bad at Nègrepelisse, and terrible at Figeac. For most of them, such variations merely showed that public opinion did not exist.[12] For those men, therefore, and for the government too, there was a definite antinomy between public opinion and popular life, as there was between innocent unity and criminal plurality. Popular life swarmed with disparate intentions; but public opinion was the concrete unity of a multiplicity grasped in an indivisible act.

This means that one could not be content simply to allow public opin-

ion to emerge: it had to be *formed*. This explains the constant demand
found in these reports for philosophical circles and clubs, schools, festivals—in short, for "Republican institutions." The idea that the general
will never makes itself heard without a social network that collects it,
canalizes it, and embodies it was familiar to all the commissioners. Au-
gustin Cochin, who has so often been criticized for the thesis that without
societies in which one votes, corresponds, disputes, canvasses, there is no
public opinion, merely takes up their explicit admission. Convinced that
public opinion cannot be subjected to observation but only to incitement,
the product of a constitutive effort, the commissioners pulled it in the
direction of an energetics. Their vocabulary is that of gymnastics or med-
icine: it is always a question of reanimating or retraining, enlivening or
inuring.

All this teleology was not conducive to acute observation, especially
since these men of the town were inclined to see the countryside as simply
the negation of urbanity. Of the beliefs of a whole century that saw the
city as destructive of wealth, populations, and morals, while attributing
to the countryside all that was most fruitful, very little survives in these
writings. Here and there one finds a picture of good village folk, a trust
in the countryman's good sense, which is seen as less easy to seduce than
the sensibility of the trivial-minded city dweller. Though simpler in his
morals, said the commissioner for the Vienne, the countryman has more
discernment. But on the whole, this is a rhetorical evocation, hardly
touched with nostalgia.[13] These pedagogical texts—and this is one of the
surprising things about them—make hardly any proper references to the
pastoral. Peasant slowness is simply treated as a demoralizing obstacle.
How can the village be made to get used to "a new calendar, new mea-
surements, new markets, new fairs, when these institutions present problems even for the educated man," wonders the commissioner for the
Creuse in desperation. How could one make the peasants forget their
festivals? Sometimes the commissioners seem utterly discouraged: "The
stubbornness of the country people is incredible. Their minds do not seem
to be made for truth."[14] For social life, civic festivals, and Republican
meetings, the towns always offered resources that could not be compared
with those of the rural cantons.

This helps us to understand the difficulty with which these men perceived regional differences. And yet they had been asked to set out in
search of them, and indeed some of these officials realized what had to be
done: "One has to have traveled to the most lonely hamlets, to have seen

everything that is happening." The journey through the départements of France, which in a few years was to become a highly popular literary genre, was still an adventure. This is borne out by the sense of wonder to be found in the accounts of the delegates to the Federation. At their modest scale, the logbooks of their journeys through the départements ought also to provide a picture of the variety of customs found throughout the territory. But this is not at all the case.

Yet the comparatist point of view is not entirely absent from the descriptions: each of the commissioners saw his département in terms of what he knew, or thought he knew, of the neighboring départements, even quite distant ones. Thus, the commissioner for the Meurthe, eager to convey the shades of opinion in his département, wanted to use only a subtle range of tints, for "the differences that characterize the two extreme parts are not at all as pronounced as in the southern regions." But this attempt to situate oneself within French territory as a whole failed. Generally speaking, the commissioners were quick to label the immense range of customs as mere superstitions and prejudices (contemptuous and convenient terms, since they made dismissal of the customs they describe all the easier), and revealed an incredible lack of curiosity. After all, scarcely six years later, the questions posed by the investigations of the Celtic Academy, which were sufficiently detailed to be used even by Van Gennep, were drawn up by men of similar education. A curiosity about folk customs seems to have been born in that brief interval, with justifications that we are familiar with today: "Collect those customs that have survived the ravages of time." recommends Dulaure, adding that one should not disdain noting down even what may seem like "tiny details." And Mangourit, one of the founders of the Academy, urged the investigation to get moving: "We must make haste in drawing up our questions, because the code and other institutions now governing France will necessarily lead to the disappearance of a large number of curious practices." So it was the forecast of an inevitable disappearance, at what seemed like a chronological threshold, that led the Celtic Academy to reflect on anthropological variety.

But it was this very presentiment of death, too, that justified the commissioners' indifference. In their eyes, the peculiarities that they encountered were signs of the temporary, and it was pointless to note down what was about to disappear. The commissioner for the Côtes-du-Nord does not use a single word of the Breton language. The commissioner for the Morbihan makes only a few allusions to it. The commissioner for the

Finistère makes only a single mention of it. The commissioner for the Pyrénées-Orientales, who met nothing but incomprehension during the tour in which he tried to spread the gospel of François de Neufchâteau, drew only one conclusion from the fact: "They realized how necessary education was."[15] This was because here one was not content to foresee the disappearance of customs; in the very terms of the futurology postulated by the request for public opinion, it was actually wished for. Indeed, this fanaticism was in proportion to the deep-rootedness of the local customs and minority languages. According to the commissioner for the Meurthe, the map of insubordination was identical to that of the German language;[16] the commissioner for the Finistère considered that "the barbarous idiom that in many cantons is the exclusive language of the governed is the reef against which all our efforts break up."[17] The commissioner for the Basses-Pyrénées noted the effect of distance produced in his département by the language of the three former Basque districts, "which make their neighbors strangers, as if communication between them were of the utmost difficulty."[18] The commissioner for the Pyrénées-Orientales, who nevertheless had been in the region long enough to converse on familiar terms with the citizens in the local idiom, could no longer recognize his own people: "They still seem to form a people apart."

Behind such descriptions was the vision of a more smoothly running society from which somatic and cultural differences would disappear because they were not grounded in reason. If, therefore, such customs survived, if such practices persisted under one's very eyes, if there was often still an "invincible habit, a kind of need for old practices," it was because there are different rational ages: hence the constant references to the notion of a child-people, still swaddled up in its prejudices. But that people would grow up. Hoping to see in the future the fine achievements of this group, the commissioners found nothing worth recording in the present. Hence their profound confusion.

If anyone doubts this, he has only to look at the reports themselves, with their frequent linguistic detours and rhetorical obscurity. Thus the great moments of the traditional calendar are never described directly, as if Christmas, Easter, or All Saints' could be grasped only with the tweezers of quotation marks or with the help of periphrasis: "the festival known as 'the patronal feast,'" "what in the Vaucluse is called the *carri* [charivari]," while the carnival becomes "that season that the peculiar prejudices of the ancien régime once devoted especially to noisy pleasures, as if to justify the use of the following season, which the same prejudices devoted to privations and penitence." Such precautions are an attempt to distance.

In them, the commissioners made it clear that they would themselves have nothing to do with "the former language" and were eager to mark a break. The use of quotation marks also allowed them to suggest—perhaps by way of wish fulfillment—that the traditional language was declining, as if one were on the edge of seeing the disappearance of "what used to be called 'the mass'" or "what was called 'Lent.'"

When, in spite of everything, circumstances forced the commissioners to look into the details of popular life, they tended to resort to theatrical vocabulary. Their accounts are filled with such terms as "religious tricksters," "Catholic tumblers," "masquerades." A commune in the Basses-Pyrénées was visited by a prophetess—a "supposed" prophetess, of course. Unfortunately, the commissioner, paying little attention to the content of the prophecy, commented: "There fanaticism had erected its stage; there the most ridiculous farces were played out. In the end all the fantasmagoric tricks had so disturbed the minds of the spectators that many poor unfortunates thought they had witnessed miracles."[19] Everywhere celebrations were seen as spectacles, the celebrants as spectators, and the people as audience.

Of course, in this reduction of traditional life to the theater, we find once again the suspiciousness of the men of the Enlightenment, which the Revolutionary sensibility carried further. Nevertheless, there is something else: the externality of something that has actually lost all meaning. One must take literally the term, so frequently used, of "meaningless ceremonies." The only meaning apart from defeat that the commissioners sometimes managed to allow the ceremonies was that of an entertainment for the youth of the communes. Generally speaking, they regarded such ceremonies as so many riddles. Moreover, from this point of view, the commissioners were the heirs of the Enlightenment. One has only to think of the blindness shown by the eighteenth-century pastoral, which, when it did describe festivals, borrowed from utopian writings rather than from folklore. It showed scant regard for local customs, even when it set out to capture a regional atmosphere, as in the case of Estelle and Némorin's Provençal pastorals, for example. This must be remembered if we are not to be too severe on our commissioners' ethnology.

History of a Failure

Indeed, what we are asking them is not to provide us with information on customs—for this their language is altogether too oblique[20]—but to show us what their repressive militantism came up against: what they failed to repress or stem, and which, against their will, breached the barrier of their careful sentences, thus perhaps laying down the lines of force of a resistance. Let us look for the signs of this rebellious popular life; they will help us to understand better, with the renewed vivacity of the popular festival, the difficulty that the Revolutionary festival had in establishing itself.

What the commissioners were unable to understand was the demonstration. A child-people, defined by its ability to be moved, had innumerable occasions to fill the streets and to occupy the public squares. The commissioner for the Morbihan notes that "a single man with a drum would get the whole canton running," and we sense his distress at finding his subjects so easily led.[21] Not that all forms of demonstration were disturbing. A very punctilious typology allowed the commissioners to distinguish between the *rassemblement* (gathering) and the *réunion* (meeting), with its *attroupement* (riotous assembly). The term *réunion* was reserved for references to the civic festival, as if its ordered, peaceful purpose could not but be Republican. Much more confused in their eyes was the *rassemblement,* which caused them a lot of trouble; one was never sure what it might lead to. So the commissioners expressed fears about the market, the fair, the patronal feast, and even the invasion of the commune on Sundays by a crowd that would spill out into the walks, cafés, taverns, and lanes, where games of bowls were played (nothing better conveys the atrophy of the Revolution than the fears felt by the men of the Revolution about an occupied street or the obstruction of a public highway). Hence, the commissioners' concern to lock up worship in the place assigned to it, to shut the doors of the churches, and to prevent the flood of worshippers from kneeling in the square—their obsession with containing any gathering within the confines of the village. Never did they prove more vehement than when condemning sorties to places of worship, chapels or oratories, outside the village. The rush to the chapels, so often mentioned in these accounts, may have been all the more frequent in that the parish church was shut or that the "Romans," who had no desire to coexist with the "Constitutionals," increased the number of places of worship outside the commune boundaries. Perhaps, too, the impoverishment of religious life drove the faithful to the more popular worship of the chapels. In any case, we have a paradoxical heritage here: the commissioners took over from the parish priests, far more than they fought them, in seeking "to concentrate all religious practices in one place" and to combat, for the benefit of the parish, the fragmentation of the places of popular devotion.

Lastly, more disturbing even than the gathering, because cruder and less disciplined, was the *attroupement*. Unlike the *rassemblement,* whose dates and frequency could be predicted, the *atroupement* was triggered by some unforeseeable event: a conscript leaving, a detachment of gendarmerie crossing the village, the disturbance caused by the falling of the Liberty Tree. And those who took part were even more difficult to identify than those involved in a *rassemblement.* They came together to make their recriminations or to "chant" their demands, or worse, to take up pitchforks and form groups that were indissociable enough for its members to be caught in the cement of a noun: the commissioners called them, quite simply, the *attroupés.*

Just as they failed to purge the communal territory of such disturbances, so also did they fail to extirpate their "signs." We should pause for a moment at a term that recurs obsessively in the official accounts. In the grand days of Jacobinism, the term was only beginning to find its meaning. The "signs" were the fleur-de-lis, coats of arms, crucifixes, statues, pictures: such a proliferating set of symbols that, sometimes, when the people's clubs received instructions from Paris, they were hard put to decide which of all these signs were the surest expression of superstition. Thus at Aubas, in the Dordogne, the municipal officers, who had just received orders to remove them, deliberated; then, "considering that the first and most characteristic sign of superstition was our parish priest, we went off to his house and, after briefly offering our compliments, threw him out." At that time too it was not thought that one could speak of signs without saying that they were signs *of* superstition or *of* monarchy. With the coming of the Directoire, the administrative language became so stretched that one spoke not so much of the signs of superstition as of signs *tout court* or even of "external signs": as if beneath those signs, which, nevertheless, one was supposed to extirpate more than ever,[22] one was no longer aware of the deep mass of beliefs and practices. They were "external,"[23] moreover, in the quite simple sense that they struck the eye and ear: in this very wide acceptance of the term, the church bells and crucifixes were the most common objects of attack.

To abolish all the crucifixes was an enormous undertaking: "I have finally got rid of all the calvaries in this arrondissement," the commissioner for the Landes notes with satisfaction. But reports of such a complete cultural revolution are rare. Generally speaking, the commissioners came up against the indefatigable resistance of the villagers. As the commissioner for the Creuse remarks,[24] "There are stone and wooden crosses; the credulous villagers accredit virtues to them and expect protection from them. So fanaticism has hidden them." Thus, a war broke out: crosses taken down during the day were put up again at night. Sometimes, even, there was no need to put them back up, for, as the commissioner for the Nord remarks with surprise, it was enough for the country people to gather "at the places where the crosses once stood." Such places then became doubly visited, as if by virtue of being missing, the crosses had become even more visible. The same man, during the tour ordered by François de Neufchâteau, observes that, although the crosses were removed from crossroads and churches, they survived in the graveyards, where they grew over the tombs like "mushrooms after a storm." He continues his cynical metaphor, "I have been out several times collecting them, to the great scandal of the fanatics." He adds, with a realism stripped of any illusions, "Since the seeds of those crosses are in their heads, I am sure they have already grown again." His colleagues, by contrast, stopped short their purge at the cemetery gates. After noting with satisfaction the progress made elsewhere, the commissioner for the Haut-Rhin admits, "The graveyards of the rural cantons alone preserve some signs of religion on the tombs; veneration for the dead seemed to require this tolerance."[25] This confirms the fact that the graveyard became, for the village, far more than the church, which had already been partly or totally taken over by the celebration of the *fêtes décadaires,* the sacral place par excellence, protected without policing, uncrossable by the Republican administration, the soul of the village.

Sign as sound, an incitement to assembly, was even more difficult to grasp and was no sooner prohibited than it reappeared. For these townsmen, noise had something uneducated and savage about it.[26] They are unanimous in contrasting the disciplined chanting of the Republican festivals with the atrocious shouts of the village festivals, with the ritual cries ("yells" and "hoots"), the indecent songs, the immoderate use made of such instruments as the farandole clarinet[27] and even "the din of household implements."[28] One can understand the commissioner's struggle against noise, that essential element of communal life, since it was he who was making public what without him would have remained private; it was he who was extending and propagating what was a limited social phenomenon. A contrary proof may be seen in the fact that no Republican ceremony seemed to the commissioners to have been a festival if it did not include at least one peal of bells.

Indeed, of all these sounds, the one that was most bound up with traditional popular life was that of the bells, the "priests' drum." Since the law of 3 Ventôse, Year III, they ought to have disappeared everywhere. But with that prohibition, how many accommodations had been made! This resulted in a variety of practices throughout the region that was again a source of recriminations. In some villages, there were no more bells at all; the reformers had even gone so far as to remove the clappers. Elsewhere, as in the Côte d'Or, the sound of the bells was tolerated to announce the various "points" of the day, but there was silence at the dawn and evening Angelus. In other places, the bells also rang out at midday "according to the ancient customs." But everywhere the commissioners noted the peasants' passionate attachment to their bells. The commissioner for the Aude says that the Narbonnais, deprived of their bells, "have fallen into a deep sadness." The country people, declared the commissioner for the Doubs, "have such passion for that music that they will be deprived of it only by breaking those instruments. It would be impossible to count the number of incidents involving the bells." Any occasion, any pretext—fear or happiness, a storm or hail—would set them in motion, for they were regarded as prophylactic. A sort of emotional contagion would then spread from village to village. The armed forces would dash to the belltower, but the ringers would already have left, and the bells of the next village would be ringing, then another, then another. Harassed and not entirely convinced of what they were doing, the National Guard exhausted itself against an ever-elusive adversary. The commissioners often considered that the sickness could be cured only by more radical treatment: the bells themselves should be removed, and, sometimes, even the belltowers should be demolished. Even that was not always enough; the commissioner for the Alpes-Maritimes reports that the Catholic priests, inconsolable at losing their great bells, tried to make up for the loss by substituting hand bells, which they did not hesitate to use, and "they were loud enough to be heard outside."

"Unquestionably what the people most regret in the Revolution is the loss of their bells," concluded the commissioner for the Somme. Additional proof of this may be found in the fact that even the commissioners draw a very clear distinction between the disappearance of the audible and that of the visible. They hardly dreamed of setting up the tricolor flag where the cross had once stood,[29] but they certainly wanted to use the bells to mark the hours. They too had difficulty imagining a life in which the day would not be broken up by the bell, so they usually gave in to the request that the "points and middle of the day" should be marked by the bell—or, as they reported the words of the local people, "les repas, le réveille, et le couché"—and they were most anxious to use them to mark the solemnity of Republican time itself. "To announce the *fêtes décadaires,*" wrote the commissioner for the Oise, "we have so far used the drum. I would have preferred to use bells; apart from the fact that it is often difficult to find someone in the communes who can beat a drum properly, the citizens who live in these hamlets cannot all hear it, whereas the sound of the bell can be heard at a great distance . . . I would imagine that the bell ringing for a quarter of an hour in each commune and at the same time would produce a strange effect. It would be known that, throughout the Republic, the *décadi* is being celebrated at the same time." It would seem, then, that the bell was fated to be the privileged instrument of a Revolutionary ambition that was to be carried to obsessional lengths— that of simultaneity. Meanwhile, something had to be done to keep the lack of bells marking the traditional calendar from being a cause of latent insurrection.

This is the sorest spot of peasant rebellion and of the failure of the administration to change popular life. Throughout the whole territory, and even in communes reputed to be patriotic, what the community re-jected, in a reaction of brutal or obstinate opposition, was the division of time imposed on it by the Republican calendar. This was made all the more frequent a source of incidents by the fact that the commissioners, convinced that "educated Europe envies us an institution that derives the division of time from nature," were unanimous in thinking that there was no better arrangement than one, as in weights and measures, calculated on the decimal system. It was a poor argument against a people quite unimpressed by this new masterpiece, for whom regularity was not nec-essarily the origin of rites, and who continued to count in weeks, to mark out the year with dates drawn from folklore and the liturgical calendar, without seeming to care that the vulgar year began at no remarkable date or that the months were guilty of "inequality."[30] The commissioners were waging a hopeless struggle against the propagation of calendars and al-manacs that followed the old system and against an even more widespread sickness; for even if, in going to the market or fair, one followed the Republican calendar, in conversation people were led irresistibly back to the old system and terminology.

The most bitter failure, because it was constantly brought home to these men, was the persistent contrast between Sunday and the *décadi*. On Sundays people put on their best clothes and did their hair, whereas on the *décadi,* the commissioners constantly complain, citizens "wear dirty clothes." Thus the commissioner for the Alpes-Maritimes fulminated one *décadi* against "Citizen Derode's eldest son, wearing his ordinary work clothes, driving an ass before him, bearing all his work tools." Sunday was also the day of rest ("everyone," observed the commissioner for the Calvados, "maintains constant idleness and anyone doing any form of work would be decried"), whereas the *décadi* echoed with the recriminations of those who would like to work but could not or dared not do so, and who denounced those who were fortunate enough to do so with impunity. Sunday still meant the walk to the former church, whether or not there was a priest. Lastly, unlike the *décadi,* which was marked by an overwhelming sense of boredom, Sunday was the day for public games, for tennis, bowls, the swing, and, above all, dancing, which the commissioners were as keen to suppress as the priests had been, but with no more success.[31] The young people, who instigated it, felt the prohibition as an attack on their traditional prerogatives and showed yet again that no law would prevent them from dancing when they wanted to.

The commissioners were probably not really surprised that Sunday was always seen as the end of the week. It is more interesting to observe that the opposition of the Revolutionary authorities was directed against a weekly celebration that was not always deeply rooted: "Sunday is celebrated almost everywhere," said the commissioner for the Oise. "It has even won as proselytes those who before the Revolution despised it." "Its observance," says the commissioner for the Calvados, "is half as much again what it was under the ancien régime," while the commissioner for the Indre observes that Sunday is "now" celebrated with a kind of enthusiasm. All these reports testify to the fact that the Revolution had revived the Sunday celebration and given it a quite recent festive character.

The social disturbance that the commissioners tried to contain was never so strong as during those two high points of the popular calendar, the carnival and the patronal feast. The carnival was greeted by the commissioners with the same sort of disconsolate sense of impotence that the priests had once shown; indeed, in recalling the failure of the ecclesiastical authorities to discipline the carnival, the commissioners found a justification for their own failure, since "even the terrifying eloquence of the preachers had been unable to shake the reign of the carnival."[32] The carnival, whose ineradicable character was stressed in so many accounts,[33] was doubly suspect in the eyes of these men. Like any popular festival it resisted rational utopia, but, more than any other, it was the appointed expression of insubordination, owing to the facility offered by its masks, its disguises, its customary dramatization. The traditional forms served, therefore, the interests of political resistance; seditious songs directed against the municipal authorities could be sung under cover of fancy dress. Hence the overdetermination of the carnival dummy, as at Clermont-l'Hérault, where the dummy carried in procession to the bonfire wore the clothes of a National Guard (the commissioner, describing the festival, sighed, "The true Republican was stuffed inside it"), or at Marvejols, where the effigy of a Constitutional priest was carried in procession before being riddled with bullets.[34]

The patronal feast, too, attracted every kind of insubordination. In the very simplified calendar, in which so many celebrations had disappeared, the patronal festival shone with particular brightness. On this day people took to the road from commune to commune, traveling for four or five leagues in noisy groups.[35] Prohibited pictures were taken out, and sometimes the meetings of forbidden confraternities were advertised and attended (as at Dunkirk, where, in Year VII, a poster urged citizens to meet at the house of the "Prince of the Confraternity of Saint Crispin" and to parade the effigy of the saint around the town); minstrels, tumblers, puppeteers, and sellers of food and drink were seen in broad daylight; lastly, administrators were molested, ill-treated, led ironically to the town halls by half-threatening, half-joking processions (like the one at Dun-sur-Auron, which led the municipal agent to the commune building to the sound of music). Indeed, they were defenseless against those unidentifiable "people of all kinds," who emerged from the confusion[36] permitted and even encouraged by the festival. When confronted by it, the commissioners, like the priests, found themselves in the grip of both repugnance and pusillanimity.

Yet, as good sociologists, the commissioners perceived the polyvalent functions fulfilled by the patronal festival, of which the commissioner for the Vendée provides a threefold definition: worship, the affairs of the commune, and the pleasures of the people. The commissioner for the Indre describes "the very populous assembly" of the commune of Vatan: "It attracts a large number of merchants, wine sellers, fiddlers, bagpipe players . . . In my opinion its purpose is either devotion or pleasure. People come from far around to invoke Saint Loup; women bring their children in the hope that they will take them home cured of the vapor of fevers, after exposing them under the shadow of the gospel stole. They also avail themselves of another motive: it is said that on that very day the farmers come to pay off their harvest workers and to make arrangements with others concerning winter tasks."[37] Others observe that the festival was the occasion for reconciliation in families,[38] even of parties in a dispute,[39] and for the pairing of couples. The patronal festival, then, was seen as an occasion of religious, civic, and secular rejoicing, a time for ceremonial, commercial, and fraternal exchange, in which everything, even dancing and feasting in the inn, fulfilled a precise function. Even the sacralizing justification of an immemorial past was not missing.[40]

The commissioners' perspicacity, however, did not stop them from shamelessly interfering with the traditional calendar to set the local festival according to the Republican calendar, without taking into account either the name of the patron saint or complaints from parishioners. It is no accident that the most determined insubordination to the order that the commissioners wanted to establish concerned the calendar. The commissioners brought their troubles on themselves with their insensitivity to the particular coloring of certain days, their obstinacy in treating the calendar as an empty form, and their determination to confine the year within a regular grid, with identical alternations of work and rest. Their uneducated adversaries show us that the calendar is an institution infinitely more resistant than the ideology that sustains it, that the latter may be easily forgotten without ceasing to make the calendar that it seems to justify the locus of myth and the object of a spontaneous sacralization.

As we bring this examination of their failure to an end, let us not be too hard on these men; we have discovered the profound consensus that linked them to those whom they nevertheless appeared to be persecuting. In their purge of "superstitions," the men of the Revolution were preceded, a long way back, by the clergy, who, throughout the century, had been imbued with the same determination to eradicate superstition. Perhaps they radicalized the enterprise by extending the notion of superstition to cover all forms of religious activity. Apart from that, their reports and decrees, which dismiss popular life as a collection of superstitions in exactly the same way, constitute a continuity rather than a break.

Then there was their enormous failure. Some of them tried to overcome it by considering how best the popular festival could be transformed gradually into the Revolutionary festival.[41] It would be enough to eliminate its religious aspect, which, in any case, was already half-effaced,[42] and to canalize the merrymaking into the ideal Revolutionary festival. The commissioner for the Loret wanted to keep it as "a civil gathering and public entertainment, under the name of *fête champêtre.*" The commissioner for the Bas-Rhin considered that if one consecrated each temple "to a Republican virtue or to a tutelary deity of our liberty," the inhabitants of the commune would be left with opportunities to gather together. The commissioner for the Lot-et-Garonne hoped that the Republican administration would have the intelligence to transfer the patronal festival to the nearest *décadi* and take over its significance: "Inaugurate the new festivals yourselves together with the good citizens." The commissioner for the Indre announced that he was keeping "the Magdalen assembly that used to be held in our commune," on condition that it would henceforth be referred to as the Assembly for Ceres. But there were few administrators sensitive or clever enough to try to turn to the advantage of a Republican ceremony the emotion aroused by the popular festival: throughout the Revolution the two existed side by side without ever merging.

Revolutionary Symbolism and Peasant Tradition

Was there not, however, an exchange at a quite different level? Can we not find in the Republican festival borrowings from the popular festival—unconscious, perhaps, but which, if they were established, would make it less alien than it is often perceived to be to the popular sensibility? The search for these bridges between two alien worlds—that of folkloric tradition and that of political and pedagogical innovation—is, for many reasons, a very difficult one.[43] Let us nonetheless make such an attempt in the case of the Liberty Tree. The example is a privileged one, for of all the acknowledged symbols of the Revolution, this one enjoys a particular status.[44] Furthermore, even contemporaries considered that a link had successfully been made between the Liberty Tree and popular May traditions: Revolutionary legend assures us that on May 1, a priest from the Vienne planted the first Liberty Tree. Grégoire uses this false information as early as Year II,[45] and it was subsequently accepted as true.

But such a link is more often supposed than demonstrated. Indeed, it is not enough here simply to juxtapose two parallel sets of documents. What we really want to find is the mediating document that would make it possible to move from one to the other. It is to be found, it seems, in the files devoted to provostal proceedings by series B of the archives of the Dordogne,[46] complemented by various other documents.[47] These papers include, for the year 1790, indictments against "persons charged with sedition and public disturbance and forced contribution demanded under armed menaces," together with their examinations and witnesses' state-ments. Now these files make it clear that the setting up of *mais* as a central element in the rural insurrections of the Périgord and Quercy in the winter of 1790. It certainly seems that these are the rare, much-sought-after intermediary documents that we have all been looking for. For the *mai* set up by the peasants in the winter of 1790 certainly appears to be the transition between the maypole of folklore and the tree made official by the Revolution. In any case, it was erected at the juncture of tradition—there is reference only to *mais* in the evidence—and innova-tion: it was also seen (we shall have to decide by whom and why) as a "Revolutionary" or "insurrectional" maypole.

Thus it is tempting to expect these documents, in a precise case, to show how Revolutionary symbolism might be articulated on peasant tra-dition.

The Mai sauvage

The wild plantings described by these texts took place in two waves. The first broke in the winter of 1790 (and even, according to certain witnesses, in the autumn of 1789)[48] with the popular uprisings[49] caused by a mis-understanding on the night of August 4: the peasants, who had been under the impression that rents had been abolished, rioted when it seemed that they would have to pay them after all. "In a large number of parishes," wrote Godard and Robin, the commissioners sent by the king to investigate, "the people are convinced that they have been emancipated from rents; in others, they will pay only after a strict check on the deeds." In any case, whatever they thought, the rioting peasants set up trees, which at first the authorities tolerated until around carnival time. Then they became alarmed, and with a great deal of clamor, but very little success, they demanded that the trees that had been set up during the riot be removed. The Federation and its succession of ceremonies imposed a truce. Then, as summer advanced, the trees reappeared, this time espe-cially in the Lot; in the end, the departmental directory, at the request of the district of Gourdon, dispatched a detachment of grenadiers to roam the countryside and destroy the *mais,* and to reestablish order. The col-umn, commanded by M. de Saint-Sauveur, left Gourdon on November 25, 1790. It left, in its wake, riots and looting. But the peasants' most spectacular riposte to this official attempt to tame the countryside was the conquest of the town that served as the column's operational base: Gourdon was invaded by peasant crowds and sacked. It was at this point that the civil commissioners sent by the king arrived on the scene with the double mission of information gathering and pacification.

The account of these events, at the center of which the maypole raises its enigmatic stature, varies a great deal, depending on the sources consulted. They all have a repressive character, but to varying degrees. The accounts emanating from the departmental directory of the Lot and the letters from notables quite simply interpret the maypoles as an incitement to riot, owing to an identification, which for them was irresistible, between the irrational and the pathological. Here is the account given by the representatives of the commune of Sarlat to "Nosseigneurs du Comité des Rapports": "They plant maypoles, which are signals of disobedience to the laws, loot the houses of the rich landowners, and do not respect any more the cottage of the poor man if he refuses to be an accomplice in their insurrections."[50] The tone of the civil commissioners, by contrast, is very liberal. Godard and Robin chose to go without an armed escort and attributed the warm welcome given them to the fact that they were unarmed. Those Paris lawyers, members of the Jacobin Club, saw themselves as messengers of the Enlightenment[51] whose task was, above all, to illuminate those poor, distracted souls; they were determined to use force only as a last resort, and above all were very eager to understand the deeper significance of the maypoles. Their report is a veritable work of anthropological research. Between these two types of documents, the answers coming from the priests provide a middle opinion. Most of them, forced under protest to speak, managed at least to compromise themselves as little as possible; but one also finds the occasional priest willing to denounce by name the ringleaders in his parish, and the rebellious priest who refuses to read from the pulpit the warning issued by the provost general and who leads his parish's resistance to the removal of its maypole.

The maypole, the object of so much emotion, indignation, justification, and interrogation, seems to be caught up in a complex of social behavior from which it is difficult to dissociate it. All the documents agree that the erection of the maypole was always carried out during a riot or an armed expedition to a neighboring village, which was then forced to adopt the maypole whether or not it wanted to. So the tree emerged in scenes of violence. According to the evidence given by Bertrand Bugeaud, a blacksmith at Sainte-Mesme,[52] his village was upside down: men "were carrying pews and chairs to a place in the graveyard in front of the church; the eldest son of the said Bernard Lafaye, who smashed the pews with a wooden mallet, the said Janisson, who arranged the wood for a fire, putting the broken chair underneath and the bits of pew on top, and who then went to look for fire and straw from the man named Bouissou, a wine seller of the said township, in order to burn all the said objects." Furthermore, all the evidence stressed the contagion that ran from commune to commune. Again at Sainte-Mesme, the villagers offered the defense that they had been persuaded "all the more easily in that all the parishes of the canton had done likewise. And threatened the parish of Sainte-Mesme in which the suppliants live, to go and make them pay for their journey if they did not set up a maypole and burn their church pews."[53]

When one tries to make out the structure of these events from an account that varies from commune to commune, depending, for example, on whether or not the lord of the manor handed over the weathercock, did or did not provide bread and wine for a simple feast,[54] and eliminating from the account all the circumstantial details, one sees that there were always at least three types of act: the removal of the weathercocks and the burning of the church pews[55] (sometimes the villagers were content to change their function and meaning by just taking them out into the open air, where they would sit on them and drink)—that is to say, the destruction of two privileges and their restoration to the community, and the erection of a maypole. All three acts were usually accompanied by the sounding of the tocsin bell.

During these episodes, the social group was, at one and the same time, torn apart by confrontation and welded together by solidarity. The evidence given by witnesses reveals hidden antagonisms. The captain commanding the National Guard at Grun declared, "A man of the name of Berni struck me several times in the face, treating me in the most humiliating way, saying that they no longer wanted Gentlemen and wanted to do as they liked."[56] The accounts often begin with some such provocative declaration as "saying that they were all equal . . ."

The insurgents also felt bound together by an increasing solidarity, and the unanimity of the communes (apart from a few recalcitrants, but even they were functionally indispensable to the sense of unanimity) was felt as legality. The blacksmith of Sainte-Mesme reports that, to the question "Who should lead the march?" the hotheads of the village replied, "Everybody must march, young and old alike."[57] The major argument of these bands armed with sticks and poor rifles, when they erupted into the villages, was that all the other parishes had taken down the weathercocks, burned the pews, and planted maypoles. It was therefore simply a question of conforming to the rules.[58] This is supported by a good deal of evidence: the riots subsided when it was seen that everything was "in order."[59] The demand made to the priests and lords was that they too should follow the rules.

These scenes were no doubt violent: they were also ritualized. The band that wanted to obtain their lord's weathercock by threats marched to the chateau in procession, the municipal drummer at their head: around the bonfire of church pews they danced. This mixture of violence and rejoicing was seen by "enlightened" nobles as collective madness: "They are like madmen who ought to be tied up, or rather like bacchantes," said the mayor of Leguillac."[60] "They danced around like Hurons and Iroquois," remarked the astonished Seigneur de Montbrun.[61] The authorities wanted to see in these scenes nothing more than disorderly energy, not the beginning of disorder. Indeed, if they did see it as such, it would seem to them to be an added provocation. "They were accompanied by bagpipes," exclaimed the notables of Lamonzie-Montastruc indignantly, "no doubt to defy those persons who had just been subjected to such a loss."[62]

Exactly what part did the maypole play in such scenes? What strikes one at first is that it emerged without the slightest justification. Witnesses found innumerable reasons, some of them highly insignificant, for the seizure of the weathercocks and the burning of the church pews: "They had the misfortune to allow themselves to be guided by bad counsel, by which they were assured that there were decrees of the National Assembly authorizing the inhabitants of parishes to remove all pews from the churches."[63] In an anonymous report on the disturbance in the Périgord, we read: "The first thing that persuaded the inhabitants of the parishes to behave as they did was a story that the king, wearing peasant's clogs and coat, turned up at the church in a pew that belonged to a lord, who shamefully chased him away and this was why the king ordered all his subjects of the Third Estate to burn the church pews."[64] In other places another story was used, namely, that the king had ordered the removal of the weathercocks. The peasants took such pleasure in the task "that they felt freed of any subordination."[65]

The setting up of the maypole was accompanied by no excuse. There was no witness to assure people that putting up a maypole was the wish of the king or had been decreed by the National Assembly. No one thought it necessary to explain why he took part in erecting the maypole. This seems to argue in favor of a spontaneous gesture, but it does not make any easier the task of those who have to decipher the meaning of the maypole. Was it, like the seizure of the weathercock and the burning of the pews, an act of insurrection, or simply evidence of collective celebration? Are we to see it bound up with the divisions caused by violence or the unanimity brought about by joy? Was it a signal of revolt or a symbol of liberation? These questions recur as we move from the repressive interpretation to the liberal interpretation; by examining the phenomenon more closely, we must now try to arrive at a conclusion.

The "wild" maypole, or *mai sauvage,* was like "a very tall, straight tree." Godard and Robin, who carefully examined it, assure us of this. It was indeed very straight, since we hear that Périer, one of the ringleaders at Montignac, cut off one branch of a forked tree to make it worthy of being a maypole; it was very tall, too, and this is enough to show that the peasants did not care in the least about the survival of the tree. There was never any question of letting it take root. In this, the maypole erected by the rioters is similar to the maypole of folklore, which could be a tall painted pole, or a crowned mast, or again a tree on which the topmost branches remained (as was the case in the Quercy and the Périgord). In any case, it was always a trimmed, painted, decorated tree. The maypoles of 1790, which were also more like greasy poles than trees and were erected rather than planted, were sometimes so brutally bare that they were more like gibbets. This may even be something more than an allusion, since some of these trees were, it was said, "erected in the form of gibbets."

Was the *mai sauvage* a maypole or a gibbet, a tree erected to signify life or to threaten death? The documents provide ambiguous answers on this point. Those most hostile to the peasants' demands saw sinister gibbets everywhere,[66] of course, and described the maypole as if it were indistinguishable from a gibbet, erected as a warning to those who paid their rents, in front of the houses of priests or big landowners. Such a gibbet certainly had an intimidating effect. It could kill before being used: "This lord was so seized at the sight of it that he suddenly died."[67] Godard and Robin, however, distinguish scrupulously between the erection of gibbets and of maypoles and sometimes even see the maypole, erected here and there after the gibbet, as a belated triumph of reason over violence. Nevertheless, what emerges from the documents is that the difference between maypole and gibbet was often very tenuous. Two members of the mounted constabulary traveling through the parishes of Chignac, Saint-Crépin, and Saint-Gérat reported that, as they passed the church door,

they saw a maypole bearing the inscription "final discharge of rents" and
"M. de Gérat's weathercock."[68] This maypole they described as "a tall tree
whose crest was in the shape of a gibbet." Another ambiguous example:
when one gibbet was removed on orders from above, it was replaced by a
maypole loaded with grapes, cakes, and goblets, and decorated with ribbons and such reassuring, conformist inscriptions as "Long live the Nation, the Law, the King." When an armed detachment arrived to remove
this less disturbing maypole, the peasants massed around the tree in a
hostile group, ready to defend it. Was what they were protecting the new
maypole or the gibbet it had replaced? Indeed, sometimes it is impossible
to make a distinction. Near Cahors an inscription was placed on a tree
that read: "This gibbet is for the reestablishment of liberty in France and
the happiness of all good citizens and to hang that aristocrat . . ."[69]

The same ambivalence is to be found in the decoration of the maypole.
Once again, different witnesses saw very different things. A student in
surgery tells us that he had noticed "a tree planted beside a church, having
at its top a weathercock and several utensils, such as a peck measure and
a riddle" and presumed that "it was as in all the other parishes where a
half-bushel measure, a peck, a strickle, a riddle, an inkwell, and two pens
were attached to a tree, with an inscription nailed onto it at the bottom
declaring that rents had been discharged."[70] As such, the maypoles were
obviously a concrete form of *doléances* or "complaints"; for instance, they
remind us that the beneficiaries of the rents used a special riddle to sieve
the grain delivered, and "in so advantageous a way," says Godard and
Robin, "that the grain handed over in lieu of rent was always worth some
30 sols more than the grain sold in the market." Godard and Robin,
however, do not accept that the decoration was always seditious. According to them, what they saw were generally maypoles decorated with laurel, flowers, and ribbons, and bearing innocent civic inscriptions. (Of
course, it is possible that the peasants, warned from village to village of
their arrival, got rid of any seditious ornaments.) They distinguish, then,
between two types of *mais,* the *mais insurrectionnaires* and the *mais libres,*
the latter being more numerous than the former. Indeed, they make it
quite clear that all the trouble in the département of the Lot was due to a
stubborn refusal to distinguish between them. But, contrary to their evidence, the documents provide innumerable examples of contamination
between "innocent" and "guilty" maypoles: a league away from Cahors, a
maypole bore the inscription "Long live the Nation, the Law, the King"
but also "No more rents."[71] It would seem doubtful that in the peasants'
minds there were two types of maypole.

The maypoles were erected in the public squares or in front of the chateaus, presbyteries, and estates. It is easy to see this as irrefutable proof of the provocative character of the maypole, in this sense related to the "recrimination trees" of folklore, intended to warn or to threaten, like those maypoles that carried horns for married men or faggots of thorns for ill-tempered daughters. But it must also be remembered that in certain parts, particularly in the southwest, there was an immemorial custom of setting up the maypole before the law courts and the houses of notables or simply of individuals whom the community wished to honor. Moreover, those "trees of honor" might, in certain cases, carry an implication of moral judgment: a recall to order mixed with homage.[72] So it is not at all certain that the maypole, even when set up in front of a priest's or mayor's house, even when laden with farm tools, was necessarily intended as an insult.

The documents tell us nothing about the rites accompanying the erection; it was, of course, a simple enough matter to fix a dry tree in the ground. The decoration and arrangement of the "wild" maypole were more important, however, than its erection. In this, it followed folk tradition; it was quite different, however, in the case of the Liberty Tree.

Furthermore, the circumstances of the insurrectional events within which the raising of the maypole took place cannot be irrelevant. Did the erection of the maypole occur before the other violent episodes or after them? This point in the investigation is fundamental, for if the erection took place before violence broke out, this means that the maypole was a trigger of revolt. One is not surprised to find this interpretation in the local authorities' reports. One anonymous document, which is very repressive in tone, claims to be a "picture of the insurrections that have taken place in the Sarladais," and declares that the riots "began with the setting up of maypoles in each parish by way of signals."[73] This interpretation was shared by the notables, but it leaves one problem unsolved: how could that signal have been deciphered? In the light of what tradition could the peasants interpret that signal so rapidly? Folk scholars say nothing about a tree that might have been a signal of rebellion or riot. But in the strikes at Epinac-les-Mines in 1871, the workers set up a maypole in front of the factory before beginning the strike.[74] Here we have something very similar to what the authorities of 1790 saw in the maypole: a call to riotous assembly, a sort of visual tocsin bell. If one examines the texts of the provostal proceedings closely, however, the cause seems to have been well understood: the erection of the maypole usually took place after other riotous actions. It completed the riot, put the final seal on the scene.[75]

With the weathercock that was tied to it, the maypole was not so much a signal as a symbolic recapitulation of what had just taken place. Godard and Robin were unaware of this fact: nevertheless, it supports their thesis.

Priests, lords of the manor, notables, investigators, commissioners, in the letters and reports with which they besieged government bodies and the National Assembly, provide a very wide range of opinion on the maypoles, including such terms as, on the one hand, "insulting witness," "symbol of revolt," "arrogant tree," "monument of insurrection," "mark of insurrection," even "monster," and, on the other, "monument of liberty," "sign of joy at the happy revolution." These terms are not without interest, especially in their repeated use of the word *monument,* which elevates the tree into a model of cultural fixity. But, obviously, one would like to know how those who erected the maypoles referred to their tree. The wine sellers, blacksmiths, and peasants, when questioned, spoke quite simply of the *mai,* never of *arbre de la liberté,* not even of *arbre de liberté,* and sometimes, though rarely, *mai de joie.* This is doubly instructive, first, because the terms associated with the maypoles by the simplest of witnesses were words expressing joy, and second, because there is a long distance from that *mai de joie* to the *arbre de la liberté,* via *arbre de liberté* (a term that competed with *arbre de la liberté* until about 1793). Indeed, in *arbre de la liberté,* the symbol is weakened by becoming emblematic. The relation between liberty and the tree is externalized, or lateralized: liberty has its tree. In the *mai* associated with riotous behavior, signifier and signified still have an analogical character; the joy of liberty is still mixed with the tree, and the *arbre-liberté*[76] (and even later the *arbre de liberté*) has an immediate effect. The *mai,* therefore, was an emotional instrument of participation, whereas with the *arbre de la liberté* we have already passed into a codified, not to say sclerotic, form of representation. In any case, we must agree that, given the dynamism suggested by the image of a liberty-bearing *mai* as a lucky tree, violence alone cannot cover the meaning of the *mai.*

This brings us to the question that Godard and Robin regard as decisive: what feelings did the peasants have toward their maypole? "As to what the peasants think about it," they note with the serious intrepidity that makes their work so valuable,

> we have made every possible effort to ascertain. When we ask a few questions on this subject, the words "liberty" and "sign of rejoicing for liberty" were mentioned by everybody. If we ask whether it was not believed, as

certain persons had told us, that when a maypole was erected for a year and a day one was freed of all payment of rent at the end of that time and whether that was not the reason for setting up *mais* everywhere and for the people's attachment to them . . . they replied with a smile at such a question, being unable to conceive that anyone could have such an idea. Generally speaking, the idea associated with the *mais* from our observations in the district of Gourdon, is that of the conquest of liberty.

Is this effusive interpretation of the maypole confirmed by the other documents at our disposal? What strikes us at first is the strength of the villagers' feelings toward their tree: "In the end they decided to take down the maypole of which they were so fond," sighed the parish priest of Limeuil.[77] The maypole at Loubejac bore this inscription: "It is strictly forbidden to remove this tree under pain of death." In the Bugue, when it was announced that troops were on their way to remove the trees, the men took out their knives. Even in the month of Ventôse, Year II, a priest who had been brought before the Revolutionary tribunal was criticized in particular by his parishioners for his opposition to the maypole of the winter of 1790. Everything goes to show that it was not some tawdry symbol. At Saint-Julien de Lampon, rather than see the maypole removed, a wall was built around it and it was guarded by a patrol, a community surveillance that shows that, like the maypoles of folklore, this tree had been sacralized by ceremonial unanimity.

What a reading of these documents leaves one in no doubt of is the privileged link between the maypole and collective joy. One of the priests questioned considered that the maypoles dated from well before January 1790. In his opinion, they had begun to be erected during the previous August, as a sign, he says, of rejoicing at the reunion of the three orders of the state. This is the only indication of an appearance before the winter of 1790: it obviously supports the views of Godard and Robin. Further confirmation is to be found in statements made to the National Assembly by the people's clubs of the Périgord[78] in July 1791: "In the districts of this département, bordering on that of the Lot, the farmers and inhabitants of the hamlets, considering weathercocks to be a conservative sign of feudal nobility and the church pews as irreconcilable with liberty, attacked both with some violence and in the effusion of their joy, which they no doubt believed to be legitimate, they set up maypoles in the public squares, surrounding them with all the destructive signs of the feudal monarchy." For those clubs, which were representative of enlightened and moderate patriotic opinion, there was a dichotomy in the insurrectional scene: violence, without doubt, for the weathercocks and pews, but joy for the maypoles.

Are we to leave it at that, then, and agree that the liberals were right? It seems very difficult to forget that the effusion of joy came after the violence, of which the tree still bore the marks. It also seems difficult to imagine that the event, in the consciousness of the simple actors, should have broken down as conveniently as under the discriminating pen of the men from Paris: this argues in favor of a more syncretic interpretation than the one offered by Godard and Robin.

Is any assistance to be expected from the work devoted by folklore specialists to the traditions associated with the maypole?[79] The classic article by A. Varagnac[80] divides interpretations of the maypole into two broad categories: those associated with the theme of renewal and fertility—for example, wedding maypoles, which were sometimes adorned with infants' clogs and feeding bottles,[81] and, of course, the *mais aux filles* and *mais galants*—and those associated with the idea of freedom. He reminds us that freedom was signified by the flyswatter, which symbolized the inn, and by the broom, which indicated that the dues had been paid and was in fact a wine seller's license. The *mai d'honneur* in the Quercy and Périgord marked a seat of government or an autonomous authority. This meaning is still present in maritime folklore: once the sails are hoisted, the men of the crew can no longer be prosecuted for debt. And in the harvest festival, the seasonal workers marked the end of their work by taking a maypole to the farmer, who, in return, gave them a banquet—mutual exactions, which indicated that both parties were quits. Similarly, De Wismes refers to those letters patent of Henri IV and Louis XIII, which, for a year, discharged of all distraints, tutelage, or guardianship, and of any obligation to house soldiers, all those who, on May 1, won the bird-shooting competition. The same arrangement is to be found in the regulations governing the Knights of the Arquebuse de Tournus.[82]

Between the two interpretations—fertility and freedom—Varagnac inclines to the second (for him the matrimonial taboo during May is an obstacle to the first), but nevertheless he provides several examples of practices that might be regarded as a synthesis of the two. A declaration of love and the hanging of the maypole from a girl's house might have meant that she was now free to marry, that she could now belong, potentially, to any man during the month of May. More convincing is the example of the renewal of the household, performed in May: this is the time of the statute fair, when employees are changed, as well as the vegetation. Of course one might add—and this is confirmed by all the folklore specialists on the traditions associated with May—that, in a number of ceremonies (marriage, engagement, the building of a house), the erection of the maypole symbolized a pact, the fixing of agreements.

What emerges from these studies is that the tree may combine within itself the magical sense of renewal and the social sense of liberty. This certainly makes it easier to understand the *mai sauvage* of the winter of 1790. Was it a signal, triggering off riot, or a sign of communal joy? Even if the tree were the "sign of happy revolution" and of "regeneration" that it was hailed as being by the liberals, regeneration would still be possible only if one were quits with the past. The planting of the maypole came after the violent destruction of an order. It did not conceal the violence, and indeed, it still bore it marks; but it was neither a new act of violence nor a call to violence. On the contrary, it was a sign that the violence had come to an end, a sign of an end to the reprisals. For the victory won over the weathercocks and church pews might only be temporary, and the rebels needed reassurance that everything would not degenerate into a ruthless struggle. This guarantee was the erection of the maypole, a rite both of ending and of beginning. They were quits: the notices bearing rent receipts were merely a particular illustration of this point, and therefore everything could begin again. This factitious tree, which, in any case, had little more of tree than its vertical stoicism and to which only strangers to the locality tried to give a meaning, was, therefore, a syncretic solution: it brought together and gave unity to a wide range of disparate requirements. Born out of insurrection, it was nevertheless not insurrectional in itself. It crowned excess but also brought it to an end and symbolically guaranteed that with the passing of the old order, the new order would remain in place.

A Pedagogical Tree

Four years separate those *mais sauvages* from the first law devoted to the Liberty Trees. Meanwhile, a great many maypoles had been erected; these ceremonies either constituted festivals in themselves (in which case they sprang from local initiatives or they were the work of the clubs of the Friends of the Constitution),[83] or they formed the heart of other festivals. There was as yet nothing official in these ceremonies; the official reports that describe them are not clear as to whether what had been erected were *arbres de la liberté, arbres de liberté, mais,* or "trees to commemorate the end of the abuses of the ancien régime and the reconquest of liberty." The legislation on the trees, which brought an end to these uncertainties, appeared with the first divisions in the unanimity of the nation: they were the first trees mutilated by the counterrevolution, or even removed by the revolutionaries themselves, because "owing to the day of their planting they still recall the frightful memory of monarchy."[84]

Those who erected maypoles in the countryside of the southwest were as silent about their reasons as the men of Year II were prolix. The erection of maypoles was recommended by a flood of national and departmental circulars and was always accompanied by long speeches. As all the speakers repeated, and sometimes even shamelessly reproduced, the writings of Convention members,[85] it is best to begin with those astonishing texts themselves.[86] One finds that they are a mixture of scholarly observations, advice on forestry matters, and meditations on the reasons for planting the trees and on their links with the Revolution.

Why plant a tree? The urge to do so seems to have been altogether stronger than the wish to erect other emblems, particularly those that are human creations, such as busts or statues. (One might note in passing that the statue of Liberty, sometimes associated with the tree, never replaced it; it was the tree that sacralized the statue and not the other way around. When, on 15 Germinal, Year V, it was decided to replace the worm-eaten pair formed by a bad statue of Liberty—at Châlons it was an altered Saint Catherine—and a dying tree, a living tree without a statue seemed a sufficient substitute.)[87] The practice of planting a tree derived from the mists of time, and it is remarkable that Revolutionary thought had recourse to this means of establishing a sacral necessity. Grégoire demonstrates this antiquity, the guarantee of a spontaneous symbolic universality, with a great many learned references. He recalls the mythological consecrations—the olive tree dedicated to Minerva, Bacchus' vine— and even (a remarkable feat, given the fact that the peasant tradition had become so enigmatic for rationalist thought)[88] the meanings of fertility and fraternity associated with the tree by folklore. He recognizes the link between the Liberty Tree and the maypole, to which Grégoire indeed attributes the ability to express varied historical realities. Accoridng to him, the immemorial use of the maypole may well have declined under despotism, as the deviation of the *mais d'honneur* shows. But it was regenerated when it passed "from England to the banks of the Delaware, where it rediscovered its original dignity and the maypoles became, once again, in each commune, a sign for citizens to gather together." Even in these learned justifications, however, historical consideration cannot be enough to account for the need to set up the maypole. Beyond all the reasons proffered, there is a recourse to a timeless popular verdict, a sort of transcendental spontaneity; for it is the people, Grégoire assures us, "that has itself determined the object that it regards as the type of what it most cherishes."

The second justification that runs through all these texts is related to the elementary sensualism that was the commonplace of all thought on the Revolutionary ceremonies. The tree provided a particular solution to this general problem of the connection between sense-perceptible objects and thought. For it is a mediator, a physical object, but also the seat of a power, already raised, by popular agreement, to the dignity of a symbol. The tree, therefore, is the "sensible sign of the regeneration of the French people," that much-sought-after means of linking sense-perceptible objects to political institutions. This is a theme tirelessly taken up by the festival organizers; when the central commissioner wrote to the municipal commissioners advising them not to be "indifferent to the erection of maypoles," they commented: "Signs exert over the people a power that all the legislators have used successfully and that we must not neglect. See with what care Catholicism reproduced under the eyes of its sectaries the emblems of religious belief."[89] This explains why reflection on the question drifts toward the most convenient physical aspect of a Liberty Tree. Thouin lays great stress on the conditions that the tree should satisfy if it is to be a good Liberty Tree. It must be tall, "that it may arouse admiration," and of imposing circumference, "in order to stir the senses and to speak the more strongly to the soul." Lastly, it must be long-lived: "If it cannot be eternal," says Grégoire, "then at least let it be chosen from among those trees that survive for several centuries."

This brings us, then, to the choice of essence, a concern that was completely absent from the planting of the *mais sauvages*. This discussion on suitable essences, though—as we shall see, of somewhat confused outcome—was carried out in typically Condillac-type terms. The important thing was to make trees the elements of a well-made language, to determine a language of trees in which the vocabulary would have a dual meaning, emblematic and geographical.[90] Thus, Hell proposed to draw up a list of trees signifying liberty, fraternity (chosen from among exotic trees that had adapted to the French climate, and particularly from among the "natural trees from the soil of our free brothers and friends of North

America"), and equality (chosen from among native trees). Then these trees would be distributed among the départements in such a way that each essence might, quite unequivocally, refer both to a Revolutionary value and to a portion of French territory. Similarly, Thouin distributed the trees that he had chosen for his symbolism among three very unequal Frances: that of the apple, the grape, and the orange.

The consideration given to such matters as soil and climate—even if aberrant, as when nonspecialists, such as Hell, are writing—makes it clear that utilitarian justifications were now mixed with historical and allegorical ones. At the back of the minds of all these writers was the complaint that the forests were being emptied and that there was a short-age of wood in France. The planting of Liberty Trees was seen as the starting point of a national reforestation campaign and a way of ensuring that the best species would be grown on the Republic's soil. Never before, said Thouin, had there been a more favorable opportunity for increasing the countryman's resources. The legislator was therefore killing two birds with one stone: while giving the people a way of erecting the symbol of liberty, he was establishing throughout the Republic seed-bearing trees. Hence the importance of selecting trees unknown in a particular region. So from Year II, the texts begin to turn their attention to the quality of the tree and to increase their practical advice: one must choose "a fine sapling," of "good growth"; the ground must be prepared in such a way that "the roots of the sacred tree can never reach calcareous tufa, clay, pure sand, permanent water, vitriolic soil, or other matter harmful to vegeta-tion." Consequently, the village community's symbolic point of concen-tration was abandoned for a more favorable place, near the drinking trough, or "close to the marl, which is in this place." All this suggests that utilitarian concerns had become more important than symbolic ex-pressiveness.[91]

The young rooted sapling of Year II,[92] with so much care and attention lavished upon it,[93] provides a strong contrast, therefore, with the vertical nudity of the maypole of the winter of 1790. This contrast is strongly emphasized in the official accounts: "What we have planted," said one commissioner, "is no longer an inanimate pole, but a flourishing tree."[94] "In view of the need to show the public what objects are to be venerated by the future generation," wrote another commissioner, "a hardy ash and an equally hardy elm have been planted." The organizers carefully distin-guished between the rooted fir tree that they were planting and the old pole of fir wood that it was replacing, even when the old pole, which, for a time, had been the beloved tree of the French people, was still looked on with nostalgia.[95] When the weather forced them to entertain no more illusions as to the tree's chance of survival, they stressed that the tree condemned by drought was merely temporary and would be replaced by another. But it was not without some regret that the image of power presented by the maypole was abandoned. The huge tree dreamed of by the organizers might speak to the senses, but to the senses of their great-nephews. Meanwhile, the delicate tree made to bear such hopes was often regarded as too puny.[96]

So what powers did Revolutionary thought attribute to the tree and what meanings did it bear? To begin with, the tree was a witness. It survived men, expressing a duration that was no longer theirs, stood as a memorial to the Revolutionary events with which it was contemporary, and of which it seemed to be the archive. We are planting the trees, the organizers said, "in order to remind the citizens of this canton for a long time to come of the memorable period of liberty."[97] The theme was already present in the planting ceremony, organized on May 1, 1790, by Norbert Pressac, which was to become a model: "At the foot of this tree," Pressac explained, "you will remember that you are French, and in your old age you will remind your children of the memorable time when you planted it."[98] This notion became a platitude in the speeches at the plantings: the tree, the orators assured their listeners, would relate how the National Convention had crushed royalism and recount the prodigious acts of bravery performed by the soldiers of Liberty. In this sense, it was a national monument: "A Republican monument, ancient tree of the nation," the orators of 1848 were still saying.[99] This designation was not as artificial as the obligatory rhetoric that surrounds it might lead one to believe. In it lives the ancient image of the calendar tree, and, in this obstinate recourse to the tree, one may also grasp what the tumultuous time of the Revolution demanded: an image of stability and the serene security of a slow, regular rhythm.

It represented stability, then, but this does not mean fixity: for the Liberty Tree, having become, unlike the maypole, a living individual, provided an image of growth that the Revolution wished to see as that of its own development. This motive is mixed up with a variety of beliefs and aspirations. To begin with, the idea that the destiny of an individual or a community is bound up with the tree planted in honor of a birth or inauguration derives both from popular tradition and from learned tradition. The texts that accompany the plantings—the justificatory thoughts of the organizers or versified doggerel proposed for the occasion by some obscure village schoolmaster—are thoroughly imbued with it. "Between us and the trees that we have sown, planted, and cultivated," writes François de Neufchâteau, "there is some attraction against which we are quite powerless, which identifies us in some way with them; which, as they grow, gives us each year a new joy, and binds our brief existence with their long future." [100] And, almost as an echo, we have these naive verses recited around the tree by schoolchildren: "As we see a branch grow, let us also see among French people the growth of the most open friendship." [101] But identification with the dynamism of the growing tree was not simply a matter of growth as such. Halfway between the mineral and the animal, the vegetal offered the model of an ideal growth: invisible but perceptible, irresistible but without unpleasant surprises, in which the thought of the future, always a source of anxiety, could, as Bernardin de Saint-Pierre has shown, give way to that of an untroubled development. [102] And, in identifying with the tree, the Revolution was able to endow itself with a happy, reflective growth. There again, the Revolutionary imagination returned to ancient institutions: in folk tales, vegetal metamorphosis is felt to be much less a punishment than animal metamorphosis; it may even be felt as a grace, a way of extending a happy state indefinitely.

The tree was also a refuge without an enclosure. We know the extent to which Revolutionary thinking placed value on open, bright space that the eye could range over without obstacles and how much it mistrusted darkness and secrecy. The branches of a tree shelter without imprisoning. The shade of a tree is the only beneficent shade mentioned in the writings of the Revolution, for the tree provides a shade without mystery or secrecy. It would seem impossible for a tree to shelter a plot. The woodland life is purified and purifying, so much so that despotism, a product of confined living, seems to date from its abandonment, when unvirtuous men "believed that they no longer had to expose the acts of the government to broad daylight, they abandoned the trees and retreated inside their dwellings, where they forged the chains that were to enslave posterity." "Hence," concluded the speaker[103] in a striking short cut, "the nobles, hence the priests."

Such innocence, of course, is the innocence of nature. That is why the most determined revilers of Revolutionary symbolism make an exception for the Liberty Tree. However severe he may have been with regard to the other creations of the Revolution, Sébastien Mercier remembered the planting of trees only as a leafy march spontaneously set in motion: "In the fine days of the Revolution, the Liberty Trees came from all the neighboring woods, took root at the feet of houses, and married their green hair with the balconies of different floors."[104] That is also why the verticality of the tree seemed to dominate without humiliating. It was not an artifact but a model of heroic uprightness, like the statue of Liberty, but without the artifice and heaviness of anthropomorphic representation. (That is why it was not only, after Thermidor, for reasons of political convenience that attempts were made to dissociate the Liberty Tree from the mountain on which it had sometimes—one verticality reinforcing another—been planted. The mountain, unlike the tree, opposed its massive opacity to the free movement of the eye, and was entirely dependent on man's initiative: hence its precariousness.)

The tree did not impede the eye but summoned it. It was also the anchorage point of communal effusion,[105] for a festival needed a center on which the eyes of the community could converge, and this would be marked by the tree. By making it the place where the community gathered—which meant that the altar of the fatherland would also be there—and therefore the place where marriage rites, youthful initiation ceremonies, and the distribution of civic crowns and rewards would take place, the festival organizers remembered their reading of Rousseau,[106] for whom the tree sacralized to such a degree that all felicity, whether of ideas or love or glory, could not willingly live except at the foot of the tree and beneath its branches.[107]

Lastly, by reason of all the aforementioned features, and because it is a memory, a center for the space of witness that gathers the community together, the tree is an educator, the silent pedagogue of the community. One is reminded here once more of the Rousseau of the *Essai sur l'origine des langues,* and, indeed, several of the festival organizers refer to him: "Beneath ancient oaks, conquerors of the years, ardent young men gradually lost their ferocity; they gradually tamed one another; in trying to be heard, they learned to speak. There the first festivals took place." Here Rousseau certainly brings together everything that Revolutionary thought demanded of the tree: harmony with another time, the disappearance of private interests, and an apprenticeship in the communal life, the center of a festal consciousness, and even civilization through language: "The hasty gesture was no longer enough."

From the Maypole to the Tree

As the object of so many writings and speeches, supported by so many learned justifications, showered with so many references, did the Liberty Tree still preserve something of the maypole of the winter of 1790? We must now examine the official accounts of the real plantings to determine whether they themselves constituted festivals or whether they were the center of other Revolutionary festivals.

Above all, did the tree[108] chosen by the Revolution enjoy a comparable unanimity with that aroused in the rebellious commune by its maypole? Here not everybody could take part in the planting. Hell recommended that "all those who had fallen into moderatism, federalism, or other criminal opinions" should be excluded. And, in fact, the official reports sometimes considered that the first act of a planting was, as at Beuzeville in the Eure, the exclusion of "municipal officers reputed to be aristocrats," whose presence would be a bad omen. Among those who remained, the "patriots of the country," the "Republic's arms," anyone could, in theory, perform the planting. Two categories of citizen were usually given this privilege, however: farmers (qua specialists) and young men (even children, sometimes, but generally youths). They would choose and dig up the tree in the communal woods, carry the tree in the procession, and dig the hole. Their presence was felt to be so necessary that when, for some reason or another, they were absent, the ceremony lost its meaning. "It has not fulfilled the views of the minister of the interior," wrote one commissioner from the Indre, "for the youth of that commune did not take part in the ceremony.[109] It is not excessive to see in this obligation on the part of the young people a memory of the maypole, the selection and erection of which was one of the tasks carried out by the young men of the community. Perhaps this privilege also stemmed from the fact that the young men were a group without hierarchy and, by that very fact, unanimist. The notion that some folk memory may have been at work here is confirmed, in any case, by the clever use made by certain municipalities of youth organizations in the festival. At Melle, for example, the municipality linked bachelorhood with a Festival of Youth, at the center of which was the planting of a willow in the "bachelors' meadow."[110]

They planted with precautions unknown to the planters of the winter of 1790: the official accounts are filled with advice on the soil to be used, the stakes to be chosen, the "Saint-Fiacre" ointment to be applied to the cuts, how often the tree had to be watered, none of which had been necessary in the case of the maypole. The watering, however, might have been symbolic, more in the nature of a fertility rite than a horticultural necessity. Very often wine from a barrel decorated with garlands and set up in the public square was used, just as today in the Limousin trees planted to commemorate the municipal elections are sprinkled with champagne: "We have worked to plant one," says one straightforward official report, "and we hope it will live, since we gave it a good drink. And we drank quite a lot ourselves, too."[111] The task was often entrusted to mothers: at Maroilles,[112] mothers watered the tree, and lest the symbol be lost on his audience, the president of the municipality declared, "May mothers make fertile the seed of Liberty in their children's hearts." Similarly, in the processions that accompanied the Liberty Tree to the place where it was to be planted, there were sometimes groups of pregnant women bearing banners. At Meaux, for example, one bore this proud inscription: "We are the ones who make up for the losses in the war." This was one of the few fertility symbols in the Revolutionary ceremonial and was almost always associated with the Liberty Tree.

The maypole was, of course, no more than a trunk, while the Liberty Tree was pruned after planting. "We planted it, then pruned it," many of the official accounts declare.[113] Was this solely for practical reasons, to ensure that it would survive? In this case, the pruning would have been quite different from the lopping off of branches in which, in the case of the maypole, only the topmost crown of the tree was kept. But if we examine the texts, it is not always easy to distinguish between the two forms of pruning. At Saint-Génix, in Year IV, there was resistance to planting a Liberty Tree.[114] Witnesses said that they had heard "the noise of a branchless tree falling," proof that the Liberty Tree had been prepared in exactly the same way as the old maypole. Furthermore, it sometimes happened (in the Côte d'Or, where "no tree survived because the village was situated on a mountainside, where the ground was not suitable to those trees,[115] it was even frequent) that one of the trees that already shaded the public square was adopted. In such cases, the local inhabitants were not content to decorate the tree with the cap of Liberty: it was trimmed. When this had been done, it was thought possible to announce that the tree was now "acknowledged to be the Liberty Tree." So the pruning was obviously not for practical reasons: it was of no use to a vigorous tree. Was it simply to distinguish it from other trees? But then the cap cut out of metal would have been enough. We can only conclude that the Liberty Tree preserved something of the maypole.

Apart from this cap, which almost obligatorily topped it,[116] what else was the Liberty Tree decorated with? Far fewer bunches of flowers than the maypole; tricolor ribbons were tied around the trunk on the day of planting (girdling the tree had always been seen as a beneficent gesture)[117] or added on the occasion of public or private celebrations—at weddings, for example, when the bride had "the charming idea of tying a ribbon that had been given her to the tree."[118] Sometimes too, but fairly seldom, farm tools—rakes, forks, flails—were found on the tree, so many emblems "intended to recall the wealth of the nation to industry."[119] And just as the choosing of the tree was left to the young men, its decoration became the task of the girls of the commune, another feature deriving from folklore. The decoration was less essential to the Liberty Tree, however, than to the maypole, whose very bareness seemed to call for notices and emblems. This sometimes led to a post's being placed next to the tree for the display of signs. Near the living tree planted at Villers-Cotterêts a column, painted in the three colors, carried the pikestaff, the crown, and the tricolor flags.[120] Though less richly decorated than the maypole, the Liberty Tree was surrounded (increasingly so as its existence was threatened) with railings painted in the three colors, stone walls, or thorn hedges. This was intended to deter attackers, whether human or animal. Such an enclosed area,[121] which the official reports refer to as "sacred," and which, they repeat, only the magistrates should enter, was not entirely respected, if the repeated appeals from certain municipalities that the tree should not be used for drying clothes is anything to go by.

The tree had now become *l'arbre de la Liberté,* or even (and this confirms the official character of the term) *l'arbre de la République,* even *l'arbre social.* Only in exceptional cases was it referred to as *l'arbre de liberté,* with its dynamic, emotive charge. Sometimes, however, it was still called *l'arbre de force et de liberté* or *l'arbre de concorde* and sometimes too *l'arbre tricolore.* In other places, here and there, one finds Unity Trees, Equality Trees, and Fraternity Trees. The Fraternity Tree had a special place, for it was usually the "second" tree in the village, so called because there was already a Liberty Tree, and it might be planted, for example, in the second-largest square[122] by the inhabitants of a quarter who felt neglected. Whether a Fraternity Tree or a Liberty Tree, it was invariably the "beloved" tree or "sacred" tree or even the "precious relic." The official accounts take on a maternal tone when referring to them: people gathered around the "beloved sapling,"[123] or put their arms "affectionately" around it; such terms testify to their seeing the tree as small and defenseless. Instinctively it

Le Mai des Français ou les entrées libres. Collection de Vinck no. 3903, Bibliothèque nationale, Cabinet des estampes.

was felt that the only stanza in the *Marseillaise* suitable for the young tree was that in which the fury of war is calmed—"Amour sacré de la Patrie"—and, in fact, the tree meant simply that.

When they recount the planting rites, the official reports tend to fall back into the terms of the pastoral. For the municipal officers or commissioners who wrote the reports, these plantings had the innocence that the eighteenth century attributed to country festivals: "Never was a festival gayer," wrote one of them, "or better represented the touching simplicity of the early ages." [124] Fife, drum, bagpipes, and clarinet accompanied the planting. The dance of the girls and boys wound in and out around the trunk. And games—"innocent" ones of course, such as ball or tennis— brought the ceremony to an end. Was it a daydream or an observation? It might be said that the Revolutionary festival, already poorer in simulacra, was never more so than during these plantings. Yet the tree sometimes played its part in the well-tried dramaturgy of appearance or disappearance: it emerged out of the ruins of a mock Bastille, or out of the ashes of a chained monster, the image of despotism, that had just gone up in flames. But generally the naturalness that seemed to be required by the planting discouraged the use of artifice. And, at a more profound level, in the simplicity of the actions performed by the villagers (they knelt in front of the tree, they put their arms around the trunk and kissed it, [125] touched it several times in order to receive its beneficent powers), we see the resurgence of the unexpressed need that turned the Liberty Tree, like the old maypole, into a source of help.

Let us now try to bring together the various features that the planting of this official tree has in common with that of the maypole. Apart from the fundamental role, already noted, that it gave to youth, we should examine the necessarily communal character of the planting, the certainty, everywhere expressed, that in order to plant a Liberty Tree, one must have the consent of the whole community. The patriotic citizens of the commune of Chemillé[126] complained bitterly to the administrators of Cholet: "The Liberty Tree was planted secretly last Monday by the municipal officers, who, no doubt, so that there would be few citizens attending this ceremony, which ought to take place with the whole community on a public holiday, so that the inhabitants might attend without neglecting their work, and to which everybody should have been invited, so that erring men, brought back to good principles by good example, an entire union of sentiment might take place, did not announce it either at the parish mass or in notices." The documents in the archives are full of such

protests against those who planted the tree "with unpardonable abandon," [127] without raising the national colors on the civic palms[128] or alert-
ing private individuals. The planting of the Liberty Tree required "magistrates in official dress,"[129] the full pomp and ceremony of planting;[130]
even the farandoles should be danced with some degree of ceremony.[131]
When a community had to choose the "real" one among several claimants
to the title of Liberty Tree,[132] the one that enjoyed greatest allegiance
among the inhabitants was chosen, and "this tree alone could be universally regarded as the Tree of Liberty in that commune." All these documents reveal the need of, and sometimes the nostalgia for, communal
unanimity. They also show that unanimity in action, as in those parishes
where the population built a sentry box at the foot of a tree threatened by
bands from neighboring villages and, for six months, took turns mount-
ing guard.[133] There are innumerable examples of a commune coming together around a tree that it had planted as it had once done around the
communal maypole.

Furthermore, like the maypole, the tree continued to signify taking
leave of the old world and welcoming the birth of the new. This is evinced
in two facts. When, as happened in towns of some size, the tree was
carried in procession, its presence was often marked by a break in the
procession,[134] and those groups that represented the past—the stretcher
carrying the mock Bastille or the masked men with hats pulled down over
their faces and wearing cloaks under which daggers were concealed, a
veritable tableau vivant of fanaticism—preceded it. Then there was a gap
in the procession, then the tree, then another gap, and a sign that read,
"The reign of Liberty has begun." Then followed the age groups, representing that seamless social order promised by the Revolution and guaranteed by the tree.

There is another fact, whose implications are even greater: the ceremonial of the tree, which integrated all festivals without exception,[135]
nevertheless animated them in unequal measure. There were festivals at
which the presence of the tree would have been expected and to which
indeed the official circulars recommended that the planting of the tree be
linked (such as the Festival of Youth, which, according to François de
Neufchâteau,[136] was doubly suitable on account of both the time of year
and the nature of the festival), but in which nevertheless it did not necessarily feature. There were festivals that seemed to have little or nothing
to do with the ceremonial of the tree, but in which it played a part, if not
a dominant one (such as the Federation). There were, however, two festi-

vals in which the planting of the tree was an obligatory rite: the Festival of the King's Death, in which it figured in all the official instructions as an indispensable element, and the Festival of Continental Peace,[137] in which no official instructions ordered the planting, but in which it nevertheless took place. Now, more than any other of the Revolutionary festivals, that of the king's death was a ritual of ending. And the Festival of Continental Peace was an explosion of joy: it seemed to promise the establishment, forever announced and forever postponed, of the Revolution. The tree, like the maypole, therefore provided both a rite of closure and a rite of birth. It was at its festival that the Revolution saw its history, like that of mankind, begin.

This survival of meanings associated with the maypole in the Liberty Tree would be confirmed, if this were necessary, by the long uncertainties over vocabulary, the obstinacy with which participants referred to their tree as the *mai*. At Châlons-sur-Marne,[138] the volunteers of the battalions from the Indre and the Creuse, who had been divided over some internal quarrel, swore to be reconciled. They laid a tricolor flame at the town hall bearing the inscription, "The Indre and the Creuse united forever." But the true sign of regeneration that effaced the past and guaranteed the future was the planting of a tree. A tree or a maypole? As far as the official accounts were concerned, it was much the same thing. Even in Year V, at Aigrefeuille,[139] when the young men uprooted a tree, the commune was outraged, and the commissioner of the executive directory denounced the act as sacrilege. The mayor defended his local people: the tree, he said, was in no way a Liberty Tree but a "little tree trunk without roots"—in other words a *mai*—put into the earth, "according to ancient custom," on 12 Floréal (May 1) and uprooted on 12 Prairial after a ritual period. In short, it was "a youthful action . . . innocent in itself." The commissioner was not convinced. What nevertheless does emerge from the confused discussion that followed is that it was very difficult, even in Year V, to distinguish between a maypole and a Liberty Tree.

A Break

Yet it was no longer the tree of rural insurrection. Indeed, we have seen how the tree, to begin with, in its physical appearance, was no longer a maypole. We should add two more features. First, the vigorous image of liberation conveyed by the maypole had lost its vitality; the theme of conquered liberty had itself gradually declined. The tree was now associated more with equality than with liberty. Gradually there had taken place a shift in meaning the stages of which are extremely difficult to detect. Yet it seems that at least two elements contributed to it. To begin with, the tree, erected in the middle of the village square, almost necessarily imposed on the space around it the most egalitarian shape—the circle of spectators—the shape in which geometry seems spontaneously to carry its own morality. In the circle thus formed, it is difficult to imagine a hierarchical classification: it welds together age groups, sexes, trades, ranks, officers, soldiers, and sometimes even "prisoners released for the occasion of the festival."[140] The circle around the tree was welcoming, whereas people would have hesitated to integrate all those groups into the linear order of a procession. In that sense, mixing the classes in the spatial democracy that it organized, the tree was certainly Barère's "teacher of equality," endowed with the pedagogical powers referred to in the specially chosen verses recited in the festivals.[141] But the substitution of equality for liberty was effected even more by the manipulation of age groups. The appearance around the Liberty Tree of age groups was indeed an obligatory element in the Revolutionary ritual, as in all such utopias. The tree was necessarily bound up with the great moments of life. It was planted at the birth of "a new member" (of the people's club),[142] who would later be buried at its feet. It was associated with the initiation of young men into adulthood and with marriages, so that the comings and goings around the tree provided a rhythm to human life. So we should hardly be surprised if the tree emerged in the midst of a festival in which one might not expect it. Indeed, it was usually there because it was associated with the age groups, for the tree united the different age groups by assigning them symmetrical functions. The adults declared, "Our children will defend it against the ravages of time," and the children replied, "One day we will defend it against the ravages of tyrants." Thanks to the tree, each generation enacted in advance the uses that time would eventually bring it, or repeated those that it had already fulfilled. One senses what the tree brought to the chain of the age groups: it prevented it from becoming pure succession. It stood there, a silent witness of succession, going back to another time, the guarantee of biological equality; it expressed the fundamentally identical state of elders and juniors. Rather than freeing people from their conditions, it made those conditions equal.

Second, and more particularly, the Liberty Tree was not associated with the violence that had accompanied the erection of the maypole. Of course, it took a long time for that violence to be extirpated. For a long time the planting was seen as the kind of provocation felt by the notables of the Périgord in 1790. At Cassel, for example, on March 25, 1792, the spontaneous planting of a tree decorated with a tricolor flag by the volunteers caused as much consternation to the municipalities as two years before.[143] "Those people," lamented the mayor, "will surely allow a thousand things against good order, dance around the tree, and insult good citizens." "I hastened to reassure him," replied the commandant of the National Guard; "I assured him that the tree would not become the cause of any disturbance on the part of the volunteers." Nevertheless, the mayor kept to his seditious interpretation and saw no other possible response than to set out at the head of a column of townsmen from Cassel against the volunteers and knock down the tree. Up to about the first few months of Year II, the tree could still be found at the center of provocative or aggressive scenes: at Wormhout, travelers, who were always somewhat suspect, were forced to get out of their carriages, kiss the base of the tree, and pay a certain sum of money.[144] At Mantes, the Liberty Tree, which had been snapped by the wind, was replaced by an upright poplar chosen from the highway; the men involved then went off to fetch the local priests, put red caps on their heads, and forced them to dance around the tree.[145] But that same Year II, well before Thermidor, any trace of violence or even of mockery was eliminated from the festival.

Where did all the violence go? Within the Republican festival itself, it had taken refuge in daydreams about the roots of the tree, for even those rationalizing speeches continued to attach great emotion to the image of roots. Roots went down to the empire of darkness, communicated with mystery. Certain Republicans, such as Demachy at Rennes, obtained permission to be buried at the foot of that "beloved emblem," convinced that the remains of a true Republican were fit matter to aid the growth of the Liberty Tree. And elsewhere, through the whole literature of the plantings, runs the theme of the tree that had slaked its thirst on the blood of kings, an image that Grégoire was not to forgive himself for risking in his *Mémoires*. In the middle of a debate in the Convention, Barère also declared that the tree should be watered with the blood of kings. And M.-J. Chénier put this sentiment into verse: "Rois conjurés, lâches esclaves / Vous avez fui devant nos braves / Et dans votre sang détesté / Abreuvant ses vastes racines / Le chêne de la Liberté / S'élève aux cieux sur vos ruines." ("Conspirator-kings, cowardly slaves / You have fled before our brave men / And watering its huge roots / In your detested blood, / The oak of Liberty / Rises to the heavens on your ruins.") This was not only a rhetorical theme: in the tuft of roots that went down into the humus of the soil, there was something dark, disturbing, and blind, which contrasted with the quiet strength of the trunk.

Moreover, it was outside the Republican festival and, from now on, against the tree that the violence was directed. The archives are full of accounts of trees brought down by professionals with saw and axe, or mutilated by impatient amateurs content to rip off the bark as they dashed past. Such cases were difficult to deal with. Usually nobody had seen anything, and few had even heard anything.[146] Witness followed witness, each declaring his innocence, and the fruitless statements piled up. Even the mayors were eager to blame the damage on "passing travelers,"[147] on "men on the run who have no fixed abode,"[148] on those who were "here today, gone tomorrow," or even on children. This was certainly in order to divert the always unwelcome attentions of commissions of inquiry or of soldiers billeted on local inhabitants. But in the constant blaming of the offence or "crime" on travelers and children—that is to say, categories outside the community—one can also see an additional sign of the strong communal feeling inspired by the tree.

It was indeed an offense, or more usually a "crime": for what emerges in the commissioners' reports devoted to incidents involving the tree was the anthropomorphic vocabulary of violence. The tree had been insulted; called, in patois, *rebeille*[149] (*rebeille,* the official investigator notes learnedly, is "a vulgar term of contempt to designate a dry, or badly shaped branch"); "profaned";[150] given a cruel blow from a billhook. Sacrilegious hands had cut it "to the quick."[151] Lastly, whereas the sap seemed like pure blood, relieved of fantasies, here it became heavy blood, ineffaceably, criminally shed. So the attack on the tree is often described in terms of murder; sometimes the violated tree was buried, as at Amiens, where nine thousand armed men, with veiled drums at their head, carried the tree, covered by a long black veil, to its last resting place.[152] Indeed, we know what cycle of violence against people the violence against the tree set in motion: the decree that declared the commune of Bédouin to be in a state of counterrevolution, condemned sixty-three of its inhabitants to death, and ordered that the commune should be set on fire was the consequence of the digging up of the Liberty Tree. The decree was read in the public square at the precise spot where the crime had been committed.

This tree, threatened by the people and defended by officials, seems to be the exact reverse of the maypole, which had been attacked by the authorities and defended by the village community. At Noirlieu, where, on the night of 11 Floréal, the Liberty Tree was knocked down, suspicion fell on a servant. Had he not given "so-called May bouquets to girls the night before"? Yes, he had offered such flowers, and he had even invited the girls to go and see them, since, he said, "they were still in the same place." This admission made him the presumed author of the looting of the official tree. It is probably to make too much of this minor incident to see it as a divorce between the tree of the Revolution and that of peasant tradition, since whoever bowed before the one attacked the other. It is not irrelevant, however, that the commissioners thought of making the link, or that the Revolutionary tree was attacked on the night of May 1.

Nevertheless, by an ironic twist, it is the attacked tree that seems closest to the maypole associated with the riots of the winter of 1790. Certainly, in referring to it the counterrevolutionaries revived the peasants' expressive short cuts of 1790, except that it was no longer *arbre de liberté* but *arbre de malheur*, or *de misère*. "Arbre de misère / Bonnet de galère / Planté par des brigands / Abattu par des Chouans" ("Tree of poverty / Galley cap. / Planted by brigands / Felled by Chouans") went the Chouan refrain in the Contentin.[153] Also, deprived of its branches, restored to the nakedness of the maypole, and sporting a notice, the tree rediscovered its function as a warning signal: perhaps, wrote a commissioner, they have done this to discourage our young conscripts from marching to the field of honor. Finally, uprooted and replanted as a provocation before the houses of Republican functionaries and municipal officers, crudely shaped, the tree became once again the gibbet that it once had been.[154]

But the Liberty Tree left room for a verticality bearing another meaning: that of the cross. Many official accounts of plantings provide evidence that the tree was seen by the revolutionaries themselves as a substitute for the cross. It was planted at the very spot at which the cross had stood, or immediately beside it, and sometimes the ceremony was concluded with "the destruction of the pedestal of a cross that was beside the place where the tree had been planted."[155] It is all too clear that erecting the cross where the tree had stood became the act of reparation par excellence, an act that was to be repeated thousands of times in the expiatory liturgies of the Restoration. At Savignac, for example, there was a riotous assembly on 3 Pluviôse, Year III, on the occasion of the planting of a tree.[156] A tree? A visiting municipal officer approached and, to his stupefaction, saw that it was a cross. Standing there was an unknown man (Was it a priest? It is by no means certain) brandishing a paper, in which it was stated that those who had degraded or destroyed public monuments would be punished. Was this not a sign "that no time should be lost in restoring the crosses?" These crosses, made of maplewood or hazel, which sprang up next to trees lying on the ground, often crudely shaped because made in haste, also, on occasion, carried meassages, notices, or "folded papers placed above the cross point,"[157] whose content, according to the official accounts, remained mysterious, for, as usual, none of the villagers was able or willing to decipher it. But what did that matter? Such a cross spoke without benefit of writing.

THE entire Revolutionary ceremonial, complained Edgar Quinet, was unable "to displace a single village saint." This admission of complete failure was all the more mortifying in that these men of the Revolution were guilty often of destruction and always of an inability to understand (but in this, we must remember, they were certainly not the first): throughout the Revolutionary decade, the official documents provide us with ample evidence of both. Is this enough to convince us? We certainly have to go beyond what the festival organizers so smugly said and wrote if we are to understand the needs fulfilled by their ceremonial arrangements. Here things changed a little: the documentation on the Liberty Tree seems to argue for a survival within the Revolutionary festival, however overladen it may have been with rationalist discourse, of authentically archaic popular practices. So it would seem to be clear that the actions associated with the planting—choosing the tree in the woods, planting it, decorating it, dancing and singing around it—were at least as important as the pedagogical lessons that accompanied it and the rational ideology that sustained it. But is this so difficult to understand? One might conclude that, at the unconscious level at least, the Revolutionary symbolism was less alien to peasant tradition than has often been supposed.

· X ·

The Revolutionary Festival:
A Transfer of Sacrality

THE official religious life was a long time dying. In many regions, parishioners would have been justified in thinking that their church still survived. Long after the orders banning "external manifestations of worship," the processions continued to fill the streets of the towns, winding their way out to the fields for the rogations, provided a juring priest was willing to lead them. At Toul, on August 6, 1792, for the feast of Saint Mansuy, the solemn transfer of the relics from the former abbey to the cathedral was worthy of the most fervent years, except that the "constitutional bishop" had replaced the Benedictines. At Marseille, on June 3, 1792, the juring priest of Saint-Augustin presented the young citizens of the parish who had made their first communion to the Club of the friends of the Constitution. Five days later, it was the turn of the young citizenesses to return in procession from Notre-Dame de la Garde. The assembly showed its satisfaction: "Did we ever enjoy the charms of such union under the old order?"[1]

The association of the religious ceremony with the Revolutionary festival, an alliance formed during the Federations, was itself a very firm one. The date of August 10, 1793, was still celebrated in many regions with an open-air mass, the exposition of the Blessed Sacrament, and the release of birds into the air. At Eze, one might think that the official account of August 10 was that of a Federation: vespers at the usual time, benediction of the Blessed Sacrament, loud peals of bells.[2] Le Coz's credo and that of the constitutional clergy as a whole—"may our holy religion gain much from this Revolution"[3]—found ample justification, therefore, right up to the middle of the terrible year of 1793. And that was not the end of it: six months later, in the midst of religious persecution, there

were communes in which the Festival of the Taking of Toulon was celebrated by sung masses and a *Te Deum*. Blutel, a member of the Convention, on holiday in a commune of the Calvados, happened to find himself
in the midst of preparations for a celebration: "Those good people believed
that a *Te Deum* would embellish their festival and proposed to go to the
church to sing it. Though I was not of the same opinion, I did not think
it politic to flout their decision by a refusal. I gave in to their wishes, but
I took advantage of the occasion to rail against fanaticism."[4]

A few months later this syncretism was disappearing; nevertheless,
manifestations of the religious life never entirely disappeared and would
suddenly emerge here and there as if from a subterranean life. The traces
of this resistance, of which the women were the secret agents, are to be
found even in the writings of the revolutionaries themselves,[5] in the *rapports décadaires*, for example. Their evidence, emanating from men whose
task it was both to assess and to construct social conformity, is all the
more significant. Where official envoys and commissioners very obviously
failed, in their own opinion, was in confining baptisms, weddings, and
funerals to the darkness of the church, so strong remained the need to
sacralize, from the cradle to the grave, the great moments of human
life—not only by religious rituals, for these, as such, were outside the
authority of the civil servants, but also by the public demonstrations attaching to them. For the people there was no true ceremony without a
public procession. The commissioner for the Seine-et-Marne waged a constant battle against the drums that continued to accompany future husbands or infants about to be baptized on their way to the church. The
commissioner for the Maine-et-Loire complained that the dead were always taken to the cemetery in procession, with the viaticum of sung prayers. Others complained of the soldiers, who, on such occasions, believed
it their duty to "make the powder speak," a form of eloquence that the
priests never used to care much for either. The inventory of these offenses
has the advantage of revealing the necessary interconnection, for a sensibility that had not changed, between the religious ceremony and the social act. A young couple might appear before the municipal officer with
the witnesses required by the law and wearing ordinary clothes, but in
that case they might as well not be married: the night after such a ceremony, complained the commissioner for the Alpes-Maritimes, a young
bride would not sleep with her husband. For a real "wedding" to be
celebrated, as opposed to this legal marriage—the commissioners were
careful to distinguish between the two terms—two more things were

required: the religious ceremony and public festivities. As good anthropologists, the commissioners knew, even when they lamented its excesses, the importance of the wedding meal as a social consecration of the
marriage. Furthermore, although they might have been careful to forbid
celebratory processions, they showed less repressive zeal where funeral processions were concerned. In the face of death, they were held back by what
they called "decency," but this may be interpreted as a more visceral than
social fear.

The pulse of the religious calendar, with its high points competing
with those that the Revolutionary calendar had tried to establish, is still
perceptible in these writings. In that sacral time of Christmas—or rather
the Christmas cycle, for Epiphany, with its bonfires on the hilltops and
its exchange of cakes, was just as keenly celebrated and was, in any case,
a more exhibitionistic, more communal festival—shone brightest. It was
a cycle marked from end to end, groaned the commissioners, by "persistent inaction in the countryside" and, in the towns, a holiday lasting
several days. Furthermore, the commissione.s, always in search of benevolent actors and consenting spectators for their own dramatic productions, had to admit, to their own astonishment, the spontaneous welcome
given to sacred drama at Christmastime, whether this took the form, here
and there, of midnight masses, in which the talents of a parish were
employed to represent angels and shepherds, or, as happened in Brittany,
the arrival of traveling players, who came at Christmas to play, in Breton,
the lives of the saints or the story of the Three Kings (twenty-five years
later, their arrival at Saint-Jean-Brévelay was to strike the imagination of
the young Jules Simon). One can imagine the feelings of the civil servants, themselves hardly welcome in the community, toward these actors,
who were often mobile artisans, always male, who played the female roles
in "appropriate costume." This was yet another sign of their profound
accord with the enlightened priests of former days: they too had suspected
these spectacles of being unedifying; they too had vituperated against
those drunken actors, incapable of speaking their lines, and, above all,
had expressed the mistrust of sedate people for those uncontrollable individuals, forever moving from village to village under cover of their sacred
frippery, bringing upon themselves a double mistrust—that of the pilgrim and that of the actor.

There are few references in these writings to Easter or Lent, which are
seen not so much as high points of the liturgical year as a dead season of
the Republican spirit, which was then weakened by the "increase in eccle-

siastical power over the weakness of the vulgar." The time of All Saints, however, was one of irrepressible sacral demonstration: at this time the population braved prohibition, as if the hostility of the commissioners stopped as surely before the night of All Saints as it did before the funeral procession. Then the bells would ring out, from commune to commune, throughout a night devoted to the din of the beyond. Awakened, like everybody else, the commissioners resigned themselves to not interfering: death, for them too, remained a religious act, and All Saints a time that they could not touch. Indeed, beyond this established religious calendar there was another calendar of reference, which was that of expectation, traces of which can be found in these usually sedate pages: rumors ran, papers circulated, there were whisperings and hopes. Something was being planned, something would happen. This "something" was mentioned in these Revolutionary writings, grudgingly and with a sort of shudder: it was the immense hope that a new time would come that would revolutionize the Revolution.

This popular persistence in marking time other than according to the Republican rhythm suggests, in any case, a daily life broken in two, limping between Sunday and *décadi,* Christmas and the taking of Toulon, profane and sacred. Hence the problem, clearly perceived by Mathiez, of knowing whether this break was experienced as one, whether, even in those festivals that broke completely any links with religious celebration, another form of religiosity were not developing.

The positive response given by Mathiez to this question owes much to the Durkheimian identification of the religious with the communal, which obviously makes any Republican assembly more or less religious. Beyond this mechanical facility in declaring the Revolutionary festival religious, Albert Soboul tried to assess the religious feelings of those who took part in the Revolutionary ceremonies.[6] Of the two examples on which he bases his argument, let us set aside that of the patriotic saints; for if a true miracle cult did indeed develop around young patriotic women who had been raped and murdered, it was not so much the image of the young *Republican* woman, as indeed Albert Soboul himself demonstrates, as that of the tortured woman that counted here. Let us instead consider all those funerals, those apotheoses, those inaugurations of busts that proliferated in the summer and autumn of 1793. This flood is to be explained by the emotion aroused among the sans-culottes by the death of Marat and may be seen elsewhere in the emulation between sections and between the people's clubs. The interpretation of this series of festivals as a veritable cult rests on the perpetually quoted words of the orator mentioned in *Les révolutions de Paris:* "O cor Marat, O cor Jesus."[7] This had led, with the help of counterrevolutionary historiography, to the image of kneeling crowds, chanting litanies to the Sacred Heart of Marat and imploring his protection. One hesitates, however, with F. P. Bowman,[8] to conclude in this particular case—despite the altars erected in the streets, despite the invocations and incense—that Marat was being deified or even sanctified. To begin with, one should not be taken in by the vocabulary. Someone may well have said that Marat was immortal, but as much was said of Brutus or Lycurgus: in the discourse of the Revolution, immortality was not a hope but the symbol of survival in the collective memory. One also used the word *martyr* (of liberty), but this was a very common word whose religious charge had been lost in the vocabulary of Revolutionary heroics. This is shown very clearly in the speed with which the habit spread of linking Marat, in these festivals, not only with other "martyrs," such as Lepelletier and Chalier, but sometimes too with the philosophers or heroes of the past. Thus, in the festival procession, one could see Marat and Lepelletier side by side with Rousseau and Voltaire, as at Beauvais, or, at Châteauroux, "honorable men wearing hats decorated with bay and carrying tricolor flags"; these men were simply regarded as triumphant warriors. Such attributes show quite clearly what these martyrs were: they were "great figures." They argued, when Jesus was put among them—and that did happen—for the humanization of Jesus rather than the deification of Marat. Marat, Lepelletier, and Chalier were examples, not figures from a cult in which "honors" were given to certain figures, as here, with all the anthropomorphism implied in the notion of honor.

Was this vocabulary of honor, were these invocations and praises capable—Albert Soboul poses the question—of being transposed by simple minds, knowing nothing of the literary mode of praise, unfamiliar with hyperbole, and all too ready to turn these great men into saints? In the festivals involving busts there was certainly a revival of emotion. The participation of the sections and people's clubs was more noticeable here than in other festivals. There were more simulacra. There was no fear of showing the tragic bathtub, or of laying out, as at Saint-Eustache, "the simulacrum of this representative on his deathbed."[9] But we already know that this expressionism belonged, on the whole, to the mode of the funeral festival. Nor was the use of the procession or of incense proof of the specificity of these festivals. Nor were the invocations that they contained—Frank Bowman notes that they belonged to an accepted rhetorical genre—evidence of the reality of a saintlike cult: no therapeutic powers were attributed to Marat. Apart from a few isolated incidents, people did not touch the bust or kiss it or ask it to perform some action. This cult, such as it was, lacked the essential element, namely, sacralizing protection.

The "Revolutionary saints" of the summer and autumn of 1793 are poor evidence, therefore, of people's deep emotional involvement. In the festivals dedicated to them, one can detect very few signs of an irrational impulse. It is quite likely, however, that certain religious needs were nevertheless satisfied by them. But the festival was merely an indirect opportunity for doing this. So the problem should perhaps be posed differently: not by denying that a contamination may have occurred in the minds of the participants, which, in any case, can only remain hypothetical, but above all by trying to discover whether the festival was in any sense the object of a transfer of sacrality.

Horror vacui

The men of the Revolution themselves had few illusions as to the meager nourishment offered popular religiosity by the Revolutionary festivals: "The poor conditions here on earth," the commissioner for the Ardennes wrote, "often transport the souls of the inhabitants of the countryside toward other hopes."[10] This is because the authorities chose not to follow the gentle methods recommended in 1789 by Rabaut Saint-Etienne in the memoranda of the Academy of Nîmes. Instead of "gradually reducing the processions, confraternities, ceremonies in square and street"—that is to say, being content to follow the simplifying tendency of the century as a whole—they chose to empty everyday life of religious acts, brutalizing, breaking up, and prosecuting them. Such a vacuum was abhorred on two accounts: either people were convinced that without rituals, any life declines into idleness or incoherence (this was the point of view of Dupont de Nemours), or it was predicted that the vacuum thus left by the expulsion of the marvelous might be filled by something even more fearful. Corruption and immortality or, worse still, a new, revived form of Catholicism might rise from its ashes. When a cult, even an unreasonable one, is destroyed, La Révellière declared, it has always proved necessary to replace it with others; otherwise, it has, so to speak, "replaced itself in rising from its own ruins."[11] The whole thinking of the Directoire, from

Tracy to Madame de Staël, is agreed on the *horror vacui* left by the persecution of Catholicism and on the imperious need to replace it.

With what was one to replace what had been destroyed, and what could be substituted for Catholicism? How was the new religion to be established? The true answer, the leitmotif of the Revolutionary assemblies, was given by the imitation encouraged by the syncretic euphoria of the Revolutionary dawn. To replace was first of all to imitate—or to copy, said the critics. The new religion, like the old, had to have its sacred center, the altar of the fatherland, a place that was both religious and civic, on which one might, as Benoist-Lamothe suggests, expose the bread of fraternity. There, too, there would have to be the sacralizing presence of a book, the sole receptacle of all moral precepts. This book would be the Declaration of Rights, which would be all the more capable of replacing the missal on the altar in that it contained the sacred statement of origins, that of the unchallengeable principles (a "children's alphabet" according to Rabaut Saint-Etienne, a "national catechism" according to Barnave), often preciously kept in an "august tabernacle," an ark of the Constitution. There would be a need for prayers and singing; hence the flood of patriotic anthems, "civic" sermons, "divine and constitutional" prayers, such literary confections as the "Village Sheet" intended to supplant "the old, superstitious prayers." A liturgical calendar would be needed, and ceremonies: thus a civic baptism was imagined, in which one saw the godfather, wearing his cockade, unstop a bottle, pour a few drops on the forehead of the newborn child, moisten his lips as the Republican Decalogue was recited, or someone read the commandments of the perfect member of the people's club.[12] And there would be a civic Lent, during which people would fast for the sake of liberty. There would be priests, who would be chosen not from among the "celibates" but from among family men. Apart from a few conditions—white hair and an upright life—they would perform exactly the same functions as Catholic priests, presiding at weddings, witnessing births, comforting the sick.

In all these suggestions there is a desperate wish to compete with religion—even to the extent of such physical features as the columns of the law and the altars of the fatherland. This furious rush of imitation is particularly apparent in the religious impregnation of vocabulary, a study of which has hardly begun. The mountain is "holy," the assemblies are "temples" and families "churches," a father is a "pontiff" and a mother his "loving and beloved vicar," the history of the Revolution is the "gospel of the day" and Paris the "true Rome," the "Vatican of Reason." The projects for a Republican liturgy, of which there was a proliferation at this time, illustrate this to the point of pastiche: there were, for example, suggestions that the Easter communion should be given twice a year, under the species of a cake at harvest time and wine from a ciborium at the wine harvest;[13] that the rogation procession be kept under the innocent name of "tour of the territory"; that Christmas be celebrated as the Festival of Birth (if the mother of the household had had a male child in that year); that All Saints' Day commemorate the great men who had died in the family; that on Good Friday, the wishes of the community be brought to those persons who, during the year, had suffered the most physically or morally.

We may laugh at the poverty of imagination of men condemned to reproduce a banished religion. This would not be entirely fair, for, in their conviction of the necessity of rites, the men of the Revolution were not content to borrow from what lay to hand. Antiquity provided them with at least as many models. There was, for example, the funeral ceremony, which Daubermesnil borrowed from the young Anacharsis and proposed to the organizers of Republican ceremonies.[14] Before the corpse the public officer would deliver the funeral oration. Then honey would be poured around the coffin in homage to the dead man's sweetness of character, then milk in memory of his candor, wine to commemorate his strength, and, lastly, incense so that "his good actions may fill the tableau of his life" like smoke. In their looting of ancient practices, the festival organizers and the authors of projects also found the powerful drama of the oath, with the curses that would befall the perjurer and the invocations that were not only a rhetorical resource but an attempt to equal the Romans, who, these men had read hundreds of times, believed that they were under a serious obligation only when they had sworn by Jupiter. It would seem, then, that in their obsession with ceremonies, they drew their models from different sources in quite unprincipled imitation.

And in fact there were no principles, or rather there was only one. By drawing on a mass of practices, wherever they were to be found, Revolutionary creation obeyed only a single law, that of the purge, which dominated both Revolutionary thought and Revolutionary action. Abolishing coats of arms, burning papers, striking out names, removing crowns and miters: a whole enterprise of subtraction and purification was directed at Catholic worship, with what was regarded as its excessive ornamentation and superfluous regulations. All this was regarded as so much bric-a-brac that needed to be swept away, if one were to see the true cult emerging from Revolutionary times in all its fresh beauty. A curious anonymous text of 1790 entitled *Décret de l'Assemblée nationale portant règlement d'un culte sans prêtres, ou moyen de se passer des prêtres sans nuire au culte* shows clearly the direction of the operation, the elimination of what Dupont de Nemours called "superfluity"—that is to say, toward the metaphysical heights and away from the depths of superstition. That is why the descriptions of the ideal Revolutionary worship are doomed to the grammar of "only" and "without." "Without recourse to trickery," writes Lefebvre de Villebrune in *La décade;* "without lustral water, without mysteries, without images." [15] Above all, this purging is the basis of all the others, without the slightest mention of sin. For the Revolutionary cult to live, all that was needed, it seems, was a mass of renunciations. As soon as the existence of the Supreme Being was declared as the first, unsuspecting cause of a formal, organized cult, a negative logic was set in motion.

At the cost of these purges, one could keep more or less anything, including the mass, for which Sobry wrote a strange apologia. [16] He had always loved the mass, he said, and never missed one under the ancien régime. And yet, in Year II, he applauded its suppression as the boldest act of the Revolution. There was no contradiction between these two attitudes. The hated mass was the mass overladen with baroque additions, weighed down by hateful dogmas, disfigured by a doctrine of tyrannies, persecutions, torture, and blood. Very little would be needed for the mass of which he dreamed to reappear in its true guise: it would be spoken in French; the priest would be allowed to say only certain words, laid down in advance; and, above all, he would say nothing about "those insignificant persons, who, under the name of saints, offer us only bad examples to follow." It is clear that the passion to purge was in no sense iconoclastic, but was an attempt to ensure the return of a primitive model. Furthermore, in their first, hesitant steps, the theophilanthropists very nearly called themselves "primitive Christians."

Indeed, this whole movement of simplification finds its culmination in theophilanthropy. [17] The hatred of the image, so often balanced in the festivals by sensualistic conformism, was here allowed full scope: no costumes (the priest would be an ordinary family man, correctly and simply dressed; the preacher of morality would renounce his robes); no exhibitionism (the examination of conscience would be silent); and a great cleansing (the temple would be swept clean not only of the tabernacle but even of the busts of the martyrs of liberty, the benefactors of mankind). This was to give rise to a great many conflicts when theophilanthropists and Catholics had to share their churches. According to its sectaries, the theophilan-thropic temple was that austere place where one saw "neither emblems nor allegories, neither statuettes of saints nor pictures of miracles, still less *ex votos,* or offerings for the people." That was how Amaury Duval saw it.[18] The frantic desire to purge was such that it even affected the book itself, whose presence on the altar seemed to be tolerated only as a temporary measure. Once the elders who presided over the worship were assured that the basic tenets were well established in everybody's mind, they ought, according to Siauve in his *Echo des cercles patriotiques,*[19] to burn solemnly the handwritten copy of the catechism, for "no book is needed for moral belief."

Since the outbreak of the Revolution, there had been plenty of people who rejected an enterprise that involved both purgation and imitation. Salaville, for example, protested against the civil cult advocated by the section of the Réunion, with its presentation of sixteen-year-old youths, which "resembles in every feature what was practiced in the churches."[20] This criticism was echoed by the counterrevolutionaries, keen to de-nounce, beyond the voluntary impoverishment of the purgings, the invol-untary poverty of imitation. But Edgar Quinet, too, was appalled at the sterility of the Revolutionary imagination, which, in his eyes, was a di-saster. Auguste Comte thought much the same. The liturgy that, in their fear of the void, the men of the Revolution were trying desperately to establish was, therefore, even for those who suspected its religious color-ing, a failed liturgy. Very few regarded it as a transfer of sacrality.

The Meaning of a Few Borrowings

We must return, then, to those borrowings for which the organizers of the Revolutionary festival were so criticized and, above all, to that obses-sive yet mysterious recourse to antiquity. While the quarrel between the ancients and the moderns had seemed to have been settled long since in favor of the moderns and emancipation, and at the very same moment when the Revolution was bringing modernity to birth, how is one to explain the imitative return to ancient models? Indeed, this choice raises several questions: first, yet again, that of the reality of Revolutionary innovation, and second, that of the extent to which the people understood this erudite revival. On March 24, 1792, *Les révolutions de Paris* declared quite calmly that the people were being "told" that the woolen cap had been the emblem in Greece and Rome of emancipation from all servitude

and that, "from that moment, each citizen wanted to have such a cap."
But the intellectualist optimism of the statement cannot make us forget
how opaque the Revolutionary symbolism was in the eyes of even not-so-
simple citizens. Lastly, and above all, we must ask why the men of the
Revolutionary festivals chose antiquity as their source of reference.

Let us now examine this last question, to which many answers have
been given. According to Mathiez and Georges Lefebvre,[21] the enlightened bourgeois—those who were everywhere responsible for organizing
the Revolutionary ceremonial—were imbued with a classical culture that
was their lingua franca. Quite naturally, therefore, they borrowed the
objects, emblems, and devices from their memories of the classroom. Not
surprisingly, then, recourse to antiquity was the result of a thorough aesthetic and literary education, and, as Lefebvre puts it, of "the impregnation of a décor." This thesis, which assumes the cultural docility of indo-
cile men, has good arguments in its favor. We now know a great deal
more about what those men read in their schools;[22] and what they read
was exactly the same as was read by the handful of opponents of antiquity
(Volney, Condorcet) and by the overwhelming majority of its admirers.
We know how potent such an impregnation can be. Yet was it irresistible,
as Louis Hautecoeur suggests? For him, men living in that setting had
necessarily to believe that they were the successors of the ancients. Necessarily? In architecture, painting, and furnishing, antique decoration had
been current since the middle of the century, and it is difficult to understand how a Revolutionary generation could see forms that had become a
repertoire of fashion and all too widespread as representing a break. Indeed, a certain lassitude could be detected before the flood of Reguluses,
Catos, and Belisariuses at the Salon.[23]

This was no less so in the literary sphere: the image of Camille Desmoulins and Madame Roland in tears at a reading of Plutarch is often
regarded as a new one; but that is to forget that in 1740, Vauvenargues
had confided in a letter to the Marquis de Mirabeau: "I wept for joy on
reading those Lives; I did not spend a night without speaking to Alci-
biades, Agesilas, and others."[24] One also forgets that the comparison with
the Roman Republic seemed such a rhetorical device that it aroused Ar-
genson's sarcasm as early as 1764. In short, the Revolution did not invent
the Romans, and its taste for them cannot be explained by some educational peculiarity. Yet one more thing, of course, should not be forgotten.
There is something very convincing in Parker's thesis that a veneration for
the ancients was for all those people—for Brissot as well as for Madame

Roland—an episode of juvenile intransigence, followed by accommodations with present reality. Once the coming of the Revolution had suddenly swept such accommodations away, it is understandable that they should have returned to the beloved antique models of their youth. Antiquity was also the youth of history.

Another very traditional but more profound interpretation suggests that antiquity provided these men above all with models of greatness. Filling one's dreams with great examples would help one to live and sometimes—as in the case of Romme's suicide—to die. We know that Plutarch was the most frequently read author and that it was through him alone that the men of the Revolution knew Greek antiquity. This is as if to say that they were concerned not so much with knowing it as equaling it, as if, in the transparent perspective of the Enlightenment, cleansed of all "superstitions," one felt the need to cling to a few great figures. Legendary antiquity helped the men of the Revolution, therefore, to rise to the level of the events through which they were living. Yet one thing remains perplexing: why the Romans and Greeks but no other models? This world, "empty since the Romans," had not always been so. Not so long before, historians had peopled it with other exemplary figures. To take only one of those whom the revolutionaries read most assiduously— the "illustrious Mably," as they themselves said—they could find in him the model of the Franks, sovereignly free in the forests of Germany, or that of the ancient deliberating assemblies, open to all the talents, that once met in the "May fields." Why, then, when the hour of the Revolution sounded, were all traditions, even the most prestigious ones, swept aside, leaving only those of antiquity? And why that self-assurance, of which we get some idea when we listen to Babeuf, in the Committee of General Safety, glorying in having taken the name of Gracchus in preference to that of any Christian hero: "What ill can result from the fact that I took as my godfather a great man rather than a small one?"

The study of the festival can certainly throw some light on the riddle of the overwhelming choice in favor of antiquity. As we know, the festival reconstructed antique decor (usually some ideal type reduced to the simplicity of the idyll), paraded the busts of the heroes of antiquity, and heard interminable speeches in which one can glimpse what the history of Greece and Rome meant to the speakers. According to them, ancient history—and in this it is quite unlike Mably's version of the history of France—is a history of origins. Mably's history, by contrast, is a history of transition, of a period that has fallen from grace, in which one constantly notes the signs in societies of that decadence that was the century's obsession. It might be objected that Greek history and, above all, since Montesquieu, Roman history ought necessarily to initiate its readers into the theme of decline. But here we come to the type of history being taught in schools. The ancient authors then being taught, as Parker sees very clearly, described their present against the background of a republic of their dreams, and used a double palette, a dark one for their present and a bright one for their past. This has the result, which is of crucial importance for us here, of dehistoricizing early ancient history, utopian-izing it as a simple, frugal, equitable life. The antique was scarcely his-torical, and we can understand why the century that, as Koyré has shown, invested so little in the past invested so much in antiquity. Antiquity seemed to the men of the Revolution to be a quite new, innocent society, in which words were a perfect match for deeds; when they did have to confront the theme of the decline of ancient society, they defused it by moralizing it, attributing the decadence of history to a taste for wealth and the loss of virtue; and they tried to see that decline occurring as late as possible.

A very fine text by Billaud-Varenne tells us much about the ancient history so dear to the festival orators:

> In the times of the Ancients, in those times that may be called the true golden age, when every nation decided its own rights and duties, times when oppression and oblivion affected only a class of exotic slaves, then the people, gathered together in what was often a very tight circle and sharing more or less equally the advantages of a collective administration, seemed to be at the same level as far as genius, tastes, manners, and idiom were concerned. The two passions that predominated in the civil order, namely, love of glory and lust for gold, must alone have introduced a jarring note into that political government, though that contrary movement became evident only after many centuries.[25]

It is all there: nostalgic evocation (the golden age); the model to be imi-tated (equality mythically obtained at the cost of the exclusion, scarcely felt as such, of a few "exotic" slaves, as easily forgotten as those excluded from the Revolutionary festivals); the explanation of social decline by the psychology of passions and the extreme slowness of decadence to make itself felt, which makes it possible to conceive of the ancient world as stable. Billaud-Varenne shows us what the men of the Revolution wanted from antiquity: the image of an ideal Republic, purged of despotism, in which the most obscure citizens enjoyed personal liberty and were protected from arbitrary rule. It does not seem to have been very important whether the model was more Spartan or more Athenian, whether a Spartan Mountain was to be contrasted with an Athenian Gironde,[26] whether the dramaturgy of the oath was copied precisely from the antique ceremonial or whether it was young Anacharsis who provided its distorted image. There is not a great deal of scholarly application here. What matters is being able to conceive of a society in which the instituted is still not too far removed from the instituter. Indeed, it is in this sense that the festival is itself, for the men of the Revolution, their great borrowing from antiquity, for the festival is instituting. When Saint-Just tried to copy Sparta in his *Fragments sur les institutions républicaines,* he borrowed two things: the school and the festival, that is to say, the two teachers of the nation.

This also helps us to understand why those men tried to bypass their own history. The obsession with decadence drove them to eliminate the mediocrity of those intermediary stages that could not, in any case, be founding moments. Their minds were still in the grip of the omnipotent idea of beginning, and for them the initial was also the founding moment. Even Condorcet, who was more susceptible than anyone else to the cumulative effect of human knowledge, transmitted from generation to generation, considered that the American Revolution, which escaped the radicalism of the French Revolution, had not been a true revolution. The good fortune of the French Revolution was that it broke with all tradition. The ancient festival was seen, therefore, not as a tradition to be rediscovered and copied but as an eternal model of communal togetherness, simplicity, and joy. Even in Pluviôse, Year IV, a sinister time, and in a reactionary newspaper, *L'historien,* a certain Vérus continued to justify the festivals conceived by the law of Brumaire: "Here is something that conforms to the simplicity and majesty of antiquity; reading the law to which we owe such festivals, one might think that it had been drawn up by Zaleucus or Solon."

Festival, law, origin: what we have here is an association suggestive of a sacralization. The great figure invoked by the festival organizers was, as Pierre Vidal-Naquet saw very clearly,[27] that of the legislator, the possessor of the power to institute, capable of bringing about a mutation of the savage world into the civilized world. Solon or Lycurgus: it hardly mattered which for such men, seeking in antiquity a model that had the reputation then of being the highest achievement of mankind. "Legislation," says Billaud-Varenne, "is the most difficult art, so much so that from the beginning of time the greatest geniuses have almost wasted their time looking for it." A whole generation, which seemed to sense that the career that was open to all the talents in a period of revolution was that of the lawyer, played not at "if I were king" but at "if I were legislator"—so sighed Manon Philipon (not yet Madame Roland) at the age of twenty-four. The need for sacrality was concentrated entirely on the figure of the lawmaker. Jesus was not only a man, he was a legislator, declared Léonard Bourdon in rather poor verse. The humanization of Jesus was compensated here by the sacralization of the man who began or began again, placed his energies at the service of social happiness, and seemed by the same token endowed with supernatural powers. One is no longer surprised by the arrogance of certain orators, such as Camus, declaring at the session of January 1, 1790, "Assuredly we have the power to change religion."

So we may risk this conclusion: recourse to antiquity in the Revolutionary festivals expressed not only the nostalgia of the aesthete or even the moral need to replace the great examples that had disappeared with the old order. It expressed also, and above all, in a world in which Christian values were declining, the need for the sacred. A society instituting itself must sacralize the very deed of institution. If one wishes to found a new order, one cannot be sparing of the means to do so; beginning a new life cannot be imagined without faith. This is the key to the paradoxical victory that the Revolution accorded the ancients over the moderns. To opt for the moderns was obviously to opt for the instructive accumulation of experience, for the beneficent continuity of the generations. To opt for the ancients was to say that in going back to origins, no purpose is served in pausing at the intermediary stages. Thus each generation conquers its autonomy and its capacity to break with the past. Antiquity itself is not at all a moment in human history like other moments. It has an absolute privilege, for it is conceived as absolute beginning. It is a figure of rupture, not of continuity; and the fervor that it arouses is not diminished but enhanced by this.

The myth of origin is also the instrument of a teleology: to make conceivable and credible the transition to the New Jerusalem presupposes a memory of the past Eden. Indeed it is by no means certain that the memory can coexist in men's minds with the belief in human perfectibility. Madame de Staël states this better than anyone else:

It is as if we felt at one and the same time regret for the few fine gifts that we were gratuitously granted and hope for the few benefits that we may acquire by our own efforts: just as the doctrine of perfectibility and that of the golden age, combined and merged together, arouse in man both pain at losing and ambition to recover. The feelings are melancholy and the mind is audacious. One looks back and the other forward. Out of this daydream and this enthusiasm is born man's true superiority, the mixture of contemplation and activity, of resignation and will, which allows him to hitch his life in the world to the heavens.[28]

To hitch one's life in the world to the heavens: that undertaking, which is also that of the Revolutionary festival, helps us to understand the meaning of a borrowing: it is not so much an imitation as a beneficent invocation.

Can the same be said of the other elements borrowed by the Revolutionary festival? The presence in the festivals of Masonic symbols has been seen as the very signature of the "Masonic plot," almost as if caught in the act—and, by the same token, one ignored, or concealed, by those historians favorable to the Revolution. The listing of Masonic emblems in the medals and banners (the level, of course, but also the compasses, the square, the columns of the sun and moon, the eye of Reason piercing the clouds of Error, the joined hands, the triangular altar), or Masonic rituals in the ceremonies (the steel vault over the newborn infants, the goblet from which one drinks, the procession in which one carries the symbolic tools), the Masonic vocabulary in the speeches ("temples of virtues," "hiding places dug for vice") was first made by hostile commentators.[29] As soon as things were looked at rather differently, in the sense not of a political plot but of a long cultural impregnation, the enormous influence of Freemasonry on the French Revolution, the noting of detail passed into other hands. Thanks to Roger Cotte,[30] we now know more about the profound influence of Masonic musical ritual on the Revolutionary festival. And thanks to Jacques Brengues,[31] we are discovering, beyond even the borrowings from Masonic symbolism, the profound kinship between the Masonic ritual and the Revolutionary festival: in both Masonry and in the Revolution, every assembly is ipso facto a festival.

But it may be said of Freemasonry what was said of antiquity: the borrowing that is attributed to it testifies not only to a cultural inertia. No doubt, just as the revolutionaries had been initiated in school into the culture of antiquity, so, accustomed to meeting in the studios, those other classrooms of the provincial elite, they could easily pile Masonic references on classical reminiscences. The interpretation is, in both cases, a lazy one. What strikes one in the Masonic borrowings of the Revolutionary festival, far more than this or that emblem, is the reasonable religion of the lodges, the evident dialectic from the Temple-Building to the Temple-Universe, the sacralization of a life deserted by the sacred around the artisan figure of man the creator. When Daubermesnil was looking for a place that would be suitable for certain ceremonies that he wanted to establish, he imagined an "asylum,"[32] that is, a sacred place, crowned with an observatory stuffed with instruments and books, where scholars would come and study the course of the stars. With the signs of the zodiac on the walls and, inside, frescoes depicting the seasons, the temple is, significantly, both the place of astronomy and the place of the civic cult, a living illustration of the link established by the famous, and then quite recent, book by Dupuis on the origin of cults.[33] Indeed, it is here that the sacrality of a revolution, which is both a scientific and an astral figure, is most surely expressed.

The Meaning of Purging

Let us now abandon, then, these borrowings, whose eclecticism will be endlessly studied, and examine the essential operation of purging practiced by the organizers of the Revolutionary festivals on their harvest of practices. This operation is generally regarded as an attempt to extirpate the sacred. This seems to me to be a somewhat hasty judgment. In the revolutionaries' treatment of their discoveries, one is struck by the obstinate search for an elementary anthropology. The historical and ethnological justifications offered by so many writings on the festival bring together Chuvash, Tartar, and even Cherkess festivals with Greek and Roman ceremonies, as if, out of such a comparison of the ceremonies of these child-peoples, the fundamental would emerge. These proliferating practices give us a glimpse of the origin of all cults and the hope, too, of inferring the original cult. What the men of the Revolution were seeking was certainly the essential identity of religion as an expression of human identity. In Year IV, Rallier wrote to Grégoire: "In meditating on these objects, I remembered hearing a wise man say, long ago, that one could make up an excellent religion out of what the others have in common. Would it not be advantageous to collect the maxims common to all the religions accepted in France or likely to be and to compose out of them a formula for invoking the Supreme Being?"[34] Once the tragic, mournful, dark apparatus of religion had been eliminated, everyone seemed to believe that one would find that basis of worship in which the religious foundation gave place to the sociomoral foundation, but on which a new sacrality would have to be constructed for a newly homogeneous mankind.

It was a passion for unity and unanimity that governed this act of purging, therefore. Because it failed in this, the much-vaunted Festival of the Federation won its first detractors,[35] for whom "its oramuses, its barbarous chants in foreign idiom" seemed to condemn the non-Roman fraction of the nation to the condition of schism. A purified religion, however, freed of dogma, should be capable of sealing the unity of the human community in a sense of the sacrality of the human being. "The only true religion," wrote Cabanis, "is that which ennobles man, by giving him a sublime idea of the dignity of his being and of the great destinies to which he is called by the human orderer."[36] The festival organizers set out, therefore, to reconstruct unity. This aim was sometimes naively pursued in the detail of the rituals, as in La Révellière's essay,[37] which proposes, according to methods inspired by Frederick II, a system of signals capable of repeating sacred words to an entire amphitheater at once. And this aim was always affirmed in the overall arrangements of the ceremony; for although the festival might have had its excluded elements, they had previously been excluded from the ranks of mankind. The Revolutionary festival worked for the homogenization of mankind. This explains the meaning of its renunciations: it was not a demolition enterprise but the search for a sacralizing foundation, of the mother religion, just as others at the same time were seeking the mother language and the humanity in all men.

This laying down of human identity, which testifies to the universal, leaves man alone, of course; that is the price to be paid for this discovery. The task of the festival is then seen to be that of redeeming the platitude of that psychosociology of the homogeneous, of saving the isolated individual from himself, and of reconstructing a new sacrality on the elementary elements thus revealed. This would take place, as we have seen throughout these pages, in the triple choice of the biological, the social, and the civic. The biological because it provides the strongest image of the reciprocity of human relations in an ideal community: this explains the importance given by the Revolutionary festivals to the ceremonial of the ages, the place they gave to the rituals of exchange and giving, the eminent role they accorded to the father and mother; it was a biological that had already been socialized into the domestic, and would soon be sacralized into a religion. We then come to the social link in its almost pure state, as revealed, throughout the Revolutionary festival, by the unusable scenography of the oath. Once again, one senses that this is not purely and simply a plagiarism from antiquity. The sacrality of the oath, for the men of the Revolution, derived from the fact that it made visible the act of contracting, which was conceived as the fundamental feature of sociability. Combined with those invocations that linked it to a necessary transcendence and those curses intended to show the extent to which the contractual commitments presupposed individual abdication, the oath of the Revolutionary festival was the sacred theater of the social contract.

Lastly, we come to the civic, the fatherland. This was the long-lost sacral reality. In 1754, the Abbé Coyer complained that this "old word of fatherland" had been purged from the language under the ministry of Cardinal Richelieu.[38] "Children have never learned it," he said sadly, and he went on to define it very confidently in terms of power: a superior power, based on nature, a divinity that accepts offerings only to redistribute them. It was a forgotten power, then, that was rediscovered by the Revolution and was henceforth recognized, proclaimed, sworn by. It was all the more unchallengeable in that it was eternal, more able than any other to oppose its resistance to the decline inherent in history. The fatherland may have been physically absent from the Revolutionary festival, in which, as we have seen, the tutelary female figures were Liberty, Victory, Reason, or the Republic, but never France, never the fatherland. Never shown, the invisible fatherland was nonetheless the focal point of the whole festival: the altar was the altar of the fatherland; the defenders were the defenders of the fatherland; the battalion of children was the hope of the fatherland; the duty of every citizen, as every speech hammered home, was to be worthy of the fatherland; and the injunction on all the banners was to live and die for the fatherland. Between this invisibility and the heroics of the festival there was an obvious link; and it is not irrelevant to this subject to note that the festivals in which the victories of the fatherland were celebrated maintained to the end of the Revolutionary decade a very special enthusiasm. The fatherland, the commonwealth, was the true expression of collective unity.

It was not difficult to find servants for these new values, domestic, social, and civic, sacralized by the festival: family men, schoolteachers, legislators, a whole benevolent team of "ministers of nature." The priests of the new cult were so solely by virtue of the fact that they possessed the power to engender: the family man, at once progenitor and teacher; the schoolteacher, a father of the collective family; the legislator, the father of the fatherland. This conjunction of terms shows the extent to which Revolutionary sacrality was a sacrality of birth. It also explains what precisely was the function of the festival for the men of the Revolution, whatever political tendency they belonged to: it was to demonstrate to man the transcendence of mankind and to establish mankind in his humanity.

So the Revolutionary festival referred to a world of perfect intelligibility, order, and stability. In this it was faithful to its utopian aim of redeeming society from the obsession with decline that had haunted the entire century. There were few thinkers who, like Condorcet, considered with lucid pessimism that the ancient legislators, who had aspired "to render the constitutions that they presented eternal, in the name of the gods, to the enthusiasm of the people," had, by that very fact, placed "a seed of profound destruction" in those perpetual constitutions. His was an isolated voice, so strong did the connection between origin, law, and the sacred then seem. The Revolutionary festival, which saw itself as establishing an eternal society, was an immense effort to conjure away decadence, that sickness of society, to regularize the time of the Revolution, and to conceal its false starts and sudden changes.

After this, one would hesitate to call the festivals of the French Revolution "revolutionary," since such a charge of emotion and subversion has been invested in the adjective of social turbulence. One may agree that these festivals were "revolutionized": their break with the ancient rituals and their contempt for the traditional, popular religious festival are sufficient evidence of this. Whether they were "revolutionizing" is another matter: their organizers did not expect them to be. Once the immense event had taken place (which they obstinately conceived in terms of order, not of disorder), they saw the festival as doing no more than strengthening the Revolution, expected of it no subversion, and attributed it to no more than a power of conservation. On 8 Thermidor, Year VII, Grenier expressed this purpose in a striking formula: "We had to be revolutionaries in order to found the Revolution; but, in order to preserve it, we must cease to be."[39]

Must we, then, at the end of this book on the "revolutionary festival," abandon the magic of the adjective and be content simply to speak of the festivals of the French Revolution? One would be tempted to adopt this solution, which would avoid any suggestion of contempt, were it not that the men of the Revolution, already struck by the abuse of the adjective, had themselves taken the trouble to say exactly what they meant by "revolutionary": "A revolutionary man is inflexible, but sensible; he is frugal; he is simple, but does not display the luxury of false modesty; he is the irreconcilable enemy of all lies, all affectation. A revolutionary man is honorable, he is sober, but not mawkish, out of frankness and because he is at peace with himself; he believes that grossness is a mark of deception and remorse, and that it disguises falseness under exuberance." The virtues listed by Saint-Just[40] in defining the private man may also, when magnified, define the public festival. That was certainly how the festival was seen and was intended to be. So why not dare to call it revolutionary?

Furthermore, if it was revolutionary in the eyes of the men of the Revolution, it was because it seemed better equipped than anything else to reconcile the rational and the sense perceptible, time and eternity, the savage and the civilized. The festival announced the advent of that unified man of whom Diderot declared that he had traveled through the history of the centuries and nations and failed to find. He had seen men "alternately subjected to three codes: the code of nature, the civil code, and the religious code and forced to transgress alternately each of those three codes, which were never in agreement; hence it is that there has never been in any land either man, citizen, or religion." What the festival tried to do was to demonstrate the compatibility of the codes, and its result seemed to be the emergence at last of the reconciled man.

Yet it will be said, it failed to create him. But Brumaire, which saw this astonishing system of festivals disappear, nevertheless did not see the disappearance of the new values that it had sacralized. Rights, liberty, and the fatherland, which the Revolutionary festival bound together at the dawn of the modern, secular, liberal world, were not to be separated so soon. The transfer of sacrality onto political and social values was now accomplished, thus defining a new legitimacy and a hitherto inviolate patrimony, in which the cult of mankind and the religion of the social bond, the bounty of industry, and the future of France would coexist. How can it be said that the Revolutionary festival failed in that? It was exactly what it wanted to be: the beginning of a new era.

Abbreviations
Notes
Bibliography
Index

Abbreviations

Arch. dép.   Archives départementales
Arch. nat.   Archives nationales, Paris
Bibl. nat.   Bibliothèque nationale, Paris
Imp. nat.   Imprimerie nationale, Paris

Notes

Source citations in this volume follow the form used in the original French edition.

Introduction

1. Faiguet de Villeneuve, *L'ami des pauvres, ou L'économe politique* (Paris: Moreau, 1766).

2. Montesquieu, *De l'esprit des lois* (Geneva: Barrillot et fils, 1748); *The Spirit of the Laws*, trans. Thomas Nugent (New York: Hafner, 1949); *The Spirit of Laws: A Compendium of the First English Edition*, ed. David Wallace Carrithers (Berkeley: University of California Press, 1977).

3. Abbé de Saint-Pierre, *Ouvrages politiques* (Rotterdam, 1734): "If, when the first canons on the cessation of labor were formed, the bishops who formed them had seen wine shops and gaming houses established, if they had foreseen all the disorders that idleness and the cessation of daily occupations were to cause, they would have limited themselves to hearing mass and to attending morning instruction."

4. Marquis de Villette, *Lettres choisies sur les principaux événements de la Révolution* (Paris: Clousier, 1792).

5. On this point see J. Y. Ribault, "Divertissement populaire et turbulence sociale: les fêtes baladoires dans la région de Thaumiers au XVIIIᵉ siècle," *Cahiers archéologiques et historiques du Berry* (1967).

6. G. B. Mably, *Lettre à Madame la Marquise de P . . . sur l'Opéra* (Paris: Didot, 1761).

7. Voltaire, *Dictionnaire philosophique* (Paris: Garnier, 1954): "Here is how the feast of Christmas was celebrated in some cities. First a half-naked young man with wings on his back appeared; he recited the *Ave Maria* to a young girl who responded, 'Fiat,' and the angel kissed her on the mouth; then a child

enclosed in a large cardboard cock cried, in imitation of the cock's crow, 'Puer natus est nobis.'"

8. See Madame Roland, *Mémoires:* "When I was witness to this sort of spectacle, which the capital often presented at the entrances of the queen or the princes or in ceremonies of thanksgiving after a childbirth, I was pained when I compared this Asiatic luxury, this insolent pomp, with the misery and abjection of the foolish people, who came running as these idols passed."

9. These are themes treated throughout the treatise *Des fêtes en politique et en morale* of J.-M. Coupé, a native of the Oise (Paris: Baudouin, n.d.): "Be careful not to recall in your humble churches that opulence of the temples and all the trappings that have dishonored them; preserve yourself from this luxury of ornamentation and gilding."

10. Diderot, *Paradoxe sur le comédien, précédé des entretiens sur le fils naturel* (Paris: Garnier-Flammarion, 1967); Lee Strasberg, *The Paradox of Acting by Denis Diderot, and Masks or Faces? by William Archer* (New York: Hill and Wang, 1957).

11. L.-S. Mercier, *Du théâtre* (Amsterdam: E. Van Harrevelt, 1773).

12. Madame Campan, *Mémoires sur la vie privée de Marie-Antoinette* (Paris: Baudouin, 1822).

13. Marquis de Mirabeau, *L'ami des hommes* (Avignon, 1756–1760).

14. J.-J. Rousseau, *Essai sur l'origine des langues* (Geneva, 1781); *On the Origin of Language,* ed. and trans. John H. Moran and Alexander Gode (New York: Ungar, 1967).

15. The posthumous publication of N. A. Boulanger's famous book, *Antiquity Unveiled,* dates from 1766. Boulanger, *L'antiquité dévoilée par ses usages, ou Examen critique des principales opinions, cérémonies et institutions religieuses des différents peuples de la terre* (Amsterdam: M. M. Rey, 1766).

16. P. H. Mallet, *Introduction à l'histoire du Danemarc* (Geneva, 1763).

17. Mirabeau, *Travail sur l'éducation publique, trouvé dans les papiers de Mirabeau l'aîné, publiés par Cabanis* (Paris: Imp. nat., 1791).

18. May trees were used in America after 1765 to support anti-English protest and as a place to post slogans and caricatures. They had already become known as Liberty Trees, as shown in a poem by Tom Paine published in 1775 and widely distributed:

> The fame of its fruit drew
> > The nations around
> To seek out this peaceable shore
> Unmindful of names and distinctions
> > They came,
> For freemen like brothers agree
> > With one spirit endued

They one friendship pursued
And their temple was Liberty tree.

19. *Correspondance complète de J.-J. Rousseau,* vol. 9 (Geneva: Institut et Musée Voltaire, 1969).

20. N. M. Karamzine, "Voyage en France, 1789–1790," *Revue de la Révolution* (1884).

21. E. Lockroy, *Journal d'une bourgeoise pendant la Révolution* (Paris: C.-Lévy, 1881).

22. La Révellière-Lépeaux, *Mémoires* (Paris: J. Hetzel, 1873).

23. L. A. Beffroy de Reigny, *La constitution de la lune* (Paris: Froussé, 1793).

24. Bernardin de Saint-Pierre, *Etudes de la nature* (Paris: P. F. Didot le jeune, 1784).

25. J.-J. Rousseau, *Lettres sur le gouvernement de la Corse,* in *Oeuvres,* vol. 3 (Paris: A. Belin, 1817).

26. This interest first appeared in American historiography in a fascination for political and propagandist reports. See, for example, Stanley J. Idzerda, "Iconoclasm during the French Revolution," *American Historical Review* 60 (1954); David L. Dowd, "Jacobinism and the Fine Arts," *Public Opinion Quarterly* (Autumn 1951); David L. Dowd, "Art as a National Propaganda in the French Revolution," *Public Opinion Quarterly* (Autumn 1951); David L. Dowd, "Jacobinism and the Fine Arts," *Art Quarterly* 16,. no. 3 (1953); David L. Dowd, *Pageant-Master of the Republic: Jacques-Louis David and the French Revolution* (Lincoln: University of Nebraska Press, 1948); James A. Leith, *The Idea of Art as Propaganda in France, 1750–1790* (Toronto: University of Toronto Press, 1965); Jack Lindsay, "Art and Revolution," *Art and Artists* (August 1969).

In France, a conference on the Revolutionary festival was organized at the University of Clermont, June 24–27, 1974, by the Centre de Recherches Révolutionnaires et Romantiques (hereafter referred to as the Clermont Conference). The introductory reports and the summaries of this conference have been published in a special number of the *Annales historiques de la Révolution française* 47, no. 221 (July–September 1975). See also Y.-M Bercé, *Fête et révolte* (Paris: Hachette, 1976), and Michel Vovelle, *Les métamorphoses de la fête en Provence de 1750 à 1820* (Paris: Aubier-Flammarion, 1976).

27. See Harvey Cox, *The Feast of Fools: A Theological Essay on Festivity and Fantasy* (Cambridge, Mass.: Harvard University Press, 1969); and Jürgen Moltmann, *Die ersten Freigelassenen der Schöpfung-Versuche an der Freiheit und das Wohlgefallen am Spiel* (Munich: Kaiser Verlag, 1971).

28. The events of May 1968 inspired a good deal of lyrical comment. See, for example, Jean-Marie Domenach, "Idéologie du mouvement," *Esprit* 8–9 (1968); B. Charbonneau, "L'émeute et le plan," *La table ronde* 251 (1968) and

252 (1969); René Pascal, "La fête de mai," *France-Forum* (October-November 1968).

29. A. M. Lemierre, *Les fastes, ou Les usages de l'année* (Paris: P. F. Gueffier, 1779).

30. Jault [a member of the Commune of Paris], *Discours sur l'instruction publique* (Paris: Société typographique des Trois-Amis, n.d.).

I. The History of the Revolutionary Festival

1. Daniel Halévy, *Histoire d'une histoire* (Paris: Grasset, 1939).

2. Lamartine, *Histoire des Girondins* (Paris: Furne W. Coquebert, 1847).

3. J. Michelet, *Le banquet* (Paris: Calmann-Lévy, 1879). On this theme see also *Nos fils* (Paris: A. Lacroix, Verboekhoven, 1870): "We have no festivals that relax and gladden the heart. Just cold salons and frightful balls! They are the very opposite of festivals. Next day, one feels even more desiccated, even more tense."

4. J. Michelet, *Histoire de la Révolution française* (Paris: Chamerot, 1847–1855). Unless otherwise stated, the quotations from Michelet in this chapter are from this source.

5. C. Péguy, *Clio* (Paris: Gallimard, 1932): "Nobody was ordered to storm the Bastille. Nobody was required, nobody was supposed to storm the Bastille. Anyway, I was there, says History. We all know perfectly well how the storming of the Bastille happened. It was on July 14, of course. It was a fine, warm day. Old Paris was getting hotter under the blazing sun. The good people did not know what to do, but they knew that they wanted to do something."

6. Halévy, *Histoire*.

7. That is also why June 20 was a festival: the people had no intention of forcing their way into the chateau. "What did they really want to do? Go somewhere. They wanted to march together, to shout together, forget for once in a while their hardship, have a great civic promenade on that fine summer's day. For them the mere fact of being allowed into the Assembly was itself a festival." Michelet, *Histoire*.

8. Ibid.: "People went before them from the towns and villages, men shook their hands, women blessed them, everywhere they were asked forgiveness in the name of France.

"This national deed is sacred. It must remain free of the violent polemics that this subject has given rise to, of the eloquent fury of the Feuillants, of the Philippics of André Chénier, Roucher, and Dupont [de Nemours], and also from Collot's declamations for the soldiers of Châteauvieux, from the keenness of Tallien and other intriguers to seize upon the event, and to turn the people's good hearts to the benefit of party spirit."

9. Michelet recounts the victory at Jemmapes as a series of marvels: "O

youth! O hope! The infinite strength of conscience and of the sense of right! Who could resist them? . . . How much God was in France! What miraculous virtue she then had! The sword with which she struck, instead of wounding, cured the nations. Touched with steel, they awoke, gave thanks for the salutory blow that had interrupted their fatal sleep, broken the deplorable spell in which, for over a thousand years, they have languished like beasts grazing in the fields."

10. Indeed, we learn the unconscious aim that drove the *fédérés* on their march. They were marching not so much to this or that town, and not so much to Paris even as toward that "Jerusalem of hearts, a holy, fraternal unity . . . , the great living city that was built of men in under a year." Michelet, *Nos fils.*

11. With similar insistence, an identical faith in the pedagogical virtues of the festival, and meeting, too, the same difficulty in combining in the festival *dirigisme* and spontaneity.

12. On this theme, see Michelet, *Le banquet* and *Nos fils.*

13. Edmund Burke, *Reflections on the French Revolution* (London, 1790).

14. Thus, for Michelet, September 2 was a terrible "festival of the dead." And he mentions Barbaroux's words "a fearful festival" on the insurrection of August 10, 1793.

15. This is what happened in the case of August 10, 1793.

16. Péguy, *Clio:* "The taking of the Bastille, says History, was the first celebration, the first commemoration, and already so to speak the first anniversary of the storming of the Bastille; or at least the zero anniversary. We were wrong, says History; we were looking only in one direction and we should have looked in the other. We saw. It was not the Festival of the Federation that was the first commemoration, the first anniversary of the storming of the Bastille. It was the storming of the Bastille that was the first Festival of the Federation, a Federation *avant la lettre.*"

17. F. A. Aulard, *Le culte de la Raison et le culte de l'Etre Suprême, 1793–1794* (Paris: F. Alcan, 1892).

18. H. Taine, *Les origines de la France contemporaine,* vol. 2, *La Révolution* (Paris: Hachette, 1878–1881).

19. A. Duruy, *L'instruction publique et la Révolution* (Paris, 1886).

20. E. Cabet, *Histoire populaire de la Révolution française* (Paris: Pagnerre, 1839–1840).

21. J. Jaurès, *Histoire socialiste de la Révolution française* (Paris: Librairie de l'Humanité, 1922–1924).

22. E. Quinet, *La Révolution* (Paris: A. Lacroix, Verboeckhoven, 1865).

23. A. Sorel, *L'Europe et la Révolution française* (Paris: Plon, Nourrit, 1885–1911).

24. Claude Mazauric, "La fête révolutionnaire comme manifestation de la politique jacobine à Rouen en 1793 (an III)," contribution to the Clermont Conference, June 1974.

25. M.-J. Chénier, *Rapport sur la fête des Victoires, 27 Vendémiaire, an III* (Paris: Imp. nat., Year III).

26. Auguste Comte, *Système de politique positive* (Paris: L. Mathias, 1851–1854).

27. Daniel Guérin, *La lutte de classes sous la Ire République, 1793–1797* (Paris: Gallimard, 1968).

28. A. Mathiez, *Les origines des cultes révolutionnaires, 1789–1792* (Paris: G. Bellais, 1904).

29. For Mathiez, then, it was the anonymous success of the Federation that inspired such individual projects as those of Mirabeau and Talleyrand; it was the great original reference that saved the festivals from the creation and intervention of politicians. It was because they had been dazzled spectators of the Revolutionary cult that had already been formed in the Federation that it occurred to them to turn it into a political tool.

30. Quinet, *La Révolution.*

31. Indeed, this boredom is conveyed by a great many texts from the Revolutionary period itself. On 19 Messidor, Year VI, Thiessé wrote: "But readings! Readings from newspapers! Even readings from the *journaux décadaires!* Have we the good fortune to possess a warrior, the honor of his country? We should not be reading his praises, but seeing his father embrace him in the midst of magistrates who are crowning him . . . We should not be painting words, but our eyes should be struck and our soul penetrated by things themselves. Everything must be in action." *Opinion de Thiessé sur le deuxième projet présenté par la Commission des Institutions républicaines* (Paris: Imp. nat., Year VI).

32. E. de Pressensé, *L'église et la Révolution française* (Paris: Fischbacher, 1889).

33. Joseph de Maistre, *Considérations sur la France* (London, 1797).

34. E. Renan, *Questions contemporaines* (Paris: Michel-Lévy Frères, 1868).

35. P. Lanfrey, *Essai sur la Révolution française* (Paris: F. Chamerot, 1858).

36. Guérin, *La lutte de classes.*

37. D. L. Dowd, *Pageant-Master of the Republic.* Dowd distinguishes among "three general types: funeral fêtes of Jacobin heroes, triumphal fêtes in celebration of republican accomplishments, and religious fêtes, of which the fête of the Supreme Being is the leading example."

II. The Festival of the Federation

1. *Lettres choisies du marquis de Villette.*

2. Louis Blanc, *Histoire de la Révolution française* (Paris: Langlois et Leclerq, 1847–1862).

3. *Relation de la fête du pacte fédératif, célébrée à Chercy le 14 juillet 1790* (n.p., n.d.).

4. Speech by the Abbé de Patry, dean of the chapter of Bordeaux, C 120, Arch. nat.

5. *Six lettres à S. L. Mercier, sur les six tomes de son "Nouveau Paris," par un Français* [Fortia de Piles] (Paris, Year IX).

6. *Mémoires de Madame la duchesse de Tourzel* (Paris: Plon, 1883).

7. H. Taine, *La Révolution*, vol. 1, *L'anarchie* (Paris: Hachette, 1878).

8. F. Furet and D. Richet, *La Révolution française* (Paris: Hachette, 1973).

9. On this point see Michel Vovelle, *La chute de la monarchie, 1789–1792*, vol. 1 of *Nouvelle histoire de la France contemporaine* (Paris, Le Seuil, 1972).

10. These documents are nonetheless valuable. They provide us with inexhaustible information on problems of precedence—between towns, between the district and the département, between various administrative bodies. They also swarm with endless questions: Should the national volunteers mount guard in every municipality or only in the principal towns of the canton? Is it or is it not in accordance with "the conduct that the military laws prescribe for the troops of the line" to brandish their hats on the end of bayonets? What will be the order of the deputations? It is laid down most meticulously, as are the words of the oath, so as to leave no room for improvisation. Demanded incessantly of the municipality by the district directories and often written up in response to some imperious order in stiff, solemn, straitlaced language, decked out with the self-important signatures of notables, lawyers, or tax farmers, the official accounts seldom provide any glimpse of those "citizens merging with one another" that the festival promised. They stress hierarchical distinctions, never forget to mention ranks and titles. The processions that they describe stress separation more often than unanimity. Even when they plan to mix the participants, they do so by carefully calibrating the mixture in advance, as at Vendôme, for the blessing of the flags of the local militia: "The battalions were mixed in such a way that there was a municipal officer in each, followed by a Croatian officer, a burgess, a gentleman, a student from the military school, an ecclesiastic, a member of the Croatian horse, a magistrate . . ."

11. Michelet, *Histoire de la Révolution française*.

12. Fédération de Saint-Cyr-d'Estrancourt, 14 juillet 1790, C 120, Arch. nat.

13. M. Lambert, *Les Fédérations en Franche-Comté et la fête de la Fédération, 14 juillet 1790* (Paris: Perrin, 1890).

14. G. Bussière, *Etudes historiques sur la Révolution en Périgord* (Paris: Lechevalier, 1903).

15. A. Sommier, *Histoire de la Fédération dans le Jura* (Paris: Dumoulin, 1846).

16. B 1688, Arch. dép. Dordogne.

17. Enquête par le procureur du roi sur l'affaire de Bar, D XXIX, Arch. nat.

18. To distinguish them from the festivals of the Federation themselves, which were July 14 festivals.

19. Dupont de Nemours, *De l'origine et des progrès d'une science nouvelle* (Paris: Desaint, 1768).

20. Mably, *Observations sur les lois et le gouvernement des Etats-Unis d'Amérique* (Amsterdam: J. F. Rocard, 1784).

21. A. Duchatellier, *Histoire de la Révolution dans les départements de l'ancienne Bretagne* (Paris: Desessart, 1836).

22. Fédération de Nègrepelisse. Cf. P. Archer, "La fête de la Fédération en 1790 dans la commune de Montauban," in *Actes du 79ᵉ congrès des Sociétés savantes* (1954).

23. Archives communales de Bourges, Registre des délibérations, 23 juin 1790.

24. The federative festival of Cravant and Vermenton was proposed as "a reconciliation between the inhabitants of the town of Cravant and the town of Vermenton, who, for two hundred years, have lived in a state of continual hostility with one another."

25. Extract from the records of the municipality of Meljac, C 120, Arch. nat.

26. *Révolutions de France et de Brabant*, no. 34.

27. *Discours de M. de La Tour du Pin, ministre et secrétaire d'Etat au département de la Guerre, à la séance du 4 juin 1790,* (Paris, n.d.).

28. D IV 49, Arch. nat.

29. Manuscrits français 11697, Bibl. nat.

30. *Avis aux Confédérés des LXXXIII départements sur les avantages et les dangers du séjour à Paris* (Paris, n.d.).

31. C 82, no. 817, Arch. nat.

32. Madame de Villeneuve-Arifat, *Souvenirs d'enfance et de jeunesse, 1780—1792,* (Paris: E. Paul, 1902).

33. A. Mousset, *Un témoin ignoré de la Révolution, le comte de Fernan Nuñez, ambassadeur d'Espagne à Paris, 1787—1791* (Paris: Champion, 1924).

34. G. Bapst, "Lettres d'un attaché saxon, 11 juillet 1790," in *Revue de la Révolution* 4 (1884).

35. See Brongniart's letter to Madame Vigée-Lebrun, quoted in J. S. de Sacy, *Brongniart* (Paris: Plon, 1940).

36. *Révolutions de Paris* no. 52.

37. T. Lindet to R. Lindet, 8 juillet 1790, in Robert-Thomas Lindet, *Correspondance* (Paris: Société d'Histoire de la Révolution française, 1899).

38. *Enterrement du despotisme, ou Funérailles des aristocrates, seconde fête nationale dédiée à nos patriotes bretons* (n.p., n.d.).

39. *Révolutions de France et de Brabant* no. 34.

40. Archives communales de Caen, pièces sur la Révolution, *liasse* 36.

41. *Discours adressé à M. Rame, ministre des protestants de Vauvert, après le serment civique et fraternel, en présence de la municipalité et du peuple et aux pieds de l'Autel de la Patrie, par J. B. Solliers, curé de Vauvert* (n.p., n.d.).

42. Quinet, *La Révolution*.

43. F. Uzureau, "Une relation inédite de la fête de la Fédération," *Annales de la Révolution* 15 (1923).

44. Marquis de Ferrières, *Mémoires* (Paris: Baudouin fils, 1821).

45. See *Description curieuse et intéressante des 60 drapeaux que l'amour patriotique a offert aux 60 districts de la ville et des faubourgs de Paris, avec l'explication des allégories, devises, emblèmes, et exergues dont ils sont ornés* (Paris: Sorin, 1790).

46. *Révolutions de France et de Brabant* no. 35.

47. Mirabeau à M. de La Marck, *Correspondance*, vol. 2 (Paris: Vve. Le Normant, 1851).

48. Comte d'Escherny, *Correspondance d'un habitant de Paris avec ses amis de Suisse et d'Angleterre sur les événements de 1789, 1790, et jusqu'au 4 avril 1791* (Paris: Desenne, 1791).

49. Hemsterhuis notes in his Dialogues that "the soul regards as most beautiful what it can conceive of in the shortest possible time." F. Hemsterhuis, *Oeuvres philosophiques* (Paris: H. J. Jansen, 1792).

50. Brissot de Warville, *Correspondance universelle sur ce qui intéresse le bonheur de l'homme et de la société* (Neufchâtel: Société typographique, 1783).

51. *Fédération du Mont-Geneviève près Nancy* (Nancy: Hoener, 1790).

52. C 120, Arch. nat.

53. *Bulletin du Comité des travaux historiques et scientifiques, Section des sciences économiques et sociales, 1892*.

54. C 119, Arch. nat.

55. J.-B. Lépine, *Histoire de Château-Porcien* (Vouziers: Duchêne-Dufrêne, 1859).

56. *Société hist. lett., sciences et arts de La Flèche* vol. 8.

57. A. Desmasures, *Histoire de la Révolution dans le département de l'Aisne* (Vervins: Flem, 1869).

58. F. Uzureau, "La fête de la Fédération à Beaufort-en-Vallée," *Andegaviana* 11 (1904).

59. "La fête de la Fédération à Cherbourg, 14 juillet 1790," *Revue de Cherbourg* (1906–1907).

60. H. Richebé, *Journal d'un bourgeois de Lille pendant la Révolution, 1787–1793* (Lille: Prévost, 1898).

61. L 224, Arch. dép. Drôme.

62. S. de Girardin, *Mémoires* (Paris: Moutardier, 1829).

63. B. Poyet, *Idées générales sur le projet de la fête du 14 juillet* (Paris: Vve. Delaguette, n.d.).

64. "La fête de la Fédération, 1790, lettre d'un délégué," *Revue rétrospective* 8 (1890).

65. G. Maugras, *Journal d'un étudiant pendant la Révolution, 1789–1793* (Paris, 1890).

66. *Journal de la cour et de la ville,* July 14, 1790.

67. *Arrivée de 4000 citoyens bretons pour la Conféderation, avec leurs armes, bagages, tentes, et provisions pour leur séjour* (Paris, n.d.).

68. Marquis de Ségur, *Mémoires* (Paris: Emery, 1827).

69. *Souvenirs du baron de Frénilly* (Paris: Plon-Nourrit, 1909).

70. Blanc, *Histoire.*

71. F. Uzureau, "Les fêtes de la Fédération à Angers," *Andegaviana* 3 (1905).

72. La Tocnaye, *Les causes de la Révolution en France* (Edinburgh: Manners and Miller, 1797).

73. W. Wordsworth, *The Prelude, or Growth of a Poet's Mind* (London: Oxford University Press, 1928):

> We chanced
>
> To land at Calais on the eve
> Of that great federal day; and there we saw
> In a mean city, and among a few,
> How bright a face is worn when joy of one
> Is joy of ten millions. Southward thence
> We held our way, direct through hamlets, towns
> Gaudy with reliques of that festival,
> Flowers left to wither on triumphal arcs
> And window-garlands . . .
>
> A lonely pair
>
> Of strangers, till day closed we sailed along,
> Clustered together with a merry crowd
> Of those emancipated, a blith host
> Of travellers, chiefly delegates, returning
> From the great spousals newly solemnized
> And their chief city, in the sight of Heaven,
> Like bees they swarmed, gaudy and gay as bees;
> Some vapoured in the unruliness of joy,
> And with their words flourished as if to fight
> The saucy air . . .

74. See *Journal de la cour et de la ville,* 17 juillet 1790.

75. Procès-verbal du dépôt de la bannière du département de l'Yonne, dans la salle de l'administration de ce département (Auxerre: L 25 Arch. dép. Yonne).

76. L 352, Arch. dép. Loire-Atlantique.

77. C 120, Arch. nat.

78. *Révolutions de France et de Brabant* no. 35.

79. C 120, Arch. nat.

80. See, for example, the official account of the Federation of the Ile-d'Alby in the Tarn, C 120, Arch. nat.

81. Official account of the Federation of d'Esterpilly, C 120, Arch. nat.

82. F. Uzureau, "Les fêtes de la Fédération à Angers."

III. The Festival above the Parties

1. There is a problem of attribution surrounding these thoughts. Were they the work of Mirabeau or Cabanis? The question is settled in favor of Mirabeau, but in a rather confused way, by H. Monin in his article "Le discours de Mirabeau sur les fêtes publiques," *La Révolution française* 25 (1893). By contrast, J. Gaulmier, in a contribution to the Clermont Conference, "Cabanis et son discours sur les fêtes nationales," attributes the thoughts to Cabanis and accepts only that Mirabeau ordered that they be recorded. Cabanis was, of course, one of Mirabeau's "ghosts." The four speeches that he wrote for Mirabeau so obviously express the latter's political intentions, however, that one may well regard them, as I do here, as writings inspired by Mirabeau.

Furthermore, Gaulmier notes in the Cabanis-Mirabeau vocabulary the obsessive presence of the terms *enthusiasm, happiness,* and *passion.* This is not how I see it. Beneath the brilliance of the official vocabulary, a compulsory concession to the rhetoric of the time, the prudent, reserved character of the text is to be found in the very restrictive arrangement laid down for the festival.

2. The festival of September 20, 1790, was celebrated at the Champ-de-Mars in honor of the national guardsmen who had died at Nancy repressing the rebellion of the Swiss regiment of Châteauvieux, which had mutinied against its commanding officers.

3. The description of their action as "resistance to the misled agents of despotism" is obviously euphemistic.

4. Speech on the Civil Constitution of the Clergy, November 26, 1790.

5. "Since the severe majesty of the Christian religion does not allow one to participate in the profane spectacles, the songs, dancing, and games of our national festival or to share their noisy enthusiasm, there will henceforth be no religious ceremony in these festivals."

6. "They must not be planned too far ahead, nor presented with too much certainty; they must not be ordered, for joy like sorrow obeys nobody's orders."

7. Though in Mirabeau's much more highly developed work there is a sense of moving away from this model, for the simple festivals of antiquity suited simple subjects: "the formation of society, its first labors, the succession and return of certain stars, which serve to measure time . . ."

8. *Société des jacobins,* Friday, April 6, 1792: "As for the ingenious decorations presented by the arts, I respect them . . . But would all those decorations be lost if they were not all borrowed? Will we lack other occasions of avenging

the misfortune of the oppressed? After the soldiers of Châteauvieux, will we not have a few crimes of aristocracy to expiate? Then David and the other artists will have the pleasure of seeing their talents contribute to the triumph of liberty."

9. Maximilien Robespierre, député à l'Assemblée nationale, *Le défenseur de la Constitution* no. 4 (June 7, 1792).

10. "The scandalous festival that they have given for their brothers in the galleys has crushed them in the opinion of the public. One has to have seen that festival to conceive to what degree of baseness the nation has fallen. All we know of the saturnalia falls short of the masquerade of April 15. We shall spare our readers so disgusting a description." *La rocambole ou Journal des honnêtes gens* 19 (April 19, 1792).

11. "The march was delayed at departure by a few, wise, moderate arrangements, which gave the festival a different character, without entirely changing its original intention. The soldiers of Châteauvieux, who were to have been on the chariot, together with the women and children and the symbol of Plenty, all marched in a group with other citizens." Lockroy, *Journal d'une bourgeoise pendant la Révolution*.

12. *Correspondance de Le Coz, évêque constitutionnel d'Ille-et-Vilaine* (Paris: Picard, 1900).

13. Madame Jullien, in Lockroy, *Journal*.

14. The organizers of the festival, fearing that the national guardsmen would be stirred up by the Feuillant propaganda, insisted on excluding weapons from the festival, stating that their prohibition included "all kinds of weapons," and were not slow in explaining the thought behind this measure. In the records of the sessions of the municipal body of Paris for Wednesday, April 11, 1792, we read: "The municipal body . . . convinced that no sign of constraint should inhibit these generous outpourings, that the abandonment of trust must take the place of the machinery of force, that the festivals of Liberty must be as free as she is, that it is time the people were shown that it is esteemed, that one believes in its reason and virtue . . ."

15. R. Schneider, *Quatremère de Quincy et son intervention dans les arts, 1788–1830* (Paris: Hachette, 1910).

16. Dowd, *Pageant-Master of the Republic*.

17. As Dulaure reports it, on June 5, 1792, in *Le thermomètre du jour:* "The Feuillants were greatly mortified to see that what was most applauded in the procession was the mayor of Paris, whom they detested as much as the people loved him."

18. On this point see Dowd, *Pageant-Master of the Republic*.

19. Quatremère attributes to the civic ceremonies—and this a few weeks after the festival of Châteauvieux—the same pedagogical virtues as do Mirabeau, Thouret, Talleyrand, and even David: "The periodic festivals, at times devoted to such great events, are the most powerful instruments that can be used to bring [men] to the imitation of what is beautiful." F. 131935, Arch. nat.

20. "A bas-relief," wrote Quatremère, "must be in the form of a procession"; see Schneider, *Quatremère de Quincy.*

21. *Courier de Gorsas,* June 9, 1792.

22. J. A. Dulaure, *Esquisses historiques des principaux événements de la Révolution française depuis la convocation des Etats généraux jusqu'au rétablissement de la maison de Bourbon* (Paris: Baudouin frères, 1823–1825).

23. This is true only of the great Paris festivals. In the provinces, many of the ceremonies were still both religious and civic.

24. Although the pantheonization of Mirabeau himself was interrupted by a mass at Saint-Eustache.

25. "It is certainly thought that there were no Catholic priests and that the priests of the dead did not tire the ears of the living." *La rocambole ou Journal des honnêtes gens* (June 7, 1792).

26. For the moment, this was especially true of Paris, at a time when the festivals had not yet been the subject of a national decree. But the idea was developing rapidly; on April 21, 1792, the Committee of Public Instruction announced that before long it would present a bill on the national festival. It was, therefore, the big city above all that gave the procession its decor and "supers." Reproduced in the smaller communes, with a few participants lacking costumes and brandishing cardboard emblems, the model of the Revolutionary festival was to prove difficult to export.

27. Madame de Tourzel, *Mémoires* (Paris: Plon, 1883).

28. On this point see *"La Marseillaise,"* Jean-Louis Jam's contribution to the Clermont Conference.

29. In November 1788, in the Grand Orient, a funeral service for Voltaire was celebrated in which all these features, among others, were to be found: the temple draped in black, devices illuminated from behind, urns, broken columns, and a burial pyramid, which disappeared with a loud noise, to reveal a painting of the apotheosis of Voltaire.

30. Rastadt Festival at Brest, 10 L 154, Arch. dép. Finistère.

31. Lasource, an advocate of postponing the festival, gave his reasons: "Let us wait for the institution of an annual festival, or for any other that we be surrounded by free people; then we shall rejoice with a great spectacle, then we shall celebrate the Festival of the Universe."

32. *Détail des cérémonies qui auront lieu au Champ-de-Mars en l'honneur des citoyens morts au siège de Nancy* (Imprimerie patriotique, n.p., n.d.).

33. I. Kant, *Critique of Judgment:* "The sense of the sublime is a pleasure that springs forth only indirectly, being produced by the sense of a cessation of the vital forces for a brief instant, followed immediately by an even stronger out-pouring of them . . . That is why this pleasure is irreconcilable with attraction; and since the mind is not only attracted by the object, but is in turn repulsed by it, the satisfaction that proceeds from the sublime comprises not so much a

positive pleasure as rather admiration and respect; and thus it deserves to be called a negative pleasure."

IV. Mockery and Revolution

1. But the committee went no further than establishing the principle of a Paris festival, dedicated to the celebration of the armies' principal victories and the progress of liberty (November 17, 1792). It left the details of the festival to the executive power.

2. The text was not, in the end, debated; the conditions of admission to the festival were to be included in the decree on the mode of summoning the French people to the primary assemblies, each assembly having to depute a citizen on August 10 to the Festival of Reunion.

3. Indeed it was felt as such. The administration of the district of Cognac wrote on August 7 to the administration of the département: "We have regarded this festival as the postponement of the Federation of July 14 to August 2." L 143, Arch. dép. Charente.

4. The provincial programs stressed the need not to tolerate any longer in the festival "differences that seem imprinted in Nature." The processions must no longer accept "any division between persons and functionaries, or any prescribed order or regularity in their march." L 659, Arch. dép. Puy de Dôme.

5. On this theme see A. Mailhet, "Une fête révolutionnaire en 1793 à Crest, ville du Dauphiné," *Bulletin de la Société archéologique, historique, et artistique, Le Vieux Papier* (1905).

6. Formality, role reversal, masquerade—these are the three forms of festivals distinguished by Leach. See E. R. Leach, *Rethinking Anthropology* (London: Athlone Press, 1961), pp. 132–136.

7. On Sébastien Mercier's testimony see "L'anti-fête dans le nouveau Paris," Catherine Lafarge's contribution to the Clermont Conference.

8. Official account of the municipality of Foix. See L. Blazy, *Les fêtes nationales à Foix sous la Révolution* (Foix: Pomies, 1911).

9. As the people's club of Guéret did on the twenty-fourth day of the first month of Year II, at the news of the taking of Lyon. See L. Lacrocq, "Notes sur les sociétés populaires de la Creuse," in *Mém. Creuse,* vols. 12–16 (1901–1906).

10. See "Une fête civique à Creyssac sous la Révolution," *Bulletin de la Société historique et archéologique du Périgord* 45–46.

11. See, for instance, the festival improvised by the people's club of Grenoble, in A. J. Parès, *La reprise de Toulon et l'opinion publique* (Toulon: Société nouvelle des Imprimeries toulonnaises, 1936).

12. Cf. Breque, "Une fête à Lescar pendant la Révolution," *Escole Gaston Febus* (1902).

13. In J. Annat, *Les sociétés populaires* (Pau: Lescher-Montoué, 1940).

14. E. Roy, *La société populaire de Montignac pendant la Révolution* (Bordeaux: Delgrange, 1888).

15. In B. Morin, *Histoire de Lyon pendant la Révolution* (Lyon: Salvy jne., 1847).

16. As also in the Comminges: J. Dhers, "La Déesse Raison du Mont Unité," *Revue de Comminges* (1960).

17. At Vermeton, 7 Pluviôse, Year II, DXXXVIII3, Arch. nat.

18. J. Berland, *Les sentiments des populations marnaises à l'égard de l'Angleterre à la fin du XVIIIᵉ siècle et au début du XIXᵉ siècle* (Châlons-sur-Marne: Rebat, 1913).

19. See E. Bourgougnon, "La fête de Toulon à Cusset," *Notre Bourbonnais* nos. 61–69.

20. See J. Sauzay, *Histoire de la persécution révolutionnaire dans le département du Doubs, de 1789 à 1901* (Besançon: Tubergues, 1922).

21. Abbé P. J. B. Deloz, *La révolution en Lozère* (Mende: Imprimerie lozérienne, 1922).

22. Registre de la société populaire d'Auch, L 694, Arch. dép. Gers.

23. See E. Dubois, *Histoire de la Révolution dans le département de l'Ain* (Bourg: Brochot, 1931–1935).

24. L. Missol, "La Révolution à Villefranche, le temple de la Raison et les fêtes d'après les archives communales," *Bulletin de la Société des sciences et des arts du Beaujolais* (1904).

25. As at Alès. See F. Rouvière, *Histoire de la Révolution française-dans-le-Gard* (Nimes: Catélan, 1887–1889).

26. F¹ CIII Eure II, Arch. nat.

27. See Parès, *La reprise de Toulon.*

28. L. Dorcy, "La société populaire de Montaigut-en-Combraille," *La Révolution française* 59.

29. R. Cobb, *Les armées révolutionnaires* (Paris: Mouton, 1961–1963).

30. See Mgr. Gaume, *La Révolution, recherches historiques sur l'origine et la propagation du mal en Europe depuis la Renaissance jusqu'à nos jours* (Paris: Gaume Frères, 1856–1859).

31. Registre de la société populaire d'Auch, L 694, Arch. dép. Gers.

32. *Bulletin de la Société archéologique du Gers, XXXIᵉ année* (1930).

33. 67 L I, Arch. dép. Landes.

34. L 1037, Arch. dép. Bouches-du-Rhône.

35. See, for example: *Le courrier républicain* (4 Pluviôse); *La gazette française* (4 Pluviôse); *Le messager du soir* (4 Pluviôse); *Le narrateur impartial* (3 Pluviôse).

36. Cf. L. Testut, *La petite ville de Beaumont-en-Périgord pendant la période révolutionnaire* (Bordeaux: Féret et fils, 1922).

37. Blois, report of the central office, 25 Thermidor, Year VI.

38. J. Perrin, "Le club des femmes de Besançon," *Annales révolutionnaires* 10 (1917–1918).

39. See J. Tiersot, *Les fêtes et les chants de la Révolution française* (Paris: Hachette, 1908). Unfaithful to its title, this book deals not so much with the festivals as such as the school of French music under the Revolution. In this more limited respect, it is highly useful. Indeed, music has been the best-studied aspect of the Revolutionary festival. See also C. Pierre, *Musique des fêtes et des cérémonies de la Révolution* (Paris: Imp. nat., 1904).

40. The day before, the Convention had decided that citizens had the right to adopt whichever form of worship suited them and to suppress those ceremonies that displeased them. See J. Guillaume, "La déesse de la Liberté à la fête du 20 brumaire an II," *La Révolution française* (April 1899).

41. See the official account of the Convention.

42. 67 L I, Arch. dép. Landes.

43. "Procès-verbal de l'organisation de la fête de la Raison à Meyssac, le 18 nivôse an II," *Bulletin de la société historique de la Corrèze* 65.

44. Sauzay, *Histoire de la persécution révolutionnaire dans le département du Doubs.*

45. C. Fauquet, "La célébration du culte de la Raison dans le Perche," *Bulletin de la Société percheronne historique et archéologique* (1907).

46. This is how the official account of the Lot-et-Garonne lays down how the "supers" should appear: "This citizeness will be dressed in white; a tricolor scarf will be tied around her waist; her hair will fall loose upon her shoulders; her right hand will rest on a column; she will hold an unrolled scroll, on which will be inscribed the Declaration of Rights and the Constitution of 1793 (old style). With the other hand, she will point out, on a globe placed to her right, France, the United States of America, Switzerland, the Republic of Martinique, and the other free states of the world. These various states alone will be illuminated. The rest of the globe will be in darkness." From this point of view, Reason is a Liberty, even if one adds, for good measure, broken sceptres, croziers, and miters.

47. A. Dufour, "La fête de la Raison à Corbeil (1793)," *Bulletin de la Société historique et archéologique de Corbeil, d'Etampes et du Hurepoix* (Year 17).

48. "Already your commune / Has signaled its ardor / The truth is one / And will replace error."

49. L 598, Arch. dép. Indre-et-Loire.

50. As Jules Renouvier sees very well in his *Histoire de l'art pendant la Révolution* (Paris: Veuve Renouard, 1863): "Beneath their antique costume, their Phrygian caps, their Athenian helmets, and their Roman diadems . . . one can always see the same woman, whose eye lights up and whose arm extends to the rising breeze."

51. The orator of the Festival of Reason at Pujol exclaimed, on 30 Frimaire, Year II: "O Reason, sublime essence of a superior intelligence! Reason lifts the veil and shows us a Supreme Being, who watches over oppressed innocence and punishes crime." L 530, Arch. dép. Lot-et-Garonne.

52. Judith Schlanger, "Théâtre révolutionnaire et representation du bien," in *Poétique, revue de théorie et d'analyse littéraire* no. 22 (1975).

53. The ceremonial of appearance and disappearance is so present in the Festival of Reason that it was the subject of a debate in the people's club of Saint-Omer, on 10 Ventôse, Year II: "The members of the people's club reminded the Commune Council that there were reforms to be introduced into the program . . . The veil that must conceal Reason until the moment of the celebration must rise and "reconceal" her to announce the end of the ceremony. Those citizens find that once reason has been uncovered she ought not to be concealed from our eyes." C. Bled, *Les sociétés populaires à Saint-Omer pendant la Révolution* (Saint-Omer: H. d'Homont, 1907).

54. Thus, the ladies of the city of Beaune, who met on July 14, 1790, "to take the oath to bring up their children according to the principle of the new Constitution," were severely reprimanded by the municipal officers, who threatened them, if they continued, to put their sashes into their pockets and exclaimed: "So august a ceremony must not be turned into a carnival farce."

55. Brongniart writes: "In the evening, I lit up the church in my own way: that is to say, on entering it was perfectly light without a single lamp being seen. So the mountain that had been erected at the end of this temple had a surprising effect. It was greeted by applause on all sides." Quoted in J. F. de Sacy, *Les Brongniart* (Paris: Plon, 1940).

56. René Girard, *La violence et le sacré* (Paris: Grasset, 1972).

57. For 26 Brumaire, Year II.

58. 10 L 55, Arch. dép. Finistère.

59. L. Jouhaud, *La grande Révolution dans la petite ville. Blancs et rouges: Eymoutiers, 1789–1794* (Limoges: Société des journaux et publications du centre, 1938).

60. B. Barère, *Mémoires* (Paris: J. Labitte, 1842).

61. Indeed, one could sense this in all the speeches delivered in the festivals of Frimaire and Brumaire, Year II, in which the orators declare that the Revolution, far from being complete, is being slowed down by innumerable obstacles, and invite the revolutionaries to become "the unleashed torrent that, springing from the mountainside, overturns, takes with it, precipitates." Speech delivered on 20 Brumaire, Year II, by Citizen Pierron, president of the section du bonnet rouge.

62. Robespierre, speech in the Convention, May 26, 1794.

V. Return to the Enlightenment

1. On 11 Germinal, the Committee of Public Instruction appointed Mathiez "to come to an agreement" on this point with the Committee of Public Safety. In doing so, he finally lost control of the bill.

2. Robespierre, *Rapport . . . sur les rapports des idées religieuses et morales avec les principes républicains, et sur les fêtes nationales . . .* (Paris: Imp. nat., n.d.).

3. M. Dommanget, "Robespierre et les cultes," *Annales historiques de la Révolution française* 1 (1924).

4. Aulard, *Le culte de la Raison, et de l'Etre Suprême.*

5. See Jean Deprun, "Les 'noms divins' dans deux discours de Robespierre," *Annales historiques de la Révolution française* (April-June 1972).

6. "The most ambitious . . . seemed to be divided into two sects, one of which stupidly defended the clergy and despotism. The more powerful and more illustrious was the one whose members were known as the Encyclopedists. It included a few estimable men and a greater number of ambitious charlatans . . . This sect, as far as politics were concerned, always fell short of the rights of the people; as far as morality was concerned, it went well beyond the destruction of religious prejudices." Robespierre, *Rapport.*

7. Boissy d'Anglas, *Essai sur les fêtes nationales* (Paris: Imprimerie polyglotte, Year II): "Philosophy has sometimes rejected the sacred opinion that you have been so hasty to adopt. But it did so, you may be sure, only because it was terrified of innumerable calamities that had followed it: it would have hastened to declare it if institutions, all as reasonable as those that emanate from you, could have guaranteed that it would never be used to cause evil on earth."

8. In this matter, his intervention of December 12, 1793, at the Jacobin Club is very instructive: "I wish to speak of the movement against worship, a movement that, matured by time and reason, could have become an excellent one, but whose *violence* could have brought with it the greatest ills." And addressing Clootz he said: "We know your visits and your *nocturnal* plots. We know that under cover of the darkness of the night you have planned with Bishop Gobel this philosophical *masquerade.*"

9. On June 14, 1793, at the Jacobin Club, trying to calm the speakers after Beauharnais had been summoned.

10. The ground had been prepared for a long time. One need cite only this intervention by Collot d'Herbois at the Jacobin Club on 9 Floréal, Year II: according to him, the French soldiers were animated not by that reason "that one wanted to turn into a maleficent divinity to stifle the gentlest sentiments, but a majestic, august reason, that enlarges the circle of ideas, sustains solid virtues, a reason that emanates directly from that sublime being toward whom our thougts are carried. Let him who wishes to deny it tell me why the wretch who escapes from a shipwreck on the frailest piece of debris raises his hands to heaven."

11. Charles Nodier, *Oeuvres complètes,* vol. 7 (Paris: E. Renduel, 1832–1837).

12. 10 L 155, Arch. dép. Finistère.

13. On this point see Tiersot, *Les fêtes et les chants de la Révolution française.*

14. G. Brégail "La fête de l'Etre Suprême à Auch," *Bulletin de la Société archéologique du Gers* 21 (1920).

15. H. Chardon, "La fête de l'Etre Suprême au Mans," *La Révolution française* 10 (1886).

16. Boissy d'Anglas, *Essai*.

17. B. Bois, *Les fêtes révolutionnaires à Angers de l'an II à l'an VIII* (Paris: Alcan, 1929).

18. Lépine, *Histoire de Château-Porcien*.

19. Those of Viala, Bara, Le Peletier, Marat, and the heroes of the Revolution, "La fête de l'Etre Suprême à Calais," *Société historique du Calaisis* (Sept.-Oct. 1924).

20. V. Grandvaux, "Souvenirs de la période révolutionnaire à Poligny," *Bulletin de la Société d'agriculture, des sciences et arts de Poligny* (1888–1889).

21. A. Sorel, *La fête de l'Etre Suprême à Compiègne* (Compiègne: Edler, 1872).

22. Bois, *Les fêtes révolutionnaires à Angers*.

23. "La fête de l'Etre Suprême à Theys," *Bulletin de la Société archéologique historique et artistique, le vieux papier* 16.

24. A. Lécluselle, *Histoire de Cambrai et du Cambrésis* (Cambrai: Régnier-Farez, 1873–1874).

25. S. Thomas, *Nancy avant et après 1830* (Nancy: Crépin-Leblond, 1900).

26. E. Herpin, "Les fêtes à Saint-Malo pendant la Révolution," *Annales de la Société historique de Saint-Malo* (1908).

27. A. Campion, *Les fêtes nationales à Caen sous la Révolution* (Caen: Le Blanc-Hardel, 1877).

28. Michel Golfier, "Culte de la Raison et fêtes décadaires en l'an II au Bugue," *Bulletin de la Société historique et archéologique du Périgord* 96 (1968).

29. "Ye of little faith, / who would see and hear the Supreme Being, / may do so, with morality in your hearts. / But you must go out into the fields, / two by two, bearing a flower. / There, by pure waters, / one hears a God in one's heart, / as one sees him in Nature." Léonard Bourdon, *Recueil des actions héroiques et civiques des Républicains français*, NAF 2713, Bibl. nat.

30. Jaurès, *Histoire socialiste:* "The scaffold filled the city with a glow of immortality."

31. R. Palmer, *Twelve Who Ruled* (Princeton: Princeton University Press, 1941): "Yet however much planned by art, and imposed by the government, the doings of 20 Prairial expressed something deeper and were a climax to those festivals that had arisen spontaneously for five years. They were indeed a consummation to the century. Was it not the aim of the philosophes to make wisdom arise from the ashes of error and to free the Supreme Being from the disguises of the God of priests? The philosophes would not have enjoyed the festival of Prairial, they would perhaps have found it vulgar and rather noisy, or complained that in detail it was not precisely what they expected. Whether they would have found it naive is more doubtful, and it is certain that the ideas expressed were theirs."

32. L. Maggiolo, "Les fêtes de la Révolution," *Mémoires de l'académie Stanislas* 5th ser., 11 and 12 (1893–1894).

33. Letter of 22 Prairial, AF II 195, Arch. nat.

34. This is not true of everybody, however. Take the testimony of Grétry, on his return, in that spring of Year II, from the Champs-Elysées, where he had gone to enjoy "the most beautiful lilac in blossom that one could ever see": "I approached the place de la Révolution, the former place Louis XV, when my ear was struck by the sound of instruments. I moved forward a few steps: there were violins, a flute, and a tabor, and I could make out the dancers' shouts of joy. I was reflecting on the contrast of the scenes to be found in this world, when a man who was passing near me pointed out the guillotine: I looked up and I saw in the distance the fatal knife rise and fall twelve or fifteen times in succession. On the one side, country dances, and, on the other, rivers of blood: the scent of the flowers, the gentle influence of the spring, the last rays of the setting sun would never be renewed for those unfortunate victims . . . Such images leave ineradicable traces." A. E. M. Grétry, *Essais sur la musique* (Paris: Imprimerie de la République, Year V).

35. J. Saige, *Opuscules d'un solitaire* (Bordeaux: Bergeret, Year XI).

36. It was at the Jacobin Club, on 16 Germinal, Year II, that Garnier de Saintes made his extraordinary intervention on the subject of the purge: "If we purge ourselves, it is to have the right to purge France. We shall leave no heterogeneous body in the Republic . . . It is said that we wish to destroy the Convention. No, it will remain intact; but we wish to lop off the dead branches from that great tree. The great measures that we are taking are like gusts of wind that shake the worm-eaten fruit to the ground and leave the good fruit on the tree."

37. *Rédacteur,* 11 Thermidor, Year VI: "Rare animals from the four corners of the globe seemed to represent the ferocity chained up on 9 Thermidor by the hands of mankind."

38. It was to remain so throughout the Directoire: "I believe," said Duplantier on 28 Messidor, Year VI, "that we are erecting only a weak monument if each of us is allowed to meditate on the whole of an object on which depends the destinies of burgeoning Republics, and the happiness of future generations."

39. "The degree of 18 Floréal places at the beginning of the year those that ought to be at the end, in summer, those that call for meditation; in winter, those that call for display, spectacle, exercises in the open air." J. F. Barailon, *Organisation et tableau des fêtes décadaires* (Paris: Imp. nat., Year III).

40. Merlin de Thionville, *Opinion sur les fêtes nationales prononcée à la Convention, 9 Vendémiaire an III* (Paris: Imp. nat., Year III).

41. P. T. Durand de Maillane, *Opinion sur les fêtes décadaires* (Paris: Imp. nat., Year III).

42. Mathieu de l'Oise, *Projet de fêtes nationales* (Paris: Imp. nat., Year II).

43. *Discours prononcé par le citoyen Daunou, président de la Convention nationale, pour la fête du 10 août* (Paris: Imp. nat., Year III).

44. One should nonetheless correct this judgment by pointing out that, however difficult they may have been to organize, there were celebrations throughout France. The absence of Republican festivals under the Directoire is, it must be repeated, an illusion owing to the fact that the great Paris spectacles disappeared and also to the fact that, as L. S. Mercier recounts in a famous passage, "There was dancing in the Carmelite monastery, where throats were being cut, there was dancing in the Jesuits' novitiate." Spectacles, balls, a revival in fashionable receptions competed with the utopian festival to the extent of giving the impression—quite wrongly—that the latter had disappeared.

45. François de Neufchâteau, *Recueil des lettres circulaires, instructions, programmes, discours et autres actes publics* (Paris: Imprimerie de la République, Years VI–VIII).

46. Indeed, the historian of festivals owes his source material to this systematic determination, for it was from the setting up of the system of Brumaire, Year IV, that there began to circulate throughout France, from Paris to the département, from the département to the municipality, and from the municipality to the commune, the model imagined by a few individuals, while the official accounts, endlessly demanded by the authorities, traveled in the opposite direction, toward Paris. So we should pause to examine exactly what the official account of a festival was like. Very often the writer would begin by reeling off the cascade of official orders concerning the festival, before going on to what actually happened in the commune (there may be many reasons for this legalistic attitude: the wish to pad out the account to an imposing length, to avoid having to dwell on the enthusiasm of the commune, or to seek to enhance the sense of national unanimity). The writer himself—he was often the president of the municipal administration, his secretary in the larger communes, or sometimes also the commissioner of the executive directory—obviously had everything to gain by adhering to the norm: thus he would avoid investigations, recriminations, the irritated incomprehension with which oversincere accounts were met in high places. That, no doubt, was why so many of the official accounts are content to remark that the festival passed off with "order and decency," two terms that do not imply festive enthusiasm. This also explains the crushing monotony of these documents—and probably certain anomalies too, such as those curious accounts written in the conditional, as if the municipalities of the communes were content to copy a departmental model in which a program of festivals might have been suggested; as if the cleverest of the writers turned this optative into an indicative, the less astute keeping the model as it was. This produces something like the following: "We therefore would proceed at the said hour, accompanied by the captain of the National Guard, who would have his company under arms, and followed by a large crowd of people of both sexes and of every age. The procession

having thus formed, we would proceed, led by fifes and drums, to the public square, where, having arrived, we would light a bonfire prepared for this festival and would dance the farandole around the Liberty Tree." Did a festival ever take place? One very much doubts it.

Yet one has to take the cultural stereotypes into account. For these men, writing was in itself an event. The official account has a naturally heavy style. The account of a festival lacking pomp may call up schoolboy rhetoric to provide the missing solemnity: "There a venerable old man applauded in his feeble accents the holy institutions by which we are governed; here a young citizen, the hope of the Republic, trembled with joy at being one day the ornament of the common weal." That is why, too, in the accounts of the winter festivals, in which so many documents attached to the official accounts testify to rainstorms, snowstorms, and freezing weather, which paralyzed so many processions and prevented the planting of so many Liberty Trees, there were always writers who declared without turning a hair that "the author of Nature parted the sky of clouds and shone his sun on the children of Liberty."

Can such straitlaced documents, with all their gaps, be of any use? There are their avowals, voluntary or involuntary (obviously we should place less trust in their assurance that "there was a great concourse of people" than in the material details they include: how many men were posted in the bell tower, from what time the music was played, how much had to be paid to the tapestry maker). Lastly, there are their additions to the official norm, whether these take the form of an interpretation of the instructions from Paris, or something that went beyond strict instructions: for example, instead of being celebrated in the canton municipality, as laid down by law, the festival is celebrated—why is not made very clear—in all the communes; hence the archives are sometimes full of innumerable documents that often seem freer and more innocent in tone with those emanating from the more important communes.

47. In a contribution to the Clermont Conference.

48. On this point it seems clear that La Révellière's thinking is based on Robespierre's. When La Révellière considers the existence of a form of worship, he pleads for a very simple form of worship that would accept the immortality of the soul, the existence of a God who rewards virtue and avenges crime, but he inveighs against pomp in religious worship, concluding: "Only the assembly of a large number of men animated by the same sentiment, all expressing themselves at the same moment and in the same manner, has an irresistible power over souls. The result is incalculable." J. F. Dubroca, introduction to La Révellière, *Discours sur les divers sujets de morale et sur les fêtes nationales, lus à l'institut le 12 floréal an V.*

49. La Révellière, *Essai sur les moyens de faire participer l'universalité des spectateurs à tout ce qui se pratique dans les fêtes nationales* (Paris: H. J. Jansen, Year VI).

50. J.-J. Rousseau, *Considérations sur le gouvernement de Pologne* (Paris: Defer de

Maisonneuve, 1790): "It would not be believed the extent to which the heart of the people follows its eyes, and the extent to which the majesty of ceremonial impresses it. This gives authority an air of order and rule and inspires confidence and avoids the ideas of caprice and whim attached to those of arbitrary power."

51. L 668, Arch. dép. Puy de Dôme.

52. As if anarchy required a more radical purification than monarchy.

53. The relation between the *fêtes décadaires* and the national festivals varied considerably throughout the decade. It was all the closer in that there was a strong wish to fill the gap left by the decline of the religious festivals. For Robespierre and Mathieu, the national festivals and the *fêtes décadaires* were inseparable. In Brumaire, Frimaire, and Nivôse, Year III, a battle raged around plans for *fêtes décadaires* to be drawn up by M.-J. Chénier, who conceived them as the surest way of placing an obstacle in the way of the offensive return of the Catholic party. The somersaults of Germinal and Prairial, Year III, delivered a fatal blow to the plans, which Daunou unambiguously abandoned on 3 Brumaire, Year IV: "What had hitherto prevented the establishment of public festivals are the names that such festivals are sometimes given . . . The plan that I am entrusted with the task of presenting to you has this advantage at least, that it makes quite clear that the national solemnities can exist without competing with private forms of worship." It was the coup de'état of 18 Fructidor that was to revive the project for the *fêtes décadaires* and, throughout Year VI, return the festival organizers to the inspiration of Robespierre and Mathieu.

VI. *The Festival and Space*

1. Memorandum on the circuses, written by the Abbé Brottier and read by him at a meeting of the Academie des lettres. Quoted by E. L. Boullée, *Architecture, essai sur l'art,* ed. J. M. Pérouse de Montclos (Paris: Hermann, 1968).

2. S. Thomas, *Mémoire adressé à l'Assemblée nationale, accompagné de deux projets pour un palais national,* N III, Seine 789, Arch. nat.

3. J. G. Fichte, *Considérations destinées a rectifier les jugements du public sur la Révolution française* (Paris, F. Chamerot, 1859) (*Beitrag zur Berichtigung der Urtheile des Publikums über die französische Revolution,* 1793).

4. P. V. Vergniaud, *Manuscrits, lettres et papiers, pièces pour la plupart inédites, classées et annotées par C. Vatel* (Paris: Dumoulin, 1873).

5. We are reminded of this by Jean Starobinski, who remarks that one of the first victories of the Revolution lay in not allowing the three orders to deliberate separately." J. Starobinski, *1789, Les emblèmes de la Raison* (Paris: Flammarion, 1973).

6. Marquis de Villette, *Lettres choisies.*

7. See Duchatellier, *Histoire de la Révolution dans les départements de l'ancienne Bretagne.*

8. Speech delivered by M. de Marsanne, lieutenant colonel of the National Guard of Montélimar, to the national guardsmen assembled under the walls of that city, on December 13, 1789.

9. Declaration by Sarrette, 30 Brumaire, Year II.

10. Anonymous, "Fédération des Vosges," *Bulletin du Comité des travaux d'histoire vosgienne* 3.

11. Years later, Michelet testified again to this sensibility when describing the funeral festival of March 4, 1838, in honor of the victims of February. He criticized that fine festival for forcing the people to "stand tightly together" and "to form a long column" when going up to and entering the narrow door of the Greek temple. Michelet remained outside: "Ah! I did not go up. I had my own church there, the great church of the sky." Michelet, *Nos fils*. Furthermore, his account of the Federation returns repeatedly to the same image: "No longer an artificial church, but the universal church. A single dome, from the Vosges to the Cévennes and from the Pyrenees to the Alps." Michelet, *Histoire de la Révolution française*.

12. Cf. *La chronique de Paris,* June 20, 1790.

13. *Fédération du mont Sainte-Geneviève à Nancy.*

14. General Duplessis: "Fête de la Confédération des gardes nationales de l'ancienne Bourgogne, le 18 mai 1790," *Mémoires académiques Dijon* (1922).

15. "Fédération des Vosges."

16. *Fédération du mont Sainte-Geneviève à Nancy* (Nancy: Hoener, n.d.).

17. *Les gardes nationales de Saint-Brice, Cravant, Vermenton, Noyers, Vézelay, Asquins, Lille, Montréal et Avalon* (n.p., n.d.).

18. *Opinion de M. Malouet sur la Déclaration des Droits, dans la séance du 2 aoôut 1789* (n.p., n.d.).

19. Cf. R. Etlin, "L'architecture et la fête de la Fédération, Paris, 1790," contribution to the Clermont Conference.

20. Boullée, *Architecture, essai sur l'art.* Furthermore, this was one of the leitmotifs of projects for theaters and circuses throughout the century.

21. See, for example, David Le Roy, *Histoire de la disposition et des formes différentes que les chrétiens ont données à leurs temples* (Paris: Desaint et Saillant, 1764).

22. Cf. De Wailly: "The audience placed in the front of the boxes thus becomes a superb spectacle, in which each of the spectators seen by all the others contributes to the pleasure that he shares." *Observations sur la forme la plus avantageuse aux salles de spectaclss,* NAF 2479, Bibl. nat.

23. M. Linguet, *Adresse au peuple français concernant ce qu'il faut faire et ce qu'il ne faut pas faire pour célébrer la fête mémorable et nationale du 14 juillet 1790* (n.p., n.d.).

24. G. Thiémet, *Projet d'une cérémonie fixée au 14 juillet prochain et pacte fédératif des troupes de tous les départements réunis à l'armée parisienne pour célébrer l'époque de la Révolution* (Paris: Potier de Lille, 1790).

25. *Observations du sieur Blondel, architecte et dessinateur du cabinet du Roi, sur le projet de fête de la Confédération patriotique du 14 juillet 1790, dont M. de Varenne, huissier de l'Assemblée nationale a donné l'idée et dont les plans et dessins ont été présentés par les dits sieurs à M. M. Bailly et Lafayette* (Paris: Imp. nat., 1790).

26. *Mémoire sur le remplacement de la Bastille, et différents projets pour l'arsenal joint aux plans et élévations d'une place Nationale à la gloire de la liberté présentée à l'Assemblée nationale le 9 Avril 1790, par le sieur Mouillefarine le fils, de Troyes en Champagne,* N IV, Seine 87, Arch. nat.

27. F. L. d'Escherny, *Correspondance d'un habitant de Paris avec ses amis de Suisse et d'Angleterre, sur les événements de 1789, 1790 et jusqu'au 4 avril 1791* (Paris: Desenne, 1791): "By dint of seeing too many objects, one saw none . . . It was too broad a field for men of five or six feet. The proportion between spectacle and spectators was entirely broken."

28. It conquered distance, like the telegraph. Lakanal explicitly criticizes both as agents of simultaneity: "Above all two discoveries seem worthy of note in the eighteenth century: the aerostat and the telegraph. Montgolfier traced a route through the air, as the argonauts had forged one through the waves, and such is the interconnection of the sciences and arts that the first vessel to be launched prepares the ground for the discovery of the new world and the aerostat was to serve liberty, in our time and, in a famous battle, was to be the principal instrument of victory . . . The telegraph, that rapid messenger of thought, brings distances closer" (Paris: Imp. nat., n.d.).

29. *Rédacteur,* 12 Thermidor, Year VI.

30. *Details de toutes les cérémonies qui vont être célébrées dans toute l'étendue de la République française, une et indivisible, en l'honneur de l'Etre Suprême, Auteur de la Nature et de la Liberté, présentés par David et décrétés par la Convention nationale suivis de l'Ordre de la Marche des cérémonies, des décorations pour l'embellisement de cette fête, de la Religion Naturelle des Vrais Républicains, de la Déclaration Solennelle de l'Homme Libre à l'Eternal* (Paris: Provost, n.d.).

31. *Procès-verbal tres intéressant du voyage aérien qui a eu lieu aux Champs-Elysées le 18 septembre, jour de la proclamation de la Constitution* (Paris: Bailly, 1791).

32. A theme superbly treated by Barère in "Discours sur les écoles de Mars qui fait l'apologie du dénuement" (*Le moniteur universel,* 15 Prairial, Year II): "For the royal military school, it was necessary to erect, with the sweat of the people's brow, a great edifice that testified only to the insolent pride of the master who had it built . . . For the Revolutionary school of Mars, all that was needed was a piece of arid land, the plain of Sablons, some tents, some weapons, and cannons."

33. Circular of 10 Fructidor, Year VI.

34. As is shown, for example, by the title of the anonymous pamphlet *Songe patriotique, ou le monument et la fête* (Paris: Didot le Jeune, 1790). See also De Mopinot: *Proposition d'un monument à élever dans la capitale de la France pour trans-*

mettre aux races futures l'époque de l'heureuse révolution qui l'a revivifiée sous le règne de Louis XVI (Paris: Laurens jeune, 1790).

35. E. P. A. Gois, *Projet de monument et fête patriotique* (Paris: Imp. nat., n.d.).

36. On this theme one might consult, for example, *L'abréviateur universel,* 18 Pluviôse, Year III, "Extrait de la République française": "Modern barbarism, by stupidly and impudently calling itself reason, enlightenment, genius, virtue, regeneration, strove to replace the masterpieces that were for so long the glory of our nation and has been capable of giving us nothing but grotesque conceptions, plaster casts, ceilings, canvases smeared to look like marble or rocks, imposing, fragile symbols of our ephemeral theories."

37. *Projet d'un monument pour consacrer la Révolution, par M. Gatteaux, graveur des medailles du roi,* C 120, Arch. nat.

38. *Confédération nationale du 14 juillet ou Description fidèle de tout ce qui a précédé, accompagné et suivi cette auguste cérémonie* (Paris: J. M. Chalier, 1790).

39. Extract from a letter written by a member of the National Assembly to one of his friends, reproduced in *Le Journal de Paris,* July 15, 1790.

40. See *Projet de décret au sujet des statues de la place des Victoires, présenté à l'Assemblée nationale par Alexandre de Lameth,* C 41, no. 363, Arch. nat.

41. For this theme see also the motion proposed to the Council of the Five Hundred by Desaix on 3 Vendémiaire, Year VIII, proposing "to honor the talents of Republican artists": "And we, too, should have, as at Athens, in a series of monuments and statues, a complete course in morality and civic instruction."

42. Linguet, *Adresse au peuple.*

43. *Projet d'un monument à élever dans le champ de la Fédération proposé par M. Sobre le Jeune, architecte* (n.p., n.d.).

44. Gatteaux, *Projet d'un monument.*

45. De Mopinot, *Proposition d'un monument.*

46. On this theme, which is a leitmotif of the century, see, for example, Bernardin de Saint-Pierre, *Etudes de la nature* (Paris: P. F. Didot le Jeun, 1784).

47. Sometimes even two verticalities are associated. This is the case when, as at the Federation of Lyon, a statue of Liberty crowned a mountain, or when, as at the Paris Federation, the altar surmounted a "mountain," though one of modest proportions, and when, as was the case in so many projects for patriotic squares, a Louis XVI was placed on top of a mountain, or a "temple open to the heavens" was erected on a pyramid.

48. Sobre le Jeune, *Projet d'un monument.*

49. Abbé Morellet, *Mémoires* (Paris: Ladvocat, 1821). The Abbé Morellet is very typical of the majority opinion, the conformist view that "it is a defect in an admirable monument not to produce its impression immediately."

50. On this theme, out of innumerable pieces of evidence, one might choose Montesquieu: "A building of the Gothic order is an enigma for the eye that sees

it and the soul is troubled, as when it is presented with an obscure poet." *Essai sur le goût* (Paris: Delalain, 1766).

51. As, for example, at Douai, for the arrangement of the temple of Reason, Nord L 5050, Arch. dép.

52. See Laurent-Hanin, *Histoire municipale de Versailles, 1787–1799* (Versailles: Cerf. 1885–1889).

53. David's program for the Republican reunion of August 10, 1793, is highly illuminating in this regard.

54. Why Caen? Because the municipal archives provide—which is not often the case—very detailed itineraries and because the administrators were obviously extremely careful not to allow the festival to be swallowed up by the local *décadaire* and to lay down the great dates for the civic promenade; because, too, the ancien régime routes are very well known through series B.B. and because, between 1683 and 1786, there was a record of the city's ceremonials. Lastly, I owe a great deal for this study to the masterly thesis by J.-C. Perrot, *Genèse d'une ville moderne: Caen au XVIIIe siècle* (Paris: Mouton, 1975).

55. On this map of the ceremonial routes at Caen during the ten years of the Revolution are missing the routes about which the archives say nothing, those for the processions in, for example, the festivals of Old Age, in which the old people chosen for their civic spirit and their virtues were led from their houses to the municipal building. This gap is not of much importance, however, since these routes were used only occasionally. Also lacking are the itineraries followed as a result of various proclamations (danger to the fatherland, for example), which would nevertheless be very interesting to know, first, because we know those adopted under the ancien régime for processions celebrating the proclamation of peace, and second, because such processions combine better than any others practical intention and symbolic expressiveness. Unfortunately, the official accounts confine themselves to saying that people gathered at the "principal squares" and crossroads. Lastly, the routes for several civic *promenades décadaires* are also missing.

56. With this exception, however: these ancien-régime routes, unlike the Revolutionary routes, which centered on the west of the Ile Saint-Jean, often took in the east side, the more aristocratic part of this residential island.

57. On this point see Campion, *Les fêtes nationales à Caen sous la Révolution.*

58. When the Revolution broke out, the law courts had still not been finished. On this point see J.-C. Perrot, *Cartes, plans, dessins et vues de Caen antérieurs à 1789* (Caen: Caron, 1962).

59. The departmental administration played a large role in the organization of the festival and was housed at the time on the place Fontette.

60. We know that from the middle of the century, the ramparts were doomed: repairs were no longer made to sections that had fallen into ruin; breaches in the walls made by private landowners went unpunished; and the old gates were

demolished. In several places the fortifications had completely lost any military appearance; games of bowls and popinjay shooting had become established in the Saint-Julien moats; and since the works for the place Fontette had begun, the city was exposed on a broad front on the Bayeux side. On all these points see Perrot, *Cartes, plans, dessins*.

61. Indeed, the works on the harbor tolled the death knell for the city's towers and walls along the quayside.

62. The guillotine had made its appearance in the place Sauveur in November 1792 for the punishment of some sordid crime. After Ventôse (the procession took place on 20 Ventôse, Year II), the spring of Year II was to see it put to other uses.

63. In Perrot, *Cartes, plans, dessins*.

64. The Montagnard representative's arrival from Cherbourg.

65. The hexagonal canopy over the altar of the fatherland was thus supported by six cocked cannon.

66. In Perrot, *Cartes, plans, dessins*.

67. When the Comte d'Artois, who, in May 1777, went from Harcourt to Avranches, arrived at Caen, the company went from the town hall to welcome him on the place Dauphine and abandoned the place Fontette; this, despite the disappearance of the porte Millet and the quite recent destruction of the Châtimoine tower, was to keep to what had now become imaginary city boundaries.

68. P. D. Huet, *Les origines de la ville de Caen* (Rouen: Maurry, 1706).

69. For example, for the taking of Marengo, the victory over the English at Saint-Cast, the reestablishment of the dauphin.

70. But more than to the symbolism of the Palais de Justice, the place Fontette owed its choice as the starting point of certain processions (in particular that of July 14) to the role played by the departmental administration, which was housed there.

71. Classical town planning had proven more timid at Caen than elsewhere, and the square, which was too open, lacked the intimacy that would have concentrated all eyes on the royal statue.

72. It should be added that certain circumstances favored the choice of the place Royale, specifically the conversion of the elegant classical buildings of the seminary into municipal premises. The municipal council chose as its meeting place the Church of the Eudistes, where the authorities were content simply to close off the arms of the transepts.

73. A few words should also be said about the passing of the procession, when it left the place Royale for the cours National, across the fairground, whose access roads and buildings had just been erected. The fairground was a traditional meeting place: its terrace looked over the harmonious perspective of the meadows and

watercourses. It was also a place of leisure, for the traveling actors would set up their stage to the southeast, and there too concerts were given after the festival. The rows of stone stalls, however, made it unsuitable for festive arrangements.

74. Huet, *Les origines*.

75. Those of the pantheonization of Mirabeau and of 9 Thermidor, Year IV.

76. Michelet, *Histoire de la Révolution française*, preface of 1847.

77. See *Conservateur décadaire*, 30 Messidor, Year II.

78. The place de l'Hôtel de Ville thus lost its ceremonial privilege: it had already been condemned, it is true, by a century of writing on town planning, and many architects considered removing the Hôtel de Ville (Stalz and Contants wanted to house it on the quai Malaquais and De l'Estrade on the quai Conti). The accounts of the ancien régime festivals celebrated at the Hôtel de Ville stress the insecurity as well as the unimpressiveness of the place. Above all, remarks Boullée, who commented on the festivals given by the city in 1782, when the festival ought to announce "general happiness," one has to be imprisoned in such a small place that it can scarcely contain the king's carriages and suite. See Boullée, *Essai sur l'art*.

79. This was why it was decided not to make the Cordeliers district, as would seem natural enough, the starting point of Marat's pantheonization: the streets of the Cordeliers were too narrow and winding for a large gathering of people.

80. Those places are generally ones that suggest depth, which was always suspect for anyone wishing to take possession of a horizontal space, as at the Palais-Royal, usually described as possessing a fantastic basement containing shops with "air grates through which one could see circles of little girls jumping." On this theme see L. Sébastien-Mercier, *Paris pendant la Révolution* (Paris: Poulet-Malassis, 1862). In 1790 the police warned the provincial *fédérés* about this gloomy sewer. And the only Festival of the Revolution to be celebrated there— it was on 20 Brumaire, Year II, and was a festival in honor of Liberty—was finally moved by a departmental order.

81. Maximilien Robespierre, *La défenseur de la Constitution* no. 9.

82. Abbé Sieyès, *Discours à la célébration de l'anniversaire du 10 août* (Paris: Imprimerie de la République, Year VII).

83. Honoré de Balzac, *Une ténébreuse affaire* (Paris: H. Souverain, 1843): "Those who read histories of the French Revolution today will never know what enormous intervals the thought of the public put between events that were actually very close in time. The general need for peace and tranquillity, which everybody felt after such violent commotions, made people completely forget the most serious of recent facts. History suddenly aged, constantly matured by violent events."

84. When, on June 25, 1793, Lakanal presented to the Convention a bill to decide the way in which the national guardsmen would be summoned to Paris,

he named the festival—it was in any case moved from July 14 to August 10—
Reunion and not Federation. Federalism, the flag of those départements that had
risen up against the Convention, now excluded the use of the word *federation*
(Paris: Imp. nat., n.d.).

85. It forces the spectator to choose his point of observation and therefore
limits his vision. Emilie Brongniart, the architect's daughter, experienced this.
In all the enthusiasm of her thirteen years, she wanted to see everything on the
day of the Festival of the Supreme Being, whereas the women who accompanied
her wanted to see only the burning of Atheism and therefore insisted on the
observation point of the Tuileries. To achieve her ends, she therefore had to give
them the slip and join the girls who were following the chariots of Agriculture.
De Sacy, *Les Brongniart.*

86. J. B. Gence, *Vues sur les fêtes publiques et application de ces vues à la fête de
Marat* (Paris: Imprimerie de Renaudiere le Jeune, Year II).

87. A festival celebrated at a time when the entire Republic is described by
Barère as "an immense besieged city." The official occasion of the festival, the
acceptance of the new Constitution and the anniversary of August 10, were
merely pretexts. The real purpose was to confront federalism with national unanimity. Furthermore, the ceremonial of the festival, though hesitating between
several competing intentions, tried to represent that unanimity: the president of
the Convention bound together into a bundle the pikestaffs brought separately
into the procession by the envoys of the primary assemblies and placed it on the
altar of the fatherland. This "Republican reunion" made a profound impression
on contemporaries, as newspapers and pamphlets show. It was regarded as the
"grand beau," embodied at last, that the Revolution had seemed to promise.

88. *La Journal de la Société populaire des arts,* Pluviôse, Year II, conveys the
uncertainty into which it plunged the people. It relates a conversation between a
wig maker and an architect on the day of the festival of August 10. The architect
did his best to explain at length the ornamental arrangements of the festival, but
the wig maker retorted: "I think that, despite everything you've just told me
about the temple, the altar, and the boundary stones at the entrance of the
Champ-de-Mars, I can only say that I am astonished. Why have those in charge
of the festival given those figures that you describe an Egyptian style? Take the
woman I saw yesterday on the place de la Bastille. Well, I would like to know
why her hair was dressed in that way. We are French, and under the pretext that
we have been corrupted in our morals and in our monuments, they want to turn
us into Egyptians, Greeks, Etruscans. I think we must do better than all those
peoples, and I tell you, citizen artist, I would much prefer a figure such as my
imagination represents it, after nature."

89. Only a "Siege of Lille" was to be shown to the participants.

VII. The Festival and Time

1. Here, out of thousands, is one testimony to the abyss that continued to separate Sunday and *décadi*. It comes from the police commissioner of Château-roux, writing to the commune's municipality, in Year VII:

"The former Sundays and holidays of the old calendar are the only true days of rest; during those days, all the workshops, whether inside the home or out, are shut; such public places as walks, cafés, billiard-rooms, wine shops, etc. are frequented by considerable numbers of people, who meet on the public highways and set up games of bowls there, despite your order.

"On the *décadis,* however, the artisan shuts up his shop and works inside his house. The merchant, too, turns to work in the home, while manufacturers, many of whose workshops are not in view of the public highway, remain open; labor that is done particularly outside, such as cultivation of the land, masonry, carpentry, wool spinning, etc., continues uninterrupted; a sort of coalition exists to protect those who break the law and to hide them from my surveillance. Warned in advance by other citizens of the time of my visits, they disappear even before I have time to notice them and often I find nothing but tools on the premises."

2. On this point, see the letter of a printer of Issoudun, 21 Thermidor, Year VII, L 300, Arch. dép. Indre.

3. *Articles complémentaires de la Constitution,* proposed by P. F. Charrel, deputy for the département of the Isère, in the National Convention (Paris: Imp. nat., Year III).

4. Up to the end of the Revolutionary years, one sees a resurgence of the plan to reorder historical time. For example, on 12 Thermidor, Year VI, Sherlock proposed henceforth to calculate everything on the Republican era: "Thus, instead of saying that Lysippus lived in the fourth century B.C., one would have to say, if my amendment were adopted, that this artist lived in the twenty-first century before the Republican era." *Opinion de Sherlock, sur le project de résolution relatif au calendrier républicain* (Paris: Imp. nat., Year VI).

In Year VI, again, Romme's arguments would be taken up by those who insisted on marking the break. There was no need, they said, to reform the chronology of the ancients: "We must respect the diversity of the chronologies as monuments appropriate to the annals of each people, as beacons placed in the light of the centuries to illuminate and mark the great historic periods." *Rapport de Lenoir-Laroche au conseil des Anciens, sur l'annuaire de la République* (Paris: Imp. nat., Year VI).

5. G. Romme, *Rapport sur l'ère de la République* (Paris: Imp. nat., n.d.). Indeed, it is Romme who stresses most forcefully the scandal that would arise from using the "same tables" for the era of monarchy as for the Republican era: "Would one not see on the same tables, engraved sometimes by a degraded burin,

sometimes by a faithful, free burin, the honored crimes of kings and the execution to which they are now doomed?"

6. Thus everything is reconciled in the choice of 1 Vendémiaire: the celestial movements, the seasons, ancient tradition, and the course of events. "How could such an accord," which Romme stresses, "fail to rally the entire nation to the new order of things"? Romme, *Rapport*.

7. Speech of the commissioner of the executive directory attached to the central administration of Aurillac, 1 Vendémiaire, Year VI: "This annual festival will assume its character by identifying with the course of the sun; consequently the old customs associated with the first day of the year will be transferred to it." L 648 bis, Arch. dép. Cantal.

8. N. Parent-Réal, *Motion d'ordre tendant à faire consacrer, par la fête du 1ᵉʳ vendémiaire, l'accord parfait qui existe dans l'histoire de la Révolution française* (Paris: Imp. nat., Year VII).

9. Charrel, *Articles complémentaires*, develops the idea that the day that saw the birth of the Republic should be consecrated by the Constitution of that Republic, "so that its memory may thereby be protected against all the blows that posterity would surely subject it to."

10. Gregory XIII "only corrected the ancient formula in order to maintain it in perpetuity, that is to say, to make the abuse eternal: furthermore, Easter nevertheless remained a very moveable feast, which continued to bring with it into most of the annual series that depend on it all the disordered variations that dishonor our calendar. It is still that of a barbarian people." Boulanger, *L'antiquité dévoilée par ses usages*.

11. On this point, see Heurtault-Lamerville's second report on the Republican calendar: "The division of Time is one of the boldest and most useful conceptions of the human mind . . . Man must be given a faithful guide that can lead him with certainty to past events and to the centuries to come." (Paris: Imp. nat., Year VI).

12. On this point, see J. Guillaume, *Procès-verbaux du Comité d'instruction publique* (Paris: Collection de documents inédits sur l'Histoire de France, 1891–1907): "Either inadvertence or amour-propre led the *rapporteur* to place the festival of genius before that of virtue. Robespierre asked that each be put back in its place. Caesar, he observed, was a man of genius, Cato was a virtuous man, and, indeed, the hero of Utica is worth more than the butcher of Pharsalia."

13. The only reminder of the carnival in the projects for festivals came from the imagination of Fabre d'Eglantine: "On this single, solemn day of the Festival of Opinion, the law opens its mouth to all citizens on the morality and actions of public servants; the law gives free rein to the gay, whimsical imagination of the French. On this day public opinion is permitted to express itself in every possible way: songs, allusions, caricatures, lampoons, the salt of irony, and the

sarcasm of folly are to be the wages on that day of those of the people's elected representatives who have betrayed it or who have become despised or hated."

14. As at Saint-Omer, where there was a festival to mark the inauguration of the calendar "on the first rest day of the second month of the second year of the one and indivisible Republic."

15. The most rigorous attempt of the kind was J. F. Barailon's plan for the organization of the *fêtes décadaires* presented in Nivôse, Year III. He made provision for a great festival each month, and to maintain this regular division, he did not hesitate to amalgamate various commemorations: thus Messidor became the "month of the French heroes," in order to recall at once two memorable times in the history of the Republic. Barailon, *Organisation et tableau des fêtes décadaires.*

16. Rouillé d'Orfeuil, *L'alambic des lois, ou Observations de l'ami des Français sur l'homme et sur les lois* (Hispaan, 1773).

17. M.-J. Chénier, *Rapport sur les fêtes du 14 juillet et du 10 août* (Paris: Imp. nat., Year IV).

18. "There [in the festival] the child will come and read the names and glorious deeds of the heroes, there their souls will be imbued with love of country and a taste for virtue." F. A. Daubermesnil, *Rapport au nom de la commission chargée de présenter les moyens de vivifier l'esprit public* (Paris: Imp. nat., Year IV).

19. Even side by side with the schools set up for children, the Republican festivals were strictly schools for adults: "For it is there that the image becomes embodied, that the living example becomes the most eloquent of teachers. Thus all ages will be instructed successively." Heurtault-Lamerville, *Opinion sur les fêtes décadaires,* Cinq-Cents (Paris: Imp. nat., Year VI).

20. P. C. Daunou, *Discours pour l'anniversaire du 10 août* (Paris: Imp. de la République, Year III).

21. In this sense, the ancient festivals were truly a model of fertility: "You have read a hundred times the account of those military games, those triumphs that hatched heroes." Daubermesnil, *Motion d'ordre sur les moyens de vivifier l'esprit public.*

22. Lanthenas declares that it was in the festival that the Convention ought to find "the strength and means" to end the Revolution. F. Lanthenas, *Développement du projet de loi ou cadre pour l'institution des fêtes décadaires . . .* (Paris: Imp. nat., Year III). This is also the theme of the *Réflexions* that Félix Le Peletier offered to the National Convention in Floréal, Year III. He proposed, through the festivals, "to lead the Republican revolution, without crises, without convulsions, to the aim that we attributed to it." F. Le Peletier de Fargeau, *Réflexions sur le moment présent* (Paris: Imp. de R. Vatar, n.d.).

23. *Discours prononcé par Laveaux, président du Conseil des Anciens, le 9 Thermidor an VI* (Paris: Imp. nat., Year VI).

24. "I swear by duty and honor, you will never be seen to regress toward

any kind of tyranny; the bloody yoke of Terror will no longer weigh on France, and 9 Thermidor, Year II, will not have been in vain." J. Dumolard, *Discours sur la fête du 9 Thermidor an V* (Paris: Imp. nat., Year V).

25. *Discours du président du Conseil des Anciens prononcé le 5ᵉ jour complémentaire an V* (Paris: Imp. nat., Year VI).

26. J. Debry, *Motion d'ordre sur la célébration d'une fête consacrée à la souveraineté du peuple* (Paris: Imp. nat., Year VI).

27. The festival is "one of the most effective ways of fixing in everybody's head the idea that one should have of this Revolution and of operating in people's minds so desirable a unity." F. Lanthenas, *Moyens de consolider la Révolution du 9 Thermidor et de rétablir la concorde entre les vrais Républicains* (Paris: Imp. nat., Year III).

28. Ibid.

29. On this theme, one might also read M.-J. Chénier: "Doubtless there will be no question of bringing annually before our eyes the image of the rapid but characterless events that belong to any Revolution; but we shall have to consecrate in the future the immortal time when the different tyrannies have collapsed under the threat of the nations, and those great steps of reason that are crossing Europe and will strike to the ends of the earth." *Discours prononcé à la Convention nationale par M.-J. Chenier, député du departement de Seine-et-Oise, séance du 15 Brumaire an second de la République une et indivisible* (Paris: Imp. nat., n.d.).

30. L. T. Dubois-Dubais, *Discours à l'occasion de la fête du 9 Thermidor* (Paris: Imp. nat., Year VII).

31. F. Maugenest, *Motion d'ordre sur le projet de fête du 18-Fructidor* (Paris: Imp. nat., Year VI).

32. M. Lecointe-Puyraveau, *Discours prononcé pour la célébration des événements des 9 Thermidor, 13 Vendémiaire et 18 Fructidor* (Paris: Imp. nat., Year VI).

33. L. A. Rallier, *Opinion sur la formule du serment* (Paris: Imp. nat., Year VII).

34. J. Dusaulx, *Discours prononcé à la Convention nationale le 17 germinal an III* (Paris: Imp. nat., Year III).

35. Portiez de l'Oise, *Rapport et projet de décret présenté au nom du Comité d'instruction publique par Portiez de l'Oise sur la célébration de la fête du 9-Thermidor* (Paris: Imp. nat., Year III).

36. Maugenest, *Motion d'ordre*.

37. This is the theme of a certain *Opinion de Desplanques sur les institutions républicaines:* "It is therefore because the French people are free, it is because they are powerful that we must take care not to prepare them for war, and extinguish in them all seeds of ambition" (Paris: Imp. de Baudouin, n.d.).

38. J. B. Leclerc, *Nouveau projet de résolution sur les cérémonies relatives au mariage et à la naissance* (Paris: Imp. nat., Year VI).

39. Dumolard, *Discours*.

40. L. F. Grelier, *Discours en réponse aux orateurs qui ont combattu le projet de résolution relatif à la fete à célébrer le 18-Fructidor* (Paris: Imp. nat., Year VI).

41. Maugenest, *Motion d'ordre;* J. F. Philippes-Delleville, *Motion d'ordre prononcée le 10 août de la Vᵉ année républicaine* (Paris: Imp. nat., Year V).

42. Maugenest, *Motion d'ordre.*

43. "In the navigation of life, festivals are like islands in the middle of the sea, places of refreshment and repose." Dubois-Dubais, *Discours.*

44. J. M. Lequinio, *Des fêtes nationales* (Paris: Imp. nat., n.d.).

45. C. Lamy, *Motion d'ordre relative à la journée du 9-Thermidor* (Paris: Imp. nat., Year V).

46. "It is an army that, without enlistment, without leaders, and without pay, is formed in the midst of battle and is organized by a triumph." P. Baudin, *Discours pour l'anniversaire du 14 juillet* (Paris: Imp. nat., Year VII).

47. *Discours prononcé par Marbot, 26 Messidor an VI* (Paris: Imp. nat., Year III).

48. J. Debry, *Sur les fondements de morale publique* (Paris: Imp. nat., Year III).

49. When the symbol of the Bastille was missing, people complained: "Is it not true that this festival would have been more interesting if Chalgrin, who was in agreement with the minister, whose means often fall short of his zeal, had raised, in place of those columns and those insignificant canopies, a simulated Bastille that could have been stormed! This is what has just been done at Chartres . . . It is thus that, through the magic of the arts, events depicted life-size leave profound and lasting impressions in the memory." *Le patriote français,* 28 Messidor, Year VI.

50. Moreau de l'Yonne, *Motion d'ordre sur le 14 juillet* (Paris: Imp. nat., Year VI).

51. "From that day an incradicable line of demarcation was traced between the friends and enemies of Liberty . . . The debris of the Bastille became material for a separating wall erected from that moment between men who, born on the same soil, speaking the same language, nourished in the same habits, no longer had the same country." Baudin, *Discours.*

52. "Fine days of the Revolution, you saw the French nation united as a people of brothers . . . Having only one feeling, one aim, one intention." Ibid.

53. J. Debry, *Motion d'ordre sur l'anniversaire du 14 juillet* (Paris: Imp. nat., Year V).

54. Sometimes ingenuously stressed: "These two memorable times would naturally be placed side by side if, more practiced in revolution, the Constituent Assembly had been able to take advantage of the first wave of popular enthusiasm for liberty by proclaiming the Republic." Speech by Leterme-Saulnier, president of the département of the Maine-et-Loire, in Bois, *Les fêtes révolutionnaires à Angers de l'an VII.*

55. J. F. Duplantier, *Motion d'ordre sur la célébration de la fête du 10 août* (Paris: Imp. nat., Year VI).

56. "The night preceding that great day was fine; the weather was clear and serene, the greatest tranquillity reigned in Paris . . . However that gloomy silence, that profound calm had something imposing and even terrible about it." L. T. Dubois-Dubais, *Discours à l'occasion de la fête du 10 août* (Paris: Imp. nat., Year VII).

57. Ibid.: "The worm-eaten throne fourteen centuries old fell into dust, the monarchy and its false glory vanished; liberty triumphed and terrified despotism recoiled, fled, and disappeared forever from the soil of France."

58. Thus *Le journal des patriotes de 89, 25* Thermidor, Year VI: "did not the day of August 10 possess some features that record its great, terrible result?"

59. Dubois-Dubais, *Discours.*

60. *Discours prononcé par le citoyen Daunou, pour l'anniversaire du 10 août.*

61. Ibid.

62. From Pluviôse, Year II, the death of the king was celebrated. But these were then sporadic celebrations, very largely improvised, free of the superstition of the precise anniversary and indeed announced, well before the physical disappearance of the king, here and there, by festivals of "the disappearance of monarchy." It was Robespierre's great speech of Floréal, Year II, that made the festival official and gave it a national character. Thermidor made it, like the other celebrations of Robespierrist inspiration, unsure of its future; but in Nivôse, Year III, it acquired its final shape, thanks to the six articles of the order, which, for the rest of the Revolutionary period, laid down its main outlines, if not its details.

63. P. J. Audoin, *Motion d'ordre pour la formation d'une commission qui soit chargée de présenter un travail sur les institutions républicaines* (Paris: Imp. nat., Year V).

64. J. P. Boullé, *Opinion sur le projet de consacrer par des monuments et des fêtes publiques la mémorable journée du 18-Fructidor* (Paris: Imp. nat., Year VI).

65. M. P. Luminais, *Discours sur le rapport fait par Grelier sur un monument à élever et sur une fête perpetuelle à célébrer en mémoire du 18-Fructidor* (Paris: Imp. nat., Year V). Luminais contrasted this unconsidered commemoration with the others: "You have wisely turned July 14, August 10, 1 Vendémiaire into festivals. July 14 saw the formation of the first knot of fraternity among all the French people; August 10 saw the overthrow of the monarchical colossus; 1 Vendémiaire saw the foundation of the Republic; 9 Thermidor annihilated anarchy, brought back order, and prepared the fine Constitution that we are happy to celebrate today."

66. Thus Maugenest, *Motion d'ordre:* "We have overthrown the throne; let us not rejoice the hearts of princes' friends by offering them the spectacle of our divisions: these impolitic festivals can only embitter people's minds, arouse feelings of revenge, bring back reaction, and delay the return of that inner peace for which we all yearn."

67. E. Pérès, *Opinion et projet de résolution . . . concernant l'institution d'une nouvelle fête relativement aux événements du 18-Fructidor* (Paris: Imp. nat., Year VI).

68. J. Garnier, *Opinion sur l'institution d'une fête nationale pour célébrer la mémoire du 18-Fructidor:* "La conspiration était jusqu'alors inconnue et entourée de toute l'influence que la légalité donne à l'ascendant de l'opinion publique." ("Conspiracy was hitherto unknown and hedged about by all the influence that legality gives to the ascendancy of public opinion.")

69. *Rédacteur,* 20 Fructidor, Year V.

70. P. C. Daunou, *Discours sur l'anniversaire du 18-Fructidor* (Paris: Imp. nat., Year VI).

71. J. B. Leclerc du Maine-et-Loire, *Rapport sur les institutions relatives à l'état civil des citoyens* (Paris: Imp. nat., Year VI).

72. Garnier, *Opinion.*

73. "All eyes turned to the man who, on 9 Thermidor, commanded the phalanxes of free men. Barras was appointed and immediately coopted Bonaparte. Then everything changed; lukewarmness and tottering mediocrity gave way to ardent, enlightened patriotism and to the masterly genius of victory." Lecointe-Puyraveau, *Discours.*

74. Speech delivered by J.-P. Quirot, *Discours sur la fête de la liberté et les événements des 9 et 10 Thermidor* (Paris: Imp. nat., Year VII).

75. "But the great mass of the Convention, pure as the driven snow, had like him to dissipate the storms and revitalize France." A. Rollin, *Rapport sur la célébration de la fête du Ier Vendémiaire* (Paris: Imp. nat., Year VII).

76. "The sincere friend of your country does not confuse your benefits with horrors that do not belong to you." This invocation was addressed on 9 Thermidor. Y. C. Jourdain, *Motion d'ordre pour la célébration de la fête du 9-Thermidor* (Paris: Imp. nat., Year VI).

77. Quirot, *Discours.*

78. Jourdain, *Motion d'ordre.*

79. Speech by Citizen Bourgeois, president of the municipal administration of Angers, in Bois, *Les Fêtes révolutionnaires.*

80. "The legislative body at last seized its bludgeon and swore, in the month of Prairial, to save the fatherland as the French people on July 14 had sworn to love liberty and to maintain its rights. Here the nation resumed its place, which had been usurped for centuries by the hereditary supreme magistracy; there the legislative body rose to the first constitutional rank, which had been seized for months by the supreme elective magistrates." B. Guyomar, *Discours sur la célébration de la fête du 14 juillet* (Paris: Imp. nat., Year VII).

81. Boulay de la Meurthe, *Discours pour la fête du 18-Fructidor an VII* (Paris: Imp. nat., Year VII).

82. Ibid.

83. Ibid.

84. F. Lamarque, *Opinion sur la formule du serment,* Cinq-Cents (Paris: Imp. nat., Year VII).

85. Boulay de la Meurthe, *Opinion sur la formule du serment* (Paris: Imp. nat., Year VII).

86. P. J. Briot, *Discours sur la formule du serment civique* (Paris: Imp. nat., Year VII).

87. "You dare to make of the anarchists an equal fraction, opposed by you to that of the royalists, which you have counterbalanced with it for three years in your appalling political scales, which you insist on enlarging in order to impose the most solemn oaths upon it . . . You remind us constantly of the reign of terror; show a little good faith at last; add up the times and the crimes; oppose blood with blood, bones with bones, daggers with scaffolds, and ask yourselves, if you wish to hate what is horrible and destructive, which, reaction or anarchy, deserves priority in your oaths." Briot, *Discours.*

88. A. Français, *Opinion sur la fête du Iᵉʳ Vendémiaire* (Paris: Imp. nat., Year VII).

89. Eschassériaux, *Motion d'ordre,* Cinq-Cents, 16 Thermidor, Year VII.

90. Y. C. Jourdain, *Opinion sur la formule du serment civique* (Paris: Imp. nat., Year VII).

91. Boulay de la Meurthe, *Opinion.*

92. A. Montpellier (of the Aude), *Opinion sur la proposition faite par Jourdan de supprimer dans le serment la formule de haine à l'anarchie sur le serment civique,* Cinq-Cents, 8 Thermidor, Year VII.

93. J. F. Curée, *Opinion sur la motion de changer la formule du serment civique* (Paris: Imp. nat., Year VII).

94. And yet (and this reinforces the contradiction) this recital continued to be regarded as oddly useful to republics: "Republics, more than any other form of government, are subject to variations. And if one is not particularly careful to secure opinion to certain ideas, in such a way that it can neither waver nor become unsafe, intriguers will never fail to manipulate it at their will." A. Duhot, *Motion d'ordre sur les institutions républicaines* (Paris: Imp. nat., Year VII).

95. Series F′ CIII, Arch. nat. Each of the bundles contains over two thousand official accounts.

96. This was so in the Festival of the Sovereignty of the People, which was largely based on the contrast between young and old. Thus, in the Sieyès, "the twelve old men went off to dinner together, while the young followed the same principles." L 365, Arch. dép. Basses-Alpes.

97. The need for it was sometimes recalled at the bottom of the programs for the processions, like some guilty afterthought, something that one omitted to say because it went without saying, but that it would be better to clarify all the same.

98. 44 L 8, Arch. dép. Bas-Rhin, official accounts of the commune of Truchtersheim.

99. J. B. Boyer, *Méthode à suivre dans le traitement des maladies épidémiques qui règnent le plus ordinairement dans la généralité de Paris* (Paris: Imprimerie Royale, 1761).

100. See J. Debry, *Rapport et projet de résolution pour l'etablissement des écoles de Mars* (Paris: Imp. nat., Year VI).

101. See W. Butte, *Prolégomènes de l'arithmétique de la vie humaine, contenant la classification générale des talents, l'échelle des âges de l'homme et une formule d'évaluation de toutes les situations géographiques, d'après un même système* (Paris: J. G. Dentu, 1827): "There is no series of years that agrees so well with observation as the series of nine years taken as the square root of life. When one agrees that nature loves perfect multiplication, speculation united with observation allows us to see clearly that it was not able to choose any other root to effect the articulation of life." But the root of the sexual life of women was the figure 7, which imposed a new "carve-up." And that is why the "sexual death" of women occurs at forty-nine (7 times 7) and that of men at sixty-three (7 times 9).

102. Local practices also confirmed the importance of this age: in the Meuse, one moved at the age of sixteen into a different group for the game of bowls.

It was also the age at which, according to Saint-Just, one should assume the "costume of the arts," after an initiation that consisted of swimming across a river, in full view of the people, on the day of the Festival of Youth. Saint-Just, *Fragments sur les institutions républicaines* (Paris: Fayolle, 1800).

103. At Gimont, in the Gers, the instructions concerning "the duties to be fulfilled by young men of the three classes" distinguished between young men who had reached the age of twenty-one, those who had reached the age of sixteen and, lastly, "those who still attended the public schools." The first group received their civic card, the second a rifle, the third books. I. 463, Arch. dép. Gers.

104. I. 183, Arch. dép. Doubs, commune of Pierrefontaine.

105. In the Morvan, it was the age at which parents took up residence in their children's home.

106. Règlement proposé par Leclerc, du Maine-et-Loire, à la suite du rapport sur les institutions civiles.

107. *Opinion de F. Bonnaire, contre le projet de résolution présenté au nom d'une commission speciale par Roëmers, sur la cocarde nationale* (Paris: Imp. nat., Year VII). Next day, Desplanques in turn argued that the cockade should be the distinctive sign of citizenship, basing his argument on the Roman example: "Above all the right to wear the toga is perfectly relevant to the question with which I am dealing, and I would like to demonstrate to what noble sentiments it developed, what sweet celebrations took place in the family when the youth put on the civic robe, how that sign of a free, conquering people imposed respect on all nations and made every citizen proud to be a Roman . . . You would see how this simple

idea of giving a distinctive mark to the citizens of a free, powerful nation acted on the human heart."

108. Collot d'Herbois, *Quelques idées sur les fêtes décadaires, qui peuvent être appliquées à tous projets imprimés jusqu'à ce jour 30 nivôse an III* (Paris: Imp. nat., Year III).

109. Cf. L 462, Arch. dép. Côte-d'Or, official accounts of the commune of Bonnemontre.

110. The Festival of Youth involved not one rite of passage but two. The second—the delivery of the civic cards and the writing in the register of the names of those citizens who had a right to vote in the primary assemblies—was the only one that theoretically marked the passage to adulthood. Yet it was the first—the giving of arms—that, no doubt on account of the ease with which it could be represented, and perhaps too because of its coincidence with puberty, acquired the stronger emotional significance. So the wisest authors of projects for festivals wanted to combine these two initiations in one (Jean-Marie Leclerc wanted one at the age of eighteen, the average age of youth) or, on the contrary, to separate them more clearly (Pison-Dugalland wanted two quite distinct ones, the first taking place in a military festival, the second in a civic festival).

111. When Lequinio was looking for an example of an event suitable for the development of a festival, he naturally thought of a young man's enlistment in the National Guard.

112. A commensality that gave rise to some delightful accounts: "A moment later, the young men went to the table of the old men and invited them, since they were their fathers, to march at their head and to dance the farandole and to sing patriotic anthems around the Liberty Tree. Seeing this meeting, the municipal agent brought a few bottles of wine himself and invited them to drink together, which they readily agreed to do; and as they clinked glasses, they shouted, Long live the Republic."

113. F[1] C [III], Lot 8, Cajarc, Arch. nat., 2 Pluviôse, Year VII: "The old men, leaning on the shoulders of robust Republicans, seemed to regain their youth and marched gaily with a firm step."

114. Thus, many communes in the Loire-Inférieure continued for a long time to base their festivals on the occupation groups. Furthermore, there is no trace in those same communes of the ceremonial of the ages, even in those festivals of which it constitutes the entire ritual, as on the day of the Festival of the Sovereignty of the People. The most striking evidence of this mutual exclusion is provided by Mouren's manuscript, which relates the various forms assumed by the Festival of the Tarasque during the Revolution. In 1792, the National Guards of Alès raided Tarascon and burned the effigy of the Tarasque (an amphibious monster said to have haunted the Rhône near Tarascon, where its effigy is still carried in feast-day processions). In 1793 and 1794, there was no festival, and Mouren, among the reasons that he gives for this eclipse, mentions the

dissolution of the guilds: for the parade of the various trades was an essential element in the traditional festival. In 1795, there was an unexpected resurgence. "The Festival of the Tarasque," writes Mouren, "took place as usual, except that the guilds did not pass by." But what took the place of the variety of the old spectacle provided by the guilds was, as if quite naturally, the variety of the age groups: "The adult men ran with the Tarasque in the usual way; this race was followed by two other small Tarasques, that of the fifteen-year-old young men and that of the young ones." Was this simply evidence of the need to fill the void left by the disappearance of the guilds?

115. Old age and youth, furthermore, may themselves be seen as allegories of equality. One thinks of Bernardin de Saint-Pierre's remark, "Old age, like childhood, brings all men to the same level and returns them to nature." Saint-Pierre, *Etudes de la nature*.

116. P. Esparron, *Essai sur les âges de l'homme* (Paris: Imprimerie de Crapelet, 1803).

VIII. The Future of the Festival

1. J.-J. Rousseau, *Discours d'économie politique* (Geneva: E. du Villard fils, 1758).

2. Heurtault-Lamerville, *Opinion sur les fêtes décadaires*, 28 Messidor, Year VI: "Your commissions are entrusted with two great tasks: the one to instruct children in the schools and the other to form men in institutions." (Paris: Imp. nat., Year VI).

3. Gay-Vernon, *Opinion sur les institutions relatives à l'état civil des citoyens et le projet de la commission présenté par Leclerc*, 21 Frimaire, Year VI (Paris: Imp. nat., Year VI).

4. On this point, see J. C. Bailleul's speech to the Council of the Five Hundred, in the great debate concerning public education: the national festivals serve "to fill the void in men's hearts." They assist books, "which certainly do not provide all that is needed." J. C. Bailleul, *Motion d'ordre sur la discussion relative à l'instruction publique*, 13 Germinal, Year VII (Paris: Imp. nat., Year VII).

5. S. Sherlock, *Opinion sur la nécessité de rendre l'instruction publique commune à tous les enfants des Français* (Paris: Imp. nat., Year VII).

6. This was the wish of Collot d'Herbois, *Quelques idées sur les fêtes décadaires* (Paris: Imp. nat., Year III).

7. Jean Guineau-Dupré, *Opinion sur la résolution relative aux fêtes décadaires* (Paris: Imp. nat., Year VI).

8. "A power," said Français, "that is born in the contact between souls." *Opinion sur la fête du 1 Vendémiaire*, 17 Fructidor, Year VII (Paris: Imp. nat., Year VII).

9. F1 CIII Rhône 5, Arch. nat.

10. B. Barère, *Rapport sur la suppression des repas civiques et des fêtes sectionnaires,* 28 Messidor, Year II (Paris: Imp. nat., Year II).

11. J. B. Leclerc, *Rapport sur les institutions relatives à l'état civil des citoyens* (Paris: Imp. nat., Year VI).

12. Creuzé-Latouche, *Opinion sur le second projet de la commission concernant les fêtes décadaires et la célébration des mariages* (Paris: Imp. nat., Year VI).

13. Ibid.

14. Thus, at Lyons-la-Forêt, in Year VII, advantage was taken of the festival of August 10 to make a solemn distribution of the first fifty copies of the "Metre," intended for the merchants of Lyon. See M. A. Dollfus, "Les Fêtes et cérémonies populaires à Lyons-la-Forêt à la fin du siècle," in *Revue des sociétés savntes de Haute-Normandie* (1958).

15. Creuzé-Latouche, *Opinion.*

16. "Speeches bore, spectacles entertain," said M. N. Brothier, *Rapport sur la résolution du 3 thermidor ayant pour objet de faire observer comme jours de repos décades et fêtes nationales* (Paris: Imp. nat., Year VI). And N. F. Thiessé: "Readings! Readings of newspapers! And readings of *journaux décadaires,* what is more!" *Opinion de Thiessé sur le 2ᵉ projet présenté par la Commission des institutions republicaines, le 19 messidor an VI* (Paris: Imp. nat., Year VI).

17. 12 L 6, Arch. dép. Bas-Rhin.

18. Ibid.

19. On this theme, see the speech delivered at Tulle by Citizen Chauffour, president of the central administration of the Corrèze, on 2 Pluviôse, Year V, FICIII Corrèze, Arch. nat. Citizen Chauffour sees the festival as an open-air history lesson, a summary in images: "What the study of history teaches to a few men in the silence of the study, the public commemoration of major events of concern to them engraves in the memory of good citizens. Like a work of painting, whose reduced proportions nevertheless offer a resemblance to the model, the series of national festivals is a small but proportioned frame, in which nothing truly essential to the instruction of the people that observes it is omitted . . . Without work, without expense, the people can follow the chain of events that preceded it."

20. "We learn while playing": this was the motto carried at Péronne, on 30 Vendémiaire, Year III, by the schoolchildren. See G. Ramon, *La Révolution à Péronne* (Péronne: Quentin, 1878–1880).

21. See, for example, Mortier-Duparc: children and adolescents receive "like soft wax the impressions that one skilfully gives them." *Rapport sur la distribution proposée du portrait du général Marceau* (Paris: Imp. nat., Year VI).

22. This is one of Jean Debry's favorite themes: "The French nation, of all the most susceptible to the culture of all the talents and capable of all the virtues, is at the same time, if I may say so, endowed with so great a mobility that to keep it at its tasks, to preserve its tastes and best qualities, it seems that they

have to be transformed into passions and always surrounded with some marks of prestige." *Motion d'ordre sur la célébration d'une fête consacrée à la souveraineté du peuple* (Paris: Imp. nat., Year VI).

23. L. Joubert, *Opinion sur le projet de résolution présenté par la Commission d'instruction publique sur l'organisation des écoles primaires* (Paris: Imp. nat., Year VII).

24. On this theme, see Eschassériaux l'aîné, *Réflexions et projet de décret sur les fêtes décadaires* (Paris: Imp. nat., Year III).

25. See J. B. Leclerc, *Rapport sur l'établissement d'écoles spéciales de musique* (Paris: Imp. nat., Year VII).

26. In *Lettres d'un fermier de Pennsylvanie,* a work published in the middle of the upheavals of the American Revolution, Diderot comments: "Can one not sense how easily souls endowed with a little generosity must drink of these principles and become intoxicated by them? Ah! My friend! Fortunately tyrants are more stupid than evil. They disappear; the lessons of great men fructify; and the spirit of a nation grows great."

27. Michel-Edme Petit, *Opinion sur l'éducation publique, prononcée le 1ᵉʳ octobre 1793* (Paris: Imp. nat., n.d.).

28. Cf. R. de Barennes, *Opinion sur la résolution du 6 Thermidor, relative aux fêtes décadaires* (Paris: Imp. nat., Year VI). Barennes, who notes the power exerted over men by "the crudest images," expresses concern at the "nudity of the Revolutionary festivals."

29. On this theme, see J. F. L. Grobert, *Des fêtes publiques chez les Modernes* (Paris: Imprimerie de Didot Jeune, Year X). "Studied gestures, concerted movements, and all that seemed ridiculous to the short-sighted, is indispensable in representation and above all in that of the festival."

30. J. J. L. Bosquillon, *Discours prononcé en présentant au Conseil des Cinq-Cents un exemplaire de la Constitution de l'an III* (Paris: Imp. nat., Year VII).

31. Leclerc, *Rapport sur l'établissement d'écoles.*

32. See, for example, G. M. Raymond, *De la peinture considérée dans ses effets sur les hommes en général et de son influence sur les moeurs et le gouvernement des peuples* (Paris: Pougens, Year VII); F. R. J. de Pommereul, *De l'art de voir dans les beaux-arts* (Paris: Bernard, Year VI); Emeric-David, *Musée olympique de l'école vivante des beaux-arts* (Paris: Imprimerie de Plassan, 1796); J. B. Chaussard, *Essai philosophique sur la dignité des arts* (Paris: Imprimerie des sciences et des arts, Year VI).

33. J. B. Gence, *Vues sur les fêtes publiques et appréciation de ces vues à la fête de Marat* (Paris: Imprimerie de Renaudière j., Year II). There is also the Chevalier de Jaucourt's statement in the *Encyclopédie:* "Those who have governed the peoples in every period have always made use of paintings and statues, the better to inspire in them the feelings that they wanted to give them, whether religious or political." There is also the view, repeatedly expressed, that in painting anyone can judge, since doing so requires no particular competence.

34. M. de Girardot, "Les fêtes de la Révolution, de 1790 à l'An VIII," in

Annales de la Société Académique de Nantes et du département de Loire Inférieure, vol. 28 (Nantes, 1857).

35. Raymond, *De la peinture.*

36. E.-M. Falconet, *Réflexions sur la sculpture* (Paris: Prault, 1761).

37. See C. L. Corbet, *Lettre au citoyen Lagarde, secrétaire général du Directoire executif, sur les esquisses et projets de monuments pour les places publiques de Paris . . . , suivie d'une réponse au citoyen Mercier . . .* (Paris: Desenne, Year V).

38. Even when the writings on the festivals do not bear out such a radicalism, the dependence on spectacle of the festival is always clearly stressed: "Theaters and spectacles of all kinds are merely entertainments after the festival. One cannot consider them essential parts of the festival itself, unless plays especially written for the subject of the day were performed in one of the theaters." Grobert, *Des fêtes publiques.*

39. Where the criticism of the footlights is concerned, nothing could be more significant than those texts in which it is proposed to convert the churches into venues for the festivals, to abolish all separation, and to move the altar to the center of the ceremonial space. See, for example, *Projet de cérémonie à l'usage des fêtes nationales, décadaires et sans-culottides de la République française, saisies dans un but moral, combinées dans leur rapports généraux et rendues propres à être célébrées dans les moindres communes . . .* (Paris, Year II).

40. Mercier, *Du théâtre.*

41. See A. Français, *Idée de la fête qui doit être célébrée à Grenoble le 20 prairial en l'honneur de l'Etre Suprême* (Grenoble: A. Giroud, 1794).

42. One can detect the same kind of repugnance in the clear reluctance to use such expressions as "theater of events" and "theater of the Revolution," with their implication that the Revolution was no more than a theatrical stage. Bernardin de Saint-Pierre, gave early voice to this view: "The Maréchal de Saxe, our historians tell us, was crowned with bay on the theater of the nation; as if the nation were composed of actors and its senate was a theater."

43. Merlin de Thionville, *Opinion sur les fêtes nationales* (Paris: Imp. nat., Year III).

44. Gay-Vernon attacks those who wanted to ban from the Republic anything that might strengthen it: "To forbid liberty chanting, forms of words, and ceremonies that might add to its charms on the grounds that monarchy and fanaticism have had theirs; to banish from the Republican temple the attractions of the arts, eloquence, poetry, and music because the king's chapel echoed to their sounds . . ." Gay-Vernon, *Opinion.*

45. P. Courteault, *La Révolution et les théâtres à Bordeaux* (Paris: Perrin, 1926).

46. As was done at Niort, on October 9, 1791, for the publication of the Constitution. Cf. H. Clouzot, *L'ancien théâtre en Poitou* (Niort: Clouzot, 1901).

47. M. Laurain, "Une fête civique à Clermont (de l'Oise)," *Mémoires de la Société archéologique et historique de Clermont* 1 (1904).

48. *Révolutions de Paris,* 20 Brumaire, Year II, article attributed to Momoro.

49. Quatremère de Quincy notes that allegory is the very language of the Revolution. This declaration is all the more interesting in that one finds it in a renegade report of 1801, to the general council of the département of the Seine, which abandoned festivals but kept July 14 and the sensualist ideology. Broadly speaking, it is a good indication of the Revolutionary consensus. F¹ C IV Seine 1, Arch. nat., Procès-verbaux du Conseil général.

50. J. Lacombe, *Le spectacle des beaux-arts* (Paris: Hardy, 1758).

51. See *L'ami des lois,* 9 Ventôse, Year IV.

52. See, for example, L. S. Mercier's commentary on the statue of Descartes: "What does it matter to the people that the author of vortices and subtle matter, Descartes, was a novelist or an exact genius? When it sees the statue pass, it will look no different to it than the statue of the Great Lama." *Discours sur René Descartes* (Paris: Imp. nat., Year IV).

53. The connection between saying and showing is charmingly expressed in these verses (F¹ CIII Eure 11, Arch. nat.), sung at Conches, to the tune of the nuns of the Order of Visitation, for the Festival of the King's Death:

> Français si vous voulez apprendre
> L'horreur des rois à vos neveux
> Tous les ans *montrez*-leur la cendre
> Du Roy tyran de leurs ayeux
> Qu'ils *lisent* sur le bois tragique
> Ces deux mots en lettres de sang
> Mort au monstre mort au tyran
> Qui trahira la République . . .

> (Frenchmen, if you wish to teach
> A horror of kings to your nephews,
> Show them every year the ashes
> Of their ancestors' tyrant-king,
> Let them read on the tragic wood
> These two words in letters of blood:
> Death to the monster, death to the tyrant
> Who betrayed the Republic.)

54. L 140, Arch. dép. Charente.

55. For Bernardin de Saint-Pierre, inscriptions were the means for the dead and for inanimate objects to speak to the living, thus establishing a correspondence "from an invisible nature to visible nature; from a distant time to the present." *Etudes de la nature* (Paris: P. F. Didot le Jeune, 1784).

56. See Cabanis's speech when, on 18 Brumaire, Year VII, he offered the Councils the dictionary of the Academy (Paris: Imp. nat., Year VI).

57. See, for example, what Charles Villette wrote about it: the aerostat must carry "various small packets of pamphlets, suspended by so many strings. To the strings would be stuck wicks of various lengths that would burn at various speeds and finally break the string; as a result, there would fall, at intervals, the Rights of Man or the Constitution, the Reform of the Clergy or the Suppression of the Religious Orders, measures taken to suppress feudalism or nobility. So simple a method would sow those leaves here and there throughout the German country-side until some good peasant picked them up. Of course it would be necessary to translate them previously into the language of the enemy country. This would be a crusade of a new kind, a means of conquering the peoples for Liberty without even striking a blow." *Lettres choisies.*

58. In a contribution to the Clermont Conference, Judith Schlanger offers a similar study of the three programs for festivals drawn up by David and of the commentary that David devoted, in the Convention, to the projects for raising a statue to the French people on the Pont-Neuf. Now, the visual expressiveness of that statue ought to be sufficient in itself, for what was proposed was a colossal statue, fifteen meters high, which was to dominate by its sheer mass a compli-cated pediment made up of an amalgam of statues removed from Notre-Dame. It would be, therefore, a Hercules, an association that would be strengthened still more by the presence of a club. In the hand holding the club would be the figures of Liberty and Equality, "holding each other tightly" (a curious ratio in propor-tion between these tiny allegories, crouching in a giant hand, but they were to bring out the filial relationship between the French people and Liberty and Equal-ity). But this allegorical overdetermination still did not satisfy David; he also wanted to write, "in capital letters," on the statue's forehead "Light"; on his breast "Nature, Truth"; on his arms "Strength"; on his hands "Labor." Taking this ex-emplary body, which carries words, and the programs for festivals drawn up by David, Judith Schlanger examines the relationship between the verbal and the visual, which seems to her to be a double one. On the one hand, the inscription reinforces the figuration in a redundant manner, but, on the other hand, the visual figuration cedes to the inscription, which is not, therefore, simply an or-nament that the vision could do without, but the very basis of the vision, at one and the same time its raw material and its purpose.

59. David, *Discours prononcé le 29 mars 1793, en offrant un tableau de sa compo-sition représentant Michel Lepelletier au lit de mort* (Paris: Imp. nat., n.d.).

60. Peguy, *Clio.*

61. Robespierre comments: "These movements might lead opinion to the point at which it must be directed by more tranquil discussion."

62. See, for example, *Considérations sur le gouvernement de Pologne* (Paris: Defer de Maisonneuve, 1790): "I regard it as fortunate that they have a particular dress. Take care to preserve this advantage; do exactly the opposite of what that so vaunted tsar did. Let neither the king nor the senators nor any public man ever

wear any other clothes than those of the nation, and let no Pole dare to appear at the court dressed as a Frenchman."

63. Schlanger, "Théâtre révolutionnaire."

64. J. P. F. Duplantier, *Opinion sur l'établissement des écoles primaires nationales* (Paris: Imp. nat., Year VII). Duplantier regards substitution as much more difficult than institution, for it requires a successful graft, that of a free state on a corrupt trunk."

65. J. Rameau, *Aperçu philosophique et politique sur la célébration des décadis et des fêtes nationales* (Paris: Imp. nat., n.d.).

66. J. Terral, *Réflexions sur les fêtes décadaires* (Paris: Imp. nat., Year III).

IX. Popular Life and the Revolutionary Festival

1. On this point, see Jam, "*La Marseillaise.*"

2. A. Varagnac, *Civilisation traditionnelle et genres de vie* (Paris: Albin Michel, 1948).

3. Not, of course, that the Revolution invented statistical investigation, but the latter was certainly begun, well before the obsession with policing took root, through the dividing up of the country into départements, as if this dividing up, this fragmentation, required specifically the collection of data and created an urgent need to draw up a table of the new fragmented France.

4. This was the order proposed to the commissioners of the directory by the printed questionnaires of the minister of the interior: the public spirit, public education, general policing, harvests and food supplies, country policing, laws concerning worship, almshouses, houses of detention, contributions, highways, agriculture, commerce, armed force, epidemics, epizootics. It was under the heading "public spirit" (or, occasionally, "general policing") that the commissioners were invited to fill in their observations on customs.

5. One may follow the stages of this will to knowledge: the studies accumulated under the Constituent Assembly to determine the extent and configuration of the départements, then the obligation that, in its obsession with surveillance, the Convention laid on its representatives and administrations to account for local resources, commerce, and industry (regulated by the decree of 14 Frimaire, Year II, the same that organized the Revolutionary government and that required of all civil servants, in every branch of the administration, an exact and detailed account of their operations); and lastly, the attempts made by François de Neufchâteau during his two periods at the Ministry of the Interior to obtain annual accounts from the departmental administrations ("an excellent way of bringing before the eyes of the executive directory a general picture of the state of France"), then, in his second ministry, his attempts to invite the commissioners of the executive directory attached to the departmental administrations to make personal tours of their départements.

6. On this collection of information, see A. Saint-Léger, *Le bibliographe moderne* (1918–1919); Mathiez, *Revue d'histoire moderne et contemporaine* 4 (1902); and J.-C. Perrot, *Annales historiques de la Révolution française* no. 224 (1976).

7. Much less incomplete and with far fewer gaps than Mathiez says, they are to be found in the boxes of the series F¹ C III, Arch. nat.; they are often arranged as an overall view of the département; they give an important place to political affairs and show great concern to define, or rather to diagnose, "public opinion."

8. Neufchâteau, *Recueil des lettres circulaires*.

9. The commissioner for the Maine-et-Loire, F¹ C III, Maine-et-Loire VI, Arch. nat.

10. We have a lot of information about the men who wrote. At the municipal level, certain files provide a list of the commissions, together with a note on the degree of civic fervor. They include middle merchants, notaries, officers of health, married priests, clerks of the court, post office managers, records officers, and a whole intermediary, hard-working world of small-town bourgeois. With the central commissioners one rises a notch in the social hierarchy to reach the communication network of the Enlightenment: enlightened bourgeois, who are members of the academies, correspond with the Institute, have a knowledge of agronomy (like Heurtault de Lamerville), and are concerned about public education and law.

11. The term, which had come from England, where the language of politics had borrowed it in the eighteenth century from the language of religion, was, in France, quite new. There is no listing for *esprit public* in Trévoux or in the *Encyclopédie*. The dictionary of the Academy does not include it until the sixth edition. But its career in France was not to be very long. In the 1877 edition, the term has already become neutralized; defined in 1823 as "the opinion that is formed in a nation about matters of concern to its glory and prosperity," it was, by 1877, no more than "the opinion that is formed concerning objects of general interest." We are already moving toward the verdict of Robert's dictionary: "obsolete."

12. On this point we have the opinion of the commissioner of the Bouches-du-Rhône: "Here public opinion is the supreme arbiter, and the bloody vicissitudes of our political stage, the continual divergence of opinions, and all the pretensions of self-seeking have substituted the man for the fatherland. There can be no public opinion where there is nothing but speculations." F¹ C III, Bouches-du-Rhône 7, Arch. nat.

13. The commissioner for the Pas-de-Calais expressed surprise at no longer finding in his territory simplicity of morals, docile obedience to the laws, and rustic virtues: F¹ CIII, Pas-de-Calais 8, Arch. nat. The commissioner for the Hautes-Pyrénées declared that ten years before, the people of his area had still been "in the state of nature." F¹ CIII, Hautes-Pyrénées 6, Arch. nat.

14. F¹ C III, Cher 6, Arch. nat.

15. F¹ C III, Pyréenées-Orientales 4, Arch. nat.: "I have found cantons in which, because they did not understand the French language, citizens had been unable to grasp what I have said when running over the various objects contained in the letter instructing me to make tours."

16. F¹ C III, Meurthe 7, Arch. nat.

17. F¹ C III, Finistère 3, Arch. nat.

18. F¹ C III, Basses-Pyrénées 7, Arch. nat.

19. F¹ C III, Hautes-Pyrénées 6, Arch. nat.

20. It would be overhasty to believe, as an excessively trusting Mathiez suggests, that it would be enough in many cases to publish the series of monthly accounts of the central commissioners in order to have "a complete, authentic, and living political history" of that département. This would be to underestimate the men put in charge of the investigation and the circumstances in which it took place. It is also to ignore the pressures involved: the investigators had to please their superiors, and their judgment would be judged. So reality can be grasped in these texts only in an infinitely less direct way, and the positive information that they provide is not so much objective evidence as information geared to administrative requirements.

21. F¹ C III, Morbihan 6, Arch. nat.

22. Here, for example, is the commissioner for the Alpes-Maritimes complaining of the inertia of his municipal officers: "They have turned a blind eye to the illuminations of the bell towers and church doors, to bonfires on days of celebration, all external signs . . . they have also ignored the ringing of bells in the mountain communes." F¹ C III, Alpes-Maritimes 2, Arch. nat.

23. These signs were now regarded as "external" in another sense: they were no longer prosecuted inside the churches. This was a result of the law of 7 Vendémiaire, Year IV, a legacy from the Convention to the Directoire. Worship was henceforth free, no one was to disturb it, but none of it was to appear in public: neither costume nor calvaries nor crosses in the cemeteries nor bell towers, and there was to be no external sign to indicate a church.

24. F¹ C III, Nord 7, Arch. nat. The same remark is to be found in a report by the commissioner for the Vendée.

25. F¹ C III, Haut-Rhin 6, Arch. nat.

26. As A. Baudouin was to show only a few years later in his study *Les signaux des Gaulois:* "In the cities one has no notion of what the piercing clamor of our countrymen is like."

27. A sworn enemy, it seems, of the commissioner for the Hérault. F C III, Hérault 9, Arch. nat.

28. This probably refers to a charivari; but the commissioner for the Côte-d'Or prefers to speak of "an insurrection lasting five hours." F¹ C III, Côte-d'Or 6, Arch. nat.

29. Although there are examples of this, notably in the Allier.

30. See F¹ C III, Cher 6, Arch. nat.: "Is it not a saddening thing that the Republican calendar, a masterpiece for dividing up the year, so simple, so easy, has not been universally adopted and that people persist in following the vulgar era, which begins at no remarkable time of the year and in which the months are not equal?"

31. At the beginning of the Revolution, the administrators often hesitated to forbid dancing. Having first forbidden it, they sometimes agreed to alter their decision. On this point, one might consult F. Rouvière, *Dimanches révolution-naires: Etudes sur l'histoire de la Révolution dans le Gard* (Nîmes: Catélan, 1888), who relates incidents that occurred at Bagnols (Gard) in 1791 after the prohibition of the votive festival, and reproduces an interesting petition from the citizen-esses of the town of Bagnols to the administrators forming the directory of the département of the Gard: "In accordance with a custom whose origin is lost in the mists of time and which is almost general in this province, the young men of the town of Bagnols hold each year a local festival or vote on September 8 or on the following Sunday, according to the wishes of the municipal officers at the time. All the inhabitants, without distinction, may share the amusement of this festival, which, by virtue of the variety of its exercises, is suitable to all ages, to people of every temperament, and to both sexes." The plea met with success.

Throughout the Revolution, administrative severity increased against dancing. On this point, see the file on the festival from Year VI to Year VIII in the departmental archives of the Rhône (L 454). In Germinal, Year VII, it took nothing less than a major general to succeed in "preventing any kind of music that might have dancing for its object."

32. F¹ C III, Landes 5, Arch. nat.

33. See F¹⁷ 1243, Arch. nat., the letter to the minister of the interior from a watchmaker of Dijon in Pluviôse, Year VII: "The carnival days have been celebrated this year in such a way as to make it quite clear that it will be impossible to stop them."

34. F¹ C III, Lozère 5, Arch. nat.

35. On this point see F¹ C III, Morbihan 6, Arch. nat.

36. This theme is not new. This was how the procurator Bignon, in a letter written in 1764 to the judge chatelain, describes the patronal festivals of the region of Thaumiers: "It is there that the confused assembly of local people and foreign workers, mingling together to enjoy at once abundant debauchery, becoming tumultuous in very little time, provides the spectacle of the most cruel fury. It is there that sometimes the young inhabitants of a neighboring parish come and exchange defiance and insults with the young men of another parish; it is there that this populace, no less terrible than guilty, takes umbrage at the sight of the ministers of the law." See Ribault, "Divertissement populaire et turbulence sociale, les fêtes baladoires dans la région de Thaumiers au XVIIIᵉ siècle."

37. L 300, Arch. dép. Indre.

38. F¹ C III, Mine-et-Loire 6, Arch. nat.: "To the advantages already cited," writes the commissioner, "should be added the fact that these assemblies were often an occasion for reconciliation between the families."

39. On this theme, see L 286, Arch. dép. Bouches-du-Rhône: the municipal agent of Cuges comments on 28 Prairial, Year V, on what had taken place on the feast day of Saint Anthony, the local patron saint: "The two parties met and marched together with us to celebrate this festival according to the wishes of the inhabitants."

40. It was in their name, for example, that the citizens of the Lot-et-Garonne submitted a petition for "the reestablishment of the times of the old year." See F¹ C III, Lot-et-Garonne 11, Arch. nat.: "The citizens have explained to us that from time immemorial their fellow citizens were in the custom of meeting in their commune squares, where dancing took place."

41. On this theme, see the letter already cited from the Dijon watchmaker (F¹⁷ 1243, Arch. nat.) to the minister of the interior: "It is your responsibility to make certain that these noisy festivals have no connection with popery; and since it is impossible to destroy them, to identify them with the Republic. You would achieve this by fixing their dates; this would upset the priests' calculations by destroying the connection that exists between them at Easter.

"If you declared that 1, 2, and 3 Ventôse were to be the only days on which the carnival may take place and that those who wore masks, disguises, or travesty on any other days than those would be punished, the purpose of those festivals would be rejoicing that winter was over and that fine weather was returning."

42. See, for example, the criticism made by Rouillé d'Orfeuil of the patronal festival, so typical of the thinking of the Enlightenment, in *L'alambic des lois*.

43. Indeed in one case, we have an enormous mass of documentation at our disposal; in the other, since the facts of folklore had the greatest difficulty in gaining entry into historical texts, and generally, as Van Hennep reminds us, in a repressive way, as when they led to disorders that required punishment, we have only local monographs on the Maytime traditions, and even these do not necessarily deal with regions for which there is abundant documentation from the Revolutionary period.

44. This is evident in its tireless resurgence in times of revolution (1830, 1848, 1871) and even, on a more modest scale, in times of Republican struggle (1902, 1906); or again, this time in the opposite direction, by the determination with which Liberty Trees were extirpated during periods of restoration—the return of the monarchy, or to order in 1815, or in the years immediately after 1848. There is something extraordinary in this determination: when, in 1852, the mayor asked the prefects that certain of these trees be spared—on the grounds that, in this village it was a beautiful feature, or in that village gave welcome shade on fair days—the same brutal answer came back: "Remove it!" There is also something extraordinary in the resistance aroused among the inhab-

itants against the removal, or even the lopping, of their trees: at Bayeux, a peaceful place if ever there was one, the decision taken by the prefect in 1820 to cut off a few branches from the Liberty Tree started a riot. We should also remember that the major crime imputed to M. de Rénal by the liberals of Verrières was the mutilation of the plane trees in the main avenue.

45. Abbé Grégoire, *Essai historique et patriotique sur les arbres de la liberté* (Paris: Desenne, Year II).

46. This was brought to my attention by G. Bussière's *Etudes historiques sur la Révolution en Périgord* (Bordeaux: Lefèvre, Chollet, 1877–1903).

47. Several other documents have made it possible to augment this repressive source: a quite special place is accorded to letters from the parish priests of the Sarladais (these are their answers to the investigation carried out on the seditious May trees by M. de Ronchamp, the provost general), to be found in the Archives nationales and in the printed report, which was very well known, though its wealth was not sufficiently exploited by the civil commissioners sent by the king into the département of the Lot to investigate the disturbances: *Rapport de MM. J. Godard et L. Robin, commissaires civils envoyés par le roi dans le département du Lot* (Paris: Imp. nat., 1791).

I have also used letters to the National Assembly from the administrator of the directory of the Lot describing the disturbances in their département and denouncing those municipalities that were too slow in reacting and punishing: series D XIV, Arch. nat.; also in series D XIV, there is a memorandum for the provinces of the Périgord, the Quercy, and the Rouergue.

48. E. Sol, *La Révolution en Quercy* (Paris: A. Picard, 1930–1932).

49. On this point, see Pierre Caron, "Le mouvement antiseigneurial de 1790, dans le Sarladais et le Quercy," *Bulletin d'histoire économique de la Révolution* no 2 (1912).

50. D XXIX 73, Arch. nat.

51. Godard and Robin, *Rapport.* The key words of their text are "to enlighten" and "to cure." What they had in mind was curing fears and spreading enlightenment. The first part of their report ends with a hymn of trust in the progress of the Enlightenment: "Since the mind of man is the same in every country, it is also capable everywhere of receiving such enlightenment if offered it, and only a few measures are still required to dissipate the clouds that, in certain places, still obscure it."

52. B 845, Arch dép. Dordogne.

53. B 844, Arch. dép. Dordogne.

54. An astute lord left this amusing account: "I had my pew taken out of the church of Lherm by a joiner under the pretext of having it repaired. I likewise had a pew that I have in the church of Saint-André removed and had the weathercocks taken down from the chateau roof." The insurrectional troops arrived nonetheless, but "they were given, with such good grace, as much to eat and

drink as they wished, that this did much to help the good people who were there to contain the others, who, after asking for riddles and rent measures loudly demanded the deeds." And what was the outcome of this astute behavior? "Thank God, there was only a May tree planted on the hill, a few faggots burned, and, that evening, the lane from here to Lherm was strewn with individuals drunk on the wine that I had had to lavish on them." Baron de Vassal de Saint-Gily, *Souvenir des troubles occasionnés par la trop célèbre Révolution de 1789*, 10 J, Fonds des familles de Vassal et de Saint-Gily, Arch. dép. Lot.

55. This was a typical reaction to the presence of private pews inside churches: "In several parish churches, one sees too many fixed pews and armrests, belonging to ordinary private individuals, All these pews mask part of the churches and make them too small; they interfere with divine service and are places of distinction that must be banned from the temples of the Lord and in his presence, except for his ministers." Letter sent on February 17, 1790, to the National Assembly by a barrister of Langogne in the Gévaudan, D XIV, Arch. nat.

56. B 845, Arch. dép. Dordogne.

57. Ibid.

58. An interpretation that is confirmed by many of the priests' questions. "My parishioners were led astray," wrote the parish priest of Aubas. "They followed the torrent," said the parish priest of Cazenac. D XXIX 73, Arch. nat.

59. On this point, see the deposition of a student in surgery at Saint-Léon de Rouffignac, February 2, 1790, B 844, Arch. dép. Dordogne.

60. Arch. dép. Dordogne, deposition of A. Rastouil, mayor of the parish.

61. D XXIX 73, Arch. nat.

62. Letter from the principal inhabitants of the parish of Lamonzie-Montastruc "to denounce the disturbances, church pews burned, chapel railings removed." D XXIX 73, Arch. nat.

63. This was the defense offered by the inhabitants of Sainte-Mesme. B 844 Arch. dép. Dordogne.

64. D XXIX 73. Arch. nat.

65. Ibid.

66. They are "uniform signs of insurrection," wrote the administrators of the directory of the Lot to the National Assembly on September 24, 1790. D XIV 5, Arch. nat.

67. Loys, deputy of the Périgord, *Mémoire pour les provinces du Périgord, du Quercy et du Rouergue* (n.d.).

68. January 31, 1790. B 844, Arch. dép. Dordogne.

69. Godard and Robin, *Rapport.*

70. At Saint-Léon de Rouffignac. B 844 Arch. dép. Dordogne.

71. D XIV 5, Arch. nat.

72. On this point see M. Dieudonné, prefect, *Statistique du département du*

Nord, vol. 1 (Year XII): "The planting of a May tree was still in many places a sign of fondness for the magistrate, the lord, the parish priest of the place when they were worthy of this feeling. Happy the times when so simple a practice was an effective judgment!"

73. D XXIX 73, Arch. nat.

74. I owe this information to Jacques Rougerie.

75. On this point, see D XXIX 73, Arch. nat., "Pièce adressée à Monsieur le Prévôt général de Guienne."

76. The statues of Liberty, or the girls and women entrusted with the task of representing Liberty, were also quite often, at least until the spring of 1794, referred to as "liberty-women."

77. D XIX 73, Arch. nat.

78. On the initiative of the Société des amis de la Constitution of Périgueux.

79. Out of an enormous bibliography, several works are worthy of particular mention: A. Van Gennep, *Le folklore du Dauphiné* (Paris: G. P. Maisonneuve, 1932–1933), and *Le folklore de la Flandre* (Paris: G. P. Maisonneuve, 1936); G. de Wismes, *Coutumes de mai en Bretagne* (Bergerac: J. Pouget, 1908), and *Les fêtes religieuses en Bretagne* (Nantes: Biroche et Dautais, 1902); E. O. James, *The Tree of Life: An Archaeological Study* (Leiden: E. J. Brill, 1966); L. Guillemin, *Chroniques locales: Pendant la Révolution, chronique d'un bourgeois d'Aire* (Aire: L. Guillemin, 1894–1900); E. Sol, *Le vieux Quercy* (Paris: E. Nourry, 1929); G. Rocal, *Le vieux Périgord* (Toulouse: E.Œ. Guitard, 1927); E. Traver, *Les bachelleries, du Poitou, du Berry et de l'Angoumois* (Melle: Traver, 1933); J. H. Philpot, *The Sacred Tree in Religion and Myth* (London: Macmillan, 1897).

There are also several useful articles: P. Sébillot, "Usages du mois de mai," *Revue des traditions populaires* 3 (1888); H. de Barrau, "Mais plantés devant les églises," *Mémoires de la Société des lettres, sciences et arts de l'Aveyron* 4 (1842–1843); J. Bédier, "Les fêtes de mai et les origines de la poésie lyrique au Moyen Age," *Revue des deux mondes,* May 1, 1896; L. Bonnaud, "Note sur les mais d'honneur élevés en Limousin après les élections municipales," *Bulletin de la Société archeologique et historique du Limousin* (1960) A. Perrier, "Les arbres de mai et les arbres de la liberté," ibid.

80. *Revue du folklore français* 11 (Jan.-March 1940).

81. Interesting symbols because they imply a recrimination or at least a summons. See J. Vandereuse, "A propos d'une coutume matrimoniale du département de la Loire," *Le folklore Brabançon* (March 1951).

82. A Bernard, *Recherches sur les chevaliers de l'Arquebuse et les chevaliers de l'Arc de Tournus* (Mâcon: L. Chollar, 1884).

83. At Guéret, on May 17, 1792, a procession went and planted a sixty-foot-tall tree. A notice read, "Citizens, friends of the Constitution and of Equality have consecrated this tree to liberty and concord . . ." Villard, *Les arbres de la liberté à Guéret et dans le département de la Creuse.*

84. *Bulletin de la Société historique et artistique du diocèse de Meaux* (1968),

extract from the records of the municipality of Montévrain. As the Revolution advanced, the number of these suspect trees increased, either because they were planted under the patronage of great persons (one, for example, was planted in front of the Duc de Penthièvre, on the terrace of the Château de Bisy), or because, since the Girondin trees were condemned by the Montagnard clubs, they shared the curse of the "faction" that had baptized them.

85. In March 1793, the Convention sent to its Legislation Committee a letter whose purpose was to facilitate a penal law against those who destroyed the Liberty Trees. Six months later, it entrusted to the Subcommittee of Agriculture (and not, significantly, to the Committee of Public Instruction), the task of drawing up a complete, didactic, and practical report on "the Liberty Trees." Hell, Cels, Flandrin, Vilmorin, and Thouin, who made up this subcommittee, set to work. Of their efforts some texts remain—thoughts on the links between the tree and the Revolution—and a law of 3 Pluviôse, Year II, even more irenic in tone: "In all the communes of the Republic in which the Liberty Tree has perished, a new one will be planted on 1 Germinal." The planting and maintenance of the tree was left "to the care of the good citizens, so that in each commune the Liberty Tree may flourish under the protection of French liberty."

At about the same time, the Convention confirmed an order from the département of the Tarn by which an altar to the fatherland was to be erected around the Liberty Tree, at the expense of those who had brought down the tree. On 22 Germinal, Year IV, the increase in attacks (the words "acts of sacrilege" were beginning to be used) brought about an increase in repression. It was decided that the perpetrators of attacks on the trees would no longer be punished solely under the order of September 1791 on rural administration (which laid down the penalties for those who destroyed the grafts of fruit trees or cut or in any other way maimed standing trees); the crime would now be punished by a fine that was double the cost of the tree and a period of confinement lasting up to six months. Despite the severity of these measures, Years IV and V saw a decline in the symbolism of the tree, which was to be revived by Fructidor. Government instructions now began to bear the mark of François de Neufchâteau's sylvicultural enthusiasm: "What is one tree per commune? Let us have rather two before each house. Let us plant whole woods, vast forests; let us erect to Liberty natural temples, under verdant arches; and may the Republic, growing in strength with the trees that will make it up, transmit to posterity the shade of those sacred woods." All this was to find expression in the law of 24 Nivôse, Year VI: "Considering that respect for the signs of liberty is bound up with respect for liberty itself, all Liberty Trees that have been knocked down or perished by natural causes will be replaced if they have not already been so at the expense of the communes." The law laid down 2 Pluviôse (the day of the Festival of the King's Death) as the time of planting and set the punishment of four years' detention for any individual found guilty of harming the tree.

86. Grégoire, *Essai historique*. Hell's text was also printed as *Suite de notes sur*

les arbres de la liberté (Paris: Imprimerie des 86 départements, n.d.); Thouin's text is in manuscript (Bibliothèque centrale du Museum d'Histoire naturelle, manuscript 312).

87. *Les arbres de la Liberté dans le département de la Marne.*

88. One could cite innumerable examples of this incomprehension. At Châlons, a mayor harangued the national guardsmen on the day of the planting of the Liberty Trees: "He told them that up until that day the planting of the maypole had been one of those absolutely insignificant childish games, but that in the present circumstances it represented the most imposing, the most majestic of spectacles."

89. Letter dated 9 Pluviôse, Year VI, L 301, Arch. dép. Indre.

90. Or again, emblematic and practical: the Festival of Youth on 10 Germinal, Year VII, at Versailles is a good example of this. The pupils of the horticultural school presented various trees and plants "as images or emblems of the rural economy," to be distributed "in a symbolic order." Thus the bay was handed to the general, the poplar to the commissioner of the executive directory, the dwarf elm to members of the Agricultural Society.

91. For example, on 29 Nivôse, Year III, the police commissioner for the section du Pont-Neuf deplored the desiccated condition of the Liberty Tree in the cour de la Fontaine. He began, mechanically, attributing this catastrophe to "the impure breath of aristocracy." Unless, he corrected himself, one must blame "the ineptitude of those who planted it on a height in such a way that the roots could never be watered by the beneficent rains, which merely flowed away from ground that was never turned." NAF 2694, Bibl. nat.

92. It should be noted, however, that this took a long time to become established and only gradually took the place of the maypole of the early days of the Revolution. Thus the "four national trees" planted at Colmar on July 21, 1793, had their trunks painted in red, white, and blue, from top to bottom of their forty-four-foot height. Report by Dominique Schutz, locksmith of Colmar, *Revue d'Alsace* 3 (1899).

93. The tree became an object to protect far more than an object to show. The Montagnard club of Fleurance abandoned any attempt to turn it into an ornamental and processional theme and preferred to enclose it in a box in order "to protect it from attacks from another town"; Archives communales, municipal debates of 27 Pluviôse, Year II. Another indication of the fact that the tree called irresistibly for planting was that there were very few trees that were used only in procession. See, however, an example in Archives municipales de Châlons, I, 199, dossier de la société populaire de Brest. Furthermore, the official accounts are sometimes obsessively detailed. See, for example, F¹ C III, Maine-et-Loire 13, Arch. nat., on the planting of a tree inside the walls of Beaufort.

94. L 1264, Arch. dép. Nord, declaration by the commissioner for Lesdain.

95. See the discussion that began on this theme on 30 Ventôse, Year II, at

Beaufort-en-Vallée. G. Hauteux, *La Société populaire de Beaufort-en-Vallée* (Angers: Germain et Grassin, 1907).

96. See, for example, on 2 Pluviôse, Year VII, the official account of the planting at Belin, in the Gironde; F¹ C III, Gironde, Arch. nat.

97. At Pierrelatte, on 19 Pluviôse, Year VI; L 230, Arch. dép. Drôme.

98. See *Le Moniteur*, May 25, 1790.

99. At Guéret. See Villard, *Les arbres de la liberté à Guéret et dans le département de la Creuse.*

100. Neufchâteau, "Circulaire du 26 Vendémiaire an VII," in *Recueil des lettres circulaires.*

101. At Landrecies; L 1264, Arch. dép. Nord.

102. Bernardin de Saint-Pierre, "Les arbres étendent dans l'infini mon existence circonscrite et fugitive," in *Etude de la nature.*

103. Speech by Citizen Guiboust at the peoples' club of the section de la République; N.A.F. 2713, Bibl. nat.

104. Mercier, *Le nouveau Paris.*

105. On this subject, I am indebted to R. Etlin for showing me, in manuscript, his "J.-J. Rousseau: A Natural History of the Human Condition."

106. And of the place held in childhood memories by the care lavished on the tree: "Each day, ardent spectators of this watering, my cousin and I were confirmed in the very natural idea that it was more beautiful to plant a tree on the terrace than a flag in the breach; and we were resolved to win that glory, without sharing it with anybody." J.-J. Rousseau, *Confessions* (Geneva, 1782).

107. See Hélène Vianu, "La lumière et l'ombre dans l'oeuvre de J.-J. Rousseau," *Revue des sciences humaines* (April-June 1963).

108. The species of tree chosen for these festivals was usually the oak. This preference was officially expressed in the debate of Frimaire, Year II, in the Convention. The oak had two virtues: the hardness of its wood, which suggested strength, and longevity, "for it would be desirable that these trees, a symbol of liberty, should be eternal." No doubt these advantages had to be paid for in slow growth: there was a case, therefore, for resorting to more rapidly growing trees. Nevertheless, the Convention decreed, in the first paragraph of the law, "The oak is the tree of liberty." Yet on 7 Nivôse, a member challenged this authoritarian identification and suggested an amendment, "so as not to shackle the liberty of citizens in the communes in the choice of these trees." As a result of this intervention, other trees—elm, ash, poplar (chosen by virtue of an incorrect etymology), fir—were chosen, though the oak was by far the most common. There were few birches or hornbeams, although the tree itself was often surrounded by a hornbeam hedge. There were a few acacias, an obvious Masonic allusion. In the northeast of France there were a great many limes. A single notable absentee from the official account is the chestnut. But what, precisely, is the meaning of

this exclusion, which is confirmed by Y. Letouzey's article "Les arbres de la liberté en l'an II," *Revue forestière française* (1961)?

109. At Pallau, on 18 Pluviôse, Year VII; L 301, Arch. dép. Indre.

110. On this point see Traver, *Les bachelleries*.

111. L 1264, Arch. dép. Nord.

112. Ibid.

113. See the official accounts for the commune of Virnet, 10 Pluviôse, Year VI; L 671 Arch. dép. Puy-de-Dôme: "And after the Liberty Tree was planted, it was trimmed to the sound of the drum."

114. L 379, Arch. dép. Savoie.

115. L 477 Arch. dép. Côte-d'Or.

116. So much so that the tree was sometimes referred to as "the tree of the cap of Liberty." See L 352, Arch. dép. Loire-Atlantique.

117. See "Suite de l'enquête sur les végétaux, à propos des arbres ceintures," *Ethnographie* no. 43 (1945).

118. W. 395, Arch. nat.

119. *Mémoires de l'Académie d'Arras* 10, 2d ser. (1878).

120. Official account of the civic festival that took place on the occasion of the inauguration of the Liberty Tree in the public square of the commune of Villers-Cotterêts, July 19, 1792.

121. These enclosed areas became all the more elaborately protected the larger the town. At Maubeuge, it consisted of railings painted in the three colors (L 1264, Arch. dép. Nord). At Lyon, a certain Citizen Chinard was commissioned to decorate the surrounding wall with "oil paintings" (L 451, Arch. dép. Rhône).

122. The favorite site for the planting was in the main square "close to the church." On this subject, see H. Libois, *Les délibérations de la société populaire de Lons-le-Saunier* (Lons-le-Saunier: Declume, 1897). Sometimes, too (and here one senses to what extent, for the Revolutionary sensibility, the verticality of the tree was a substitute for that of the cross), at the crossroads. See "Une fête civique à Saint-Jean-Poutge en 1793," *Bulletin de la Société archéologique du Gers* 22 (1921). Things were quite different in the cities, where the sites were suggested by the positioning of various monuments; the courtyards of the hospital, school, or municipal buildings were favorite sites, which also suggests a sense of privacy that makes the urban ceremony less exemplary.

123. See the official account of the planting at Bannalec, V W 395, 916, no. 70, Arch. nat.

124. W 395, Arch. nat.

125. L 671, commune of Monton, Arch. dép. Puy-de-Dôme.

126. 1 L 411, Arch. dép. Maine-et-Loire.

127. At Pressigny, 11 Nivôse, Year VII; L 272, Arch. dép. Haute-Marne.

128. At Palluau, L 301, Arch. dép. Indre.

129. At Saint-Nectaire, L 671, Arch. dép. Puy-de-Dôme.

130. At Rochetaillée, L 451, Arch. dép. Rhône.

131. L 230, Arch. dép. Drôme.

132. L 453, Arch. dép. Rhône.

133. Ibid.

134. As at Arras. Cf. *Mémoires de l'Académie d'Arras* 10, 2d ser. (1878).

135. This is an important clue, for, distributed throughout the year, some of these festivals offered conditions that were very unfavorable to planting; but this did not stop people from planting, a sign that agronomical concerns had not entirely triumphed.

136. Circular of 17 Ventôse, Year VII: "What more convenient time to choose for this purpose than that of the festival, when the elite of the youth will itself be entrusted with the task of planting this beloved tree, whose progress will remind citizens of the image of the national festival when it was planted." *Recueil des lettres circulaires.*

137. In Vendémiaire, Year VI.

138. Châlons, Archives municipales, registre des délibérations.

139. L 355, Arch. dép. Loire-Atlantique.

140. See 1 L 411, Arch. dép. Maine-et-Loire, letter from the procurator-syndic of the district of Saumur to the general procurator-syndic of the département of Maine-et-Loire.

141. At Guéret, the following verses were recited by a citizeness to the Liberty Tree:

> De nos faits, instruisez nos fils d'âge en âge
> Heureux par nos nouvelles lois
> Ils viendront sous votre feuillage
> Entendre et bénir nos exploits . . .

and to the Fraternity Tree:

> Sous vos yeux cet arbre adorable
> Doué de plus nobles pouvoirs
> Ne nous coûtera nulle fable
> Mais nous apprendra nos devoirs.

> (Of our deeds instruct our sons from age to age.
> Happy in our new laws,
> They shall come under your foliage
> To hear and bless our exploits.)

> (Under your eyes this adorable tree,
> Gifted with nobler powers,
> Will cost us no fable,
> But will teach us our duty.)

142. See N.A.F. 2713, Bibl. nat., peoples' club of the section de la République, speech by Citizen Guiboust, 4 Ventôse, Year II.

143. L 1264, Arch. dép. Nord.

144. Ibid.

145. M. Potié, "Les fêtes de la Révolution à Mantes et à Limay," *Mantois* 11 (1960).

146. There is an example on which thousands of depositions were based. It occurred at Saunt-Génix, in Savoie. The owner of a wine shop that stood opposite the tree, when questioned as to whether on the night of 11 Germinal anyone had come to drink at his shop, replied: "I saw nobody that day or night. Indeed the little wine I do sell is on Sundays, Old Style." L 379, Arch. dép. Savoie.

147. Official account of the commune of Arthon, L 301, Arch. dép. Indre.

148. At Saint-Benoît du Sault, ibid.

149. At Brisle, L 272 Arch. dép. Haute-Marne.

150. At Brisle, 17 Nivôse, Year IV, ibid.

151. At Vatan, for example, in Year VII. Cf. L 301, Arch. dép. Indre.

152. La 393, Arch. dép. Somme, Rousseau's project for the ceremony of the replanting of the Fraternity Tree. Indeed it is a ritual of substitution: when the old tree arrived at the municipal building, a new one was taken out and decorated with the national colors.

153. J. Buisson, "L'arbre de la Liberté de Lingeard," *Revue du département de la Manche* (1962).

154. As in the Quesnoy, L 1264, Arch. dép. Nord.

155. F[1] C III, Haute-Vienne, Arch. nat., commune de Saint-Saturnin.

156. See E. Poumeau, *La société populaire de Périgueux pendant la Révolution* (Périgueux: D. Joucla, 1907).

157. For example at Saint-Génix, L 379, Arch. dép. Savoie.

X. The Revolutionary Festival

1. Bouches-du-Rhône, *Encyclopédie départementale,* "Etudes sur la Révolution et les cultes philosophiques."

2. C. A. Fichera, "Fêtes et cérémonies officielles à Eze sous la Révolution et l'Empire," *Nice historique* (1938).

3. *Correspondance de Le Coz, curé constitutionnel d'Ille-et-Vilaine* (Paris: Picard, 1900).

4. C 287, Arch. nat.

5. As in the previous chapter, I am using here the *comptes décadaires* (or monthly accounts) kept in series F[1] C III, Arch. nat.

6. A. Soboul, "Sentiments religieux et cultes populaires pendant la Révo-

lution, saintes patriotes et martyrs de la Liberté," *Annales de la Révolution française* (1957).

7. *Les Révolutions de Paris* no. 211 (July 20-August 3, 1793).

8. F. P. Bowman, "Le Sacré Coeur de Marat," contribution to the Clermont Conference.

9. C 266, Arch. nat.

10. F¹ C III, Ardennes 5, Arch. nat.

11. L. M. de La Révellière-Lépeaux, *Réflexions sur les cultes, sur les cérémonies civiles et les fêtes nationales* (Paris: F. J. Jansen, Year V).

12. E. Fassin, "Les baptêmes civiques," *Bulletin de la Société des amis du vieil Arles* 2 (1904–1905).

13. *Décret de l'Assemblée nationale, portant règlement d'un culte sans prêtres, ou moyen de se passer de prêtres sans nuire au culte* (Paris, 1790).

14. F. A. Daubermesnil, *Extraits d'un manuscrit intitulé "Le culte des Adorateurs," contenant des fragments de leurs différents livres sur l'institution du culte, les observances religieuses, les préceptes et l'Adoration* (Paris: Imprimerie du Cercle social, Year IV).

15. February 8, 1797.

16. J. F. Sobry, *Apologie de la messe* (Paris: Sobry, Year VI).

17. On this point, see A. Mathiez, *La théophilanthropie et le culte décadaire* (Paris: F. Alcan, 1903).

18. In *La décade*, 30 Floréal, Year V.

19. In *L'echo des cercles patriotiques* no. 14.

20. *Annales patriotiques*, 9 Frimaire, Year II.

21. G. Lefebvre, "Compte rendu de l'ouvrage de H. T. Parker," *Annales historiques de la Révolution française* (1938).

22. H. T. Parker, *The Cult of Antiquity and the French Revolutionaries* (Chicago: University of Chicago Press, 1937).

23. Faced with which Cochin suggested that the great subjects should be sought in the history of France, which is proof that the model might have had competition.

24. Letter to Mirabeau, March 22, 1740, in Vauvenargues, *Oeuvres*, vol. 3 (Paris: A la cité des Livres, 1929).

25. Billaud-Varenne, *Les eléments du républicanisme*, pt. 1 (n.p., n.d.).

26. On this theme, see E. Rawson, *The Spartan Tradition in European Thought* (Oxford: Clarendon Press, 1969).

27. P. Vidal-Naquet, preface to the French translation of M. I. Finley, *Democracy, Ancient and Modern (Democratie antique et démocratie moderne)* (Paris: Payot, 1976).

28. Madame de Staël, *De l'Allemagne* (Paris: H. Nicolle, 1810).

29. See, for example, G. Gautherot, *La démocratie révolutionnaire* (Paris: 1912).

30. In a contribution to the Clermont Conference, Roger Cotte emphasizes that the composers used by the Revolutionary authorities had almost all been initiated into lodges before 1789, as had the singers and instrumentalists also. Out of 110 teachers at the Conservatoire national de Musique, set up in 1795, sixty were unquestionably initiates. But, even more important, the Revolutionary music bore the mark of the as yet little-known Masonic music, of which one may distinguish four kinds: the lodge concert, the Masonic song, the musical ritual, and the column of harmony. The first kind did not contribute much to the Revolutionary festival, but the influence of the other three can be detected. First, this takes the form of sung Masonic poetry or cantata, "composition of a high level written for an audience including the profane." Did we know, for example, that the cantata to the Eternal, intended to be sung on 20 Brumaire, Year II, in the Temple of Reason incorporates lines from a Masonic hymn to the Eternal, presented by Nogaret during a concert of the Musée de Paris, a para-Masonic cultural organization, and that Nogaret republished it in 1807, among his Masonic poetry, under the title of *Hymn to the Great Architect of the Universe?* There is also the influence of Masonic musical ritual, often conceived as a dialogue between a soloist, the chorypheum (a term often used in Revolutionary scores, unless a representative of the people took the place of the chorypheum), and a male-voice choir: again one cannot but notice that, in the music of the Revolution, choirs are very often all male, sometimes on grounds of particular suitability, as when, for example, hymns to warriors are being sung, but also in imitation of the initiatory chants. The last constitutive element of Masonic music was the "column of harmony," a group of wind instruments that, just prior to the Revolution, consisted of two clarinets, two horns, and two bassoons, with the possible multiplication of the parts and the support of the *basso profundo* provided by the serpent. We are well aware, of course, of the preference shown by the Revolutionary festivals for wind instruments, which find a quite natural place in popular festivities. It may be noted, too, that the requirements of Masonic ritual established the practice of treating the wind instruments as the major, if not exclusive, members of the orchestra. Lastly, the Masonic influence on the very texture of the music used by the revolutionaries can be seen in the widespread use of such purely musical devices as triple time.

31. Jacques Brengues, "L'apport de la franc-maçonnerie à la fête révolutionnaire," *Humanisme* (July-August 1974).

32. Daubermesnil, *Extraits.*

33. C. Dupuis, *Origine de tous les cultes ou Religion universelle* (Paris: H. Agasse, Year III).

34. *Lettres de Rallier, membre du Conseil des Anciens, au citoyen Grégoire, membre du Conseil des Cinq-Cents* (Paris: Desenne, Year IV).

35. On this theme, see L. A. De Moy, *Accord de la religion et des cultes chez une nation libre* (Paris: Au presbytère de Saint-Laurent, Year IV): "This is how we

have behaved so far in the Festival of the Federation. We invited the priests of the Roman cult to it and said to them: 'Come with all the paraphernalia of your liturgy, your rituals, your ceremonies, your incense, your Gothic ornaments, your masses, your *Te Deums,* your *Oremuses,* your barbarous chants in a foreign idiom . . . ' and you dare to call that solemnity the Festival of the Federation."

36. P. J. G. Cabanis, *Lettre posthume et inédité de Cabanis à M. F. sur les causes premières* (Paris: Gabon, 1824).

37. La Révellière, *Essai sur les moyens de faire participer l'universalité des spectateurs à tout ce qui se pratique dans les fêtes nationales* (Paris: H. J. Jansen, Year VI).

38. G. F. Coyer, *Dissertations pour être lues: la première sur le vieux mot de patrie, la seconde sur la nature du peuple* (The Hague: P. Gosse, Jr., 1755).

39. J. Grenier, *Opinion sur la question de savoir si l'on doit supprimer de la formule du serment civique les mots de haine à l'anarchie* (Paris: Imp. nat., Year VII).

40. Saint-Just, *Rapport sur la police générale, la justice, le commerce, la législation, et les crimes des factions* (Paris: Imp. nat., n.d.).

Bibliography

Secondary Sources

Annales historiques de la Révolution française 47, no. 221 (July-September 1975).

Annat, J. *Les sociétés populaires*. Pau: Lescher-Montoué, 1940.

Archer, P. "La fête de la Fédération en 1790 dans la commune de Montauban." *Actes du 79ᵉ congrès des Sociétés savantes* (1954).

Arrivée de 4000 citoyens bretons pour la Confédération, avec leurs armes, bagages, tentes et provisions pour leur séjour. Paris: n.d.

Aulard, F. A. *Le culte de la Raison et le culte de l'Etre Suprême, 1793–1794*. Paris: F. Alcan, 1892.

Avis aux Confédérés des LXXXIII départements sur les avantages et les dangers du séjour à Paris. Paris: n.d.

Balzac, Honoré de. *Une ténébreuse affaire*. Paris: H. Souverain, 1843.

Bapst, G. "Lettres d'un attaché saxon, 11 juillet 1790." *Revue de la Révolution* 4 (1884).

Barère, B. "Discours sur les écoles de Mars qui fait l'apologie du dénuement." *Le moniteur universel*, 15 Prairial, Year II.

———. *Mémoires*. Paris: J. Labitte, 1842–1844.

Barrau, H. de. "Mais plantés devant les églises." *Mémoires de la Société des lettres, sciences et arts de l'Aveyron* 4 (1842–1843).

Baudouin de Maison Blanche, J. M. *Les signaux des Gaulois*.

Bédier, J. "Les fêtes de mai et les origines de la poésie lyrique au Moyen Age." *Revue des deux mondes*, May 1, 1896.

Beffroy de Reigny, L. A. *La constitution de la lune*. Paris: Froussé, 1793.

Bercé, Y.-M. *Fête et révolte*. Paris: Hachette, 1976.

Berland, J. *Les sentiments des populations marnaises à l'égard de l'Angleterre à la fin du XVIIIᵉ siècle et au début du XIXᵉ siècle*. Châlons-sur-Marne: Rebat, 1913.

Bernard, A. *Recherches sur les chevaliers de l'Arquebuse et les chevaliers de l'Arc de Tournus.* Mâcon: L. Chollar, 1884.

Bernardin de Saint-Pierre, Jacques-Henri. *Etudes de la nature.* Paris: P. F. Didot le Jeune, 1784.

Billaud-Varenne. *Les éléments du républicanisme,* pt. 1. N.p., n.d.

Blanc, Louis. *Histoire de la Révolution française.* Paris: Langlois et Leclerq, 1847–1862.

Blazy, L. *Les fêtes nationales à Foix sous la Révolution.* Foix: Pomies, Fra 1911.

Bled, C. *Les sociétés populaires à Saint-Omet pendant la Révolution.* Saint-Omer: H. d'Homont, 1907.

Bois, B. *Les fêtes révolutionnaires à Angers de l'an II à l'an VIII.* Paris: Alcan, 1929.

Boissy d'Anglas, F. A. (Comte de). *Essai sur les fêtes nationales.* Paris: Imprimerie polyglotte, Year II.

Bonnaud, L. "Note sur les mais d'honneur élevés en Limousin après les élections municipales." *Bulletin de la Société archéologique et historique du Limousin* (1960).

Boulanger, N. A. *L'antiquité dévoilée par ses usages, ou Examen critique des principales opinions, cérémonies et institutions religieuses des différents peuples de la terre.* Amsterdam: M. M. Rey, 1766.

Boullée, E. Louis. *Architecture: essai sur l'art,* ed. J. M. Pérouse de Montclos. Paris: Hermann, 1968.

Bourgougnon, E. "La fête de Toulon à Cusset." *Notre Bourbonnais* nos. 61–69.

Bowman, F. P. "Le Sacré Coeur de Marat." *Annales historiques de la Révolution française* 47, no. 221 (July-September 1975).

Boyer, J. B. *Méthode à suivre dans le traitement des maladies épidémiques qui règnent le plus ordinairement dans la généralité de Paris.* Paris: Imprimerie royale, 1761.

Brégail, G. "La fête de l'Etre Suprême à Auch." *Bulletin de la Société archéologique du Gers* 21 (1920).

Brengues, Jacques. "L'apport de la franc-maçonnerie à la fête révolutionnaire." *Humanisme* (July-August 1974).

Breque. "Une fête à Lescar pendant la Révolution." *Escole Gaston Febus* (1902).

Brissot de Warville. *Correspondance universelle sur ce qui intéresse le bonheur de l'homme et de la société.* Neufchâtel: Imprimerie de la Société typographique, 1783.

Buisson, J. "L'arbre de la Liberté de Lingeard." *Revue du département de la Manche* (1962).

Bulletin du Comité des travaux historiques et scientifiques, Section des sciences économiques et sociales (1892).

Bulletin de la Société archéologique du Gers 31 (1930).

Bulletin de la Société historique et artistique du diocèse de Meaux (1968).

Burke, Edmund. *Reflections on the French Revolution.* London, 1790.

Bussière, G. *Etudes historiques sur la Révolution en Périgord.* Bordeaux: C. Lefebvre, 1877–1903.

Butte, W. *Prolégomènes de l'arithmétique de la vie humaine, contenant la classification générale des talents, l'échelle des âges de l'homme et une formule d'évaluation de toutes les situations géographiques, d'après un même système.* Paris: J. G. Dentu, 1827.

Cabanis, P. J. G. *Lettre posthume et inédité de Cabanis à M. F. sur les causes premières.* Paris: Gabon, 1824.

Cabet, E. *Histoire populaire de la Révolution française.* Paris: Pagnerre, 1839–1840.

Campan, Madame Jeanne-Louise-Henriette de. *Mémoires sur la vie privée de Marie-Antoinette.* Paris: Baudouin Frères, 1822.

Capion, A. *Les fêtes nationales à Caen sous la Révolution.* Caen: Le Blanc-Hardel, 1877.

Caron, Pierre. "Le mouvement antiseigneurial de 1790, dans le Sarladais et le Quercy." *Bulletin d'histoire économique de la Révolution* no. 2 (1912).

Charbonneau, B. "L'Emeute et le plan." *La table ronde* 251 (1968) and 252 (1969).

Chardon, H. "La fête de l'Etre Suprême au Mans." *La Révolution française* 10 (1886).

Chaussard, J. B. *Essai philosophique sur la dignité des arts.* Paris: Imprimerie des sciences et des arts, Year VI.

Chevalier de Jaucourt, Louis. Statement in the *Encyclopédie.*

Clermont Conference. See *Annales historiques de la Révolution française.*

Clouzot, H. *L'ancien théâtre en Poitou.* Niort: Clouzot, 1901.

Cobb, R. *Les armées révolutionnaires.* Paris: Mouton, 1961–1963.

Comte, Auguste. *Système de politique positive.* Paris: L. Mathias, 1851–1854.

Confédération nationale du 14 juillet, ou Description fidèle de tout ce qui a précédé, accompagné et suivi cette auguste cérémonie. Paris: J. M. Chalier, 1790.

Coupé, J.-M. *Des fêtes en politique et en morale.* Paris: Imprimerie de Baudouin, n.d.

Courteault, P. *La Révolution et les théâtres à Bordeaux.* Paris: Perrin, 1926.

Cox, Harvey. *The Feast of Fools: A Theological Essay on Festivity and Fantasy.* Cambridge, Mass.: Harvard University Press, 1969.

Coyer, G. F. *Dissertations pour être lues: la première sur le vieux mot de patrie, la seconde sur la nature du peuple.* The Hague: P. Gosse, Jr., 1955.

Daubermesnil, F. A. *Extraits d'un manuscrit intitulé "Le culte des Adorateurs," contenant des fragments de leurs différents livres sur l'institution du culte, les observances religieuses, les préceptes et l'Adoration.* Paris: Imprimerie du Cercle sociale, Year IV.

Deloz, Abbé P. J. B. *La Révolution en Lozère.* Mende: Imprimerie lozérienne, 1922.

De Mopinot, A. R. *Proposition d'un monument à élever dans la capitale de la France pour transmettre aux races futures l'époque de l'heureuse révolution qui l'a revivifiée sous le règne de Louis XVI.* Paris: Laurens jeune, 1790.

De Moy, L. A. *Accord de la religion et des cultes chez une nation libre.* Paris: Au presbytère de Saint-Laurent, Year IV.

Deprun, Jean. "Les 'noms divins' dans deux discours de Robespierre." *Annales historiques de la Révolution française* (April-June 1972).

Description curieuse et intéressante des 60 drapeaux que l'amour patriotique a offert aux 60 districts de la ville et des faubourgs de Paris, avec l'explication des Allégories, Devises, Emblèmes et Exergues dont ils sont ornés. Paris: Sorin, 1790.

Desmasures, A. *Histoire de la Révolution dans le département de l'Aisne.* Vervins: Flem, 1869.

Détails de toutes les cérémonies qui vont être célébrées dans toute l'étendue de la République française, une et indivisible, en l'honneur de l'Etre Suprême, Auteur de la Nature et de la Liberté, présentés par David et décrétés par la Convention nationale suivis de l'Ordre de la Marche des cérémonies, des décorations pour l'embellisement de cette fête, de la religion naturelle des Vrais Républicains, de la Déclaration Solennelle de l'Homme Libre à l'Eternal. Paris: Prévost, n.d.

Dhers, J. "La Déesse Raison du Mont Unité." *Revue de Commonges* (1960).

Diderot, Denis. *Lettres d'un fermier de Pennsylvanie.* Paris: J.-A. Naigeon, 1798.

———. *Paradoxe sur le comédien, précédé des entretiens sur le fils naturel.* Paris: Garnier-Flammarion, 1967.

Dollfus, M. A. "Les fêtes et cérémonies populaires à Lyons-la-Forêt à la fin du siècle." *Revue des sociétés savantes de Haute-Normandie* (1958).

Domenach, Jean-Marie. "Idéologie du mouvement." *Esprit* 8–9 (1968).

Dommanget, M. "Robespierre et les cultes." *Annales historiques de la Révolution française* 1 (1924).

Dorcy, L. "La société populaire de Montaigut-en-Combraille." *La Révolution française* 59.

Dowd, David L. "Jacobinism and the Fine Arts." *Art Quarterly* 16, no. 3 (1953).

———. *Pageant-Master of the Republic: Jacques-Louis David and the French Revolution.* Lincoln: University of Nebraska Press, 1948.

———. "Art as National Propaganda in the French Revolution." *Public Opinion Quarterly* (Autumn 1951).

Dubois, E. *Histoire de la Révolution dans le département de l'Ain.* Bourg: Brochot, 1931–1935.

Dubroca, J. F. Introduction to La Révellière's *Discours sur les divers sujets de morale et sur les fêtes nationales, lus à l'institut le 12 floréal an V.*

Duchatellier, A. *Histoire de la Révolution dans les départements de l'Ancienne Bretagne.* Paris: Dessessart, 1836.

Dufour, A. "La fête de la Raison à Corbeil (1793)." *Bulletin de la Société historique et archéologique de Corbeil, d'Etampes et du Hurepoix* 17 (1911).

Dulaure, J. A. *Esquisse, historiques des principaux événements de la Révolution française depuis la convocation des États Généraux jusqu'au rétablissement de la maison de Bourbon.* Paris: Baudouin frères, 1823–1825.

————. *Le thermomètre du jour,* June 5, 1792.

Duplessis, General. "Fête de la Confédération des gardes nationales de l'ancienne Bourgogne, le 18 mai 1790." *Mémoires académiques de Dijon* (1922).

Dupont de Nemours, Pierre-Samuel. *De l'origine et des progrès d'une science nouvelle.* Paris: Desaint, 1768.

Dupuis, C. *Origine de tous les cultes, ou Religion universelle.* Paris: H. Agasse, Year III.

Duruy, A. *L'instruction publique et la Révolution.* Paris: Hachette, 1882.

Emeric-David, T. B. *Musée olympique de l'école vivante des beaux-arts.* Paris: Imprimerie de Plassan, 1796.

Emmanuelli, F. "La fête de la Fédération à Cherbourg, 14 juillet 1790." *Revue de Cherbourg* (1906–1907).

Enterrement du despotisme, ou Funérailles des Aristocrates, seconde fête nationale dédiée à nos patriotes bretons. N.p., n.d.

d'Escherny, F. L. *Correspondance d'une habitant de Paris avec ses amis de Suisse et d'Angleterre, sur les événements de 1789, 1790 et jusqu'au 4 avril 1791.* Paris: Desenne, 1791.

Esparron, P. *Essai sur les âges de l'homme.* Paris: Imprimerie de Crapelet, 1803.

Etlin, R. "L'architecture et la fête de la Fédération, Paris, 1790." *Annales historiques de la Révolution française* 47, no. 221 (July-September 1975).

————. "J.-J. Rousseau, a Natural History of the Human Condition." (Manuscript.)

Faiguet de Villeneuve, J. *L'ami des pauvres, ou L'économe politique.* Paris: Moreau, 1766.

Falconet, E.-M. *Réflexions sur la sculpture.* Paris: Prault, 1761.

Fassin, E. "Les baptêmes civiques." *Bulletin de la Société des amis du Vieil Arles* 2 (1904–1905).

Fauquet, C. "La célébration du culte de la Raison dans le Perche." *Bulletin de la Société percheronne historique et archéologique* (1907).

"Fédération des Vosges." *Bulletin du Comité des travaux d'histoire vosgienne* 3.

Fédération du Mont-Geneviève près Nancy. Nancy: Hoener, 1790.

Ferrières, Marquis de. *Mémoires.* Paris: Baudouin fils, 1821.

"Une fête civique à Creyssac sous la Révolution." *Bulletin de la Société historique et archéologique du Périgord* 45–46.

"Une fête civique à Saint-Jean-Poutge en 1793." *Bulletin de la Société archéologique du Gers* 22 (1921).

"La fête de l'Etre Suprême à Calais." *Société historique du Calaisis* (September-October 1924).

"La fête de l'Etre Suprême à Theys." *Bulletin de la Société archéologique, historique et artistique, le vieux papier* 16.

"La fête de la Fédération, 1790, Lettre d'un délégué." *Revue rétrospective* 8 (1890).

Fichera, C. A. "Fêtes et cérémonies officielles à Eze sous la Révolution et l'Empire." *Nice historique* (1938).

Fichte, J. G. *Considérations destinées à rectifier les jugements du public sur la Révolution française.* Paris: F. Chamerot, 1859.

Français, A. *Idée de la fête qui doit être célébrée à Grenoble le 20 prairial en l'honneur de l'Etre Suprême.* Grenoble: A. Giroud, 1794.

Frénilly, A. F. *Souvenirs du baron de Frénilly.* Paris: Plon-Nourrit, 1909.

Furet, F., and D. Richet. *La Révolution française.* Paris: Hachette, 1973.

Les gardes nationales de Saint-Brice, Cravant, Vermenton, Noyers, Vézelay, Asquins, Lille, Montréal et Avalon. N.p., n.d.

Gaulmier, J. "Cabanis et son discours sur les fêtes nationales." *Annales historiques de la Révolution française* 47, no. 221 (July-September 1975).

Gaume, Mgr. *La Révolution, recherches historiques sur l'origine et la propagation du mal en Europe depuis la Renaissance jusqu'à nos jours.* Paris: Gaume Frères, 1856–1859.

Gautherot, G. *La démocratie révolutionnaire.* Paris: G. Beauchesne, 1912.

Girard, René. *La violence et le sacré.* Paris: Grasset, 1972.

Girardin, S. de. *Mémoires.* Paris: Moutardier, 1829.

Girardot, M. de. "Les fêtes de la Révolution, de 1790 à l'An VIII." *Annales de la Société Académique de Nantes et du département de Loire Inférieure,* vol. 28 Nantes, 1857.

Golfier, Michel. "Culte de la Raison et fêtes décadaires en l'an II au Bugue." *Bulletin de la Société historique et archéologique du Périgord* 94 (1968).

Grandvaux, V. "Souvenirs de la période révolutionnaire à Poligny." *Bulletin de la Société d'agriculture, des sciences et des arts de Poligny* (1888–1889).

Grégoire, Abbé H. *Essai historique et patriotique sur les arbres de la liberté.* Paris: Desenne, Year II.

Grétry, André-Ernest-Modeste. *Essais sur la musique.* Paris: Imprimerie de la République, Year V.

Guérin, Daniel. *La lutte de classes sous la 1ʳᵉ République, 1793–1797.* Paris: Gallimard, 1968.

Guillaume, J. "La déesse de la Liberté à la fête du 20 brumaire an II." *La Révolution française* (April 1899).

———. *Procès-verbaux du Comité d'instruction publique.* Paris: Collection de documents inédits sur l'histoire de France, 1891–1907.

Guillemin, L. *Chroniques locales: pendant la Révolution, chronique d'un bourgeois d'Aire.* Aire: L. Guillemin, 1894–1900.

Halévy, Daniel. *Histoire d'une histoire.* Paris: Grasset, 1939.

Hauteux, G. *La société populaire de Beaufort-en-Vallée.* Angers: Germain et Grassin, 1907.

Hell. *Suite de notes sur les arbres de la liberté.* Paris: Imprimerie des 86 départements, n.d.

Hemsterhuis, F. *Oeuvres philosophiques*. Paris: H. J. Jansen, 1792.

Herpin, E. "Les fêtes à Saint Malo pendant la Révolution." *Annales de la Société historique de Saint-Malo* (1908).

Huet, Pierre-Daniel. *Les origines de la ville de Caen*. Rouen: Maurry, 1706.

Idzerda, Stanley J. "Iconoclasm during the French Revolution." *American Historical Review* 60 (1954).

Jam, Jean-Louis. "*La Marseillaise*." *Annales historiques de la Révolution française* 47, no. 221 (July–September 1975).

James, E. O. *The Tree of Life: An Archeological Study*. Leiden: E. J. Brill, 1966.

Jaurès, J. *Histoire socialiste de la Révolution française*. Paris: Librairie de l'Humanité, 1922–1924.

Jouhaud, L. *La grande Révolution dans la petite ville. Blancs et rouges: Eymoutiers, 1789–1794*. Limoges: Imprimerie de la Société des Journaux et Publications du Centre, 1938.

Kant, Immanuel. *Kritik der Urteilskraft* (Critique of judgment), 1790.

Karamzine, N. M. "Voyage en France, 1789–1790." *Revue de la Révolution* (1884).

Lacombe, J. *Le spectacle des beux-arts*. Paris: Hardy, 1758.

Lacrocq, L. "Notes sur les sociétés populaires de la Creuse." *Mém. Creuse* 12–16 (1901–1906).

Lafarge, Catherine. "L'anti-fête dans la nouveau Paris." *Annales historiques de la Révolution française* 47, no. 221 (July–September 1975).

Lamartine, Alphonse-Marie-Louis de Prat de. *Histoire des Girondins*. Paris: Furne W. Coquebert, 1847.

Lambert, M. *Les fédérations en Franche-Comté et la fête de la Fédération, 14 juillet 1790*. Paris: Perrin, 1890.

Lanfrey, P. *Essai sur la Révolution française*. Paris: F. Chamerot, 1858.

La Révellière-Lépeaux, L. M. de. *Essai sur les moyens de faire participer l'universalité des spectateurs à tout ce qui se pratique dans les fêtes nationales*. Paris: H. J. Jansen, Year VI.

———. *Mémoires*. Paris: J. Hetzel, 1873.

———. *Réflexions sur les cultes, sur les cérémonies civiles et les fêtes nationales*. Paris: F. J. Jansen, Year V.

La Tocnaye, M. de. *Les causes de la Révolution en France*. Edinburgh: Manners and Miller, 1797.

Laurain, M. "Une fête civique à Clermont (de l'Oise)." *Mémoires de la Société archéologique et historique de Clermont* 1 (1904).

Laurent-Hanin. *Histoire municipale de Versailles, 1787–1799*. Versailles: Cerf, 1885–1889.

Leach, E. R. *Rethinking Anthropology*. London: Athlone, 1961. Pp. 132–136.

Lécluselle, A. *Histoire de Cambrai et du Cambrésis*. Cambrai: Régnier-Farez, 1873–1874.

Le Coz, C. *Correspondance de Le Coz, évêque constitutionnel d'Ille-et-Vilaine.* Paris: Picard, 1900.

Lefebvre, G. "Compte rendu de l'ouvrage de H. T. Parker." *Annales historiques de la Révolution française* (1938).

Leith, James A. *The Idea of Art as Propaganda in France, 1750–1790.* Toronto: University of Toronto Press, 1965.

Lemierre, A. M. *Les fastes, ou Les usages de l'année.* Paris: P. F. Gueffier, 1779.

Le Peletier de Fargeau, F. *Réflexions sur le moment présent.* Paris: Imprimerie de R. Vatar, n.d.

Lépine, J.-B. *Histoire de Château-Porcien.* Vouziers: Duchêne-Dufrêne, 1859.

Le Roy, David. *Histoire de la disposition et des formes différentes que les chrétiens ont données à leurs temples.* Paris: Desaint et Saillant, 1764.

Letouzey, Y. "Les arbres de la liberté en l'an II." *Revue forestière française* (1961).

Libois, H. *Les délibérations de la société populaire de Lons-le-Saunier.* Lons-le-Saunier: Declume, 1897.

Lindet, Robert-Thomas. *Correspondance.* Paris: Société d'Histoire de la Révolution française, 1899.

Lindsay, Jack. "Art and Revolution." *Art and Artists* (August 1969).

Linguet, M. *Adresse au peuple français concernant ce qu'il faut faire et ce qu'il ne faut pas faire pour célébrer la fête mémorable et nationale du 14 juillet 1790.* N.p., 1790.

Lockroy, E. *Journal d'une bourgeoise pendant la Révolution.* Paris: Calmann-Lévy, 1881.

Mably, Gabriel Bonnot, Abbé de. *Lettre à Madame la Marquise de P . . . sur l'Opéra.* Paris: Didot, 1761.

———. *Observation sur les lois et le gouvernement des Etats-Unis d'Amérique.* Amsterdam: J. F. Rocard, 1784.

Maggiolo, L. "Les fêtes de la Révolution." *Mémoires de l'académie Stanislas* 11 and 12, 5th ser. (1893–1894).

Mailhet, A. "Une fête révolutionnaire en 1793 à Crest, ville du Dauphiné." *Bulletin de la Société archéologique et artistique, le vieux papier* (1905).

Maistre, Joseph de. *Considérations sur la France.* Paris: Société typographique, 1814.

Mallet, P. H. *Histoire de Dannemarc.* Lyon: P. Duplain, 1766.

Mathiez, Albert. "Les comptes décadaires des autorités du gouvernement révolutionnaire et des commissaires du Directoire." *Revue d'histoire moderne et contemporaine* 4 (1902–1903).

———. *Les origines des cultes révolutionnaires, 1789–1792.* Paris: G. Bellais, 1904.

———. *La théophilanthropie et le culte décadaire.* Paris: F. Alcan, 1903.

Maugras, G. *Journal d'un étudiant pendant la Révolution, 1789–1793.* Paris: Plon-Nourrit, 1890.

Mazauric, Claude. "La fête révolutionnaire comme manifestation de la politique jacobine à Rouen en 1793 (an III)." *Annales historiques de la Révolution française* 47, no. 221 (July-September 1975).

Mémoires de l'Académie d'Arras 10, 2d ser. (1878).

Mercier, A. "Suite de l'enquête sur les végétaux, à propos des arbres ceinturés." *Ethnographie* no. 43 (1945).

Mercier, L.-S. *Du théâtre.* Amsterdam: E. Van Harrevelt, 1773.

Michelet, Jules. *Le banquet.* Paris: Calmann-Lévy, 1879.

———. *Histoire de la Révolution française.* Paris: Chamerot, 1847–1855.

———. *Nos fils.* Paris: A. Lacroix, Verboekhoven, 1870.

Mirabeau, Victor de Riquetti, Marquis de. *L'ami des hommes.* Paris: Hérissant, 1759–1760.

———. *Travail sur l'éducation publique, trouvé dans les papiers de Mirabeau l'aîné, publiés par Cabanis.* Paris: Imp. nat., 1791.

———. (a M. de La Marck). *Correspondance,* vol. 2. Paris: Vve. Le Normant, 1851.

Missol, L. "La Révolution à Villefranche, le temple de la Raison et les fêtes d'après les archives communales." *Bulletin de la Société des sciences et des arts du Beaujolais* (1904).

Moltmann, Jürgen. *Die ersten Freigelassenen der Schöpfung-Versuche an der Freiheit und das Wohlgefallen am Spiel.* Munich: Kaiser Verlag, 1971.

Monin, H. "Le discours de Mirabeau sur les fêtes publiques." *La Révolution française* 25 (1893).

Montesquieu, Charles de Secondat, Baron de. *De l'esprit des lois.* Geneva: Barrillot et fils, 1748; *The Spirit of the Laws,* trans. Thomas Nugent, intro. Franz Neumann. New York: Hafner, 1949; *The Spirit of Laws: A Compendium of the First English Edition,* ed. David Wallace Carrithers. Berkeley: University of California Press, 1977.

———. *Essai sur le goût.* Paris: Delalain, 1766.

Morellet, Abbé André. *Mémoires.* Paris: Ladvocat, 1821.

Morin, Benoît. *Histoire de Lyon pendant la Révolution.* Lyon: Salvy jne., 1847.

Mousset, A. *Un témoin ignoré de la Révolution, le comte de Fernan Nuñez, ambassadeur d'Espagne à Paris, 1787–1791.* Paris: Champion, 1924.

Nodier, Charles. *Oeuvres complètes,* vol. 7. Paris: E. Renduel, 1832–1837.

Palmer, R. *Twelve Who Ruled.* Princeton: Princeton University Press, 1941.

Parès, A. J. *La reprise de Toulon et l'opinion publique.* Toulon: Société Nouvelle des Imprimeries toulonnaises, 1936.

Parker, H. T. *The Cult of Antiquity and the French Revolutionaries.* Chicago: University of Chicago Press, 1937.

Pascal, René. "La fête de mai." *France-Forum* (October-November 1968).

Péguy, Charles. *Clio.* Paris: Gallimard, 1932.

Perrier, A. "Les arbres de mai et les arbres de la Liberté." *Bulletin de la Société archéologique et historique du Limousin* (1960).

Perrin, J. "Le club des femmes de Besançon." *Annales révolutionnaires* 9 and 10 (1917–1918).

Perrot, J.-C. *Cartes, plans, dessins et vues de Caen antérieurs à 1789.* Caen: Caron, 1962.

———. *Genèse d'une ville moderne. Caen au XVIIIᵉ siècle.* Paris: Mouton, 1975.

———. "L'âge d'ôr de la statistique régionale (an IV–1804)." *Annales historiques de la Révolution française* no. 224 (1976).

Philpot, J. H. *The Sacred Tree in Religion and Myth.* London: Macmillan, 1897.

Pierre, C. *Musique des fêtes et des cérémonies de la Révolution.* Paris: Imp. nat., 1904.

Pommereul, F. R. J. de. *De l'art de voir dans les beaux-arts.* Paris: Bernard, Year VI.

Potié, M. "Les fêtes de la Révolution à Mantes et à Limay." *Mantois* 11 (1960).

Poumeau, E. *La société populaire de Périgueux pendant la Révolution.* Périgueux: D. Joucla, 1907.

Poyet, B. *Idées générales sur le projet de la fête du 14 juillet.* Paris: Vve. Delaguette, n.d.

Pressensé, E. de. *L'église et la Révolution française.* Paris: Fischbacher, 1889.

"Procès-verbal de l'organisation de la fête de la Raison à Meyssac, le 18 nivôse an II." *Bulletin de la société historique de la Corrèze* 65.

Procès-verbal très intéressant du voyage aérien qui a eu lieu aux Champs-Elysées le 18 septembre, jour de la proclamation de la Constitution. Paris: Bailly, 1791.

Quinet, E. *La Révolution.* Paris: A. Lacroix, Verboeckhoven, 1865.

Rallier, L. A. *Lettres de Rallier, membre du Conseil des Anciens, au citoyen Grégoire, membre du Conseil des Cinq-Cents.* Paris: Desenne, Year IV.

Ramon, G. *La Révolution à Péronne.* Péronne: Quentin, 1878–1880.

Rawson, E. *The Spartan Tradition in European Thought.* Oxford: Clarendon Press, 1969.

Raymond, G. M. *De la peinture considerée dans ses effets sur les hommes en général et de son influence sur les moeurs et le gouvernement des peuples.* Paris: Pougens, Year VII.

Relation de la fête du pacte fédératif, célébrée à Chercy le 14 juillet 1790. N.p., n.d.

Renan, E. *Questions contemporaines.* Paris: Michel-Lévy Frères, 1868.

Renouvier, Jules. *Histoire de l'art pendant la Révolution.* Paris: Veuve Renouard, 1863.

Revue du folklore français 11 (January-March 1940).

Ribault, J. Y. "Divertissement populaire et turbulence sociale: les fêtes baladoires dans la région de Thaumiers au XVIIIᵉ siècle." *Cahiers archéologiques et historiques du Berry* (1967).

Richebé, H. *Journal d'un bourgeois de Lille pendant la Révolution, 1787–1793.* Lille: Prévost, 1898.

Robespierre, Maximilien. *Le défenseur de la Constitution* no. 4 (June 7, 1792).

———. *Le défenseur de la Constitution* no. 9.

Rocal, G. *Le vieux Périgord*. Toulouse: E. H. Guitard, 1927.

Roland, Madame Marie-Jeanne Phlipon. *Mémoires,* ed. P. de Roux. Paris: Mercure de France, 1966.

Rouillé d'Orfeuil, A. *L'alambic des lois, ou Observations de l'ami des français sur l'homme et sur les lois*. Hispaan, 1773.

Rousseau, J.-J. *Les confessions*. Paris: Poingot, Year VI.

———. *Considérations sur le gouvernement de Pologne*. Paris: Defer de Maisonneuve, 1790.

———. *Correspondance complète de J.-J. Rousseau,* vol. 9. Geneva: Institut et Musée Voltaire, 1969.

———. *Discours d'économie politique*. Geneva: E. du Villard fils, 1758.

———. *Essai sur l'origine des langues*. Geneva: 1781; *On the Origin of Language,* ed. and trans. John H. Moran and Alexander Gode. New York: F. Ungar, 1967.

———. *Lettres sur le gouvernement de la Corse. Oeuvres,* vol. 3, Paris: A. Belin, 1817.

Rouvière, F. *Dimanches révolutionnaires: études sur l'histoire de la Révolution dans le Gard*. Nîmes: Catélan, 1888.

Roy, E. *La société populaire de Montignac pendant la Révolution*. Bordeaux: Delgrange, 1888.

Sacy, J. F. de. *Les Brongniart*. Paris: Plon, 1940.

Saige, J. *Opuscules d'un solitaire*. Bordeaux: Bergeret, Year XI.

Saint-Just, Louis de. *Fragments sur les institutions républicaines*. Paris: Fayolle, 1800.

Saint-Léger, A. *Le bibliographe moderne*. Les mémoires statistiques des départements, pendant le Directoire, le Consulat et l'Empire, 1918–1919.

Saint-Pierre, Abbé de. *Ouvrages de politique*. Rotterdam: J.-D. Beman, 1733–1740.

Sauzay, J. *Histoire de la persécution révolutionnaire dans le département du Doubs, de 1789 à 1901*. Besançon: Tubergues, 1922.

Schlanger, Judith. "Théâtre révolutionnaire et representation du bien." *Poetique, Revue de théorie et d'analyse littéraire* no. 22 (1975).

Schneider, R. *Quatremère de Quincy et son intervention dans les arts, 1788–1830*. Paris: Hachette, 1910.

Schutz, Dominique. "Report." *Revue d'Alsace* 3 (1899).

Sébastien-Mercier, L. *Paris pendant la Révolution*. Paris: Poulet-Malassis, 1862.

Sébillot, P. "Usages du mois de mai." *Revue des traditions populaires* 3 (1888).

Ségur, Marquis de. *Mémoires*. Paris: Émery, 1827.

Six lettres à S. L. Mercier, sur les six tomes de son "Nouveau Paris," par un Français (Fortia de Piles). Paris: Year IX.

Soboul, A. "Sentiments religieux et cultes populaires pendant la Révolution, saintes patriotes et martyrs de la Liberté." *Annales de la Révolution française* (1957).

Sobry, J. F. *Apologie de la messe.* Paris: Sobry, Year VI.

Société hist. lett., sciences et arts de La Flèche, vol. 8.

Sol, E. *La Révolution en Quercy.* Paris: A. Picard, 1930–1932.

———. *Le vieux Quercy.* Paris: E. Nourry, 1929.

Sommier, A. *Histoire de la Fédération dans le Jura.* Paris: Dumoulin, 1846.

Songe patriotique, ou Le monument et la fête. Paris: Imprimerie de Didot le Jeune, 1790.

Sorel, A. *L'Europe et la Révolution française.* Paris: Plon, Nourrit, 1885–1911.

———. *La fête de l'Etre Suprême à Compiègne.* Compiègne: Edler, 1872.

Staël, Madame de. *De l'Allemagne.* Paris: H. Nicolle, 1810.

Starobinski, J. *1789: les emblèmes de la raison.* Paris: Flammarion, 1973.

Strasberg, Lee. *The Paradox of Acting by Denis Diderot, and Masks or Faces? by William Archer.* New York: Hill and Wang, 1957.

Taine, H. *Les origines de la France contemporaine,* vol. 2, *La Révolution.* Paris: Hachette, 1878–1881.

Testut, L. *La petite ville de Beaumont-en-Périgord pendant la période révolutionnaire.* Bordeaux: Féret et fils, 1922.

Thiemet, G. *Projet d'une cérémonie fixée au 14 juillet prochain et pacte fédératif des troupes de tous les départements réunis à l'armée parisienne pour célébrer l'époque de la Révolution.* Paris: Potier de Lille, 1790.

Thomas, S. *Nancy avant et après 1830.* Nancy: Crépin-Leblond, 1900.

Tiersot, J. *Les fêtes et les chants de la Révolution française.* Paris: Hachette, 1908.

Tourzel, Madame de. *Mémoires.* Paris: Plon, 1883.

Traver, E. *Les bachelleries, du Poitou, du Berry et de l'Angoumois.* Melle: Traver, 1933.

Uzureau, F. "La fête de la Fédération à Beaufort-en-Vallée." *Andegaviana* 2 (1904).

———. "Les fêtes de la Fédération à Angers." *Andegaviana* 3 (1905).

———. "Une relation inédite de la fête de la Fédération." *Annales de la Révolution* 15 (1923).

Vandereuse, J. "A propos d'une coutume matrimoniale du département de la Loire." *Le folklore barbançon* (March 1951).

Van Gennep, A. *Le folklore du Dauphiné.* Paris: G. P. Maisonneuve, 1932–1933.

———. *Le folklore de la Flandre.* Paris: G. P. Maisonneuve, 1936.

Varagnac, A. *Civilisation traditionnelle et genres de vie.* Paris: Albin Michel, 1948.

Vauvenargues, Luc de Clapiers, Marquis de. Letter to Mirabeau, March 22, 1740. In *Oeuvres,* vol. 3. Paris: A la cité des Livres, 1929.

Vergniaud, Pierre-Victurnien. *Manuscrits, lettres et papiers, pièces pour la plupart inédites, classées et annotées par C. Vatel.* Paris: Dumoulin, 1873.

Vianu, Hélène. "La lumière et l'ombre dans l'oeuvre de J.-J. Rousseau." *Revue des sciences humaines*. (April-June 1963).

Vidal-Naquet, P. Preface to the French translation of M. I. Finley's *Democracy, Ancient and Modern (Démocratie antique et démocratie moderne)*. Paris: Payot, 1976.

Villard, F. de. *Les arbres de la Liberté à Guéret et dans le département de la Creuse*. Guéret: Bétoulle, 1906.

Villeneuve-Arifat, Madame de. *Souvenirs d'enfance et de jeunesse, 1780–1792*. Paris: E. Paul, 1902.

Villette, Marquis de. *Lettres choisies sur les principaux événements de la Révolution*. Paris: Clousier, 1792.

Voltaire, François-Marie. *Dictionnaire philosophique*. Paris: Garnier, 1954.

Vovelle, Michel. *La chute de la monarchie, 1789–1792. Nouvelle histoire de la France contemporaine*, vol. 1. Paris: Le Seuil, 1972.

———. *Les métamorphoses de la fête en Provence de 1750 à 1820*. Paris: Aubier-Flammarion, 1976.

Wismes, G. de. *Les fêtes religieuses en Bretagne*. Nantes: Biroche et Dautais, 1902.

———. *Coutumes de mai en Bretagne*. Bergerac: J. Pouget, 1908.

Wordsworth, William. *The Prelude, or Growth of a Poet's Mind*. London: Oxford University Press, 1928.

Reports and Publications of the Assemblies

Articles complémentaires de la Constitution. Proposed by P. F. Charrel, deputy for the département of the Isère in the National Convention. Paris: Imp. nat,, Year III.

Audoin, P. J. *Motion d'ordre pour la formation d'une commission qui soit chargée de présenter un travail sur les institutions républicaines*. Paris: Imp. nat., Year V.

Bailleul, J. C. *Motion d'ordre sur la discussion relative à l'instruction publique*, 13 Germinal, Year VII. Paris: Imp. nat., Year VII.

Barailon, J. F. *Organisation et tableau des fêtes décadaires*. Paris: Imp. nat., Year III.

Barennes, R. de. *Opinion sur la résolution du 6 Thermidor, relative aux fêtes décadaires*. Paris: Imp. nat., Year VI.

Barère, de Vieuzac, B. *Rapport sur la suppression des repas civiques et des fêtes sectionnaires*, 28 Messidor, Year II. Paris: Imp. nat., Year II.

Baudin, P. *Discours pour l'anniversaire du 14 juillet*. Paris: Imp. nat., Year VII.

Blondel. *Observations du sieur Blondel, architecte et dessinateur du cabinet du Roi, sur le projet de fête de la Confédération patriotique du 14 juillet 1790, dont M. de Varenne, huissier de l'Assemblée nationale a donné l'idée et dont les plans et dessins ont été présentés par les dits sieurs à MM. Bailly et Lafayette*. Paris: Imp. nat., 1790.

Bonnaire, F. *Opinion de F. Bonnaire, contre le projet de résolution présenté au nom d'une* commission speciale par Roëmers, sur la cocarde nationale. Paris: Imp. nat., Year VII.

Bosquillon, J. J. L. Discours prononcé en présentant au Conseil des Cinq-Cents un exemplaire de la Constitution de l'an III. Paris: Imp. nat., Year VII.

Boulay de la Meurthe, A. Discours pour la fête du 18-Fructidor an VII. Paris: Imp. nat., Year VII.

————. Opinion sur la formule du serment. Paris: Imp. nat., Year VII.

Boullé, J. P. Opinion sur le projet de consacrer par des monuments et des fêtes publiques la mémorable journée du 18-Fructidor. Paris: Imp. nat., Year VI.

Briot, P. J. Discours sur la formule du serment civique. Paris: Imp. nat., Year VII.

Brothier, M. N. Rapport sur la résolution du 3 thermidor ayant pour objet de faire observer comme jours de repos décades et fêtes nationales. Paris: Imp. nat., Year VI.

Cabanis, Georges. Speech on 18 Brumaire, Year VII, when he offered the Councils the dictionary of the Academy. Paris: Imp. nat., Year VI.

Chénier, M.-J. Discours prononcé à la Convention nationale par M.-J. Chénier, député du département de Seine-et-Oise, séance du 15 Brumaire an second de la République une et indivisible. Paris: Imp. nat., n.d.

————. Rapport sur la fête des Victoires, 27 Vendémiaire An III. Paris: Imp. nat., Year III.

————. Rapport sur les fêtes du 14 juillet et du 10 août. Paris: Imp. nat., Year IV.

Collot d'Herbois, Jean-Marie. Quelques idées sur les fêtes décadaires qui peuvent être appliquées à tous projets imprimés jusqu'à ce jour 30 nivôse an III. Paris: Imp. nat., Year III.

Corbet, C. L. Lettre au citoyen Lagarde, secrétaire général du Directoire exécutif, sur les esquisses et projets de monuments pour les places publiques de Paris . . . suivie d'une réponse au citoyen Mercier . . . Paris: Desenne, Year V.

Creuzé-Latouche, J. A. Opinion sur le second projet de la commission concernant les fêtes décadaires et la célébration des mariages. Paris: Imp. nat., Year VI.

Curée, J. F. Opinion sur la motion de changer la formule du serment civique. Paris: Imp. nat., Year VII.

Daubermesnil, F. A. Rapport au nom de la commission chargée de présenter les moyens de vivifier l'esprit public. Paris: Imp. nat., Year IV.

Daunou, P. C. Discours pour l'anniversaire du 10 août. Paris: Imp. de la République, Year III.

————. Discours sur l'anniversaire du 18-Fructidor. Paris: Imp. nat., Year VI.

David, Jacques-Louis. Discours prononcé le 29 mars 1793, en offrant un tableau de sa composition représentant Michel Lepelletier au lit de mort. Paris: Imp. nat., n.d.

Debry, J. Motion d'ordre sur la célébration d'une fête consacrée à la souveraineté du peuple. Paris: Imp. nat., Year VI.

————. Motion d'ordre sur l'anniversaire du 14 juillet. Paris: Imp. nat., Year V.

————. *Rapport et projet de résolution pour l'établissement des écoles de Mars.* Paris: Imp. nat., Year VI.

————. *Sur les fondements de morale publique.* Paris: Imp. nat., Year III.

Décret de l'Assemblée nationale, portant règlement d'un culte sans prêtres, ou moyen de se passer de prêtres sans nuire au culte. Paris, 1790.

Desplanques, C. *Opinion de Desplanques sur les institutions républicaines.* Paris: Imp. de Baudouin, n.d.

Détail des cérémonies qui auront lieu au Champ-de-Mars en l'honneur des citoyens morts au siège de Nancy. Imp. patriotique, n.d.

Discours du président du Conseil des Anciens prononcé le 5ᵉ jour complémentaire an V. Paris: Imp. nat., Year VI.

Dubois-Dubais, L. T. *Discours à l'occasion de la fête du 10 août.* Paris: Imp. nat., Year VII.

————. *Discours à l'occasion de la fête du 9 Thermidor.* Paris: Imp. nat., Year VII.

Duhot, A. *Motion d'ordre sur les institutions républicaines.* Paris: Imp. nat., Year VII.

Dumolard, J. *Discours sur la fête du 9 Thermidor an V.* Paris: Imp. nat., Year V.

Duplantier, J. P. F. *Motion d'ordre sur la célébration de la fête du 10 août.* Paris: Imp. nat., Year VI.

————. *Opinion sur l'établissement des écoles primaires nationales.* Paris: Imp. nat., Year VII.

Durand de Maillane, P. T. *Opinion sur les fêtes décadaires.* Paris: Imp. nat., Year III.

Dusaulx, J. *Discours prononcé à la Convention nationale le 17 Germinal an III.* Paris: Imp. nat., Year III.

Eschassériaux, J. *Réflexions et projet de décret sur les fêtes décadaires.* Paris: Imp. nat., Year III.

————. *Motion d'ordre,* Cinq Cents, 16 Thermidor, Year VII.

Français, A. *Opinion sur la fête du 1 Vendémiaire,* 17 Fructidor, Year VII. Paris: Imp. nat., Year VII.

Garnier, J. *Opinion sur l'institution d'une fête nationale pour célébrer la mémoire du 18-Fructidor.* Paris: Imp. nat., Year V.

Gay-Vernon, L. H. *Opinion sur les institutions relatives à l'état civil des citoyens et le projet de la commission présenté par Leclerc,* 21 Frimaire, Year VI. Paris: Imp. nat., Year VI.

Gence, J. B. *Vues sur les fêtes publiques et appréciation de ces vues à la fête de Marat.* Paris: Imp. de Renaudière jeune, Year II.

Godard, J., and L. Robin. *Rapport de MM. J. Godard et L. Robin, commissaires civils envoyés par le roi dans le département du Lot.* Paris: Imp. nat., 1791.

Gois, E. P. A. *Projet de monument et fête patriotique.* Paris: Imp. nat., n.d.

Grelier, L. F. *Discours en réponse aux orateurs qui ont combattu le projet de résolution relatif à la fête à célébrer le 18-Fructidor.* Paris: Imp. nat., Year VI.

Grenier, J. *Opinion sur la question de savoir si l'on doit supprimer de la formule du serment civique les mots de haine à l'anarchie.* Paris: Imp. nat., Year VII.

Grobert, J. F. L. *Des fêtes publiques chez les modernes.* Paris: Imprimerie de Didot Jeune, Year X.

Guineau-Dupré, Jean. *Opinion sur la résolution relative aux fêtes décadaires.* Paris: Imp. nat., Year VI.

Guyomar, B. *Discours sur la célébration de la fête du 14 juillet.* Paris: Imp. nat., Year VII.

Heurtault de Lamerville, J. M. *Opinion sur les fêtes décadaires,* Cinq-Cents. Paris: Imp. nat., Year VI.

Jault, P. S. J. *Discours sur l'instruction publique.* Paris: Imprimerie de la Société typographique des Trois-Amis, n.d.

Joubert, L. *Opinion sur le projet de résolution présenté par la Commission d'instruction publique sur l'organisation des écoles primaires.* Paris: Imp. nat., Year VII.

Jourdain, Y. C. *Motion d'ordre pour la célébration de la fête du 9-Thermidor.* Paris: Imp. nat., Year VI.

―――. *Opinion sur la formule du serment civique.* Paris: Imp. nat., Year VII.

Lamarque, F. *Opinion sur la formule du serment,* Cinq-Cents. Paris: Imp. nat., Year VII.

Lamy, C. *Motion d'ordre relative à la journée du 9-Thermidor.* Paris: Imp. nat., Year V.

Lanthenas, F. *Développement du projet de loi ou cadre pour l'institution des fêtes décadaires . . .* Paris: Imp. nat., Year III.

―――. *Moyens de consolider la Révolution du 9–Thermidor et de rétablir la concorde entre les vrais républicains.* Paris: Imp. nat., Year III.

La Tour du Pin, J. F. *Discours de M. de La Tour du Pin, ministre et sécretaire d'État au département de la Guerre, à la séance du 4 juin 1790.* Paris, n.d.

Laveaux, J. C. T. *Discours prononcé par Laveaux, président du Conseil des Anciens, le 9 Thermidor an VI.* Paris: Imp. nat., Year VI.

Leclerc, J. B. *Nouveau projet de résolution sur les cérémonies relatives au mariage et à la naissance.* Paris: Imp. nat., Year VI.

―――. *Rapport sur l'établissement d'écoles spéciales de musique.* Paris: Imp. nat., Year VII.

―――. *Rapport sur les institutions relatives à l'état civil des citoyens.* Paris: Imp. nat., Year VI.

Lecointe-Puyraveau, M. *Discours prononcé pour la célébration des événements des 9 Thermidor, 13 Vendémiaire et 18 Fructidor.* Paris: Imp. nat., Year VI.

Lenoir-Laroche, J. J. *Rapport de Lenoir-Laroche au conseil des Anciens, sur l'annuaire de la République.* Paris: Imp. nat., Year VI.

Lequinio, J. M. *Des fêtes nationales.* Paris: Imp. nat., n.d.

Loys (deputy of the Périgord). *Mémoire pour les provinces du Périgord, du Quercy et du Rouergue.* N.p., n.d.

Luminais, M. P. *Discours sur le rapport fait par Grelier sur un monument à élever et sur une fête perpétuelle à célébrer en mémoire du 18-Fructidor.* Paris: Imp. nat., Year V.

Malouet, P. V. *Opinion de M. Malouet sur la Déclaration des Droits, dans la séance du 2 août 1789.* N.p., n.d.

Marbot, J. A. de. *Discours prononcé par Marbot . . . ,* 26 Messidor an VI. Paris: Imp. nat., Year III.

Mathieu de l'Oise. *Projet de fêtes nationales.* Paris: Imp. nat., Year II.

Maugenest, F. *Motion d'ordre sur le projet de fête du 18-Fructidor.* Paris: Imp. Nat., Year VI.

Mercier, L. S. *Discours sur René Descartes.* Paris: Imp. nat., Year IV.

Merlin de Thionville. *Opinion sur les fêtes nationales prononcée à la Convention, 9 Vendémiaire an III.* Paris: Imp. nat., Year III.

Mirabeau, Honoré-Gabriel de Riqueti, Comte de. Speech on the Civil Constitution of the Clergy, November 26, 1790.

Montpellier, A. *Opinion sur la proposition faite par Jourdan de supprimer dans le serment la formule de haine à l'anarchie sur le serment civique,* Cinq-Cents, 8 Thermidor, Year VII.

Moreau du l'Yonne. *Motion d'ordre sur le 14 juillet.* Paris: Imp. nat., Year VI.

Mortier-Duparc, P. *Rapport sur la distribution proposée du portrait du général Marceau.* Paris: Imp. nat., Year VI.

Neufchâteau, François de. *Recueil de lettres circulaires, instructions, programmes, discours et autres actes publics.* Paris: Imp. de la République, Years VI–VIII.

Parent-Réal, N. *Motion d'ordre tendant à faire consacrer, par la fête du 1er vendémiaire, l'accord parfait qui existe dans l'histoire de la Révolution française.* Paris: Imp. nat., Year VII.

Pérès, E. *Opinion et projet de résolution . . . concernant l'institution d'une nouvelle fête relativement aux événements du 18-Fructidor.* Paris: Imp. nat., Year VI.

Petit, Michel-Edme. *Opinion sur l'éducation publique, prononcée le 1er octobre 1793.* Paris: Imp. nat., n.d.

Philippes-Delleville, J. F. *Motion d'ordre prononcée le 10 août de la Ve année républicaine.* Paris: Imp. nat., Year V.

Portiez de l'Oise. *Rapport et projet de décret présenté au nom du Comité d'instruction publique par Portiez de l'Oise sur la célébration de la fête du 9-Thermidor.* Paris: Imp. nat., Year III.

Projet de cérémonie à l'usage des fêtes nationales, décadaires et sans-culottides de la République française, saisies dans un but moral, combinées dans leur rapports généraux et rendues propres à être célébrées dans les moindres communes . . . Paris, Year II.

Quirot, J.-P. *Discours sur la fête de la liberté et les événements des 9 et 10 Thermidor.* Paris: Imp. nat., Year VII.

Rallier, L. A. *Opinion sur la formule du serment.* Paris: Imp. nat., Year VII.

Rameau, J. *Aperçu philosophique et politique sur la célébration des décadis et des fêtes nationales.* Paris: Imp. nat., n.d.

Robespierre, Maximilien. *Rapport . . . sur les rapports des idées religieuses et morales avec les principes républicains, et sur les fêtes nationales . . .* Paris: Imp. nat., n.d.

————. Speech in the Convention, May 26, 1794.

Rollin, A. *Rapport sur la célébration de la fête du 1ᵉʳ Vendémiaire.* Paris: Imp. nat., Year VII.

Romme, G. *Rapport sur l'ère de la République.* Paris: Imp. nat., n.d.

Saint-Just, Louis de. *Rapport sur la police générale, la justice, le commerce, la législation, et les crimes des factions.* Paris: Imp. nat., n.d.

Sherlock, S. *Opinion de Sherlock, sur le projet de résolution relatif au calendrier républicain.* Paris: Imp. nat., Year VI.

————. *Opinion sur la nécessité de rendre l'instruction publique commune à tous les enfants des Français.* Paris: Imp. nat., Year VII.

Sieyès, Abbé Emmanuel-Joseph. *Discours à la célébration de l'anniversaire du 10 août.* Paris: Imprimerie de la République, Year VII.

Sobre le Jeune. *Projet d'un monument à élever dans le champ de la Fédération proposé par M. Sobre le Jeune, architecte.* N.p., n.d.

Société des jacobins, Friday, April 6, 1792.

Solliers, J. B. *Discours adressé à M. Rame, ministre des protestants de Vauvert, après le serment civique et fraternel, en présence de la municipalité et du peuple et aux pieds d'l'Autel de la Patrie, par J. B. Solliers, curé de Vauvert.* N.p., n.d.

Terral, J. *Réflexions sur les fêtes décadaires.* Paris: Imp. nat., Year III.

Thiessé, N. F. *Opinion de Thiessé sur le 2ᵉ projet présenté par la Commission des institutions républicaines, le 19 Messidor an VI.* Paris: Imp. nat., Year VI.

Departmental Archives (Archives départementales)

Bas-Rhin	12 L 6, 44 L 8
Basses-Alpes	L 365
Bouches-du-Rhône	L 286, L 1037
Cantal	L 648 bis
Charente	L 140, L 143
Côte-d'Or	L 462, L 477
Dordogne	B 844, B 845, B 1688
Doubs	L 183
Drôme	L 224, L 230
Finistère	10 L 55, 10 L 154, 10 L 155
Gers	L 463, L 694
Haute-Marne	L 272
Indre	L 300, L301

Indre-et-Loire   L 598
Landes   67 L I
Loire-Atlantique   L 352, L 355
Lot   10 J
Lot-et-Garonne   L 530
Maine-et-Loire   I L 411
Nord   L 1264, L 5050
Puy de Dôme   L 659, L 668, L 671
Rhône   L 451, L 453, L 454
Savoie   L 379
Somme   La 393
Yonne   L 25

National Archives (Archives nationales)

AF II 195
C 41 no. 363, 82 no. 817, 119, 120, 266, 287
D IV 49, XIV, XIV 5, XXIX, XXIX 73, XXXVIII 3
F 131935
F^1 C III
F^1 C III   Alpes-Maritimes 2
           Ardennes 5
           Basses-Pyrénées 7
           Bouches-du-Rhône 7
           Cher 6
           Corrèze
           Côte-d'Or 6
           Eure 11
           Finistère 3
           Gironde
           Haut-Rhin 6
           Haute-Vienne
           Hautes-Pyrénées 6
           Hérault 9
           Landes 5
           Lot 8
           Lot-et-Garonne 11
           Lozère 5
           Maine-et-Loire 6, 13
           Meurthe 7
           Morbihan 6
           Nord 7

            Pas-de-Calais 8
            Pyrénées-Orientales 4
            Rhône 5
F¹ C IV   Seine 1
F¹⁷ 1243
N III   Seine 789
N IV   Seine 87
V W 395, 916, no. 70
W 395

Bibliothèque Nationale

NAF 2694, 2713, 2479
Manuscrits français 11697

Bibliothèque Centrale du Museum d'Histoire Naturelle

Manuscript 312

Archives communales de Bourges, Registre des délibérations, June 23, 1790
Archives communales de Caen, pièces sur la Révolution, *liasse* 36
Archives municipales de Châlons, I, 199

Government Papers

Bouches-du-Rhône, Encyclopédie départementale, "Études sur la Révolution et les cultes philosophiques."
Statistique du département du Nord, vol. 1, by M. Dieudonné, prefect, Year XII.

Revolutionary Journals

Abréviateur universel, 18 Pluviôse, Year III.
Ami des lois, 9 Ventôse, Year IV
Annales patriotiques, 9 Frimaire, Year II.
Chronique de Paris, June 20, 1790.
Conservateur décadaire, 30 Messidor, Year II.
Courrier de Gorsas, June 9, 1792.
La décade, 30 Floréal, Year V.
Écho des cercles patriotiques no. 14.
Journal de la cour et de la ville, July 14 and 17, 1790.
Journal de la Société populaire des arts, Pluviôse, Year II.
Journal de Paris, July 15, 1790.

Journal des patriotes de 89, 25 Thermidor, Year VI.

Le moniteur, May 25, 1790.

Le patriote français, 28 Messidor, Year VI.

Rédacteur, 20 Fructidor, Year V; 11 Thermidor, Year VI; 12 Thermidor, Year VI.

Révolutions de Paris, 20 Brumaire, Year II (article attributed to Momoro); no. 52; no. 211 (July 20–August 3, 1793).

Révolutions de France et de Brabant nos. 34 and 35.

La rocambole, ou Journal des honnêtes gens, April 19, 1792; June 7, 1792.

Index